THE POLITICAL ROLE OF MINORITY GROUPS IN THE MIDDLE EAST

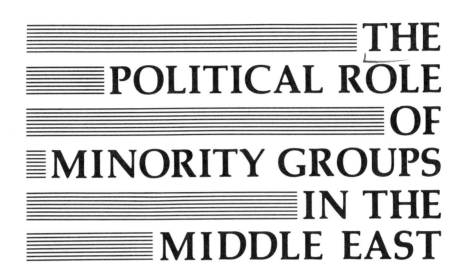

THE POLITICAL ROLE OF MINORITY GROUPS IN THE MIDDLE EAST

edited by
R. D. McLaurin

PRAEGER

PRAEGER SPECIAL STUDIES • PRAEGER SCIENTIFIC

Library of Congress Cataloging in Publication Data

Main entry under title:

The Political role of minority groups in the Middle
East.

Bibliography: p.
1. Near East--Politics and government--Addresses,
essays, lectures. 2. Minorities--Near East--Addresses,
essays, lectures. I. McLaurin, Ronald De, 1944-
DS62.8.P65   323.1'56   79-20588
ISBN 0-03-052596-9

Published in 1979 by Praeger Publishers
A Division of Holt, Rinehart and Winston/CBS, Inc.
383 Madison Avenue, New York, New York 10017 U.S.A.

© 1979 by Praeger Publishers

9 038 987654321

Printed in the United States of America

PREFACE AND ACKNOWLEDGMENTS

When we study and forecast developments in the Middle East, our disciplinary "slips" usually show. The commercial economist focuses on trade, technology transfer, and business economics; the finance economist on capital flows; the military specialist on arms transfers, armed forces, and praetorian politics; the comparative political scientist on internal functions and challenges; the international relations analyst on foreign pressures and policies. That the Arab-Israeli conflict preempted other subjects almost to their exclusion had some advantages, as well as evident drawbacks.

Since 1975, the prominence of diversity in the identification or loyalty of the Middle Eastern bodies politic has taken center stage. Not that the subject is new—minorities have been a principal political force at all levels in the region as far back as recorded history carries us. What has shifted our attention is the changing focus in which we hold the region as a whole. No longer is it dichotomous; no longer must everything be judged in terms of the prolonged confrontation between Israel and the Arab states, or of the global rivalry between the United States and the Soviet Union. Of course, inhabitants of the Middle East and the serious students of the region as well always recognized the fallacies of such caricatures. Nevertheless, much of what passed for analysis, policy, and forecasting labored under the weight of these misbegotten concepts.

There is no single explanation for, no single model of, no single key to Middle Eastern politics. Certainly, this book offers none. We do feel that too little attention has been paid to the critical political role played by many important minorities in the Middle East. If this collection serves no purpose beyond pointing out the centrality and limits of minority roles in local, national, and regional politics, it will have served a worthwhile purpose.

Most of this book's ten chapters deal with specific minorities. At the outset, we faced the issue of whether to proceed on the basis of a rigidly comparative approach or a more loosely structured volume. The latter path was chosen because data are in any event lacking for a comprehensive treatment of all major minorities across countries. Moreover, the idiosyncracies of each case are far better presented outside a rigid framework, which would appear arbitrary in its treatment (and neglect) of certain issues.

The result of the looser approach is, predictably, a collection of rather independent analyses, each treated as the author has judged he could best and most appropriately deal with issues he feels are raised in the case he presents. Several focus on politics and society at the local level; others treat the national level much more fully.

The editor's introductory chapter and Lewis Snider's concluding chapter attempt to go beyond specific cases and issues to some of the major regional issues raised in the present and future by the number and importance of minorities in the Middle East. Two chapters deal with *majorities*. The first treats the Christians in Lebanon. Although by some estimates (cf. Appendix 2) Christians as a whole constitute a majority of the Lebanese population, the essay focuses primarily on two major minority constituents of the Christian community. The second addresses the Arabs in the Israeli Occupied Territories, who are clearly a majority, but a majority whose situation in some respects resembles that of a minority. The book also contains appendixes with some estimated population data, including comparative tables, and a bibliography of referenced material.

The debt owed many in the preparation of this book are considerable. First and foremost, the editor has appreciated the other contributors' cooperation and conscientiousness. Most have made an extraordinary effort in the face of many other outstanding obligations to ensure the completion of their chapters within or ahead of schedule. No editor could fail to appreciate such consideration.

Second, several chapters have benefited from outside financial support. The editor is no less indebted for this assistance to the authors than they are themselves. In particular, then, we should like to express our appreciation to the American Philosophical Society, the Centre d'Études et de Recherches Économiques et Sociales, the Department of the Army, the Office of the Assistant Secretary of Defense (International Security Affairs), the Social Science Research Council, and the University of Wisconsin—Milwaukee. The editor also wishes to express his personal thanks to two colleagues, Preston S. Abbott and Edward E. Azar, and to two other individuals—Robert Kubal and Jerrold K. Milsted—whose assistance at various stages of the original research has been very helpful in bringing this volume together. James M. Price has helped me with many of the mundane aspects of getting the text of this book together. I am extremely thankful for his diligence in what must have seemed a tiresome and thankless endeavor. To Cathie Love, who typed or retyped—and in some cases re-retyped—several chapters, apologies for my cryptic penmanship can only effectively be expressed as gratitude for her patience, perseverance . . . and humor.

CONTENTS

LIST OF TABLES AND FIGURES

Figures

THE POLITICAL ROLE OF MINORITY GROUPS IN THE MIDDLE EAST

MINORITIES AND POLITICS IN THE MIDDLE EAST: AN INTRODUCTION

R. D. McLaurin

Virtually all the many books dealing with political dynamics in the Middle East discuss the instability often associated with the region. This instability is seen to be reflected in frequent changes of political regime by extra-legal means; in high levels of domestic political violence; in interstate conflict within the region; and in political, military, and economic intervention in domestic and regional political processes by powers external to the Middle East. There is little attempt, in most cases, at differentiating or weighting the various indexes of instability, distinguishing between time periods and identifying trends, isolating causal variables, or comparing levels of instability with other regions. If we say the Middle East is "unstable," then surely we must mean *more* unstable than other regions.

Yet, it is not at all clear that the Middle East *is* more unstable than other developing areas. Recognizing the problems with data reliability, a cursory survey of traditional indicators of political instability across developing areas seems to suggest that the Middle East has *not* been characterized in the 1970s by more regime changes than Africa or Latin America; by levels of domestic political violence as great as Africa or Southeast Asia; or by greater degrees of external political or military intervention than Africa or East Asia. It is true that the Arab-Israeli conflict, as a regional interstate rivalry, has consistently shown extremely high levels of conflict, however, levels exceeding (in their combination of consistency, intensity, and duration) for this decade those of other dyads. By itself, though, the

Arab-Israeli conflict is clearly not the focus of those who describe the region as unstable.

Alternatively, we may consider comparison over time. We would argue that by many measures, the Middle East between 1970 and 1975 enjoyed a period of unwonted stability. Since 1975, forces in the region seem to be pushing it toward a renewed period of instability. Whether this is a function of heightened ethno-religious awareness (Lebanon, Iran) or the unprecedented influx of capital and aliens (Iran), a number of countries—Egypt, Iran, Iraq, Israel, Jordan, Lebanon, Syria, and Turkey—give some evidence, at least, of greater instability than during the first half of the 1970s.

LEGITIMACY AND STABILITY OF POLITICAL POWER IN THE MIDDLE EAST

Students of political science have become imbued with the importance of power as the key concept of that discipline. Too often, however, we confuse the *acquisition* of power with politics. In most developing countries, and in some developed countries as well, politics has very little to do with the acquisition of power. The retention of power, by contrast, in all societies is the essence of politics. The principal executive position in some small states can be and in too many has been seized in a meaningless and short-lived *coup d'état.* Yet, a coup may lead to such a *force majeure* as that of the Young Officers in Egypt in 1952, changing not only the face of Egyptian politics but the nature of Egyptian society and regional development.

While not synonymous, stable power relations and the concept of legitimacy are closely related. In an outstanding recent book, Hudson describes Arab politics as a "search for legitimacy."[1] We agree that legitimacy is the key concept to understanding the politics of the Middle East, even if its salience to such understanding varies across the many countries of the region. It is important, however, to distinguish among different levels of legitimacy—the legitimacy of the political order, that of the regime itself, and the legitimacy of an individual leader. In most cases, to use a caveat so necessary to politics, regime and individual legitimacy devolve from the legitimacy of the political order. The strongest, most charismatic leaders can alter this sequence, as Nasser certainly did. Yet, legitimacy will usually be elusive to the regime or leader whose political order commands no firm allegiance. Because the states of the Middle East are relatively new, it is hardly surprising that their political systems do not enjoy any great degree of legitimacy.

Whether at the level of the political order or of regime or leader, legitimacy must mean authority, identification, and identity.[2] By "authority" in this context we mean simply "power." Although leaders out of power may command respect, popularity, and allegiance, it is meaningless to think of political legitimacy without real authority. Identification with the authority is equally important to legitimacy: it means projection of oneself. That leader, regime, or political order with which people are unable to identify is not legitimate, for it fails to capture their loyalty. One may dissent strongly on specific issues and still retain a sense of general identification. Finally, identity has been aptly explained by Hudson: "The people within a territory must feel a sense of political community which does not conflict with other subnational or supranational communal identifications."[3]

Normally, while a single leader or even a regime may quickly establish (and lose) legitimacy based upon the values of the nation (identity) and the degree to which the leader or regime communicates representation of those values (identification) and maintains control (authority), a political order requires in addition the passage of time before deep roots of legitimacy may take hold. That this places the new states in a disadvantageous position is clear.

While it is true, then, to say that as a group developing countries (in the Middle East and elsewhere) are characterized by greater levels of governmental instability and political violence (relative to their size) than developed societies,[4] it is necessary to look to the general absence among this group of the same degree of legitimacy to understand the dynamics better. That is, although the proximate cause for dissent may be relative deprivation of one or more social goods expected,[5] the deprivation would be more acceptable if the elements of legitimacy were more firmly rooted in the body politic. It is instructive to compare relatively stable governments with political processes in relatively unstable countries. Some populations in the face of great *perceived* poverty do not turn on their governments; others, confronting relatively less extreme perceived deprivation, do.

In many industrialized countries, disenchantment with government performance is accepted—and channeled into sanctioned forms of political dissent. Parties are voted out of office, new political groups are formed, demonstrations are held, and so forth. In general, unsatisfactory behavior of the regime (in terms of expectations and aspirations) prejudices the legitimacy of the leader, or conceivably the regime (party, administration); such poor performance does not move most people to consider changes in the nature of the political order.*

MINORITIES AND POLITICAL POWER

Leaders, governments, and the accepted political structure as a whole must be able to mobilize adequate support across all issues to maintain legitimacy. Or, more accurately, they must retain sufficient legitimacy to prevent the effective mobilization of opposition. Given the number and diversity of political issues confronting government at all levels, coalition fluidity could be a reasonable expectation. However, we know that people do not move freely between political groups with equal ease. Some individuals are more inclined to activity than others. Some are more rigid. Groups manifest similar differences. Moreover, some issues are more salient to the most active publics than others. Thus, we find in all societies a tendency for certain groups or parties to react rigidly with respect to certain issue areas, even if the relationship between the immediate behavior and the issue is tenuous or invisible to others. When groups behave in this manner their cohesion becomes a political factor, and if the group is large this factor can be a principal political consideration.[6]

This book deals with minority groups. Definitionally, a minority group is any body of persons with a sense of cohesion who, taken together, constitute less than one-half the population of an entity. In practice, we are considering national minorities, that is, minorities in sovereign states or otherwise autonomous polities ("entities") that see themselves as discrete and primary social groups. Minorities theoretically may include political factions, social or economic classes, religious communities, either sex, age groups, occupational groups, language or racial groups, and many more. Generally, we tend to think of minority groups as identity groups, such as religious, racial, or linguistic communities. Effective socialization often gives strength to minority identity in these groups and provides the

---

*The perpetrators of willful violence are often exceptions. "Radicals" in the United States, for example, have used violence to attempt to change the political order. Certainly, large numbers of Flemish and French-speaking activists in Belgium have been moved to violence at times. Yet, the majority has resisted violence because to most the political status quo is acceptable, *even with periodic outbreaks of violence.* Northern Ireland is a more questionable case. In Iran in early 1979, the end of the shah's regime changed the cost-benefit balance for several minorities. Although they had acceded to the shah's regime and control, they began to express particularist views more openly once the weaknesses of the successor regime became apparent.

backbone of resistance to assimilation (which would submerge that identity).

Cohesive minorities can pose major problems for governments of countries in which the political order itself, and the regime as well, do not possess established legitimacy. Minorities' group loyalties are often more real than state loyalty, and, consequently, decisions at the state level are frequently made with a view to retaining these groups' conditional allegiance. State policy is, in effect, held hostage to minority will.[7] Where there are several of such groups within a single polity, state "nationalism" may be a myth—a concept felt by no major portion of the populace.

The dominant argument of political and other social scientists surveying the global scene has convinced many observers that the power and indeed the existence of minority groups are anomalous, anachronistic, dysfunctional, and, most important, evanescent.[8] Minorities, that is, minority identity and power, are doomed, it is averred, by the forces of modernization and nationalism. The process and nature of nationalism are reviewed, its imperatives analyzed, and the verdict rendered: slowly, unevenly, and with difficulty, minorities will be absorbed—but absorbed they will be—by the emerging nation-states of which they are a part.

An elaborate facade intentionally provided by global politics since 1945 has given support to the concept of integrative modernization. The force of the decolonization movement under the rubric of what is somewhat misleadingly called "nationalism," treated non-self-governing territories, no matter how arbitrarily their boundaries were drawn, as integers, as "nations in embryo."* From 1945 until the early 1970s, decolonization has submerged the minorities issue, principally because it threatened fundamental conceptual problems and intimidating political consequences for the movement.[9]

Largely in order to avoid confronting the minorities question, colonial boundaries were accepted as sacred. At least partly to garner and maintain maximum support for the movement, moreover, minorities questions in independent states old and new were

---

*"Nationalism," like "nation," has been defined clearly enough for all social scientists, but generally used without reference to technical meaning. Nationalism, in a word, has, come to be used without reference to the concept of "nation."

We use the term "non-self-governing territories" in the sense of Article 73(e) of the United Nations Charter, as applied—i.e., all territories not sovereign. The term's application has not been entirely consistent, but the essence since the mid-1950s has been sovereignty rather than self-government.

avoided.† Few challenged this approach, and the solitary challengers were widely discounted as apologists for colonialism, colonialists who were trying to sow the seeds of division among the anti-colonialists.[10]

Yet, by the mid-1970s, non-self-governing territories were neither numerous nor populous. And a series of phenomena, long gathering momentum, was in the process of increasing minority desire for autonomy. These phenomena include

The entry into a "consolidation" phase of many new, postcolonial states. "Consolidation" is, of course, a threat to minority identity.

The undemocratic unitary nature of many of these states contrasts markedly with the tolerance toward minorities shown by some colonial rulers. France, for example, intentionally encouraged minorities in the Levant to participate actively in society in order to dilute the power and potential nationalist resistance of the majority.

The impacts of improved communication. Communication allows minorities divided by older borders to interact efficiently with fellow minority members in other states and to learn immediately of the travails and triumphs of their brethren in other states or elsewhere in their own country. Communication—the media are used by the majority—is seen as a threat, too, a means of invading the house with the "other" culture. This threat stimulates minorities to action.

New power relationships in which size is no longer essential for security.

The passage of time. Many minorities, including some in Europe and the Western Hemisphere, were willing to try—and did try—pluralism. Some have concluded, perhaps for the reasons cited above, that the experiment was not going to succeed. The appearance of an increasing vulnerability of the state to low-level violence may also have convinced them that, at the least, increased autonomy could be aspired to feasibly.[11]

The growing self-assertion and search for power of minority groups is a global phenomenon affecting developed and developing, Western and Eastern, centralized and less centralized countries. But the systemic threat to polities where institutions and traditions of political order are yet young is perceived clearly to be greater and more immediate than in older societies with an established political culture. By the late 1970s, ethnic separatism was recognized as a vital force.[12]

---

†The United States tried for some years to use the colonialism issue against the Soviet Union in the United Nations. Although the principal focus of U.S. attempts to oppose Soviet "colonialism" was Eastern Europe, some Soviet minorities were also discussed.

MINORITIES IN THE MIDDLE EAST

Although the popular American image of the Middle East envisages a region with many homogeneous Arab, Muslim countries and a single Jewish state, Israel, the Middle East is in fact peopled by numerous minorities. Moreover, the minorities have diverse bases, linguistic, religious, and racial. Recognizing the predominance of Arabism and the Sunni branch of Islam, one may usefully group them: Arab, non-Sunni; non-Arab, Sunni; non-Arab, non-Sunni.[13] (Although it was not our objective to include studies on each type of group, all are represented in this volume: the Alawis, Druze, and Lebanese Christians as non-Sunni Arabs; the Berbers and Kurds as Sunni non-Arabs; and the Maghreb Jews as non-Sunni non-Arabs.)

Of the twenty states in the Middle East,* fully nine have minorities representing at least 25 percent of their populations. Table A.2 in the appendixes to this volume shows these minorities are sometimes ethnic, sometimes religious, sometimes linguistic, and sometimes alien in nationality or origin. By "alien" we include all foreigners within a state in one group, irrespective of the fact that they often are *not* cohesive. That is, although Palestinians, in particular, have an important transnational role in the labor force of many Middle Eastern states, the presence of aliens in large numbers can by itself constitute an important variable in governmental decision making. In Kuwait, for example, there is substantial ill feeling between foreign labor per se, on the one hand, and Kuwaiti nationals, on the other.

It is often thought that a minority must constitute a large part of a country's population before it begins to have any substantial effect on elite views and decisions. However, this belief is misleading, for what is equally important are the *absolute* size of the minority and its cohesion. After a cohesive group reaches a certain size—we might conceive of it as constituting the necessary "critical mass"—it no longer seems to require relative size to be important. The Palestinians of Lebanon, for example, constitute about 10 percent of that country's population, no more, relatively, than the Iranians in Qatar (over one-fifth of the country's people) and far less than the Berbers of the Maghreb, who comprise as much as 40 percent of the popula-

---

*Definitions of the geographical scope of the term "Middle East" are, of course, varied. For our purposes here we include only those North African states on the Mediterranean littoral (thus excluding Mauritania, the Sudan, Djibouti, and Somalia); all the countries on the Arabian/Persian Gulf and Arabian peninsula; all the Levant, including Turkey; and Jordan.

tion (Morocco). Yet, the Palestinian community clearly constitutes a major ingredient in decision making, at least with respect to some issue areas. This is also true of the Kurds in Turkey (7 percent of the population) and Iran (3 percent), small groups which for a variety of historical reasons carry an importance belied by their relative size in the demographic picture. The Palestinians and Kurds are reasonably cohesive, and they are numerous enough to pose political or security problems should they attempt to do so. Finally, they *have* done so.

Cohesion and mobilization are critical to minorities if they are to exert influence. Another important factor is the group's relations with the other factions or forces inside or outside the country. The Arabs of Israel are an example. Israeli Arabs constitute about 15 percent of the Jewish State's population. If all Arabs under Israeli control are counted, Arabs constitute well over a third of the population of Israel and the occupied territories.[14] Arabs inside Israel and in the occupied territories define themselves as "Palestinians." They dislike Israeli rule. Even more than the Kurds are their numbers external to the state considerable. And, of course, the arms available to and from Arabs outside Israel are considerable. Now it may be that one day Israel's Arabs, who by the year 2015 will make up about one-quarter of the population (about 30 percent of the population of Israel, East Jerusalem, and parts of the West Bank), will pose a serious security threat to Israel.[15] But, notwithstanding Palestinian claims to the contrary, Israel certainly has been able to maintain an effective control system to date.[16] In addition to excellent intelligence and immediate and forceful response, the system has been based on isolating the Arabs internally and externally.[17] Even though internal isolation is beginning to break down[18] (with perhaps important ramifications for Israeli society) external isolation is still quite effective, particularly in view of the ability of modern technology to breach the borders of sovereign states.[19] Isolation of a minority from potential external sources of supply is a critical tactic in effective control.[20]

Given the number of cohesive, mobilized minorities in the Middle East, which represent 10 to 49 percent of the population in the 20 states, it is clear that what Connor calls "ethnonationalism" is a force to be reckoned with in the region. Yet these minorities constitute major political factors for a variety of reasons. Some are important because they pose a real or latent threat of secession, which is a *threat to the political integrity* of the states in which they are located. The secession of others is threatening less for its political than for its economic significance (*threat to economic resource base*). Apart from secession, some minorities are viewed with concern because they may be a *threat to regime stability* or a *threat to the political order* of specific states. Other minorities pose a *threat to the values of the dominant group*, but little tangible threat. These "threats" are not necessarily "real" (i. e., proximate or realistic). They may misconstrue completely the values and objectives of minority leaders and peoples. Yet, it is in the nature of a threat that the target's perceptions are conclusive. He—or, in this case, they— will act in accordance with his (their) own assessments or beliefs or attitudes concerning the views and values of the minority.

Threats to Political Integrity. The Kurds are among the most obvious potential secessionists, having already attempted on several occasions to establish their own nation-state. Whether the Kurds will succeed now is questionable. Meanwhile, the Christians of Lebanon, especially the Maronites, have already succeeded partially in seceding from the old Lebanon through bringing about a set of conditions amounting to partition, a partition which may lead to independence of the Christian-dominated areas,[21] but which in any case, seems to relegate the unified, pluralistic Lebanon to the past.

Threats to Economic Resources. To Iraq alone among the five states where the Kurds live, Kurdish secession also represents a real threat to vital elements of the national economic resource base, since the oilfields of Mosul and Kurkuk lie in Kurdish areas. In Iran, the Arabs also are much more populous around the oil-producing areas near the Gulf than they are in the rest of the country.

Threats to Regime Stability. Notwithstanding the potential threat of secession raised by some important Middle Eastern minorities, most do not constitute such a threat. Rather, the political weight of the larger minorities or their ability to articulate their interest in cooperation with other political forces of the state often constitutes a threat to regime stability, either through the positive operation of sanctioned political processes or through their ability to impede or obstruct the execution of policy. In addition, minorities have been deeply involved in the illegal changes of regime—notably, *coups d'état*—in the Levant. Unquestionably, the instability of the Syrian government before Hafez al-Assad came to power in 1970 was directly related to the complex mosaic of minorities (political, economic, ethnic) that makes up that country.[22]

Threat to the Political Order. Both Lebanon and Syria have recently witnessed fundamental changes in the political order, changes initiated by minority group considerations. In Lebanon, Maronite and other Christian separatists sought and have effected partition largely out of fear of the Muslim majority. Even before the civil war that began in 1975, the Palestinian minority exerted a powerful influence on the nature of Lebanese politics which clearly can be related to the basic changes that have resulted in Lebanon. The Alawis, although a minority, have controlled the Syrian government for almost a decade and were a significant factor in the previous government ruled by Alawi Salah Jadid.[23] The policies of this minority both before and after its ascension to power have resulted in a fundamental change in elite recruitment and structure, allocation and distribution of political power, political communication, and almost all major domestic and foreign policies, including those pertaining to economic development.[24] The Arabs in Israel, by virtue of their very presence, are a threat to the Israeli political order, for they force a choice between a democratic and a Zionist state.

Threat to Dominant Group Values. The Israeli Arabs are also therefore a threat to the predominant group's values in and for Israel. If the state is to remain Zionist, the Palestinian Arabs must continue to be treated as second-class citizens and eventually further discriminated against as their numbers represent an increasing proportion of the Israeli population. Yet surely this violates the political values of the majority of Israel's citizens. Another group that embodies a threat to majority values is the Baha'i in Iran. Representing between one-half and one percent of the populace, the Baha'i are not allowed to practice their religion; indeed , it is outlawed, so they cannot even acknowledge it. Despite the fact that many very influential members of the elite during the shah's reign were Baha'is, the movement was feared and suppressed.

MINORITY POLICIES IN THE MIDDLE EAST

Because certain minorities in each Middle East state have been viewed with antipathy, distrust, or fear, "minority policies" have frequently stressed control and have varied widely. Where decision elites have faced cohesive, mobilized minorities with nationalist aspirations they have at times

executed minority group leaders;
imprisoned or released minority leaders or militants;

deported or allowed the return of leaders;

resettled minority group members;

resettled others in minority-dominated areas;

allowed or forbidden minority languages to be used in certain circumstances;

armed or disarmed minorities;

seized the agricultural land of minority group members;

prohibited certain types of communications among minorities;

forbidden minority meetings, organizations, or membership;

used intelligence agents to penetrate minority groups;

prohibited or guaranteed minority representation in the civil service, legislatures, cabinets, or other state offices;

underdistributed or overdistributed development funds to minority districts;

forbidden the transport out of the country of minority personal property and cash;

allowed or prevented a large measure of autonomy in minority areas.

It is evident that by themselves none of the approaches noted above will ensure minority assimilation to the ethos of the state. Minorities that are tightly—or otherwise effectively—organized and that maintain a high level of internal communication are not amenable to forced absorption. They tend to react defensively to preserve an identity deemed salient enough to have given rise to that degree of organization. This is not to say such minorities cannot be *controlled*, although most developing states' structures are ill equipped and populations too heterogeneous to effect *absolute* control. We are suggesting simply that mobilized minorities are not likely to accept assimilation passively or quickly. By contrast, minorities that have neither a sense of identity nor established organization nor adequate communication may be more easily absorbed. The absence of a threat to the group's essential values or physical security also conduces to assimilation.

MINORITIES IN POWER

Two of the minority groups studied in this book have dominated their respective countries in recent years: the Maronites in Lebanon and the Alawis in Syria. In addition, the Sunnis of Bahrain and Iraq, and the Shi'a (Zaydis) of Yemen are other minority religious groups that have secured or maintained the major share of power within their countries.* (Unlike the Maronites and Alawis, however, all of these latter groups represent nearly half the population of their respective countries.) No ethnic or linguistic minorities are in power. In fully four states of the Middle East, however, aliens outnumber the nationals of those countries (in two cases by ratios of three to one or more). Thus, technically, nationals are "minorities" in power. (Indeed, in both the United Arab Emirates and Qatar, there are probably one or more specific foreign nationalities numerically superior to the number of citizens.)

There are no comprehensive or comparable statistics on the representation of minorities in the higher councils of the countries of the region. Nevertheless, it is clear that a preferred means of securing minority support is through cooptation. Similarly, minority representatives' threat to withdraw from governing coalitions or cabinets has been a technique employed by minorities to influence decision making. The approach is not at all unlike that used by minority political parties in the Western parliamentary democracies. Indeed, the leverage of minority groups is often exercised in manners quite parallel to minority parties.

The differences between sanctioned minority political parties and the minority groups studied here are psychological, both subjective and objective. Objectively, these groups may be expected to identify less fully with the extant political order and dominant nationalism than do members of sanctioned political parties. Subjectively, members of the dominant group and of other minoritiy groups *expect* such a reduced level of identification and therefore themselves behave accordingly, often reinforcing the competing loyalties in the minds of the minority group members.

MINORITIES, POLITICAL POWER, AND POLITICAL STABILITY—A REPRISE

While the issue of legitimacy is yet far from resolved in the region, the growing power of central government structures and force—which, ironically, is not synonymous with governmental stability—severly limits the likelihood of secession. The states in

---

*Bahrain's Sunnis and Shi'as are communities of approximately the same size, both numbering about 130,000. However, it is thought that the Shi'as may be slightly more numerous, even though Bahrain has long been dominated by Sunnis. (The ruling family is Sunni.) Cf. Appendix B. Like Bahrain, Iraq has traditionally been dominated by Sunnis. However, the number of Shi'as in Iraq is believed to be substantially larger

which the central government does not command sufficient strength to prevent secession are limited to Lebanon and some of the smaller Persian Gulf and Indian Ocean countries. These countries are not alone in facing a territorial secession threat if the political order should change drastically. For example, the end of Alawi rule in Syria could generate a serious secessionist threat by the Alawis. Geographical integrity of minorities' areas—as the Iraqis concluded with respect to their Kurds—substantially increases the credibility of secessionist thought.

By contrast, the political power of religious and ethnic and some national minorities is growing and may well pose increasing threats to the regime stability of countries like Iran, Iraq, Lebanon, Syria, and Turkey. Similarly, when minorities in power base their political strength on their fellow minority members the legitimacy and long-run prospects for tenure are not good. The short-run prospects for tenure, of course, may be greatly improved by strengthening the role of one's own group in the society, government, military, and economy. The inevitable resentment this strategy generates, however, is not a favorable omen for the long term. Power still is not synonymous with legitimacy.

The influx of capital and foreign workers to the Middle East introduces additional stresses to societies already besieged by pressures inherent in the process of modernization. All the countries of the Middle East save two are principally composed of Islamic peoples. These societies are burdened with traditions which so far have not been able to adapt themselves to rapid social change, though it must be said the Saudis and some others are making great strides to alter that record. It is suggested by many that Islam and modernization are incompatible, and yet in a number of states strenuous efforts toward real economic modernization coexist with energetic attempts to maintain the purity and give effect to the values of Islam. It is too early to know whether these attempts, or those of Israel's Jews to create a democratic yet Zionist state, will succeed. It is too early to be certain about the future of distinct ethnic or racial groups, whose opportunities to create their own nation-states have probably passed. It is too early to determine the conse-

---

than that of the Sunnis (Cf. Appendix B). In view of the Shi'a plurality, Iraq's Sunni leaders have experienced some concern over the resurgence of Shi'a consciousness in Iran. Yemen is the only Arab country where the Shi'as have dominated traditionally. Ironically, the Shi'as (Zaydis) of Yemen probably do not constitute a plurality in the Yemen Arab Republic. Although relatively evenly divided between Shi'a and Sunni, Yemen probably has a slight Sunni plurality.

quences of such massive immigrations of foreign labor as we are witnessing in the Gulf.

What seems clear is that minorities will continue to play an important role in determining the present and the future in the Middle East. It is apparent that strategies for dealing with the perceptions and expectations of minorities will greatly influence the course the Middle East follows over the next decade and beyond. There is little reason to forecast minority assimilation by dominant nationalisms as a function of modernization across the region, as some authorities have anticipated it around the globe. But there is every reason to expect that the political role of minorities in the Middle East will continue to be a key factor in the directions, velocity, and nature of regional social change.

NOTES

1. Michael C. Hudson, *Arab Politics: The Search for Legitimacy* (New Haven: Yale University Press, 1977).

2. We thus differ with Dankwart Rustow on only one element. Rustow suggests that the three essential concomitants of legitimacy are authority, identity, and equality. See Rustow, *A World of Nations: Problems of Political Modernization* (Washington, D.C.: Brookings Institution, 1967), *passim*, and several of his other works.

3. Hudson, *Arab Politics*, p. 4.

4. Developed, pluralist societies have suffered relatively less prominent or costly violence. The United States' racial unrest, for example, notwithstanding its sociological and political import, produced levels of violence which were, by international standards, quite low. This is true, as well, for the Belgian and Canadian cases. The major exception is Northern Ireland. See Christopher Hewitt, "Majorities and Minorities: A Comparative Survey of Ethnic Violence," *Annals of the American Academy of Political and Social Science* 933 (September 1977); 150-60, esp. 152.

5. The relative deprivation approach is most associated with Ted Gurr. See, for example, *Why Men Rebel* (Princeton: Princeton University Press, 1970); and *Cross-National Studies of Civil Violence* (Washington, D.C.: Center for Research in Social Systems, American University, 1969). See also Chong-Do Hah and Jeffrey Martin, "Toward a Synthesis of Conflict and Integration Theories of Nationalism," *World Politics* 27, no. 3 (April 1975), 361-86.

6. We are not, of course, dealing with "perfect" rigidity either. Indeed, scholars reflect increasing awareness of and interest in ethnic change, the variation in composition of ethnic group inclusion and exclusion over time. See Donald L. Horowitz, "Ethnic Identity," pp. 111-40, in *Ethnicity: Theory and Experience*, ed. Nathan Glazer and Daniel P. Moynihan (Cambridge; Harvard University Press, 1975); "Cultural Movements and Ethnic Change," *Annals of the American Academy of Political and Social Science* 933 (September 1977); 6-18.

7. "Majority rule works only when the minority has such confidence in the ultimate reasonableness of the majority and such conviction of the ultimate community of majority and minority interests that it can afford to respect the right of the

majority to rule." Inis L. Claude, Jr., *Swords into Plowshares*, rev. 3rd ed. (New York: Random House, 1964), p. 118. See also, generally, Inis L. Claude, Jr., *National Minorities: An International Problem* (Cambridge; Harvard University Press, 1955).

8. Karl W. Deutsch, *Nationalism and Social Communication: An Inquiry into the Foundations of Nationality*, 2nd rev. ed. (Cambridge, Mass.: MIT Press, 1966); Clifford Geertz, "The Integrative Revolution: Primordial Sentiments and Civil Politics in the New States," pp. 104-57, in *Old Societies and New States*, ed. Clifford Geertz (Glencoe, Ill.: Free Press, 1965); Kalman H. Silvert, *Expectant Peoples, Nationalism and Development* (New York: Vintage, 1963); Myron Weiner, "Political Integration and Political Development," *Annals of the American Academy of Political and Social Science*, 358 (March 1965); 52-64.

9. Rupert Emerson, *Self-Determination Revisited in the Era of Decolonization*, Occasional Papers in International Affairs, no. 9, (Cambridge, Mass.: Harvard University Center for International Affairs, 1964).

10. The most eloquent and erudite statesman to press for equal treatment of *all* non-self-governing peoples, whether in independent or other territorial status, was Fernand van Langenhove, proponent of the "Belgian Thesis." (*All* peoples or territories not fully self-governing on terms roughly equal to the "most" self-governing area or peoples within a polity are non-self-governing—this was the Belgian Thesis. Several anticolonial leaders, e.g., India, were vulnerable to this offensive.) See his "Le Problème de la protection des populations aborigènes aux Nations Unies," *Recueil des Cours* (Hague Academy of International Law) 89, no. 1 (1956); 319-433; and "La Question des aborigènes aux Nations Unies," pp. 126-44, in *The United Nations: 10 Years' Legal Progress*, ed. Gesina J. H. Van der Molen, W. P. J. Pompe, and J. H. W. Verzijl (The Hague: Nederlandse Studentenvereniging Voor Wereldrechtorde, 1956).

11. Cf. Anthony H. Birch, "Minority Nationalist Movements and Theories of Political Integration," *World Politics* 30, no. 3 (April 1978); 335-36, which discusses two of these points.

12. Birch, "Minority Nationalist Movements," notes the growth in concern in at least two different directions, the "internal colonialists" and the "new ethnicists" (*passim*). Some of the literature includes Cynthia H. Enloe, *Ethnic Conflict and Political Development* (Boston: Little, Brown, 1973); Glazer and Moynihan, eds., *Ethnicity*; Harold Isaacs, *Idols of the Tribe: Group Identity and Political Change* (New York: Harper & Row, 1975); Abdul Aziz Said, ed., *Ethnicity and U.S. Foreign Policy* (New York: Praeger, 1978); and Abdul A. Said and Luis R. Simmons, eds., *Ethnicity in an International Context* (New Brunswick, N.J.: Transaction, 1976).

13. Hudson uses similar categories but distinguishes between what we have called Arab, non-Sunni (e. g., Shi'a) and Arab, non-Muslim. This is, of course, a perfectly reasonable alternative. Hudson, *Arab Politics*, p. 59.

14. Edward E. Azar and R. D. McLaurin, "The Population Problem: The Demographic Imperative in Arab-Israeli Settlement," *Middle East Focus* 1, no. 3 (September 1978); 21.

15. *Ibid.*

16. Ian Lustick, "Arabs in the Jewish State: A Study in the Effective Control of a Minority Population" (Ph.D. diss. University of California at Berkeley, 1976).

17. Lustick calls this internal aspect of the control system "segmentation." *Ibid.*

18. *Ibid.*, pp. 376-415.

19. Cf. Ithiel de Sola Pool, "The Changing Soviet Union," 2:1043-50, in *The Art and Science of Psychological Operations*, ed. R. D. McLaurin et al., 2 vols. (Washington, D.C.: Government Printing Office, 1976), who discusses the difficulty of controlling information in an era in which communications complexity has made state borders extremely porous.

20. In an important, empirical study of the military effect of 183 variables on insurgency and government counterinsurgency, Condit and Cooper determined that access to external support was the single most powerful predictor of success (n=44 cases). D. M. Condit and Bert H. Cooper, Jr., *Strategy and Success in Internal Conflict* (Kensington, Md.: American Institutes for Research, 1971). Cf. D. M. Condit, *Modern Revolutionary Warfare: An Analytical Overview* (Kensington, Md.: American Institutes for Research, 1973), pp. 104-05.

21. See below and cf. Chapter 7. There are few accurate portraits of the Christian—especially Maronite—objectives. P. Edward Haley and Lewis W. Snider, eds., *Crisis in Lebanon: Participants and Issues* (Syracuse: Syracuse University Press, 1979), one of the best analyses of the conflict, is better on Palestinian than Christian perceptions. By late 1977 or early 1978, the Lebanese Maronite leaders were determined to perpetuate some form of partition that allowed for their complete control in Christian areas.

22. Cf. R. D. McLaurin, Mohammed Mughisuddin, and Abraham R. Wagner, *Foreign Policy Making in the Middle East* (New York: Praeger, 1977), pp. 231-42, and the sources identified in the notes.

23. *Ibid.*, chap. 6, *passim.* Jadid attempted to go beyond Alawi or military support to establish his legitimacy but weakened his power among the Alawi and the military in the process. Assad, attempting to achieve the same objective, has consistently concentrated on *building from a firm Alawi base in the military.*

24. R. D. McLaurin and Mohammed Mughisuddin, *Cooperation and Conflict: Egyptian, Iraqi, and Syrian Objectives and U.S. Policy* (Washington, D.C.: American Institutes for Research, 1975).

2

MINORITIES IN POWER: THE ALAWITES OF SYRIA

Peter Gubser

$\mathbf{A}$ny minority can dominate a majority if it has political, military, or economic superiority.[1] This statement was written during the French Mandate over Syria by the most famous student of the Alawites, the majority group in Latakia Province in northwest Syria who at the time were dominated by Sunni Muslims, Isma'ilis, and Christians in that province. By a curious twist of fate, the Alawites currently have the upper hand in all of Syria.

Who are the Alawites? How did this radical change come about? What does it bode for the Alawites' future? For Syria? To answer these questions, this chapter initially will describe briefly the people and their region and the distinctive Alawite religion, the key factor distinguishing this group from others in the Middle East. Then, in more detail, the sociopolitical structure and leadership of the society will be probed, and, finally, the internal and external political trends of the Alawites will be described and analyzed.

THE PEOPLE AND THEIR REGION

The Alawites are a concentrated Muslim minority group located in one major area with smaller numbers dispersed more widely in other regions of the Middle East. The greatest number live in the province of Latakia in northwestern Syria, with a significant overflow into the neighboring provinces of Homs and Hama. To the south of Latakia in the Lebanese district of Akkar are found a few Alawite

TABLE 2.1: The Alawite Community (approximate figures in thousands)

Country	Population	Year	Population	Year
Syria	495	1960	680	1970
Turkey	120	1940	185	1970
Lebanon	6	1956	9	1970
Total	—	—	874	1970

Source: Munir al-Sharif, *al-Muslimun al-'Alawiyun: Man Hum Wa'Ayna Hum*, 2nd ed. (Damascus: al-Matba'a al-'Umumiya, 1960), pp. 56, 123; Jacques Weulersse, *Le Pays de Alaouites* (Tours: Arrault, 1940), pp. 59-60; Moshe Zeltzer, "Minorities in Iraq and Syria," pp. 22-23, in *Peoples and Cultures of the Middle East*, ed. Ailon Shiloh (New York: Random House, 1969); J. C. Dewdney, "Turkey: Recent Population Trends," pp. 57-58, in *Populations of the Middle East and North Africa*, ed. by J. I. Clarke and W. B. Fisher (New York: Africana, 1972); Gabriel Baer, *Population and Society in the Arab East* (London: Routledge and Kegan Paul, 1964), pp. 82, 114; Michael C. Hudson, *The Precarious Republic: Political Modernization in Lebanon* (New York: Random House, 1968), p. 22. It should be noted that all figures are subject to doubt. Due to the fact that minority policies of the countries in which Alawites live obscure the true numbers, one has to work with extrapolations of census figures dating back to the 1930s.

villages and to the north of Latakia in the Turkish provinces of Hatay (formerly Alexandretta), Seyhan (or Adana), and Içel a much larger number of Alawites reside. Until the end of World War I, all of these provinces were part of the Ottoman Empire, without restrictive international borders, and as such the Alawites naturally migrated into these provinces just as they had into the provinces of Homs and Hama. In addition to this general region, scattered small groups of Alawites are found in the Wadi al-Taym in southeast Lebanon and in two villages north of Nablus in the Israeli-occupied West Bank of Jordan.[2] Alawite population figures appear approximately as shown in Table 2.1.

The major region where the Alawites live in Syria is characterized by three distinctive terrains: coast, mountains, and inland plains. On the Mediterranean coast are found small port towns and a narrow coastal plain. In the more northern part lies the large town of Latakia, which is surrounded by an expansive, agriculturally rich plain called the Sahal. The heart of the Alawite region, where most of the Alawites live in numerous small villages, is a mountain range, called Jabal al-Nusayriya, which parallels the coast, running from Turkey to close to the Lebanon and anti-Lebanon ranges. Although the range is less formidable than that of Lebanon, it is less developed, partially due to the lack of good water sources and fertile soils. The eastern part of the Alawite region, which lies in the provinces of Homs and Hama, is another plain.[3]

The Alawite mountains, where the bulk of the Syrian Alawites, live may be characterized as exceptionally poor and decidedly underdeveloped. Over the centuries, the Alawites have not terraced the mountains, depriving themselves of any control over their own terrain and climate. However, the land, with the exception of the Sahal surrounding the city of Latakia and the small Christian town of Safita in the south, is not blessed with a great potential for development. It is wanting in rivers and water sources; it is subject to destructive erosion from the hard rains; and it is lacking in rich soil.

Despite the impoverished nature of the land, the Alawites are primarily a rural people. In Syria, although they constitute the majority of the population of the province of Latakia, Alawites are only 11 percent of the population of the city of Latakia. Very few live in the towns of Homs and Hama, but substantial numbers live in the provinces of the same name. (The same pattern holds for Lebanon, where the Alawites live and work in the plains and low hills of the Akkar.) From another viewpoint, the Alawites live in two separate and distinctive rural patterns. The majority are mountain people, residing and earning their living in the Jabal al-Nusayriya, which stretches from southern Latakia into the Turkish province of Hatay and overlaps into the Syrian provinces to the east of Latakia, Homs and Hama. The balance of the Alawites, except for those few who live in urban areas, reside in the plains along the Mediterranean coast, from the Akkar through Latakia to Hatay, Seyhan, and Içel, and in the plains of Homs and Hama next to the Jabal al-Nusayriya.

The Alawites' rural nature is contrary to the predominant pattern found in the Islamic-Arab Middle Eastern culture which has always had a strong urban element (see Table 2.3). In Syria, significantly less than two-thirds of the population is rural. However, in Latakia province over three-quarters of the population lives in the countryside, reflecting the proclivities of the Alawites to live away from the cities.

Historical reasons best explain this Alawite pattern of living. As a persecuted religious minority from the time of the Mamluks and the Ottomans, they always sought a haven, and the mountains of Latakia proved to be their best defense. Also, even though some Alawites may have wanted to live in the cities, they were always made to feel unwelcome by the traditional urban population which was either of another Islamic sect or Christian. These groups prevented the Alawites from obtaining gainful employment except for the most menial kind and prevented them, at times physically, from taking part in the activities of the city. Finally, in the 1970s, this pattern is changing. As with the rest of the world, Syria is becoming more urbanized, and the Alawites are no exception to the rule. Many are now migrating to major urban centers in search of employment and education. The current Alawite dominance of the Syrian government additionally is facilitating this movement.

RELIGION

The key factor setting the Alawites off from the Sunni and Shi'a Muslim Arabs and other religious and ethnic groups in the Middle East is religion. This religion, founded in the tenth and eleventh centuries, contains a number of unique features which affect the Alawites' character and behavior. Thus, it is appropriate here to provide a brief summary of the salient aspects of Alawite religious belief.

The most significant belief distinguishing the Alawites from other Muslims is their strong focus on 'Ali, the paternal cousin and son-in-law of Muhammad, and his deification in their eyes. The Alawites believe in one God who manifested himself to the world seven different times. Each time God showed himself, he made use of two other persons who, with God, make up an inseparable Trinity and which are called the *Ma'ana*, the *'Ism*, and the *Bab*. The *Ma'ana* (the meaning) indicates that God is the meaning, sense, and reality of all things. The *'Ism* (the name) is also called the veil, because behind it the *Ma'ana* hides its glory, but through it, the *'Ism*, the *Ma'ana* reveals itself to the people. The *Bab* (door) is the entrance to knowledge about the *Ma'ana* and the *'Ism*. Given this breakdown, the following are the seven appearances of the *Ma'ana*, the *'Ism*, and the *Bab*.

Ma'ana	'Ism	Bab
Abel	Adam	Gabriel
Seth	Noah	Yayil ibn-Fatin
Joseph	Jacob	Ham ibn Kush
Joshua	Moses	Dan ibn Usbawt
Asaph	Solomon	Abdullah ibn-Siman
Simun al-Safa	Jesus	Ruzabah ibn al-Marzabah
'Ali	Muhammad	Salman al-Farisi

After 'Ali, God manifested himself in the Shi'a Imams. However, 'Ali is the greatest and most important manifestation of God, "so that he occupies in person and name, with respect to man, the position of the Deity himself." In addition, 'Ali's humanity was only apparent, he was not made of flesh and blood and did not act like other humans.[4]

This type of trilogy is very expressive of the nature of the Alawite religion. In each case, the 'Ism was considered at the time of his historical appearance or in the religious literature of Orthodox Muslims, Jews, and Christians as a prophet (or son of God) and undoubtedly the most important of the three. But for the Alawites, the real manifestation of God, the supreme one being 'Ali, was always hiding behind the more visible figure. Also, there is the Bab, the person who wrote or "propagandized" for the other two. It is upon some of the writings of Salman al-Farisi that the Alawites base a good portion of their beliefs and theology.

Another important beliefs of this group is the exoteric versus esoteric interpretations (called bataniya) of written religious books, the most important one being Kitab al-Majmu'a, doctrines and beliefs. Thus the exoteric is that which is apparent in the literal meaning of the word, while the esoteric is only known to those who are initiated into the mysteries and secrets of the religion, as described below in this chapter. This differentiation is apparent in the Alawites' distinction between the Ma'ana and the 'Ism, and it is carried into all phases of the religion. Other salient beliefs are as follows. First, all Alawites "were at the beginning of the world luminant lights and radiant spheres of noncorporeal nature,"[5] or, as others claim, stars. Second, when a virtuous Alawite dies, he becomes a star. But if he sins, he is transformed into a Jew, Muslim, or Christian. A soul of "one of the latter three, if relatively good, will become the soul of an Alawite and, if exceptionally good, will become a star. The number of transformations (metempsychoses) for the faithful is limited to seven; after this it will become a star irrespective of other activities. Third, Alawites are allowed to practice taqiya (the hiding of their true faith and the profession of another) for their protection and convenience. Fourth, women are inferior in a religious sense; they are neither taught the prayers nor allowed to be initiated.[6]

The origins of the beliefs of the Alawite religion are obscure and subject to considerable academic debate, but, in broad outline, they may be summarized as follows. "From paganism the [Alawites] took over the idea of a Divine Triad, of its successive incarnation in the seven cycles of world history, and of the transmigration of souls. From Shi'a Islam they adopted and exaggerated the cult of Ali, whom they regard as the incarnation of the Divinity; and from Isma'ilism, the idea of an esoteric teaching hidden from the masses and revealed only to the initiates after a complex period of initiation. From

Christianity they appear to have derived much of the ritual, the possession of which distinguishes them from other Islamic or post-Islamic sects."[7]

What is the meaning of the religion for the ordinary Alawites? On one level, there is little knowledge of the doctrine and theology, especially for the majority non-initiates. They have strong folk beliefs in talismans, magic, and *ziyaras* (burial places of holy people which are subject to pilgrimage). The common people also hold considerable faith in Khudr, a savior who can be compared to St. George the dragon killer. He may appear from time to time in corporeal form, but always is the Divinity of the sea and agriculture from which comes the livelihood of the Alawites. "In reality, Khudr is for the non-initiated people the divine appellation par excellence, as is 'Ali for the initiated people."[8] On another level, many Alawites, especially the educated non-initiated (many of whom make up the new educated middle stratum), state that they do not know and cannot know anything about their religion and therefore it means little to them. In actuality, this is a method of identifying with other members of the Alawite religion, for Shi'a and Sunni Muslims and Christians can and often do know something about their religion.[9] On still another level, many Alawites have argued that they did not identify with their religious group until the last decade. First, the isolation of the majority of the Alawites in the mountains and the lack of communication and education left them little aware of other groups, thus they had little need to be actively conscious of their religious identity. As their circumstances changed, the awareness and importance of religion was enhanced. Second, only in the last decade has membership in the Alawite sect become a political asset. Because Alawites have acceded to high positions, fellow Alawites can appeal to religious communal loyalty for jobs and economic benefits. In sum, this is what some have termed "situational selection," whereby an individual selects the group (to which he wants to belong and in which he can claim membership) that will benefit him most in a given situation. The Alawites have followed this pattern quite closely.

SOCIOPOLITICAL STRUCTURE AND LEADERSHIP

Stratification Systems

The Alawite community is subject to three forms of traditional social stratification, with the addition of a new stratum in the last two dacades. First, there is the differentiation among the religious shaykhs, the religiously initiated, and the religiously uninitiated; second, the social, political, and economic distinction between the notable families and the peasants; third, the dominance of the Sunni Muslims and Christians over the Alawites, especially along the Latakia coast plains and the plains of Homs and Hama; and fourth, the development and rise to power of the new middle stratum.

At the top of the religious stratification system are the religious shaykhs. This stratum may be considered almost a rank or caste, for only members of certain known and designated families may become religious shaykhs—no one else is allowed by religious dogma. Not all members of the shaykhly families become shaykhs, but only those who choose and are chosen to go through the initiation procedure and to study to be a shaykh. After a man has reached this position, he is treated deferentially by the larger Alawite society. His income is derived from the zakat (Islamic tithe), presents from notables and peasants alike, his own property, and fees for talismans and prayers. Socially, he tends to be bound to tradition. He is required to entertain—particularly other shaykhs—a considerable amount of time, especially at religious feasts. Over the years, a shaykh may gain a substantial reputation for solving disputes and occasionally serving as an arbiter. A few have risen to political power, rivalled political leaders, and eventually taken over a political clientele or split one with a rival leader. If the shaykh was noted for being particularly religious and/or his talismans and prayers were considered to have exceptional efficacy, upon and after his death his tomb would be subject to pilgrimage and adoration.[10] The shaykhly families are few.

The next two levels of religious stratification revolve around the question of whether an Alawite is initiated into the religious mysteries of his sect. Initiation is open to male Alawites whose parents are both Alawite. If a man wishes to be initiated, he approaches a religious shaykh who undertakes to teach him the secrets and esoteric dogma and theology of the Alawite religion. An individual who is initiated continues to function in the society as an ordinary peasant or notable. He possesses, however—and this is recognized and respected by most Alawites—a certain aura of religiosity. Finally, the bulk of the society is made up of those who are uninitiated.

In terms of socioeconomic stratification, the Alawites are by tradition divided into two major strata: the peasants and the notables. The peasants are the vast majority of the population, 90 percent in the late 1930s, but substantially less today. Their existance has been characterized traditionally by a hard, unsophisticated life with a simple pattern of birth, marriage, and death, their only social pleasures being various festivals and village life. In the mountains, the Jabal al-Nusayriya, the peasants in the past and today tend to own their own property, with only a small number sharecropping the land of notables. However, in the plains, until the Syrian government began expropriating the land of large landholders during and after the union with Egypt, very few owned any land at all: today many are still sharecropping the land of city dwellers, but a certain number are benefiting from the government's redistribution of expropriated land. Thus, within the peasant stratum, there were two quite different groups: those who owned their own land and had the relatively independent spirit of mountain people and those who were without land and were dominated by urban landowners, usually of a different religion than their own.

The notable families form the upper stratum. For the vast majority, this was an inherited position, yet some successful peasants certainly have risen to this level.* The life of the notable families is more varied than that of the peasants. Traditionally, a male member received some primary education, usually in the towns. Afterwards he returned to his village and contracted plural political marriages. He also learned how to manage his property and proceeded to help his family gather and/or maintain a political and social clientele. The notable families in the Latakia mountains have never been overly rich in land, but they always had some as the basis of their wealth. In addition, they would collect "taxes," receive presents, and gather fees for marriages from members of their clientele. Occasionally, their peasants were subject to corvée. Finally, it should be noted that these notable families are mostly located in the mountains; their presence and authority in the plains is often limited if not ephemeral due to the property being owned by non-Alawite city dwellers.[11]

The third form of stratification is the social and economic differentiation between the Alawite peasants of the plain and the absentee landowners of the towns, who are also of a different religion, usually Sunni Muslim and Greek Orthodox. As was mentioned above, prior to land expropriation in Syria, the peasants were dominated by the landowners and were forced to pay up to 75 percent of their crops in sharecropping arrangements. Because of this property arrangement, true notable families from the Alawites

---

*Sulayman Murshid is a prime example. A man of humble origins, he experienced a religious vision in the early 1920s. Based on a cultivated religious aura, he developed a large political following and formed his own tribe, the Ghasasna. In 1946, he was killed after he led a short-lived revolt against newly independent Syria.

could not arise; rather, there were intermediary families who sometimes acted as middlemen between the peasants and the landowners. For the most part, however, political and economic patrons were the landlords themselves. After land expropriation and land redistribution, some of these landlords lost much of their power. Many, though, still retain some if not substantial portions of their land in Latakia because landholdings were never particularly large there and thus not subject to considerable expropriation. In contrast, landholdings in Homs and Hama were quite large and were mostly expropriated, thus destroying the landowners' hold over the peasants and their position in an Alawite stratification system.

The new middle stratum is a recent addition to the stratification structure of the Alawites. Under many names, this feature has been recognized and investigated by students of the developing countries and the Middle East. Each has given it an important and often crucial position in the transitional societies.[12] What sets this group apart from the others is what is at best an intellectual commitment to achievement versus ascriptive criteria for professional advancement and a higher value put on modern skills and abilities derived from education. This is not to say that members of this group completely eschew ascriptive criteria and values such as the family, tribe, and religious group. However, they do emphasize them less than other members of the society. On another plane, this group as a societal entity is competing strongly with the traditional ruling stratum for leadership positions, and there is evidence that they have succeeded in many cases. Some traditional leaders whose positions were based primarily on economics have been displaced. Others who based their power on broader political assets have been able to maintain their positions, but in an altered manner. Thus members of this new middle stratum are sharing power on municipal and village councils and increasingly are taking over bureaucratic positions, where their skills are particularly valued.

Viewing the new, educated middle stratum from another viewpoint, it should be stated that it is not a corporate group, it does not have any internal cohesion, but sub-groups within it do exhibit these qualities. Thus, individuals from this general category are organized in or members of political parties, for example, Ba'th and Syrian Social National Party (SSNP), social and sports clubs, army officers corps, and informal groups gathered around one man. There is no way to estimate the size of the new middle stratum, but it is increasing in size due to the expansion of the state's educational system. This category is also composed of different kinds of individuals. Thus, lower and higher-level civil servants, teachers, army officers of various ranks, government leaders, political operatives, and professionals all have many different characteristics, but they do share certain common ones as defined above. Their distribution largely depends on where there are employment opportunities for educated individuals. Thus, they are concentrated in the cities and towns where the bureaucracy and more and better schools are located. However, many are scattered around the village and district schools in the province of Latakia and neighboring districts.

Because of their education and their positions in the government—as civil servants, in the officer corps and top government positions—they command considerable prestige among all Alawite strata and groups. As a group, they do not have a defined or definable social influence or political power. Rather their influence and power are much more a function of the nature of the organization(s) or group(s) to which they belong. Thus, many are army officers and soldiers and party members. They form part of the cadre and leadership of these groups, and, because of the political success of these organizations, they have gained the dominant political position in Syria. (It should be remembered that there are not only Alawites in these organizations.) Equally, through their functions in the bureaucracy, they are in the position of dispensing favors and benefits for their own or their political group's benefit.

Tribal System

Turning to Alawite tribal structure, it should be stated initially that it is quite different from the tribal structure traditionally associated with the Middle East, that of the bedouin. Structurally, the Alawite tribe (or at times only its subsections) may be described as a territorial group with pyramidal and segmentary patterns. The significance of the pyramidal pattern is that there is an overall *vertical* organization of the tribe, not just a series of horizontal units with the same general identity. But the Alawite tribe is also inherently segmentary; each segment at each level has a separate identity and a degree of power and authority of its own. Coupling the two concepts, pyramidal and segmentary, indicates that the tribe is organized in an ascending series of segments, each a political and social group at some times and in some events. Thus, each unit at a structurally higher level automatically contains all those groups below it. Nor does any real leadership hierarchy connect the groups; instead, for example, the shaykh of one of the subsections is in turn the shaykh of the section of which it is a part; similarly, the shaykh of one of the sections is shaykh of the tribe.

As a consequence of internecine fights among tribal sections, tribes, and tribal confederations and of the difficulties of communication within the Jabal al-Nusayriya, the structure is not always as clear-cut and discrete as the above description. Over the generations, tribes or tribal sections segment. Thus, at times, a new section forms and splits off from an old section but remains under the umbrella of the larger tribe. Equally, a tribe may split into two parts, sometimes remaining as two sections with the same tribal name and at other times forming totally different tribes. The opposite process, that is, fusion, also takes place. In this manner, two tribes may unite to make one tribe or two sections of separate tribes may split off and then unite together to form a separate section of a third tribe or to form a new tribe of their own.

The highest structural groups in the Alawite mountains are the tribal confederations, which are loose associations of tribes formed over the centuries. Because most political competition is at a lower level than the confederations, it is often observed that they have little political or social coherence. But when political activity does rise to this level, it is evident that they do play a role in the individual Alawite's loyalty.

This flexible pattern of a shifting tribal structure may be demonstrated graphically with a list of the tribes as they existed in the early 1930s in comparison to a list of them as they appeared in the late 1950s.

In the list of tribes in Table 2.2, it is obvious that the tribes with quite large populations—Kalbiya, al-Rashawana, Bayt al-Khayat, Bayt al-Haddad, Matawra, and al-Namaylatiya—have not had a coherent authority structure for any extended period of time. They may be brought together for certain political purposes, but for most of the time their sections function as the largest operative unit. In those tribes which are geographically split, there also is no single authority structure over a long period of time.

Table 2.3 below gives some indication of how the tribes and confederations have changed over one generation. Comparing the two tables, one finds that ten names have disappeared, while seven new ones have appeared. The difference should partly be ascribed to the manner in which the two cited authorities gathered information. But they did use many of the same sources so the name changes do at least reflect the dynamics of the Alawite tribal structure. Again, as in Table 2.2, those tribes in Table 2.3 should not be considered as coherent units; the subtribe level would be the most important operative unit.

Why do the tribes split into parts or join together? One of the

TABLE 2.2:   Alawite Tribes and Their Confederations in the Early 1930s

Tribe	Population
Kalbiya Confederation	
Kalbiya	8,700
Dariwasa*	4,900
Bayt al-Shilaf	5,200
Nuwasara*	4,500
al-Jurud	3,300
Kharala*	7,700
al-Rashawana	8,400
Jalkiya	2,700
Rislana	5,300
Khayatin Confederation	
Bayt al-Khayat*	26,500
'Amamra	5,600
al-Saramta	4,100
No tribe	6,500
Haddadin Confederation	
Bayt al-Haddad	29,200
al-Mahlaba	5,600
Rikawana	2,400
Banu 'Ali	6,000
Bayt Yakout	700
Bashlawa	2,700
Shamsin	2,100
No tribe	900
Matawra Confederation	
Matawra	23,300
Matawra of Banyas	1,400
al-Namaylatiya*	15,000
al-Bashargha*	5,000
al-'Arajana	1,000
No tribe	500

Note: The tribes with asterisks beside their names are not territorially coherent but are separated into two or more geographical units. Also, none of the tribes lives in the plain surrounding the city of Latakia; this is a non-tribal Alawite region.

Source: Jacques Weulersse, Le Pays de Alaouites (Tours: Arrault, 1940), pp. 330-33.

most important reasons is the demographic dynamics of the tribe over generations. Because of births and deaths, disease, famine, or prosperity, a tribe or a tribal section, on the one hand, may grow, become too large for a single leader to control, and split into two. On the other hand, a tribe or section may shrink, become too small to have much political weight on its own, and join a larger group. Another significant cause for fusion or segmentation is a dispute. If a dispute arises that cannot be solved easily, it usually splits the group, one part often leaving the geographical area. The most important cause for this tribal shifting, however, lies in the political maneuvering of the tribal leaders and their families. An ambitious chief competes with other chiefs in his tribe for a political clientele and even at times with chiefs of other tribes and confederations. As he draws men and families into his clientele, loyalties change, and over the years the clientele members often change their tribal allegiance. A graphic example of this pattern is the rise to power of Sulayman Murshid mentioned above. In Table 2.2, there is no Ghasasna tribe, but in Table 2.3 the Ghasasna tribe totals over 36,000 members. This is the result of Murshid's activities during the 1930s and early 1940s, when he gained many adherents of the Saratma in the Jabla District, Bayt al-Khayat in Talkalakh district, Matawra in Misyaf and Talkalakh districts, and Numaylatiya in Talkalakh district. After Murshid's death, because the high value of remaining a Ghasasna no longer existed, some of these tribesmen returned to their original tribes.

With this background on the structure and dynamics of the Alawite tribal system, it is now appropriate to turn to tribal leadership as such. The base of a tribal chief's power is all those political assets that give him his position and that he brings to bear in his political activities. These political assets may be categorized as economic goods and services, status, information, force, and authority.

The chief of a tribal section or a clientele has a plethora of economic resources to draw from. Through his notable family, he has an inheritance which he attempts to maintain or build up. Two decades ago, he was able to collect "taxes" and marriage fees and receive presents from his followers; a measure of this practice continues today. Through his connections with the bureaucracy, he is able to gather goods and services from the government. These resources are in turn used to enhance his own personal wealth but more importantly to gather and maintain a political following. Members of his immediate group, especially armed supporters, need to be paid; occasionally, individuals of his larger group petition him

TABLE 2.3: Alawite Tribes and Their Confederations, 1959

Latakia Province

Tribe	Latakia District	Haffa District	Jabla District
Kalbiya Confederation			
Kalbiya	1,045	7,141	15,862
al-Rashawana	—	—	2,419
al-Qarahala	—	198	10,811
Rislana	—	—	—
Bayt Muhammad	—	231	—
al-Turud	—	559	—
Nuwasara	573	179	3,026
Khayatin Confederation			
Bayt Khayat, al-Faquwara, al-'Ahadiya, al-Halahiya, al-Saramta	2,464	1,632	7,851
al-Ghasasna	—	—	20,107
Haddadin Confederation			
Bayt Haddad	1,890	3,292	26,570
Shamsin	—	—	—
al-Mahlaba	—	—	1,476
Matawra Confederation			
al-Matawra, al-Jawahara, al-Sawarma	—	—	1,487
al-Namaylatiya	7,451	1,784	8,878
al-Darawsa	—	8,347	548
al-Bashargha	—	—	675
al-'Arajna	—	434	—

Note: This table does not include very many tribal members for the plains around Latakia because of the lack of a tribal structure in this region. Dashes indicate negligible number.

Source: Adapted from Munir al-Sharif, *al-Musliman al'Alawiyn: Man Hun Wa 'Ayra Hum*, 2nd ed. (Damascus: al-Matba'a al-'Umumiya, 1960), pp. 117, 124.

for funds. The connections with the government are especially important, for he often exchanges administrative favors, government jobs, and economic benefits extended to his region for the political support of his clientele.[13]

Status and prestige, if used wisely, may help a chief to gain and maintain considerable political support. The name of his notable

Table 2.3 (continued)

	Latakia Province			Hama Province	Homs Province
Banyas District	Tartous District	Safita District	Total	Misyaf District	Talkalakh District
57	—	—	24,105	—	—
4,317	—	—	6,790	9,727	2,580
1,090	—	—	11,999	2,500	—
—	150	11,941	12,091	—	—
—	—	—	231	—	—
—	—	—	559	—	—
—	3,231	765	7,774	800	—
14,022	6,787	20,854	53,610	7,480	6,824
—	—	—	20,107	2,386	13,620
10,606	17,702	17,959	77,019	6,490	3,856
—	1,183	1,938	3,121	—	—
—	—	—	1,476	—	—
8,074	3,318	12,422	25,301	18,840	9,204
2,164	1,957	—	22,234	1,646	—
—	—	—	8,895	59	—
—	2,254	4,656	7,585	223	—
—	—	—	434	—	—

family automatically gives him a certain aura of esteem and provokes social deference.[14] The Alawite chief traditionally receives a measure of formal education, usually just at the primary level. Subsequently, he is given a practical education in managing land and more importantly in the ways and means of political life. Early in his life, a political marriage is arranged for him, and he will continue to contract political marriages for himself throughout his political career. This status gives him access to individuals of political standing and helps open doors in the government bureaucracy.[15] With respect to the general Alawite population it almost automatically gives him an opening to leadership positions if he uses most of his political assets properly.

Information is a particularly valuable political resource, and Alawite chiefs and notable families have more access to and control over it than other members of the community. They are more educated, making the printed word and all its accompanying benefits more accessible: newspapers, bureaucratic operations, correspondence. They are richer and so have a greater ability to buy radios, televisions, and publications. They are members of notable families and so are in the stratum both with the most information and where it circulates. They have contacts with the bureaucracy and so are in a position to act as the middlemen between the Alawite tribesmen and the government. With this control over some of the key information, the Alawite chief is able to gain services which he can exchange for political support, and he is in a position to give out, withhold, or manipulate information for local political purposes. Conversely, it is often upon these same men that members of the bureaucracy have relied for information about the Alawites.

The use of force as a political asset has been endemic throughout Alawite history. Alawite chiefs have access to this resource by dint of their control over political followings, and they have used it at various levels of political activity. On the local level, the chief usually has a small group of strong men who historically were the insurance that tribesmen would pay "taxes" and provide labor for the corvée; also, these men would provide protection for the chief and at times for members of his clientele. On a regional level, there have been numerous armed conflicts between chiefs, tribal sections, tribes, and confederations. On the national level, the Alawites have often challenged the authority of the government with the use of armed forces: the nineteenth century fights with the Ottomans, the rising against Prince Faysal, Shaykh Salah al-'Ali's revolt against the French during the early days of the mandate, Sulayman Murshid's challenge to the Syrian authorities before and after World War II, and rioting against Sunni Muslims in the 1960s. On each of these occasions, the chief who can prove himself by bringing force to bear attracts other followers and further enhances his power and political assets.

A tribal chief's authority is an ephemeral but important political asset. In one sense, it is the sum of all the other assets, which give him his position in the first place. In another, however, it gives him the right in the eyes of his tribal clientele to perform many significant social and political functions in the community. Admittedly, authority is often based on the threat of force, and it may disappear as one chief wins over another's following. Nevertheless, through this authority the chief has the strongest influence in dispute settling within his following, in arranging marriages (which often have the benefit of consolidating or gaining political support), and in making decisions affecting the whole community.

Alawite tribal chiefs employ these political assets in their competition with other chiefs for supporters and clients. The arena is usually the section or the tribe. Tribal members do not easily cross tribal lines in their political and social loyalty. However, when especially ambitious chiefs like Shaykh Salah al-'Ali or Sulayman Murshid attempt to gain more power and followers, tribal members will and do cross these lines. This pattern has caused students of the Alawite community to write about the decline in the importance of the tribe and its loss of social and political meaning.[16] This is a misinterpretation, however. Because most of the political resources and other geographical and demographic factors have remained relatively constant over a considerable period of time, the pattern described has remained, or rather developed, within the context of the socioeconomic changes that have affected the Alawites.

In the predominately non-tribal areas in the plains along the Mediterranean coast and in the provinces of Homs and Hama, tribal leadership and authority have long been weak or nonexistent, primarily because no Alawite can gain enough political assets to challenge the large landowners. Through the ownership of land on which the Alawite peasants work, the landowners—until their property was expropriated—were able to control the peasants politically.[17] This form of leadership was (and is, where it still exists) of a considerably different nature than that in the Alawite mountains. The landowner has a different set of assets whereby he exercises control, his primary asset being the ownership of the peasant's means of livelihood. He lacked any solidarity with the Alawite peasant through religion or tribe and had little to say about marriage arrangements. In contrast to the tribal leaders, he did not use force to subjugate the peasants; rather, he employed it in order to coerce them to obey his will. The arrangement was dictated through the ownership of land, not by any other form of loyalty. When and where the peasants had the opportunity to break away from this form of control after the expropriation of land in the 1960s, they did so.

Looking at the tribal chiefs from another standpoint, they may be considered as a group only by dint of shared characteristics; they have no common organization, internal cohesion, or political stand binding them together. They are distributed fairly equally over the Alawite mountains relative to the number of Alawites in given areas and the nature of the terrain allowing for communication. Their power is not in the numbers of the group as a whole but in their political power over a particular group of people, their clienteles. As was described above, each chief has a political following which usually includes a small number of armed retainers. These chiefs also form small, constantly shifting cliques (kutlas), which are described below.

These traditionally oriented leaders have retained a measure of political power despite the social revolution taking place in Syria. There was very little expropriation and redistribution of land in Latakia; so the political assets of the tribal chiefs remain. Where they have lost power is in the staffing and access to government bureaucracy. Previously it was through these leaders that most of the benefits of the government were funneled to the tribesmen or through whom the tribesmen gained access to the government bureaus. However, today, with the increased staffing of the bureaucracy by the educated new middle stratum and the control of the government by the party (Ba'th) the tribal chiefs' relationship with the government is being undermined. The individuals of the new stratum, working primarily through the government bureaucracy or governmentally sponsored organizations, have taken over some of the political and social functions and resources of the more traditional leaders.[18] Thus, by controlling the distribution of goods, services, and economic benefits—that is, by their staffing the bureaucracy, forming governmentally sponsored agricultural cooperatives, and gaining positions on town and village councils—they have removed partially the more traditionally oriented leaders' economic resources. And some of these actions correspond to the revolutionary policies of the Syrian government. However, deep social and political changes always take a considerable time to take root, and, consequently, it has been observed that the tribal leaders have retained a certain role in this whole process. This is especially the case with non- or little-educated peasants, whose tribal loyalty remains intact for a longer time than does that of their more educated communal brothers. In addition, there is evidence that this tribal loyalty remains in at least some form among individuals who are educated and politically active on the national scene.[19] Thus, although the Alawite tribal chiefs' position is in the process of being changed, they certainly have not been replaced completely.

As with other Alawites, tribal chiefs share certain common attitudes and values. The most salient of these are a feeling of the superiority of their religion, a desire for a measure of autonomy for the Alawites (especially when a non-Alawite-dominated government is ruling Syria), and a hearty dislike of being discriminated against and "exploited" by Sunni Muslims, Isma'ilis, and Christians. More specifically to this group, a traditionalism and desire to preserve their position is prevalent, a typical characteristic of any individual or group that is in power. It should be noted that this group of leaders, through their notable families, does evidence a significant degree of flexibility. The notable families do send sons to school so that they will become members of the educated new middle stratum and retain a political position in the new, changing structure. For example, the notable al-'Ali family, from which came Shaykh Salih al-'Ali, the leader of a revolt against the French during the mandate, had in the early 1970s a member who was commander of the Syrian army, Ibrahim al-'Ali.

Communal and Regional Solidarity

Alawite communal-political solidarity is a recent and still developing phenomenon. There has always been a sense of identity of being an Alawite on religious grounds, but not until recently was this transferred to social and political loyalty for the group as a whole.* Previously, the largest group to which an individual gave his loyalty was a tribe, a confederation, or the following of a particular chief. These groups in turn allied with separate non-Alawite leaders or groups, competed with and even fought each other on these terms. Non-tribal Alawites were the political followers of Alawite and non-Alawite leaders. With the development of communications and educational systems, a growing solidarity among Alawites is apparent. Starting with the intellectuals, it gradually spread to the peasantry by the late 1960s. Thus, today most Alawites support other Alawites over members of another religion, irrespective of most other considerations.[20] This new found solidarity certainly has contributed to the Alawites' success in gaining a large measure of control over the Syrian government in the last decade.

A phenomenon concomitant with the above is the strong regionalism prevalent in Latakia province and overlapping into the Alawite districts in Homs and Hama. Historically in the Middle East, the agro-city, a central major city with its agricultural hinterland, has been a semi-independent economic entity and a political and administrative unit with which loyalty and identity developed.[21] This loyalty intensified especially when a region was mostly made

---

*An exception to this in a different sense is the occasional Alawite revolts against outside powers in preindependent Syria.

up of one religious group like the Alawites. This regional loyalty has not been undermined with the introduction of modern education and radical political ideologies, which theoretically should be cross-regional, because the Alawites, especially the new educated middle stratum, are politicized while still in their provincial high schools; so their "political and ideological loyalties reflect the local political situation in their particular" province.[22] Thus, this active concept of regionalism has remained operative irrespective of the type of government: be it Ottoman, French, or Arab; traditional or modern; capitalistic or socialistic; non-revolutionary or revolutionary.

POLITICAL DYNAMICS

Internal Trends

The Alawites have no overall structure or organization to give them a semblance of unity or a theater for politics involving the whole group. On a traditional plane, the group is divided politically and socially into tribes and tribal confederations, the latter of which were and are very weak. Moreover, a portion of the Alawites are not even members of tribes. With respect to religion, the Alawites on the one hand are split into four different sects (Haidaris, Shamalis or Shamsis, Kalazis or Qamaris, Gha'ibis) and, on the other, there is no organized structure for the Alawite clergy even on the sect level. On another plane, the Alawites are separated by political borders. The Alawites in Turkey have no significant political contact with their neighbors to the south; also, for the most part, they are not tribal, and so lack even this tenuous tie. However, the Alawites in Lebanon do have sustained contact with their Syrian brothers and are members of the same tribes.

Despite these divisions, there exist two kinds of internal Alawite politics which interact and clash with each other. The traditionally oriented tribal chiefs and leaders of clientele groups compete with each other. Using their political assets, they attempt to build up followings or clienteles, often persuading another chief's followers (or a portion of them) to join their clientele. Among chiefs, constantly shifting alliances, called *kutlas*, are formed. A temporary bloc such as this attempts to gain more followers (even though at times and at the same time they are competing among themselves for adherents) and to gather power for its *kutla* in the politics of its district, province, or the country. In addition, they seek alliances with non-Alawite leaders in these maneuverings. At one time, all intra-

Alawite politics were dominated by this form of allegiance, activity, and exercise of power. But with the rise of the new middle stratum, a new and very important dimension was added.

The growth and politicization of the Alawite new educated middle stratum started in the high schools, primarily in the province of Latakia. The SSNP in the 1930s and the Ba'th Party in the late 1940s recruited members while they were still in high school; by the 1950s they had succeeded in mobilizing significant segments of the population. Both parties sent equal numbers to the military academy in the 1950s, but by 1960 the SSNP had been virtually totally defeated, leaving the field open to the Ba'th Party.[23] Within the Ba'th Party, especially after the union with Egypt during which the national organization was seriously damaged, the power base for the Alawite leaders was in Latakia, and upon this base they were able to reach for power on a national level. In turn, leading men, such as Salah Jadid and Hafez al-Assad (both Alawite military officers and Ba'thists), "in the 1960s repeatedly used their national power to consolidate their local base of support. Success in local level politics, then, catapults individuals into the national arena; and success in national politics enhances their appeal in their local"[24] region. Finally, in regard to the clash between the traditionally oriented tribal chiefs and the new middle stratum, it appears that the latter are in ascendancy. This group joined in a loose alliance with a portion of the peasants under the leadership of members of the former and ex-peasants like Hafez al-Assad. The purpose of this alliance was to undermine the traditional local elite, and it succeeded in completely ruining the leading economic families.[25] The latter would include Sunni Muslims and Christians and a very few Alawites. While the new middle stratum has succeeded in partially replacing or undermining the power and authority of the traditionally oriented tribal chiefs, notable or chiefly families have not lost their position entirely. Aside from retaining many of their traditional sociopolitical assets, the notable families also certainly have members in the Ba'th Party who consider themselves members of the new educated middle stratum. (This is not an atypical pattern in the Middle East, that is, for notable families to have individuals in various political camps.) In this way, these families may retain some leading positions in the Alawite society.

There is no evidence that any of these trends has spilled over into Turkey, where the Alawites identify with Arabs and interact with them as a quasi-political group, but there has been some influence on the Alawites of Lebanon. There, Ba'thists from Syria have crossed over the border and persuaded the Alawite peasants to demand land reform measures as in Syria. These same peasants also attacked local Maronite Christian villages in the Akkar region during the Lebanese civil war.

External Trends

Prior to Syrian independence, the Alawites' relations with non-Alawites may be characterized as remote, filled with potential conflict, and with the Alawite always on the lesser side of the relationship, that is, discriminated against on religious grounds and "exploited" economically. In the urban areas, there was only very minimal contact between the Alawite community and other religious communities.

> Each one of them lives apart with its customs and its laws. Not only are they different, moreover, they are hostile . . . the idea of mixed marriages appears to be inconceivable. Not one Alawite would dare enter a [Sunni or Shi'a] Muslim mosque. Formerly, not one of their [religious] shaykhs was able to go to town on the day of public prayer without risking being stoned. All public demonstrations of a community's separate identity appeared as a challenge . . . Each person lives in his quarter in a secret manner. Each quarter is virtually autonomous with its own mukhtar, religious shaykh, its council of elders, and its own police.[26]

As has been stated, the vast majority of the Alawites live in the rural areas, while the cities and towns are dominated by the other Muslims and Christians. Here, too, there was traditionally only minimal contact fraught with violence. The townspeople "knew nothing" of the surrounding area and never claimed to have roots there, unlike townspeople in many other areas of the Middle East. But the Alawites had to go to the towns for trade, and there conflict often arose.

> An injury [by a Sunni Muslim] inflicted on an Alawite peasant in the town market would rouse his religious brothers in the mountain who would then avenge themselves against the Sunni Muslim minority in their area; an explosion which would call for, in its turn, a counter-demonstration in the Sunni cities. One may say that each community thus lives in the anxious expectation of having "martyrs" to avenge by the excesses of saintly, pious, and profitable anger.[27]

Thus, social, religious, and political relations were obviously bleak, but the economic interrelations were as bad or worse. Like virtually all other Middle Eastern areas, the towns in the Alawite area imported much more from the countryside than they exported to it. In the plains area, where the land was owned by town dwellers and farmed by Alawites, the relationship was particularly onerous. The landowner took half or more (sometimes as much as three-quarters) of this produce, while the peasant had to supply the seed, farming implements, animal power, and labor. The peasants of the mountain were much freer in this respect, but again they were at the mercy of the urban traders for selling their produce.

Given this background, it is not surprising that the Alawites were slow to develop an identity with Arab nationalism or the emerging Syrian nation. During the French Mandate, the Alawites had little consciousness of being Arab. The French encouraged this by setting up a separate government of Latakia and fostering the development of an independent Alawite identity and "a more conscious particularist spirit than they had previously possessed."[28]

Pre-twentieth century Alawite history is full of revolts and secessionist movements against the Mamluks and the Ottomans. With the arrival of the French after World War I, this rebellious tradition was continued under Shaykh Salih al-'Ali, but then the French turned his antipathy around and allowed the Alawites of Latakia a separate state for a time. Upon independence, the new Syrian republic was faced with a traditional centrifugal tendency on the part of the Alawites. At the outset, the Syrian government was faced with a revolt by Sulayman Murshid, but this was quickly quelled and the rebel leader was put to death. However, this did not put a stop to the autonomous, centrifugal feelings of the Alawites. "Alawi leaders . . . among them Ibrahim al-Kinj and Munir al-'Abbas . . . called upon the government to add an Alawi minister, to appoint an Alawi governor in the province, and set free the group of Murshid. Otherwise, they said, the province would seek to attach itself to Lebanon." Alawite leaders also had contacts with Amir Abdullah of Transjordan with respect to his greater Syria scheme.[29]

Corresponding to these actions,

One of the first steps taken by the Syrian government after independence was to reduce, and eventually to abolish, communal representation in the parliament which the various minorities had enjoyed under the French Mandate. A further step in this direction was to abrogate certain jurisdictional rights in matters of personal status, which were granted to the Alawis . . . by the French authorities.[30]

In summary, the new Syrian state was acting on three levels vis-à-vis the Alawites (and other minorities). First, it needed "to assert its integrity and prove its effectiveness to the public" so it felt compelled to subdue the Alawites' atavistic centrifugal tendencies. Second, in its quest for some kind of uniformity, inspired by nationalism, it needed to eliminate legal and practical vestiges and protection for separatism. Third, its state nationalism required it first to contain and then subdue the Alawites' autonomous aspirations.[31] By the mid-1950s, especially with the crushing of the 1954 Druze revolt against the Shishakli government, the Syrian government succeeded in many of its aims, and the Alawites started to take a larger role in the life of the country.

This larger role in Syria at first consisted of joining the military and the political parties. With respect to the former, a number of steps have led to the Alawites' dominance of the officers corps and key commands, as well as the ranks of the army. First, during the French Mandate, the majority group (the Sunni Muslims) of the Syrian nation did not want to cooperate with the French authorities, as evidenced by their lack of enrollment in the French-directed Syrian forces. Second, the French specifically encouraged the recruitment of minority groups into the Syrian forces because they thought these groups would be more loyal to French policy and so that the French could more readily carry out their "divide and rule" program. The urban Sunni Muslims have traditionally disclaimed military service both during and after the mandate and thus have, for the most part, attempted to avoid the armed forces, often even to the point of buying their way out of the draft. The Alawites who were, in the vast majority, either poor plain or mountain peasants, saw in the army an opportunity to see other aspects of life. Many Alawites who had been able to attain a secondary education used the military academy as a means to continue their education, which otherwise they could ill afford. Once Alawite's gained positions in the ranks, the noncommissioned officers corps and the commissioned officer corps, they encouraged their relatives, fellow tribesmen, and fellow villagers to join the military. The political parties—the Ba'th and SSNP—encouraged their members to enroll in the army in order to secure more power for their political group within the country. As a result of the armed forces' participation in politics and the numerous *coups d'état* since independence, the Sunni Muslim officer class was greatly reduced in the 1950s by purges and transfers. This process left the Alawites (and Druze, to a lesser extent) in the important commanding positions in the 1960s. By the 1970s, for example, all army strike units were effectively controlled by Alawite personnel. With this power, they have taken over a high percentage of all authoritative positions in Syria.[32]

Concomitant with these developments was the political parties' recruitment of Alawites into their ranks. Because of the Alawites' religious minority status, they were primarily interested in secular parties, that is, the SSNP and the Ba'th. The Muslim Brotherhood had no attraction for them because of its Sunni Muslim orientation. The Arab Nationalist movement symbolized by Egypt's President Gamal Abdul Nasser also had little draw for them because of its Egyptian sponsorhip, its sometimes strong, sometimes weak Islamic overtones; and its appeal to greater Arabism, a rather remote concept for Alawites just entering the Syrian political scene. The SSNP was virtually eliminated by the late 1950s, leaving the Ba'th Party as the only organized political party for ambitious young Alawite civilians and officers. This party they joined in large numbers, and the educated new middle stratum was using it to gain power in the Latakia region in the 1950s.

Breaking this Alawite pattern both in the military and the Ba'th Party was Syria's brief union with Egypt in the form of the United Arab Republic (U.A.R.) between 1958 and 1961. The Alawites disliked the union on several counts.

> The Alawites were primarily afraid that they were going to be pushed around in favor of Egyptian immigrants. They were particularly worried that the Ghab irrigation project was going to be turned over to Egyptian peasants. This fear was undoubtedly encouraged by Younes, the Minister of Agriculture, who said that Egyptian immigration depended on the implementation of irrigation projects. The Alawites also suffered considerably from the drought in that they are principally farmers. To add to their plight they were not allowed to go freely to Lebanon to find work.[33]

Second, the Alawites, already a minority but 10 percent of Syria, did not want to be subsumed by a much larger majority of Sunni Muslim Arabs, which was one effect with the addition of Egypt. Third, the dissolution of the Ba'th Party (and all other parties) was disliked by all Ba'thists but particularly by the Alawites (and the Druze). These men had not been consulted or informed about this action, and they naturally resented it. But, much more importantly, the dissolution would destroy the one organized group through which they could bring about what they considered to be desperately needed reforms and even social revolution in Latakia and the neighboring provinces. In addition, this move "suddenly snapped the thin thread . . . so vital for provincial people . . . connecting the regional party apparatus in the provincial towns with Damascus."[34]

After the break with Egypt in 1961, the previous formal dissolution of the Ba'th Party on a national scale proved to be a political boon to the Alawites. After the coup of 1963 which brought the Ba'th to power in Syria, the party as such was not well organized, but it had maintained its organization in some of the provinces and most strongly and importantly in Latakia.[35] With this and the army as a base, the Alawites eventually were able to gain control of the government in Syria.

The military coups d'état and political maneuvering that brought the Alawites of the Ba'th Party and the army to power in the 1960s have been well described by other authors in numerous works.[36] Therefore only a brief analytical outline will be presented here.

It may be safely stated that the intermeshing of two key factors brought the Alawites into the top positions of power in the Republic of Syria. These were, first, the large number of Alawites in the military both as officers and enlisted men and, second, the Alawites' control of the well-organized Latakia branch of the Ba'th Party and their strong influence in its national organization. During the internecine struggles within the party and the military in the early and mid-1960s, Alawite officers gradually pushed their way to the top of both organizations; following a coup d'état in 1970, General Hafez al-Assad, an Alawite with truly poor origins, became president of Syria on February 22, 1971.

Alawite communal solidarity certainly aided the Alawites in their struggle for power. The question of the nature and intensity of communal solidarity is always difficult in any context, but it is particularly so in independent Syrian history. The potential for it was and is continually present, but whether or not this potential is realized depends on its value as a political asset in the given political equation. Thus, it appears that in the 1950s Alawite communal consciousness was neither great nor an overriding factor.

> Traditional religious and family loyalties have, at times unconsciously, played a role in determining policy orientation despite the individual's deep commitment to national reform. In general, however, ascriptive loyalties among the post-independence generation are weakened or surpressed while non-personal and ideological orientations have become much more salient.

But in a later period, "under the political circumstances of the 1960s and the rule of the Ba'th, Alawi primordial loyalties become important; as intra-Ba'th politics intensified, absolute personal trust became a major criterion in political alliances."[37] This was carried so far that in 1966, while the non-Alawite officers were still capable of doing so, they dismissed a large number of Alawite officers on the charge of "communal clannishness."[38] A non-Alawite Ba'thist complained strongly about the Alawites' use of communal solidarity in the struggle for power in his book, significantly called *The Bitter Experiment*.[39] In sum, being an Alawite in the 1950s was not a useful political asset, but in the 1960s and 1970s it was and is. This is not to say that all Alawites necessarily and always stick together; there are a few individuals who work with other groups and more importantly, there are internal Alawite struggles.

The Alawites' accession to power through the military and the Ba'th Party has provoked considerable conflict with the balance of the Syrian population, and particularly with the urban Sunni Muslims. Is the reason for this strife sectarian conflict or class conflict (symbolized by the urban middle and upper middle classes versus the rural peasant lower and lower middle classes)? From one viewpoint, many of the actions of the government indicate that its motives are based primarily on class differences. Land reform has been very extensive with about 28 percent of the land being expropriated and redistributed, with the effect of raising considerably the living standards of the peasants. Nationalization of industrial and commercial establishments has run broad and deep, causing directly and indirectly a high proportion of the middle and upper classes to leave Syria. (It should be noted that pressure on the commercial sector became less intense during the mid-1970s.) Investment in the public educational system, which benefits all classes but mostly the lower ones, has not been insignificant, particularly in Latakia. From another viewpoint, even though it is quite evident that each of these measures definitely benefits the lower and lower middle classes, it can also be argued that they hurt urban Sunni Muslims and Christians the most.

It is equally apparent that Syrian government investment in Latakia Province has been particularly high. Some argue that this only reflects the government's intention to concentrate development in the heretofore neglected rural areas. That Latakia Province receives proportionately more than other rural provinces, however, argues more persuasively that the direction of government investment is influenced strongly by sectarian interests. And it is worthy to note that even the (U.S.) Agency For International Development-sponsored development, due to Syrian pressures, is more concentrated on Latakia than other regions.

There has been, in addition, considerable conflict between the Alawites and Sunni Muslims on a religious plane. The Alawite-dominated government has often attempted to diminish the role of Islam and the position of the Sunni Muslim religious leaders (*ulama*) in the state and the society, usually in the name of the advancement of secularism and the elimination of the role of religion in the state and curtailing it in the society. These moves have often ended in violence. For example, the spring of 1973 witnessed rioting in Hama over the noninclusion of Islam as the state religion in the new constitution.

The Alawites themselves have not given us the answer to the above question, but probably the ambiguity of their statements paints the true picture. Many of the government leaders just echo the vague generalities of Arab socialism. However, others have been more to the point. One "veteran Arab statesman" is quoted as saying, "We, the Alawites and Druze" will not stop socialism or nationalism, for if we did, control would go back to Sunni Muslim city dwellers and anyway, what do we have to lose?" Another speaker, this time an officer, made a statement with a similar meaning. "Don't expect us to eliminate socialism in Syria; for the real meaning of such steps would be the transfer of all the political, financial, industrial, and commercial advantages to the towns, i.e., the members of the Sunni community. We, the Alawis and the Druze, will then again be the poor and the servants. We shall not abandon socialism, because it enables us to impoverish the townspeople and to equalize their standard of life to that of the villagers . . . What property do we have which we could lose by nationalization? None!"[40] A non-Alawite Syrian Ba'thist includes both elements (class and religion) in his analysis, but puts the weight on class issues. He states that it has been traditional for the Ba'th Party to have a higher proportion of minority members than their percentage of the population because these minorities are rural and they had to live under the yoke of "feudalism." This he argues is the reason for their "socialistic" measures, but then he equivocates by criticizing the Alawites in the military government for sticking together as Alawites and, thus, not as Ba'thists.[41]

By the mid-1970s and with the further consolidation of President al-Asad's power, the Alawites took another tack in their relations with Sunni Muslims. Not unlike his forefathers in the 1920s and 1930s who were attempting to prove their Arab and Muslim identity, President al-Assad has sought and received affirmation that he is a true Muslim from Syrian Sunni *ulama* and even persuaded Lebanese Shi'a *ulama* to declare that Alawites are Shi'a Muslims.[43] One should, however, interpret these moves as a broadening of his base in the overall society, not as a lessening of Alawite consciousness or distinctiveness.

The only conclusion that may be rationally drawn from the above discussion is that both factors—class conflict and sectarianism—have been operative in the 1960s and the 1970s. In this instance they overlap, but because the Sunni Muslims of the rural peasantry and urban lower and lower middle classes are largely excluded from power, the true class nature of the current ruling group is definitely blurred, and so its sectarian nature is emphasized. Irrespective of this argument, religious roles in Syria are far removed from what they were in the 1930s, when the Alawites were discriminated against and exploited. Appropriately, one of the banners carried in the 1973 spring riots read, put an end to "Alawite power."[44] Thus, the statement of the most famous student of the Alawites during the mandate; "Any minority can dominate a majority if it has political, military, or economic superiority,"[45] still holds, just with a reversal of roles from the scholar's original meaning.

Future Trends

The Alawites are a concentrated minority with considerable sectarian consciousness. They have acceded to power by dint of their own efforts and the fortunes of history. In acquiring power, they have angered other segments of society, segments which are both sectarian and class-related.

Although Weulersse argues that a (religious) minority can rule a majority, this is not to imply that this relationship will be sustained indefinitely. What will happen when the Alawites lose power in Syria? The answer lies at two interacting levels, the Syrian and the Alawite.

In the mid-1960s, when Sunni Muslims were still capable of dismissing Alawite officers because of their "clannish" behavior, it appears that due to sectarian antagonism they did so. In the event that Sunni Muslims once more gain an upper hand in Syria, a similar but broader effort would most probably be initiated. The officer corps, the Ba'th Party apparatus, and key government positions would be purged of Alawites. Their numbers would be reduced to those representative of their proportion of the total Syrian population, or perhaps much below that proportion. The process of executing such changes would almost necessarily involve some sectarian violence.

The above assumes that a Sunni Muslim takeover would be relatively rapid and that Alawites could be speedily contained. Another definite possibility is that the Alawites might react in force. As noted previously, Alawites control Army strike units. With such military power at hand, they most probably could defend themselves effectively and render considerable damage to their opponents.

But what might the Alawites attempt to create or do if they were relieved of power in Damascus? The answer may lie in recent history and the examples of neighboring states. First, after World War II during early Syrian independence, the Alawites exhibited centrifugal tendencies. As noted in previous sections, they sought or contemplated autonomy or separation. A resurgence of such thinking and action is entirely possible if the Alawites again felt they would suffer unequal treatment at the hands of an unsympathetic Syrian government. Second, in neighboring Lebanon, Maronites have seriously thought of, if not acted upon, setting up an autonomous (or perhaps independent) Maronite region in Mount Lebanon. This kind of sectarian thinking is present in the Middle East, and one must assume that Alawites are not immune to it. Third, the central government's heavy investment in the development of Latakia, it could be contended, is not only for the benefit of Alawites under a Syrian regime but in preparation for the time when Alawites fall from power.

This section is not a prediction of what is to come. It is simply an exploration of what might happen, given today's realities. Nor is it a prediction that radical changes will occur in the very near future. But, as it is now trite to say, the ever changing Middle East will witness more change in the future.

NOTES

1. Jacques Weulersse, *Le Pays de Alaouites* (Tours: Arrault, 1940), p. 77.

2. *Ibid.*, pp. 59-60; Munir al-Sharif, *al-Muslimun al-'Alawiyun: Man Hum Wa 'Ayna Hum*, 2nd ed. (Damascus: al-Matba'al-'Umumiya, 1960), p. 123; Samuel Lyde, *The Asian Mystery* (London: Longman, Green, Longman, and Roberts, 1860), pp. 3, 18-19; Muhammad al-Tawil, *Ta'rikh al-'Alawiyin* (Beirut: Dar al-'Andalis, 1966), p. 467; Phillip K. Hitti, *The Origins of the Druze People and Religion* (New York: Columbia University Press, 1928), p. 28. The Alawites of Arab origin in Turkey should not be confused with Turkish Alevis, who are Shi'a Muslim Turks.

3. Etienne de Vaumas, "Le Djebel ansarieh, étude de géographie humaine," *Revue de géographie alpine* 48, no. 2 (1960); 269-71; Jacques Weulersse, *Paysans de Syrie et du Proche-Orient* (Paris: Gallimard, 1946), pp. 260, 270; al-Sharif, *al-Muslimun*, pp. 51-54.

4. Lyde, *The Asian Mystery*, pp. 110-16; E. J. Jurji, "The Alids of Northern Syria," *The Moslem World* 29, no. 4 (October 1939); 333-38; René Dussand, *Histoire et religion des Nasairis* (Paris: Bovillon, 1900) pp. 42-76; Hasa Tankut, *al-Nusayriyun wa al-Nusayriya* (Ankara: Devlet Matbassi, 1938), pp. 42-56; Mahmud al-Salih, *al-Naba' al-Yaqin 'an al-'Alawiyin* (n. p., 1961), pp. 39-52.

5. Jurji, "The Alids," p. 338.

6. Dussaud, *Histoire*, pp. 42-76, 120-27; Lyde, *The Asian Mystery*, pp. 72-73, 112-13; al-Salih, *al-Naba'*, pp. 39-52; Tankut, *al-Nusayriyun*, pp. 42-66.

7. Albert H. Hourani, *Minorities in the Arab World* (London: Oxford University Press, 1947), p. 8. Also, see Tankut, *al-Nusayriyun*, pp. 32-46; Jurji, "The Alids," pp. 338-41.

8. Dussaud, *Histoire*, pp. 135, 128-34.

9. This is also a common phenomenon among the Druze of the Middle East. They have the distinction between the initiated and the uninitiated as well. See Chapter 5.

10. Dussaud, *Histoire*, pp. 117-19; Weulersse, *Pays*, pp. 261, 264-65; al-Sharif, *al-Muslimun*, pp. 126-28; Pierre May, *L'Alaouite* (Paris: Brokghausen, n.d. [late 1920s?]), pp. 61-67. For the names of shaykhly families and their tribal affiliation, see al-Sharif, *al-Muslimun*, pp. 126-27.

11. al-Sharif, *al-Muslimun*, pp. 130-33; Weulersse, *Pays*, p. 264; May, *L'Alaouite*, pp. 37-38. For the names and tribal affiliations of the notable families, see al-Sharif, *al-Muslimun*, pp. 118-21.

12. For example, see John H. Kautsky, "An Essay in Political Development," in *Political Change in Underdeveloped Countries: Nationalism and Communism*, ed. John H. Kautsky (New York: Wiley, 1962), pp. 22, 24; William R. Polk, *The United States and the Arab World* (Cambridge: Harvard University Press, 1965), pp. 215-88; David E. Apter, *The Politics of Modernization* (Chicago: University of Chicago Press, 1965), pp. 138-78; Edward Shils, *Political Development in the New States* (The Hague: Mouton, 1968), pp. 15-24, 87-89; Leonard Binder, "National Integration and Political Development," *American Political Science Review* 55, no. 3 (September 1964); 627-31; James A. Bill and Carl Leiden, *The Middle East: Politics and Power* (Boston: Allyn and Bacon, 1974), pp. 84-88.

13. al-Sharif, *al-Muslimun*, pp. 115-16, 130-32; Weulersse, *Pays*, p. 264; May, *L'Alaouite*, pp. 71-73.

14. It should be remembered that not all tribal chiefs come from notable families. Successful peasants with enough ambition, courage, intelligence, and luck have been known to rise to top leadership positions despite the lack of this political asset. Examples would be Sulayman Murshid and 'Ali Baddour. Weulersse, *Pays*, pp. 333-37. Also, occasionally, a religious shaykh has political ambitions and will compete with the tribal chiefs for power. al-Sharif, *al-Muslimun*, pp. 126-28.

15. al-Sharif, *al-Muslimun*, p. 115; Weulersse, *Paysans*, pp. 118, 220; Weulersse, *Pays*, p. 264; May, *L'Alaouite*, pp. 71-73.

16. Weulersse, *Pays*, pp. 264, 333; Zeltzer, "Minorities," p. 21.

17. Zeltzer, "Minorities," p. 25; Weulersse, *Pays*, p. 363.

18. Raymond A. Hinnebusch, "Local Politics in Syria: Organization and Mobilization in Four Village Cases," *Middle East Journal* 30, no. 1 (Winter 1976); 1-24.

19. Eliezer Be'eri, *Army Officers in Arab Politics and Society* (New York: Praeger, 1970), p. 160; Martin Seymour, "The Dynamics of Syria Since the Break with Egypt," *Middle Eastern Studies* 6, no. 1 (January 1970); 40.

20. Albert Hourani, *Syria and Lebanon* (London: Oxford University Press, 1946), p. 144; Be'eri, *Army Officers*, pp. 160, 336; Iliya Harik, "The Ethnic Revolution and Political Integration in the Middle East," *International Journal of Middle East Studies* 3, no. 3 (July 1972); *passim.*; Michael Van Dusen, "Political Integration and Regionalism in Syria," *Middle East Journal* 26, no. 2 (Spring 1972); 127, 134, and *passim.* Also, see the discussion of the manifestation of this point below.

21. Albert H. Hourani and S. M. Stern, eds., *The Islamic City* (Philadelphia: University of Pennsylvania Press, 1970), *passim.* See especially Hourani's introduction, pp. 16ff.

22. Van Dusen, "Political Integration," p. 127 and *passim.*

23. This defeat was a result of struggles among the Syrian political parties during the 1950s. The climax of this struggle came with the assassination of a popular army officer by a sergeant who was a member of the SSNP. The other parties, especially the Ba'th and the Communists, "clamoured for revenge: the [SSNP] was outlawed; large numbers of its members were arrested. . . . The press, the courts, the Premier himself, accused the [SSNP] of plotting with a foreign Power to overthrow the Government. Thus the [SSNP] was eliminated from Syrian public life." Patrick Seale, The Struggle for Syria (London: Oxford University Press, 1965), pp. 242-43.

24. Van Dusen, "Political Integration," p. 135.

25. The best description and analysis of these trends is ibid., pp. 125-26, 128, 132-33, 135; and Van Dusen, "Syria: The Downfall of a Traditional Elite," pp. 115-55, in Political Elites and Political Development in the Middle East, ed. Frank Tachau (Cambridge, Mass.: Schenkman, 1975).

26. Jacques Weulersse, Comptes rendus du Congrès International de Géographie (Warsaw) 3 (1934); 258, as cited in G. E. von Grunebaum, "Islam: Essays in the Nature and Growth of a Cultural Tradition," Proceedings, American Anthropological Association, 57, no. 2, part 2, Memoir no. 81 (April 1955); 156-57, fn 21. Author's translation.

27. Weulersse, Paysans, p. 87, and the quote, p. 77. Author's translation.

28. Hourani, Syria, p. 185.

29. Zeltzer, "Minorities," p. 25.

30. Moshe Ma'oz, "Attempts at Creating a Political Community in Modern Syria," Middle East Journal 26, no. 4 (Autumn 1972); 399.

31. Harik, "The Ethnic Revolution," pp. 310-11.

32. al-Hayat, December 19, 1964; George Haddad, Revolution and Military Rule in the Middle East: The Arab States, 2 vols. (New York: Speller, 1971), 2: 45; Be'eri, Army Officers, p. 337; Gad Soffer, "The Role of the Officer Class in Syrian Politics and Society" (Ph.D. diss., American University, 1968), p. 25; Seymour, "Dynamics," p. 40.

33. Peter Gubser, "U.A.R.—A Study in Unity," (M.A. thesis, American University of Beirut, 1966), p. 114.

34. Avraham Ben-Tzur, "The Neo-Ba'th Party in Syria," New Outlook 12, no. 1 (January 1969); 25.

35. Ibid., p. 27.

36. Haddad, Revolution, 2; 181-350; Seymour, "Dynamics," passim.; Van Dusen, "Political Integration," passim.; Ben-Tzur, "The Neo-Ba'th," passim.; Be'eri, Army Officers, pp. 130-70; Moshe Ma'oz, "Alawi Military Officers in Syrian Politics, 1966-1974," in The Military and State in Modern Asia, ed. H. Z. Schriffrin (Jerusalem: Academic Press, 1976), passim.; R. F. Nyrop, et al., Area Handbook for Syria (Washington, D.C.: Foreign Area Studies Division, American University, 1969), pp. 143-68.

37. Nyrop, et al., Area Handbook, pp. 127, 134.

38. al-Hayat, December 30, 1966; Be'eri, Army Officers, p. 167.

39. Munif al-Razzaz, al-Tajriba al-Murra (Beirut: Dar Ghandur lil Taba'a wa al-Nashr wa al-Tawzi', 1967), pp. 158-60.

40. See al-Hayat, February 5, and May 5, 1966; Be'eri: Army Officers, p. 337; Soffer, "The Role," p. 26.

41. al-Razzaz, al-Tajriba, pp. 158-60.

42. al-Sharif, al-Muslimun, pp. 106-08, 168-69; al-Salih, al-Naba', pp. 130-77.

43. Moshe Ma'oz, "Syria Under Hafiz al-Asad: New Domestic and Foreign Policies," Jerusalem Papers on Peace Problems, no. 15 (1975); 10-11.

44. The Economist, March 10, 1973, p. 38.

45. Weulersse, Pays, p. 77.

3

MINORITIES IN REVOLT: THE KURDS OF IRAN, IRAQ, SYRIA, AND TURKEY

William E. Hazen

The Kurds are a political ethnic minority in the Middle East that has struggled on numerous occasions to gain autonomy or independence. A short-lived, independent republic in 1946 has been the greatest extent of their efforts and triumphs but not of their sacrifices. In recent decades, each time success seemed within grasp, external pressures defeated their ambitions.

Events in Iran following the downfall of the shah's government exemplify the Kurdish experience. When the central government becomes weak, the Kurdish star of autonomy or independence rises; when the central government is rejuvenated and becomes strong, the star sinks below the horizon. Currently, the Khomeini-sponsored government is weak, faced with enormous complexities which threaten to engulf it. As a result, the Kurds in Iran are flexing their muscles and defying dicta issued by the central government. The motions being made are those which, if carried through to their logical conclusion, would bring independence. If, however, the Khomeini government or some other political group were to resolve its problems and reorganize its army, Kurdish defiance most probably would soon melt away. Any actions on the part of the Iranian government of necessity would be taken in conjunction with those taken by neighboring states with Kurdish populations.

Because the Kurd is basically in opposition to the societies in which he is a minority, those majority populations react violently to Kurdish actions that appear to threaten or undermine "national" interests, that is, the interests of the state in which the Kurds are but a minority. Alienated from pan-Turanianism and pan-Arabism and balking at Turkification, Arabization, and Iranianization, the Kurd has attempted to remain aloof and pursue his life in isolation— except when given the opportunity to seize the initiative and seek his ultimate goal, independence. Because none of the states with Kurdish minorities would feel comfortable with the establishment of an independent Kurdish state, which might attract their own Kurds, these countries would work in tandem to crush any attempted independence movement.

The Kurds have long been used by their Middle Eastern host governments as political pawns. Iran, especially, has used the Kurds to plague the Iraqi government. But in a showdown between the two countries, the governments chose not to war against one another but to sacrifice the Kurds on the altar of peace. Syria, likewise, has used its Kurdish population to pressure Iraq. But when it became expedient for the two countries to shelve their differences, the Syrian Kurds were once again leashed.

If events in Iran deteriorate to the extent that the country is permitted to fragment, then the Kurds will again have the option of seeking independence. And seek it they will. The Kurdish community of Iran could become a symbol to the Kurdish minorities in the other four countries with sizable Kurdish populations and could bring about extensive disruption and internal warfare as the Kurdish communities strove to join their territories with the Iranian independent homeland, thereby fulfilling a dream fixed within each Kurd.

DESCRIPTION

As a recognized people, the Kurds have lived in their present geographic region in the Zagros mountains since the days of the Assyrian king, Tiglath Pileser (2000 B.C.), who fought a tribe called the Kur-ti-e.[1] The Greek historian, Xenophon, in 401 B.C., mentions the Kardukai, who descended from their mountain strongholds and harassed the famous "Ten Thousand Greeks" as they fought their way to the Black Sea from Mesopotamia.

The name "Kurd" came into existence during the Arab invasion of the Sassanian Empire in the seventh century A.D. The Arabs applied this name to all the tribes that lived in this region, a name derived from several tribes that had taken the name "kordukh."[2] Although the Kurds themselves gradually accepted being called the people from Kurdistan, the tribal names remain very important to the Kurds, who prefer to be known by their tribal affiliations, such as Barzanji or Pizhdari, unless, of course, they are speaking with non-Kurds. Then they will state that are Kurdan, those who come from Kurdistan.

The Kurds inhabit a large triangularly shaped region divided among five states: Turkey, Syria, Iran, Iraq, and the Soviet Union. The westernmost tip reaches the Kurd Dagh mountain, in Turkey, near the Gulf of Alexandria; the easternmost in the Luristan mountains of Iran.[3] To the north, the Kurdish homeland stretches into Soviet Armenia.

The largest segment of Kurdish territory is found in Turkey. Seventeen provinces, all in the eastern or central-eastern part of the country, contain Kurds, who in some provinces constitute over 50 percent of the total population.[4] Some scattered pockets exist in central and southern Turkey as a result of the government's attempts to disperse the concentrated numbers of Kurds in the eastern provinces.

Most Kurds in Syria live in the north and northeast portions of the country. The largest numbers inhabit the upper Jazira and Tigris regions. The town of al-Qamishliya in the Khabar district of al-Hazakah province serves as the focal point for Kurdish activities. Others are based in Aleppo province. There is the Jabal al-Akrad (the Kurdish mountains), with the town of Afrin serving as the Kurdish center. Their numbers increased during the interwar period when Turkish Kurds underwent enforced assimilation. The Salhiya quarter in Syria's capital, Damascus, contains approximately 30,000 Kurds. But as a whole, the Kurds remain a relatively small ethnic minority in Syria.

The Kurds in the Soviet Union are located in the three south-central republics of Armenia, Azerbaijan, and Turkmen.[5] There is no great preponderance in any of these provinces, and the Kurds remain a distinct minority compared to the other ethnic communities inhabiting these republics.

This is not the case in Iraq. The Kurds inhabit what might be considered the northern third of the country. Most live in the *liwas* (provinces) of Sulaimaniya, Irbil, Kirkuk, and Dohuk. However, there are concentrations of Kurds in the Khanaqin and Mandali districts of the *liwa* of Duzala and in the vicinity of the cities of al-Kut and Baghdad.[6]

Iran was the only country ever to have within its borders an independent Kurdish republic. Although this experience was short-lived, the Kurds continue to be concentrated in this same area, in the provinces of Azerbaijan Havari, Azerbaijan Bakhtari, Kurdistan,

Kermanshah, and Khuzistan, where the southern part of the Zagros mountains is located.[7] Because of enforced dispersion, a few pockets exist in other parts of the country (Fars and Mazandaran), where they have been successfully assimilated with the indigenous population.

Kurds are to be found also in Lebanon and Jordan, but their numbers are small. Because of the recent civil war in Lebanon, their numbers have diminished drastically. Most of these families originated in Turkey and came through Syria to avoid persecution.

POPULATION

Estimates of the size of the Kurdish population vary greatly according to the sources used. A rough estimate places the number of Kurds at between 8 and 16 million. The 8 million discrepancy is the difference between Kurdish and government sources, with the Kurds claiming the greater number.[8]

Kurds are distributed by country as follows: Turkey, approximately 4 million, or 10 percent of the total population; Syria, 250,000; the Soviet Union, 120,000; Iraq, 2 million, or 20 percent of the population; and Iran, 2.5 million, or about 12.5 percent of the Iranian populace.[9] These figures generally apply to those who speak Kurdish. Kurdish figures include not only those who speak Kurdish, but, as well, those who consider themselves Kurds and have adopted another tongue. Thus, one will find Arabized or Turkified Kurds who no longer know a single word of their ethnic tongue yet who continue to claim Kurdish descent.

Kurds in Turkey inhabit approximately 30 percent of Turkish territory. Most reside in remote villages of from 50 to 300 persons. Only 100,000 live in urban centers. A few remain transients, but even these are being encouraged to settle and take up cultivation.[10]

The Turkish government has resettled hundreds of thousands of Kurds in other parts of the country in order to alleviate pressure and prevent rebellion. Because of the harsh treatment utilized during relocation, however, thousands fled to Syria.[11] Some tribes migrated to Iran and Iraq, where they found refuge with their fellow Kurds. The Turks still call their Kurdish people Mountain Turks, thereby preserving the concept of pan-Turanianism raised by the Young Turks in 1908 and carried through by the successor of the Ottoman sultan, Ataturk.

The Kurds in Iraq have undergone population dispersion since the conquest of the Kurdish strongholds in 1975. Approximately

300,000 have been resettled in southern Iraq.[12] Another 100,000 are said to have fled to Iran to avoid imprisonment.[13] About 30,000 have been imprisoned and 227 executed.[14] Nevertheless, the majority of the Kurdish community continues to reside in the northern provinces.

Within Iraq is a group of Kurds called the Yazidis.[15] They number approximately 60,000 and live mostly in the Jabal Sinjar and Shaykh Adi regions in northern Mosul province. They speak Kurdish and are recognized as being of Kurdish stock. Yet they are repudiated by the majority of Kurds, primarily because of their heretical religion. Some pockets of Yazidis are to be found in Iran, Turkey, and Syria, but their numbers are negligible.

Iraq has a large number of transhumant Kurds. In general, though, they must be classified as vertical nomads since the majority remain within the same vicinity year round, taking herds to the mountains during the summer and returning to the valleys during the winter months. As in Turkey, most reside in small villages in the remote areas of northern Iraq. War, though, has accelerated the move to urban centers. When villages were destroyed and crops burned, many found it necessary to find jobs at industrial sites or in cities as unskilled laborers. Most, however, rebuilt, preferring to remain on their ancestral lands.

The Kurds of Iran represent the largest ethnic group in that country. Their population center is around Lake Rizaiyeh. Because of the overt participation of the central government in Kurdish affairs, the Kurds of Iran are predominantly settled in small communities. In order to prevent tribal disturbances and revolt the shah's government, split up the tribes, resettling some far from their homelands. This policy had its beginnings as early as the seventeenth century, when Kurds were settled in Khorasan to prevent tribal disturbances as well as to act as guardians of the Persian heartland. Under Shah Reza Pahlavi, many tribal leaders were taken as hostages to Tehran.[16] Although permitted to live relatively luxurious lives, they were prevented from returning to their tribal homes. By eliminating tribal leadership, the government found it easy to settle the tribes in designated areas.

The Kurds in Syria are located mainly in the regions abutting Turkey. Most of these immigrated from Turkey during times of Turkish repression in the 1920s and 1930s.* While the Syrian government has stressed settlement, the Kurdish population remains

---

*There remains a great distinction within the Kurdish communities between the old families and the newly prominent, the former looking with disdain upon the latter.

divided equally among three groups: nomadic, seminomadic, and sedentary. Tribal affiliations remain very strong, probably because tribal members stayed together and did not scatter when migrating from Turkey.

Reliable figures for the Kurdish population in the Soviet Union are unavailable. Although under strict control by the Soviet government, the Kurds have fared much better than their ethnic brethren in the other four countries. They have not been relocated. Furthermore, the government has permitted the Kurdish language to flourish in the schools and local government.[17] One may surmise from this advantageous treatment that Soviet Kurds are in fact a propaganda tool to be used against the Kurds in the other countries.

As with many minorities, the Kurds' ethnic origins are obscure. One author claims them to be of Mediterranean stock, but of a heavier build than most.[18] And while there are few blonds among them, their deep jaw and large teeth are characteristic of the northern European. Most anthropologists claim the Kurd is of Aryan descent (or Indo-Aryan since their language is Indo-European).[19] It is believed that a group migrated from the north and intermixed with an indigenous group living in the mountains. The resemblance to early descriptions suggests the migrants may have been Medes or Assyrians, whose empires encompassed all or part of modern-day Kurdistan. Frequently, one will see an atavism to the earlier civilization. He is short, very stocky and robust, and has a broad face with a heavy jaw and a long upper lip. Commonly his eyes are green.[20]

Since the marriage of these two ancient groups, the Kurdish race has remained comparatively pure. Their mountain barriers and warlike characteristics deterred others from penetrating their region. Only in the plains areas is there emerging a new grouping, a mixture of Arab and Kurd; but because the migration to the plains is of comparatively recent origin, numbers of this new group are small.

HISTORY

The writings of the early civilizations that controlled the region known today as Kurdistan provide accounts of warlike tribal people (Kurds) who harassed both travellers and settled populations.[21] Down through the centuries, the role of the Kurds has changed little. Up to and including the first part of the twentieth century, Kurds continued to raid their neighbors or, for that matter, each other. Though rarely able to rise above the status and identity of petty tribal unit members, they were still able to gain prominence, primarily because of their geographic position. Kurdistan was contested for almost four centuries by the Ottoman and Safavi (Iranian) empires. The Kurds soon realized that alliances were never binding, that, rather, they shifted easily in accordance with changing interests.

As allies of first one side and then another, the Kurds were able to build up their reputation as fierce warriors. Their contingents were welcomed by their allies because of manpower needs and because of Kurdish harassment capabilities. It should be noted, however, that the Kurds did not act as a single unit. It was common practice for each tribe to pledge its allegiance to the side offering the best terms. Thus, Kurds fought Kurds; there was no sense of Kurdish unity. Each tribe looked to its own welfare, a practice that is still recognized in parts of present-day Kurdistan.

Probably history's most prominent and successful Kurd was Salah ad-Din al-Ayubbi (Saladin, 1138-93), who became ruler of Egypt, the Levant, Syria, Iraq, and parts of modern-day Turkey.[22] His allegiance was to the caliph in Baghdad. However, he was virtually an independent ruler, ridding Islam of both the heretical Fatamid dynasty in Egypt and the Christian Crusader kingdoms in the Levant. Yet, he was never able to conquer his own homeland from the Seljuk Turks. Nevertheless, his name is revered in Kurdistan above those Kurdish leaders who became semi-independent princes within their own territories.

Because of the constant state of war between the powers on either side of them, Kurdish tribal leaders were able to establish their own principalities. In 1596, a detailed account of the Kurds, the *Sharafnamah*, was written by Sharaf ed-Din, in which he listed twenty-nine Kurdish principalities.[23] Many were short-lived; others continued until the mid-1800s, when the Ottoman government rid itself of these troublesome satraps. When the power of the princes, such as Baban, Bohtan, and Hakkari, was broken, however, lawlessness invaded the region. The petty tribal chiefs began asserting their own power since Ottoman authority failed to fill the vacuum left by the defeated princes. This state of anarchy satisfied the Porte, because there was no single tribal chieftain able to challenge Ottoman authority.

It was during the nineteenth century, too, that the shaykhs, the principal religious personalities in Kurdistan, began to usurp power for themselves.[24] Nontribal in origin, they soon gained a sufficient number of followers to establish their own tribal organizations. The shaykhs of Barzan are excellent examples of this rise to power. Mulla Mustafa Barzani, the late Kurdish leader, was a descendent of the first Barzan shaykh to acquire regional power, power he himself wielded for over 20 years.

In 1880, the most important Kurdish shaykh was Ubayd Allah, the son of a religious leader who lived in Turkish Kurdistan.[25] It was he who first voiced the idea of Kurdish unity. He sought an autonomous state to offset the anarchy within the Kurdish homeland. At this time, too, there was a threat of an Armenian invasion and, with the Kurds divided as they were, he feared a piecemeal takeover of the homeland.

Attempting to realize his objective, Ubayd Allah amassed a Kurdish force and penetrated Persian Kurdish territory—all with the tacit approval of the Ottoman government, whose leaders sought every possible opportunity to embarrass and weaken the Persians. Initially successful, Ubayd Allah was soon confronted by a large Persian army. His followers abandoned him, and he was forced to flee, his dream of a Kurdish state shattered.

Kurds next came into the public eye in 1891, when the Ottoman sultan, Abd al-Hamid II, organized Kurdish cavalry units.[26] Used specifically in Kurdish districts, the Hamadiyah Brigade, as it was called, soon pacified the territory.* The Hamadiyah were also used with great success against the Armenian communities. Armenian intrigue with the Russians and the subsequent unrest among this Christian minority concerned the Porte. Harassment and eventual massacres of the Armenians by the Kurds occurred under both Abd al-Hamid II and the republican government.[27]

The Hamadiyah Brigade formed the nucleus of the 30 Kurdish regiments raised during World War I to fight against the Russians. At first successful, they were forced to retreat against overwhelming odds. When the situation became untenable, they merely disbanded and returned to their tribal homes, leaving the German and Turkish advisers to cope with the advancing Russian forces. The Russian revolution only delayed the Porte's eventual capitulation; yet, it did give the Turkish leaders a chance to extricate themselves from the eastern front.

Kurdish autonomy was fully discussed during the peace conferences following World War I. Kurdish aspirations were recognized in the Treaty of Sèvres (1920):

Article 62: A Commission . . . shall draft within six months from the coming into force of the present treaty a scheme of local autonomy for the predominantly Kurdish areas lying east of the

---

*Their loyalty to their sultan was unquestioned. In fact, when Abd al-Hamid II was deposed in 1908, units occupied Damascus for the sultan and only left that city when they were driven off by larger numbers of Turks loyal to the revolutionaries.

Euphrates, south of the southern boundary of Armenia as it may be hereafter determined, and north of the frontier of Turkey with Syria and Mesopotamia.[28]

Excluded from the proposed state were those parts of Kurdistan lying within Iran and Russia. However, the question of these regions did not arise because the Treaty of Sèvres never came into force. Instead, the Treaty of Lausanne (1923) regulated the peace between Turkey and the victors, and the Kurdish question was completely ignored.

The defeat of the Turkish forces and the occupation of northern Iran by the Russians during World War I only encouraged Kurdish tribal leaders to challenge the governments that succeeded to power at the close of the war. In Iran, Simko, a powerful tribal leader, rose against the shah and succeeded in acquiring for himself a feudal kingdom.† However, when an Iranian force under Reza Khan met him in battle, Simko's "army" was roundly defeated. Simko was to be pardoned at this time. When he revolted a second time in 1926, his popularity had waned. His success was brief, and he was soon captured.[29]

In 1925, Shaykh Sa'id, the hereditary chief of the powerful Nakhshbandi dervish sect, revolted against the Turkish administration Kemal Ataturk. Shaykh Sa'id sought to restore to Turkey the Caliphate, which Ataturk had abolished. The Shari'a had also been dislodged as the law of the land. Haranguing his followers on the godlessness of the Turkish regime, he declared a jihad, a holy war, asking all devout Muslims, not only Kurds but Turks as well, to rebel. Although he was successful at first, pious elements deserted him because of the atrocities committed by many of his troops who seized the opportunity to loot whomever they came upon, rebels as well as those loyal to the Turkish government. Soon, Shaykh Sa'id was left with only his brigands, who were no match for the Turkish forces. As in the past when the Kurds were confronted by well-organized and superior units, they dispersed. Shaykh Sa'id was captured through the treachery of one of his trusted lieutenants and hanged.[30] The Turkish Kurds then faced severe repression. A half million were relocated to other parts of Turkey, mostly to western Anatolia, where, as we have already chronicled, many soon died. Approximately 200 villages were destroyed, and 15,000 inhabitants killed.

---

†His real name was Isma'il Agha of the Shakkak tribe. He had had several altercations with the Iranian government, but because of his tribal position, had been appeased.

This was the first of three bloody revolts that took place within Turkish Kurdistan. The other two occurred in 1930 and 1937. In the aftermath, thousands were killed, but many more were forcibly relocated. Others fled to Syria where the French were sympathetic to their plight. The revolt of 1930 took on, for the first time, the characteristics of Kurdish unity, since the Kurds of Syria as well as some in Iraq offered their support to the Turkish Kurds. The mandate powers refused permission to cross the borders and took measures to seal the frontiers. The Turkish tribes found themselves alone once more. The gesture, though, had been made in the name of unity and freedom for all the Kurdish people.

The Kurds in Iraq have been in revolt against the government of the modern Iraqi state since 1919, when the Kurds rebelled against the British mandate authority. At that time, no decision had been made with respect to the disposition of the Kurds. They were fighting to rid their country of foreign invaders and to become an independent nation in the process. A hiatus ensued while the peace negotiations proceeded at their slow pace. Persuaded by the Turks that nothing would emerge to further the Kurdish cause, the Kurds began fighting again. Aided by the Turks, who were at this moment (1922) fighting for the existence of their nation, several Kurdish tribes under the leadership of Mahmud of the Barzinja captured Sulaymaniya. Then in November 1922, Mahmud proceeded to claim leadership of all Kurdish areas in the Iraqi state. His forces were known as the Kurdish National Army, and his capital was Sulaymaniya.[31] The dream of nationhood was once more short-lived, as Iraqi troops, assisted by the British Royal Air Force, dislodged the Kurds from their positions in the mountains and forced them to disperse. The revolt was over.[32]

A second revolt broke out in 1931. This time the leader was Ahmad, shaykh of the Barzani. The revolt began as tribal warfare when the shaykh of the Baradost Kurds attacked the followers of the Barzan shaykh for spreading an heretical and personal brand of Islam.[33] The revolt spread when Iraqi troops were sent into the region to quell the disturbance and to usurp Kurdish authority. Only the RAF saved the government troops from total annihilation, and, although order was restored, the Barzanis remained in control of events in this region.

World War II exacerbated conditions in Kurdistan. The presence of Russian troops in northern Iran, German influence in Iraq, and the weakening of British rule revived once more national aspirations for the Kurds. Trouble arose simultaneously in Turkey and Iraq in 1943. The Turkish revolt under Sa'id Birokh was short-lived. Mulla Mustafa, the brother of Shaykh Ahmad Barzani, succeeded in clearing the Barzan area of Iraqi troops. However, he was persuaded to agree to a ceasefire so that Kurdish aims could be aired and their problems mediated by the British. The Iraqi government under Nuri as-Sa'id was sympathetic to Kurdish grievances. Mediators were appointed and fruitful talks were held. But with the departure from office of Prime Minister Nuri as-Sa'id, the situation between the two groups worsened. In 1945, Iraqi troops were sent again into Kurdistan to enforce government rule. Mulla Mustafa regarded this as an act of war and began attacking Iraqi government positions. Outnumbered, he was forced to retreat, first to Barzan and the formidable heights that surround this town, then to Iran where he joined forces with the Kurds who were at that time establishing the first independent Kurdish national state in the city of Mahabad.

On January 22, 1946, the Kurdish Autonomous Republic of Mahabad was proclaimed.[34] The president was Qazi Muhammad, a member of a Sunni religious family of Mahabad. Although its territory was limited to Iran, Qazi Muhammad claimed to speak for all the Kurds. Behind the republic stood the army of the Soviet Union. Russian troops had occupied northern Iran in 1941, ostensibly to ensure a secure route for supplies to reach the Russian front. Shah Reza Pahlavi had been deposed and his son installed on the Peacock throne. In this state of confusion, the Soviets encouraged both the Kurds and Azerbaijanis to seek independence under Soviet auspices. It was their intention to remain in Iran and incorporate these newborn republics into their sphere of influence, either as satellites or as republics of the Soviet Union itself.

U.S. and world pressure forced the Soviets to withdraw from Iranian territory. Left on their own, the two independent states could not withstand the Iranian forces seeking to recover their lost territory. The Kurdish army, in which Mulla Mustafa had been made a general, used diversionary tactics to stall the advance of the Iranian troops. The Kurdish front collapsed, though, and the republic ceased to exist on December 14, 1946. The entire Kurdish government surrendered to the Iranians, who promptly tried them, sentencing some to prison and executing others, including the former president, Qazi Muhammad.[35]

Mulla Mustafa refused to lay down his arms and retreated toward the Iraqi border with his forces. Even in his homeland his position was untenable because of his earlier acts against the Baghdad government, however, so he and some 500 well-armed Barzani tribesmen crossed into Soviet territory and remained there until the overthrow of the Iraqi monarchy in 1958.

Throughout the 1900s, the military attempts to establish an independent Kurdish state were supported by political movements. The first organization that sought the autonomy of all Kurdistan was founded in 1908. The members of this party, Kurdistan Toali ve Terakki Jam'yate (Society for the Rise and Progress of Kurdistan) had been influenced by the Young Turk movement which overthrew Sultan Abd al-Hamid II.[36] They had not declared for independence; they sought from the Porte representation for their people.

Other parties, such as the Kurd Nashri Ma'arif Jam'iyati (Society for the Propagation of Kurdish Education) and the Hivi-ya Kurd Jam'iyati (Kurdish Hope Society), a student organization, came into existence. Their membership, composed only of the educated and army officers, was small. The bulk of the Kurdish people remained ignorant of what was taking place within those circles seeking a change in Kurdish life. Most Kurds tilled their land, pastured their flocks, and followed their tribal leaders. It was only after the religious shaykhs had begun to carry to the people the idea of a national entity that the Kurds in the small towns and rural areas felt the spirit that was spreading from the elitist circles.

Credit must go to the shaykhs for being the most ardent nationalists, be their reasons for sponsoring nationalism patriotic or personal. Of the earlier nationalist leaders, Shaykh Abd al-Salam of Barzan, the eldest brother of Mulla Mustafa, had asked from the Ottoman government in the early part of the century the following:

the adoption of Kurdish as the official language in the Kurdish areas
　　governed by the Porte;
the use of Kurdish in the schools of Kurdistan;
the appointment of Kurdish-speaking officials within the Kurdish districts;
the appointment for Kurdistan of qadis and muftis belonging to the Shafi'i
　　school;
the collection of taxes in accordance with the Shari'a;
the provision that those taxes raised should be used for the repair and
　　maintenance of roads within Kurdistan.[37]

Kurdish nationalist hopes became centered on a new organization, the Khoybun (Independence), founded in 1927. Its two principal goals were to advance Kurdish nationalism and to act as the rallying point for Kurdish activities against the Porte. This party had been the fruit of the first Kurdish National Congress, held in Paris in 1927. During its sessions, those attending resolved to dissolve all Kurdish nationalist organizations then in existence so that their membership could be joined into one new organization, the Khoybun.[38] Furthermore, in addition to a pledge to continue to struggle for Kurdish autonomy, the members established a single military command and designated locations for supply and ammunition depots.

Between 1927 and 1945, several more Kurdish national parties were established. The Hiva (Hope) Party lasted only two years, from 1935 to 1937. The Kurdish Communist Party was founded in 1945, and it, in turn, set up the Rezqari Kurd Party (now defunct). The party that was to gain the greatest Kurdish support, however, was the Kurdish Democratic Party (KDP), founded in 1945. Although Soviet-inspired, its program appealed to most of the nationalist leaders. When founded, its platform included:

the right of the Kurds to self-government and autonomy;
the use of Kurdish in the schools and as the official language;
the appointment of Kurdish officials to positions in local government within
    Kurdish areas;
the right to develop the resources within Kurdistan.[39]

These are the most salient points. Three of them harken back to those first broached by Shaykh Abd as-Salam.

Although established primarily for those Kurds living in Iraq, the KDP was to be used as a rallying point for Kurds in other countries. It remains today the principal focal point for Kurdish nationalism. Its viewpoints have changed somewhat. Russian influence is negligible within the party, which was run by Mulla Mustafa Barzani until his death in January 1979. He had originally been opposed by the party members to lead the Kurdish struggle for independence. Nevertheless, realizing that the people were rallying around the strongman of Kurdish Iraq instead of an idea, they capitulated and Barzani became president of the party. It was useful to him since it is an organization with cells in several countries outside Kurdistan that disseminate propaganda favoring Kurdish nationalism. It is also the legal tool through which negotiations for autonomy or independence can be channeled.

The Iraqi revolution of 1958 created conditions which were to affect events in Kurdistan to the present day. With the accession to power of Abd al-Karim Qassim, Mulla Mustafa Barzani and his followers returned to their homeland. It was a period of great expectations. The Baghdad government agreed to listen to the demands of the Iraqi Kurds. The Iranian government, on the other hand, was apprehensive. What would their own Kurdish population do in view of the Iraqi events?

The honeymoon between the Qassim regime and the Kurds lasted but three years. The situation, in fact, began to deteriorate as early as March 1959, when, to quell an uprising by pro-Nasserite elements in Mosul, Qassim ordered Kurdish elements loyal to Mulla Mustafa to cooperate with the communists and to put down the revolt.[40] Immediately after this massacre, thousands of Iraqi Kurds migrated to Turkey and Iran. They feared the growing power of Mulla Mustafa and believed that if they disagreed with government policy, the same might happen to them. (Another result of the massacre was the Iranian Kurds' decision to remain free from Iraqi events. In fact, subsequently the Iranian government even used their Kurdish elements to create dissension for a later Baghdad regime.)

Following the 1959 events, the Qassim government began to interfere more in Kurdish affairs, installing police positions in the Kurdish provinces, disbanding Kurdish militia groups, and evading questions of autonomous rights for the Kurds. With the hope of creating a modus vivendi, Mulla Mustafa laid before the Iraqi government his demands, among which were the following:

1. Kurdish to become the first official language in the Kurdish autonomous region.

2. The police to be entirely Kurdish, as also the army units stationed in the Kurdish region. . . .

3. The Kurdish provincial government to control education, health services, communications and municipal and rural affairs.

4. A substantial share of the oil industry of the Mosul-Kirkuk region to be spent in Kurdistan.

5. . . . the Vice Premier, the Assistant Chief of Staff, and the assistant ministers of all ministries to be Kurds.

6. The employment of Kurdish Army units outside the Kurdish region to be made only with the consent of the Kurdish Republic authorities.[41]

Kurdish districts would remain within the Iraqi state, and important functions, such as foreign policy, defense, and finance, would continue to be handled by the central government. The petition, though, was rejected. Mulla Mustafa immediately began to prepare for a confrontation since he realized that it was only a matter of time before the Qassim regime would begin to assert its authority over Iraqi Kurdistan in earnest.

The war began in December 1961, with the bombing of Kurdish villages by the Iraqi Air Force.[42] It was to persist, intermittently, until March 1970, when an agreement was reached by terms of which the central government virtually capitulated to the points demanded by Mulla Mustafa in 1961. Kurdish nationality was officially recognized, while a general amnesty was granted to those who had engaged in the fighting. In addition, the Kurds were given a vice-presidency, five ministerial positions, the promise of economic aid and development for the Kurdish districts, and permission to run their local affairs.

In the nine years between 1961 and 1970, bloody fighting took place. In the end the Kurds held the mountain tops while the central government ruled precariously in the larger valleys. A stalemate had been reached with both sides exhausted from perpetual warfare. The accord was to give each side time to re-equip and retrain its forces.

The main stumbling block to agreement on the role of the Kurds in Iraqi society was recognized by both sides to concern territorial delineation, which, in turn, hinged on the issue of control of the oil fields around Kirkuk. The Kurds claimed that Kirkuk was Kurdish and that they therefore had the right to dispose of the oil revenues from *their* lands. The central government refused to accede to this claim and began settling Arabs in the region by the thousands in order to create a majority Arab population in the district by the time of the next census.

The Baghdad regime compounded its delaying tactics to implement the accord fully by creating a National Front. The principal components were to be the Ba'this, the Communists, and the Kurds. These three groups were to work hand-in-glove for the benefit of the state, and the fulfillment of the terms of the March 11, 1970 accord were closely tied to the articles found in the charter of the front:

> The implementation of all articles in the 11 March declaration and the completion of all prerequisites for the peaceful and democratic solution of the Kurdish national issue are closely tied to the preservation of the existing revolutionary regime, the strengthening of its concept and the consolidation of its position in the struggle against imperialism, Zionism and local and neighboring reaction. They are also tied to the exercise of democratic freedom in Iraq, including the Kurdish regions, the realization of full equality in rights for all communities and minorities, the liquidation of feudalism in Kurdistan, the realization of agrarian reform, persistence in the implementation of the 11 March declaration and strengthening of the social concept in the interest of the masses.[43]

The Kurds, in turn, fearful of being outmaneuvered, did nothing on their part to implement the 1970 agreement. They distrusted the Baghdad government since its leaders conducted a campaign of intrigue against Mulla Mustafa Barzani and his KDP followers, attempting to assassinate Barzani and utilizing his Kurdish rivals as alleged spokesmen for the entire Kurdish population. Barzani, in fact, controlled all Iraqi territory from Zakho in the north to Halabja in the southwest of Iraqi Kurdistan. He had established a de facto administration answerable to him personally. His party, the KDP, had been granted official recognition as the sole representative of the Kurdish people. His Pesh Merga force of 100,000 was the sole institution for law enforcement within this territory.

Unable to persuade the Kurdish leadership to implement the terms of the accord, which was to be fully operational by 1974, the central government took matters into its own hands and unilaterally effectuated the agreement. Indeed, the document was amended on March 11, 1974: "The region, a majority of whose population consists of Kurds, is hereby granted autonomy in accordance with legal regulations."[44] These legal regulations permitted the central government to intervene in regional government work or even to dissolve the regional government, however.

Once the regulations were promulgated in this form, a renewal of warfare was likely. The Kurds foresaw ever increasing encroachment on their affairs by the central government, and the latter suspected that the Kurds had never intended to stop at autonomy but, rather, had sought independence from the outset. Independence of Kurdistan would deprive Iraq of one-third of its territory, including the oil-rich lands around Kirkuk.

The four-year hiatus had enabled the central government forces to re-equip and retrain. The Kurds, on the other hand, although they had intended to follow suit, were unable to find necessary sources of and depots for supply. There remained available to them only the traditional sources through Iran. The Iraqi army soon pushed Barzani's Pesh Merga into a corner abutting that country. While willing to permit money and matériel to reach the Iraqi Kurds, the shah's government was unwilling to use the Iranian army in their defense.

On March 6, 1975, the shah and the vice-president of Iraq, Saddam Hussein, met in Algeria under the auspices of Houari Boumedienne, Algeria's president. There they concluded an agreement of far-reaching implications. By its terms Iran would terminate military assistance to the Kurds in exchange for riparian rights to the Shatt-al-Arab, thereby ending all border disputes between the two countries.

As a result of this agreement, the Kurds were forced to capitulate to the Baghdad government by the end of April 1975. On May 3, 1975, Barzani said (from Iran, where he had taken refuge) that the Kurdish struggle in Iraq had ended and would not be resumed. (Barzani was soon to leave for the United States. Terminally ill, he blamed the United States for pressuring Iran into signing such a pact.)

The immediate consequences of the end to the fighting were the resettlement of 300,000 Kurds in southern Iraq, the imprisonment of 30,000 Pesh Merga fighters, and the execution of 227 Kurdish leaders.[45] In addition, 35,000 men fled to Iran with Barzani. The number of refugees was swelled to 100,000 by the families of these fighters.[46] To ensure that it retained control over Kurdish territory, the central government razed 63 Kurdish villages on the Iranian border, thereby creating a no man's land; established non-Kurdish belts around the northern cities; and began an intensive campaign to populate the north with thousands of Arabs.[47] In order to effect this strategy, Kurdish lands have been sequestered and families evicted, to be resettled in the south or in other parts of Kurdistan.

By the end of 1976, it seemed that Kurdish dreams of independence in Iraq had died forever. Yet the central government seems to be unilaterally implementing the 1970 accords as amended. The Kurdish provinces are considered autonomous. Kurds have their own representative government, their own leaders, and even their own police force. Kurdish is allowed in schools, and a university has been established in Sulaymaniya.[48] To ensure quiescence, though, the Kurdish homeland has been receiving the bulk of the development funds for the past several years,[49] and, of course, Iraqi troops are always present in large numbers.

In spite of the monetary largesse and strict control, and notwithstanding Barzani's departing remarks, the dream of Kurdish independence in Iraq has not died. Since 1977, incidents of a guerrilla nature have been perpetrated against Iraqi military forces and installations and against government-appointed development contractors. Most important to Kurdish aspirations is the regrouping of Kurdish political forces into a unified command. Following Barzani's defeat in 1975, several small rival groups sprang up to attract the Kurds' backing. The Socialist Movement of Kurdistan, the Association of Marxist-Leninists of Kurdistan, and the Kurdistan Action Command, formed by dissidents from the KDP, are three which have vied for political power. All were absorbed by the Patriotic Union of Kurdistan (PUK), founded by Jalal Talabani, a former rival of Mulla Mustafa Barzani. Talabani is an avowed communist and at one time was used by the Baghdad government to supplant Barzani as head of the KDP.[50] Led by Talabani, who had come back from self-imposed exile in Syria, and Ali Askari, a founder of the Socialist Movement of Kurdistan, who became the second-ranking PUK leader, the PUK challenged the KDP, currently led by Mustafa Abdul Rahman and Idris Barzani, a son of the late Mulla Mustafa. The result was heavy fighting within the Turkish province of Hakkari and the total defeat of the PUK forces.[51] While Talabani escaped into Syria, 400 of his PUK fighters, including Ali Askari, were captured. Agitation in Iraqi Kurdistan can only be increased, too, because of current events in Iran and Turkey.

With the departure of the shah and the establishment of a government under the power of the religious leader Ayatollah Khomeini, events in Iran again stimulate the Iranian Kurds' latent political aspirations. The country is in a chaotic state, with a weak government challenged by diverse Marxist groups. Kurdish tribesmen seized control of the cities of Sanandaj and Mahabad, ousted the Khomeini forces, and presented a list of demands to the government. These demands included:

joint control of military installations in Kurdistan;
self-determination within a framework worked out by Kurdish and government officials;
government boycott of the remnants of Barzani's ill-fated KDP;
recognition of Shaykh Ezzedine Hosseini as the sole representative in any negotiations;
Kurdish to be an official language and to be taught in schools.[52]

In spite of the attempt to boycott the KDP, its presence is very much in evidence since many of the rebellious Kurdish leaders are members or former members of this banned party.

By placing any future negotiations in the hands of a conservative religious leader, the Kurdish autonomous movement is attempting to circumvent radical elements, which could push the Iranian Kurdish community into an extremist situation such as that of 1946, as well as endeavoring to establish credibility with what it sees as the religious tenor of current Iranian politics. Kurdish leaders understand that extremism may unite the remainder of Iran's currently fragmented society against them and force it, as well, into a rigid stance. Instead of rushing to embrace a goal of independence, the groundwork for self-government is being laid first. While the central government at present shows signs of total disintegration, there is no assurance that a future government opposed to autonomy may not seize power and once again crush Kurdish self-rule. The spark for independence has been ignited, however, and could burst into flame, engulfing not only the Kurds in Iran, but those in Iraq and Turkey as well.

During the past decade, extensive unrest has been reported in Turkish Kurdistan. As early as May 1971, the Turkish government admitted that the Kurds living within its borders had begun to stockpile arms and ammunition for a future revolt aimed at the establishment of an independent Kurdistan.[53] Martial law was declared for most of Turkish Kurdistan but has since been lifted from almost all the provinces affected.

The Kurds have allied themselves with other dissident groups, such as communists and terrorists, in their bid to rid their areas of military rule. (For example, a Turkish People's Liberation Army was organized to employ guerrilla tactics against government installations. And although the entire liberation is Marxist-oriented, the Kurds are clearly exploiting the ideological movement as a tactic to achieve their own goals.)

In addition to having proclaimed martial law for Kurdish regions, the Turkish government imprisoned many educated Kurds, accusing them of spreading Kurdish national propaganda.[54] While the acts by these dissidents were probably hostile to the central government in sentiment, these activities afforded the military an excuse to rid itself of the Kurdish leaders, a goal quite apart from the specific incidents.

Nevertheless, as resentment against the Turkish government builds throughout the country, Kurdish independence sentiments rise accordingly. Certainly, the fighting between Iraqi Kurdish forces on Turkish soil shows an increasing sympathy in Turkey among Kurds for the national aspirations evoked by Kurdish leaders beyond Turkey's borders.

In both Syria and the Soviet Union, the relatively peaceful existence enjoyed by the Kurds can be explained by the size of their communities in those countries. There have been reports emanating from Damascus that suggested extensive military assistance was being given by the Syrian Kurds to the Iraqi Kurds, and that over 300 armed Kurds from Syria joined forces at one time with those of Barzani.[55] However, this was presumably an extension of the feud between the Ba'th regimes in Syria and Iraq, which has, at least temporarily, ended. Nevertheless, Syria has been a refuge for Kurdish dissidents from both Turkey and Iraq, with Talabani a prime example. Since the Syrian Kurdish community is small, intracommunity communication can be presumed to be relatively universal. Events taking place in other parts of Kurdistan will most certainly be discussed within the Kurdish community of Syria. Still, efforts for Kurdish autonomy outside Syria's borders must remain limited given the community's size and the control of the central government over its activities.

KURDISH POLITICS

Kurdish aspirations for independence have been centered in the Kurdish Democratic Party (KDP). Cells of this party are to be found in Iran, Turkey, Iraq, and Syria, and offices in countries outside the Middle East: Austria (Vienna), France (Paris), West Germany (West Berlin), the Netherlands (Amsterdam), Switzerland (Geneva, Lausanne), the United Kingdom (London), and the United States (Chicago, Los Angeles).[56] Membership is open to all Kurds. Elections to office are conducted democratically. Formerly established as a communist-oriented party, the KDP altered its position when Barzani was elected its head. Although a leftist wing does exist, most of this faction bolted the party and joined the PUK.

While the center of the Kurdish nationalist movement was for many years Syria, the Syrian Kurdish population has ignored party politics. The most prominent Kurdish politician in Syria was Khalid Bakdash. Born in the Kurdish quarter of Damascus—which also happens to be one of the poorest sections of the city—he entered politics in the 1940s and won a seat in the parliament during the 1950s. His cause, however, was that of the Communist Party. He eventually became secretary-general of the Syrian Communist Party, a development which alienated him from the majority of Damascus's Kurdish population.[57]

Kurdish politics in Turkey have been primarily underground. The Turkish army's intensive persecution of Kurdish nationalists has forced Kurdish leaders to operate with great care. There is no Kurdish party as such except the illegal KDP. The Kurds have instead participated with other parties in an attempt to gain more freedom for themselves. For example, they supported Adnan Menderes; but after his execution in 1960 and the abolition of his Democratic Party, they turned inward once more. In the 1970s the Kurds have supported the outlawed Turkish Workers' Party as well as the Kurkish People's Liberation Army.[58] However, because of the military's heavy-handedness, the success of these two groups has been limited. Instead there are indications that the Kurds are once more acting on their own and, through the Turkish branch of the KDP, have begun to agitate for Kurdish rights more openly in the name of the KDP.

In the past, cooperation among the Kurdish populations of the various countries has been limited. Intense localism tended to isolate the various communities. Being a transhumant society, movement over the borders was quite common for several tribes since their winter grazing grounds might be in one country and the summer pasture in another. The proximity of the border also afforded places of refuge. Since there was little cooperation among the central governments, it was common to have a dissident tribal leader cross the national boundary of his state into another without fear of repercussion from the government of the country into which he moved. When the situation became favorable, the self-imposed exile would return to his tribal lands, content with the knowledge that he would always have a home with his brethren across the border.

The first major act of cooperation among the various Kurdish populations came in 1946 with the establishment of the Mahabad Republic in Iran. Under Barzani, a small contingent of about 500 men was attached to the armed forces of this short-lived state. A few Turkish Kurds joined with the forces of Mahabad. However with the demise of the state, these Turkish and Iraqi nationalists returned to their homelands or to exile, as in the case of Barzani and his men.

In his revolt against the Iraqi regime in 1961, Barzani received support from Turkish Kurds who saw a chance to strike a blow for their own people who were, at this time, undergoing repression following the death of Menderes.[59] But the support given was meager. Nevertheless, constant contact was maintained. Barzani also received assistance from the Iranian Kurds, but it was sporadic, since the Iranian government opened or closed its borders depending upon its relations at the time with the Iraqi regime.[60]

The conclusion of the March 11, 1970, agreement between Barzani's forces and the Iraqi government gave new hope to Kurdish nationals in other countries. They saw that Barzani's success or failure to achieve autonomy would have repercussions in their own communities. If successful, pressure would be applied on the central governments to conclude similar pacts with their own Kurdish populations. If the Iraqi government failed to carry out its promises, then Kurds everywhere would be forced to remain in a status quo situation.

Shortly after proclamation of the 1970 agreement, the clandestine Iranian Democratic Party of Kurdistan reaffirmed its determination to fight against the Iranian central government.[61] It paid homage to the Iraqi KDP, citing the Iraqi Kurds as inspiration for the Iranians to achieve similar goals. In July of 1970, a Kurdish congress was held in northern Iraq to commemorate the pact.[62] In attendance were Kurds from Lebanon, Western Europe, Turkey, Iran, Syria, and even the United States. For the first time, solidarity was being shown.

In 1971, the Turkish military uncovered a Kurdish nationalist movement. This in itself was not new, but the military command

reported that the Turkish movement had as its goal the establishment of liaison with Barzani's forces who were assisting in the
stockpiling of arms.[63] The Syrian government reported a year and a
half later (January 1973) that there was extensive military cooperation between Syrian and Iraqi Kurds, including the dispatch of 300
armed Syrian Kurds to Barzani's command.

RELATIONS WITH THE GENERAL SOCIETY

Throughout the Middle East the Kurds have been regarded by
Middle Eastern majorities with suspicion. This is a natural attitude
to take since the Kurds set themselves apart from the people, not
only physically but by their customs as well. A Kurdish woman can
readily be spotted in an Arab city by her dress—gaudy clothes,
usually a long dress, the older woman in white kerchiefs, and
wearing numerous trinkets. The men are less distinguishable, but
their headpieces differ from the Arabs' in the way they are worn or in
shape.

The Kurds have also gained a reputation as petty thieves. In
general, therefore, the Kurd is looked down upon by the masses. Not
that there is overt criticism; instead, he is ignored. He represents a
traditional, conservative group which, in most modern societies, is
derided. He is considered backward and slow-witted. At times,
because of his dress, he is labeled slovenly.

In spite of this disapprobation, the Kurd has been tolerated by
these societies, mainly because he is a pious Muslim and willing to
work at menial tasks. The Kurds in turn regard the non-Kurdish
societies in which they live with scorn. In their opinion, the Arabs do
not keep their promises. Furthermore, they consider Arabs lazy in
their work habits and lax in their religious duties. As a result, each
side distrusts and disapproves of the other. Yet, they have lived
together for centuries and will continue to do so, regardless of a
continuing air of coolness and suspicion between the two groups.

RELATIONS WITH INTERNATIONAL POWERS

Because of its proximity to the Kurds, the Soviet Union has had
close relations with this minority. In connection with its southward
expansion and attempts to break its containment, Moscow used the
Kurds to further Soviet aims. Sponsoring the Mahabad Republic is
one example of Soviet techniques. Another is the asylum offered to

Barzani and his men from 1947 to 1958. These Kurds were always a trump card to be used against Iraqi governments. Even the Kurdish population in the Soviet Union could be described as hostages to Soviet policy. Through them, the Soviet Union has attempted to influence the Kurdish people in other countries. Some Kurds did become communists. The majority, though, held fast to their tribal ways and refused to embrace communist ideas emanating from the Soviet Union.

In spite of generally good Soviet-Kurdish relations over time, the cooperative and close ties between Baghdad and Moscow poses the distinct possibility of alienating the Kurds. In an attempt to circumvent any rupture, the Soviets have invited Kurdish leaders to the Soviet Union for amicable discussions. Soviet Vice-Premier Novikov, for example, met with representatives of Mulla Mustafa Barzani in Iraq in July 1971, to explain the detente between Iraq and the Soviet Union.[64] Yet, he failed to persuade Barzani to visit the Soviet Union for closer talks. In 1972, the invitation was extended two more times, still without success.[65]

By normalizing relations with Turkey and Iran and establishing close military ties with Syria, the Soviet Union has jeopardized its relations with the Kurds in these countries. At the same time, because of its past activities, Soviet relations with the Kurds must be suspect to Middle East governments. Moscow has in the past supplied weapons to the Kurds to use against these governments and could again if its relations with the Middle Eastern states deteriorated once more.

The Iranian government has also used its Kurdish population against the Iraqi government. Whenever Iraq tried to put too much pressure on Iran, the latter merely opened its borders so that Iranian Kurds could enter Iraq and support Barzani's forces. Iran was also the means by which arms reached the Iraqi Kurds. The Soviets were not the only nation to send arms to the Kurds, however. Israel, to keep Iraqi forces pinned down within their own country, sent shipments of arms via Iran.[66] This policy was successful in the 1967 Arab-Israeli conflict, for example, when major contingents of Iraqi forces were pinned down in Kurdistan. Radio announcements on October 12, 1973, citing new fighting between the Kurds and Iraqis, may have shown another attempt to prevent Iraqi forces from entering the fray.

Mention should be made of the appeal by Mulla Mustafa Barzani to the United States for support. In a personal interview, Mulla Mustafa outlined the factors favoring U.S. assistance.[67] Oil was the prime reason the United States should intervene, in his view, apart from the moral issue. Barzani would guarantee that the United States would receive oil from the Kirkuk fields. U.S. policy would not permit a close relationship with the Kurds, however. Eventually, the U.S. government abandoned its clandestine support—through Iran and Israel—for Kurdish separatism. Washington did accept 700 Kurds, including Barzani, as a token contingent of refugees following the 1975 debacle in which the United States curtailed its support for the Kurds as part of the Iran-Iraq settlement.

THE FUTURE

With the regional unrest persisting in the Middle East, turmoil in Iran, and disorder in Turkey, Kurdish aspirations for a national state may yet be realized. Much depends upon events now taking place in Iran. If the central government accedes to the demands put forth by the Kurdish community, a new autonomous Iranian Kurdistan could rise from the ashes of the ill-fated Mahabad Republic. Such an emergence would have clear repercussions for both Turkey and Iraq, whose leaders would most probably be faced with increased agitation by their Kurdish communities.

The Kurds are currently undergoing social change. Detribalization is spreading throughout Kurdistan. Policies promulgated by the various central governments to assimilate the Kurdish population, whether called Arabization, Turkification, or Iranianization, have decreased the percentage of migratory tribes so that sedentary living is now the norm. War, modern communications, and economic development have also accelerated the process of detribalization.

Detribalization has not meant a weakening of Kurdish solidarity. It has, in fact, strengthened the idea of nationhood, for allegiance is being transferred from the tribal leaders to the nationalist parties seeking Kurdish autonomy. The Pesh Merga itself has been reduced to a few hundred fighting men, the rest scattered or imprisoned. However this is not to say that they could not be regrouped and become a force of 100,000 again.

Following World War I, international public opinion encouraged a number of ethnic minorities to seek autonomy. Most failed. However, events in the present era are once again creating interest in and impelling toward self-determination for ethnic communities.[68] Combined with world pressure and internal chaotic conditions, Kurdish aspirations for an independent Kurdish homeland could at last be realized. Independence, though, cannot be achieved through force of arms. Today, given the *military* power (even in chaos) of the five nations in which the Kurds are found, it must be brought about by political means.

NOTES

1. Hassan Arfa, *The Kurds: An Historical and Political Study* (London: Oxford University Press, 1966), p. 3.

2. *Ibid.*, p. 6.

3. Wadie Jwaideh, "The Kurdish National Movement: Its Origins and Development" (Ph.D. diss., Syracuse University, 1960), p. 1.

4. Hugh Hutchinson, Jr., "Kurds in Turkey" (M.A. thesis, Columbia University, 1967), p. 4.

5. Moshe Zeltzer, "Minorities in Iraq and Syria," in *Peoples and Cultures of the Middle East*, ed. Ailon Shiloh (New York: Random House, 1969), p. 18.

6. *Ibid.*, p. 14.

7. B. D. Clark, "Iran: Changing Population Patterns," in *Populations of the Middle East and North Africa*, ed. John Innes Clarke and W. B. Fisher (New York: Africana, 1972), p. 71.

8. Derk Kinnane, *The Kurds and Kurdistan* (London: Oxford University Press, 1964), p. 2; S. S. Gavan, *Kurdistan: Divided Nation of the Middle East* (London: Lawrence and Wishart, 1958), p. 11; and George S. Harris, "Ethnic Conflict and the Kurds," *Annals of the American Academy of Political and Social Science*, 483 (September 1977); 112.

9. Harris, "Ethnic Conflict." One author places the Kurdish population in Turkey at 8 million. See Bernard Brigouliex, "Kurds Seek Way as Violence Rises," *Manchester Guardian*, August 13, 1978, p. 13.

10. J. C. Dewdney, "Turkey: Recent Population Trends," in Clarke and Fisher, eds., *Populations of the Middle East*, p. 57.

11. It has been estimated that over a half million were deported to western Anatolia after the 1925 Kurdish revolt. Because of the lack of government support for resettlement purposes, over one-third of these people died during the first year. See Jwaideh, "The Kurdish National Movement," p. 602.

12. U.S. Department of State, Office of the United States Coordinator for Refugee Affairs, *1979 World Refugee Assessments*, Washington, D.C., March 14, 1979, p. 44.

13. Eric Pace, "Iran Reported Offering Sanctuary to Kurds from Iraq," *New York Times*, May 15, 1975, p. 7.

14. U.S. Committee for Refugees, *1978 World Refugee Survey Report*, Washington, D.C., 1978, p. 33.

15. R. I. Lawless, "Iraq: Changing Population Patterns," in Clarke and Fisher, eds., *Populations of the Middle East*, p. 103.

16. Zeltzer, "Minorities," pp. 13-14.

17. Zeltzer, "Minorities," p. 14.

18. Carleton Coon, *Caravan: The Story of the Middle East* (New York: Henry Holt and Company, 1951), p. 158.

19. Hutchinson, "Kurds," p. 11.

20. Coon, *Caravan*, p. 158.

21. Arfa, *The Kurds*, p. 3.

22. Jwaideh, "The Kurdish National Movement," p. 34. History has recorded this name as Saladin, the nemesis of Richard the Lion-Hearted during the Third Crusade.

23. Arfa, The Kurds, pp. 17-19.

24. Jwaideh, "The Kurdish National Movement," p. 214.

25. Ibid., p. 218.

26. Arfa, The Kurds, p. 25.

27. The Armenians retaliated during World War I by organizing an Armenian volunteer corps, armed by the Russian forces, and massacring more than 600,000 Kurds in eastern Turkey. See Arfa, The Kurds, p. 25.

28. Ibid., p. 29.

29. Jwaideh, "The Kurdish National Movement," p. 400.

30. Arfa, The Kurds, p. 37.

31. Jwaideh, "The Kurdish National Movement," p. 588.

32. Mahmud continued to create trouble during the 1930s on several occasions, emerging from his sanctuary in Iran. However, these engagements were of a limited nature and involved only his immediate forces. At no time was he successful in his endeavors to establish a Kurdish state. See Arfa, The Kurds, p. 119.

33. Ibid., p. 118.

34. Ibid., p. 84.

35. Ibid., p. 99. The story of the episode has been told best by William Eagleton in The Kurdish Republic of 1946 (London: Oxford University Press, 1963).

36. Jwaideh, "The Kurdish National Movement," p. 297.

37. Ibid., pp. 304-05. For his pains, Shaykh Abd al-Salam was eventually captured and executed,

38. Ibid., p. 616.

39. Ibid., pp. 731-32.

40. Arfa, The Kurds, p. 132.

41. Arfa, The Kurds, p. 134. Edgar O'Ballance, The Kurdish Revolt 1961-1970 (Hamden: Archon, 1973), provides a detailed account of some of the military developments.

42. Arfa, The Kurds, p. 137.

43. Foreign Broadcast Information Service (FBIS), Daily Report; Middle East and Africa, no. 172, supplement 30, September 5, 1973, pp. 9-10.

44. Roger Hardy, "In Iraq: Independence is the Watchword," The Times (London), July 17, 1978, p. 15.

45. U.S. Committee for Refugees, 1978 World Refugee Survey Report, pp. 32-33.

46. Pace, "Iran Reported Offering Sanctuary to Kurds from Iraq."

47. The Times (London), September 8, 1977, p. 13.

48. Ferdinand Hurni, "Report from Iraq," Swiss Review of World Affairs (February 1978); 17.

49. "New Modus Vivendi," The Middle East, no. 43 (May 1978); 46.

50. "Setting the Record Straight," ibid., p. 47.

51. Edward Mortimer, "Veteran Kurd Group in New Clashes with Iraqi Forces," The Times (London), July 18, 1978, p. 6.

52. Jonathan Randal, "Kurds' Autonomy Cries Rekindle Ethnic Flashpoint in Iran," Washington Post, March 2, 1979, p. A-13.

53. John Cooley, "Ankara Admits Kurdish Threat," The Christian Science Monitor, May 3, 1971, p. 1.

54. "Mass Trial in Turkey Draws Concern in Europe," The Christian Science Monitor, January 15, 1973, p. 12.

55. FBIS, Daily Report, Middle East and Africa, no. 49, August 2, 1973, p. 13.

56. Uriel Dann, "The Kurdish National Movement in Iraq," The Jewish Quarterly, no. 9 (Fall 1978); 144. These European and U.S. cities are used primarily as propaganda offices to further Kurdish interests.

57. Michael Van Dusen, "Political Integration and Regionalism in Syria," *Middle East Journal* 26, no. 2 (Spring 1972); 128-29.

58. John Cooley, "Election Tests Turkey's Military," *The Christian Science Monitor*, March 16, 1973, p. 4.

59. Hutchinson, "Kurds," pp. 51, 52.

60. *Ibid.*, p. 59.

61. "Le P.D.K. appelle les Kurdes d'Iran à la révolte," *L'Orient*, April 26, 1970, p. 6.

62. John Cooley, "Journey to Kallala," *The Christian Science Monitor*, July 15, 1970, p. 18.

63. Cooley, "Ankara Admits Kurdish Threat," p. 1.

64. John Cooley, "Russians and Iraqis Forge Links," *The Christian Science Monitor*, July 7, 1971, p. 5.

65. *An-Nahar* (Beirut), November 1, 1972, p. 2.

66. Cooley, "Journey to Kallala."

67. "Barzani Speaks Out," *Daily Star* (Beirut), June 29, 1973, p. 4.

68. Walker Connor, "Nation-Building or Nation-Destroying?" *World Politics* 24, no. 3 (April 1972); 319-55.

4

MINORITIES IN CONTAINMENT: THE ARABS OF ISRAEL

Suhaila Haddad, R. D. McLaurin, and Emile A. Nakhleh

The half million Arabs who have lived in Israel since 1948 have for most of these three decades been a relatively quiescent minority in the state, with no input into or influence on the Arab-Israeli conflict or the Palestine question—none, that is, until March 1976. These "Israeli Arabs" are those Arabs who came under Israeli rule in 1948 and who since then have become Israeli citizens, either by birth or by naturalization. These "pre-1967 Arabs" have lived in large concentrations in Galilee in the north and in the Triangle region of the central plains of Israel. Some bedouin have also lived near Beersheba in the Negev. (Under U.N. Resolution 181[II] of 1947, partitioning Palestine into two states, Galilee was to be a part of the Arab state which did not come into being.) They do not live in the territories that Israel has occupied only since June 1967. They possess Israeli citizenship and have experienced life in Israel intimately. Both youths and adults invariably speak Hebrew in addition to Arabic. While Israeli Arabs have identified emotionally and historically with the Arab nation as a whole, between 1948 and 1967 they were cut off culturally from the Arab world; the only linkage was maintained through radio and television programs broadcast from the Arab world, a linkage that was dramatically reinforced after the 1967 war.

From 1948 until the mid-1970s, Israel's Arab minority, whose numbers rose from roughly 156,000[1] to 455,000[2] during the same period, was widely perceived as a docile populace which had adjusted peacefully to its status as a cultural rather than a political minority. Over the years, through a systematic policy of "institution-alized segmentation," successive Israeli governments have ensured, that Israel's Arabs remained a cultural minority in a Jewish-dominated state, with no opportunity or encouragement to develop any sense of political consciousness regarding their non-Jewishness in the state of Israel.

Across Israel's frontiers, Arab governments and peoples perceived Israel's Arabs as a helpless minority which had been either co-opted or persecuted into submission to Israeli rule. Just as Israeli Arabs were cut off from the mainstream of Arab thinking, the Arab world was generally unaware of the literary output of the Arabs inside Israel, or "occupied Palestine," as it was often called. Again, contacts were reestablished following the June 1967 war.

Israel's Arabs have often been treated as second-class citizens, and they have been told repeatedly that their existence in Israel, a state in which Arab nationalism has no place, depends on their good behavior as a tolerated minority. They were free to speak, worship, assemble, and write so long as those freedoms did not involve political action in any form. Violations were dealt with harshly, as in the late 1950s and early 1960s with the *al-Ard* group (see below). The only forms of political action tolerated by the authorities were those activities invited by the authorities themselves as a form of token-ism.

Until recently, relatively little analysis has been directed at the Arab Palestinians who remained in Israel. This chapter assesses the evolution of Israeli Arabs' self-perception, goals, attitudes toward Israeli governance, and political behavior. It examines their views of their possible futures, and the critical factors that have influenced these attitudes over time. The analysis is based upon four principal sources. Although each provided different perspectives, the conclusions have been integrated for the purposes of this chapter.

The first source consists of observations derived from a number of largely unstructured, open-ended interviews with Israeli Arabs in the summers of 1976 and 1977. The interviews involved most Israeli Arab leaders and many others as well and touched on a variety of subjects. A number of the most salient observations have been given in greater detail in a separate volume.[3]

A similar series of discussions was held by Edward E. Azar among Israeli Arabs and their leaders in the fall of 1976. These form a second basis for this chapter.

The third source of data was the writings of Israeli Arabs. This literature appears in English and other Western languages to a limited extent, but principally in Arabic. We have reviewed and synthesized the Arabic language writings in newspapers and periodicals, as well as the English, French, and Hebrew writings by Arabs in books, newspapers, and periodicals.[4]

Fourth, we have followed carefully the *Daily Report* (for the Middle East and North Africa) of the Foreign Broadcast Information Service (1976-77).

Finally, the assessments of Israeli and foreign observers in books, newspapers, and magazines have been drawn upon when these shed additional light on the evolution of Arab perceptions.

HISTORICAL OVERVIEW OF ARAB ATTITUDES

There are rarely easy and clear-cut turning points in the evolution of attitudes. In the present case, however, external events have facilitated the identification of—admittedly somewhat artificial—temporal stages. These external considerations are the major Middle East wars of 1948, 1967, and 1973.

Stage 1: An Isolated, Leaderless Minority, 1948-67

The 1948 conflict resulted in the establishment of Israel as a sovereign entity, thus introducing the problem of Arabs in the Zionist state. But Israeli demography was not created, after all, simply by the massive influx of large numbers of Jews from other parts of the world. The major demographic change from 1947 to 1948 was the national flight of the Palestinian Arabs from that part of Palestine occupied or threatened by Jewish forces.

The magnitude of the Arab exodus is still unknown with any precision. Estimates, indeed, vary widely. A reasonable figure for the number of Arabs who fled Israeli Palestine might be approximately 700,000-1,000,000.[5] That the nature and not just the size of the mass evacuation is important must be evident, for in a Palestine which had known large urban Arab population centers, such as Jaffa, Haifa, Lydda-Ramle, and Nazareth, only the last named remained. The others became mixed cities with small Arab minorities (2-3,500). Of the 550 Arab villages in Israeli Palestine, only 121 remained.[6] Table 4.1 presents some population data for Arab settlements before and after the 1948 war.

Thus, only a fraction of the original Palestinian Arab population remained in what was to become the State of Israel, and this fraction constituted the margin rather than the core of the Palestinian

TABLE 4.1: Arab Urban Population before and after the 1948-49 War

City	Before	After
Haifa	71,200	2,900
Jaffa	70,000	3,600
Lydda-Ramle	34,920	2,000
Nazareth	15,450	16,800
Acre	15,000	3,500
Safed	9,530	negligible
Tiberias	5,310	negligible

Source: Ian Lustick, "Arabs in the Jewish State: A Study in the Effective Control of a Minority Population" (Ph.D. diss. University of California at Berkeley, 1976), p. 71. These figures diverge somewhat from those available in the Statistical Abstract of Palestine, 1944-45.

community. Among those who fled were most of the extant Arab elite. The Arabs who remained were, as Khalil Nakhleh has written, "leaderless with a depressed and suppressed cultural symbolic repertoire."[7] Although a variety of resistance and interest groups formed among Israeli Arabs, their effectiveness was limited by the purposeful isolation of the Arabs and restrictions on their activities.

After 1948, the Arabs were isolated from each other and from the Jewish population by a series of measures and social phenomena. Most obvious and prominent was the military government that remained in force until 1966. Under the military government, the military governor could "proclaim any area or place a forbidden area." To enter or leave such an area one needed "a written permit from the military commander or his deputy . . . failing which he is considered to have committed a crime."[8] All the Arab villages and towns, even in the Negev, were declared "security zones" (forbidden areas); so Arabs required permits from the military government to leave and enter. Each village constituted, in effect, a separate zone, making travel between villages subject to permission of the military governor. Article 109 of the military government regulations allowed the military government to banish individuals—in effect to force them to live in designated areas. Other such regulations permitted imposition of partial or complete curfews in any area.[9]

Far more important than the arbitrary rule of the military government in isolating Arabs in Israeli society has been the self-consciously Zionist nature of that society.

When considering the position of the Arab minority in Israeli society one must remember that these institutions all developed in an antagonistic relationship of one sort or another with the Arabs of Palestine. Their organizational ideologies, and the personal commitments of the individuals who control them, are rooted in bitter struggles, fought with Palestinian Arabs, for Jewish land ownership, Jewish immigration, Jewish labor, and Jewish political rights. The men and women who filled the bureaus and agencies of the new Israeli Government ... experienced this struggle as the determining fact of their socio-political existence. Spurred then by individual commitment and endowed finally with the sanction and encouragement of the Government, these insititutions, after 1948, continued the struggle with Israel's Arab minority that they had waged ... with the Arab majority of Palestine.[10]

These observations apply even more wholly to the "National Institutions," the Zionist institutions (such as the Jewish National Fund, responsible for acquisition and leasing of Israeli land; the Jewish Agency; the Histadrut) which exist in parallel—and share power with—government agencies and departments. Thus, "Israeli Arabs are cut off from the mainstream of public power and purpose in Israeli society."[11] Participation in the Israel Defense Force (IDF), for example, is perhaps the single most important institution of social integration and personal mobility in Israel. Muslim Arabs, except the bedouin, are excluded, but Christians can volunteer and Druze and Circassians are conscripted. Indeed, while Israel is a state of a multiplicity of overlapping institutions molding the traditional Zionist objectives and national administrative needs, there are no similar "national" institutions representing Arab perspectives, needs, or values, in spite of the fact that Arabs are in every meaningful way excluded from all of the routes and accesses to power and influence.

Beyond the isolation of the Arab community from the Jewish majority, the internal segmentation of the Arab community has been until recently an important result of Jewish strategy and existing social institutions. Israeli Arabs include Christians, Muslims, and Druze, and some smaller minority groups (such as Circassians) may also be included. Divisions among these religious groups are very deep, and the attitudes of each group toward Israel and their role are consequently quite distinct. There are similar profound differences between urban and rural Arabs; among Arabs from Galilee, those from the Triangle area, and the bedouin of the Negev; and between family and tribal groups. The military administration from 1948 to 1966 reinforced these divisions within the Arab community in its travel restrictions and by reacting quickly and sternly to any attempt to *organize* Arabs, even for sports groups.

In addition, the Israeli administration has assiduously pursued the objective of diluting the Arab concentrations in Galilee and the Little Triangle. It is in this connection that Arabs see the Judaization of the Galilee program as a threat.[12]

One means used by the government to discourage coalescence of the Arab community has been to strengthen the internal divisions of that community. Thus, the Druze have received a status of far greater autonomy than any they have experienced in the past. Special privileges and legal systems are applied to the Druze in Israel, and economic support to their community is far greater than to the Christian and Muslim Arab groups. Christian and bedouin groups are also treated with special favors, however.

We do not suggest that Israeli Arabs lacked any political cohesion or leadership during the 1948-68 period, only that they were circumscribed under the conditions that obtained. For example, from the founding of the League of Poets in 1952, a group of activist Israeli Arabs was involved in the establishment of conferences, committees, and other organizations dedicated to the defense of the Arab minority's rights and Arab lands. As a result of these activities, a small "Arab Front" was formed in 1957, later called the "Democratic Popular Front." The nationalist movement began to publish a newspaper, *al Ard*, on an intermittent basis, established the al-Ard Company, Ltd., and engaged in various organizing activities (most were clubs of various types). After sending a memo to the United Nations, the group formally set itself up as the al-Ard movement. The leaders requested to register it as a party, but several of them (including Sabri Jiryis) were arrested soon thereafter and accused of establishing contacts with the fedayeen and the Palestine Liberation Organization (PLO) and of founding a secret movement. The al-Ard Company and the movement were banned. After a series of further confrontations, the leaders were forced to leave the country, and the members continued to be watched closely by the Israeli government for some time thereafter. Although the group dissolved after 1965, it is remembered as the largest and most visible of Arab protest organizations during the military administration.[13]

Thus, educational, social, and partisan structures have all been used to divide the Arabs by sociological, family, income, sectarian, geographic, and other factors, and to prevent the emergence of a common Arab identity. In the absence of leadership and under the restrictions of the military administration, there was little possibility for such a consciousness to arise. However, the military government was terminated in 1966. The end of the military administration and the major Arab-Israeli war of June 1967 ushered in a new era for Israel's Arabs.

Stage 2: Discovery, Organization, Communication, and an Arab Identity, 1967-73

The June War, despite the crushing defeat of the Arab states, did directly affect the political consciousness of the Arab minority in Israel. Several surveys taken before and after the brief conflict demonstrate a clear-cut change in the Arabism, Palestinianism, and goals of the minority. A much greater proportion of Israeli Arabs was oriented toward militant Palestinian goals or held secessionist aspirations after the war.[14]

The post-June War period in Israel was characterized by a general economic boom, a feeling of political and military self-confidence vis-à-vis the Arabs, and substantial social change in the relationships of the different elements of the Jewish population. In the course of these developments, little attention was paid to the Arab minority. For all intents and purposes, Israel considered the minority to be without importance in Israel—and acted accordingly, an existential denial of a minority proportionately larger than the Blacks in the United States. Thus, land expropriations continued, and the multiplicity of other forms of discrimination, some subtle and some less subtle, and control continued apace.[15]

The disestablishment of the military government did not end the application of emergency regulations, and some applications were more severe than they had been under the previous situation. Administrative detentions, for example, tended to be much longer after 1967. Yet, on the whole, government control of the Arab minority was unquestionably less severe after 1967 than before.[16]

The Israeli Arabs, for their part, also experienced important social changes between 1967 and 1973. First, with the lifting of the restrictive controls in place throughout the military government period, Israeli Arabs were able to interact with each other and to travel throughout Israel.

A second critical factor influencing Israeli Arab perceptions has been contact between Israeli Arabs and the residents of the occupied territories.[17] Similarly, the end of the isolation of Israeli Arabs engendered more widespread exposure to currents of thought developing throughout the Arab world. Throughout the period after the June War and before 1973 the Arab world reflected the humiliation and defeatism that arose from the June War.

State 3: Identity, Consciousness, and Palestinianism, 1973 to the Present

The major changes witnessed after 1973 in the role of the Arabs in Israel are probably attributable both to developments in the 1966-73 period, on the one hand, and to the effects of the October War, on the other. Arab-Israeli wars have consistently raised the group consciousness of Israel's Arab minority, and the new feeling of Arab worth and self-confidence current throughout the Arab world removed some of the other constraints on Arab identification.

Probably at least as important as the war, however, has been the further development of trends begun in the previous period. Contacts with the Arab world and with West Bank Arabs have proliferated. Contacts between and among Israeli Arabs through institutionalized channels of communication have increased, taken cohesive shape, and, for perhaps the first time, been heard. This fact has reinforced the utility of these new channels and methods. The concept of the new phase, however, has increasingly been *Palestinian* identity rather than Arab identity, with all the cultural and political symbolism such specificity implies.

In sum, the current stage sees increasing Arabism and Palestinianism confronting Israeli officialdom and organizing to exploit perceived weaknesses. These two themes, continued and more institutional and visible organization and active confrontation dominate the post-October War period.

POLITICAL SITUATION

The most important new issue after 1948 became state security, and for years Israel's Arabs were viewed not in the context of an ethnic minority whose rights needed protection but rather as a potential fifth column. Indeed, it may be argued that Israel's Arab minority has always been regarded in this perspective: almost all of the advisers to the Prime Minister on Arab Affairs and predecessor offices have had backgrounds principally in security or intelligence. The seizure of Arab lands and other resources, the establishment of Jewish settlements in the Galilee and along the armistice lines segregating Arabs from themselves and Jews, and other actions formed part of a natural, well-orchestrated strategy of social control and exploitation. As Ian Lustick has admirably synopsized:

> According to its major objectives the leadership of the new State wanted to prevent the Arab minority from serving as a fifth column or abetting large scale infiltration; to acquire from Israeli Arabs a

large percentage of their land holdings; to take advantage of Arab resources for the absorption of new immigrants; to harness Arab economic power for the rapid development of the Jewish controlled Israeli economy; to aggregate political support among Israeli Arabs for partisan advantage; and to prevent the Arab minority from becoming a burden in the arena of international politics. These goals . . . resolved themselves into the one overriding objective of the Israeli leadership vis-a-vis the Arab minority—control.[18]

Control, as Lustick has also pointed out, was operationalized in three components: segmentation, dependence, and co-optation. The first of the three tools involves both the isolation of the Arab minority from the Jewish majority and the encouragement of schisms within the Arab community. By "dependence" is meant the strategy of cultivating Arab reliance on Israeli Jews and the dominant sociopolitical system for political, economic, and social benefits. The third element is the process by which Arab leaders and groups are penetrated and "bought" by the dominant majority group.[19]

We have already discussed the Arab's early years (1948-66) in Israel. A study of editorials and columns written by Arabs in three prominent Arabic newspapers in Israel—al-Ittihad, the Arabic organ of the Communist Party; al-Mirsad, published by Mapam, the left-wing Zionist party which concerns itself with Arab problems; and al-Yom (now al-Anba), sponsored by the government and the Histadrut (the General Federation of Workers)—observes that although the writers had limitations arising from their sponsorship, by the Communist Party and Mapam, they nevertheless did try to express the views of the Israeli Arabs. The Arab columnists of al-Ittihad and al-Mirsad raised voices of constant protest against and criticism of defense regulations, military government, land expropriation, individual displacement and isolation, and other symbols of what they saw as repression of a minority. The commentators spoke out against undemocratic treatment. Implicitly, and frequently explicitly, they rejected the concept of Israel as a Zionist state; their objective was a secular, democratic country treating Jews and Arabs equally.[20]

Thus, even before the June War, Israeli analysts sensed the views of Israeli Arabs and recognized the problems they faced in dealing with Israeli society. The principal tool employed to control the Arab sector was the military government. That the government and leaders of Israel generally viewed Israeli Arabs as suspect was taken for granted by and acceptable to Israel's majority. This basic distrust of the Arabs, which has underlain the approach to and management of them, is a constant in national policy. As we and others have indicated, the post of adviser to the prime minister on Arab affairs—the chief position concerned with the drafting and implementation of government policy towards the Arabs—has generally been filled by individuals with extensive experience in the intelligence or security services.[21] Although military administration has ended and the surface tenor of government relations with and approaches to Israeli Arabs have evolved substantially, security is still the principal factor in Israeli planning, policy, and behavior with respect to its Arab minority.

Political Representation

> In Israel political power is concentrated in the governing bodies (the Central Committees, the Secretariats, the nomination committees, etc.) of the Zionist political parties. These are the arenas in which party policy is hammered out and slates of candidates for the Knesset, for the Executive Council and the Central Committee of the Histadrut, and for the governing bodies of the Jewish agency and the World Zionist Organization are drawn up. In each of these institutions the same set of six or seven Zionist political parties compete for control.... Control over these institutions by these political parties ... has been exerted by means of an intricate network of interlocking directorates and a constant rotation of party elites.[22]

The existing parties in Israel are largely the contemporary incarnation of the pre-Israeli Zionist political clubs and organizations. Because their history has been oriented toward and their policies aimed at achieving particularist Zionist objectives, Arab representation is not merely peripheral to the operation of these parties; it may be subversive of their goals. Thus, such representation is minimal and is perceived by many as mere tokenism.[23] The Israeli political system is based on a multiparty concept. Given the societal fragmentation, governments frequently emerge as coalitions. Arab political representation has traditionally been through the "Arab lists" (officially, "affiliated lists") sponsored by the various political parties of which Mapai (Israel Labor Party since 1968) has set the standard. These lists were drawn up on the basis of residence and religious affiliations from among the party's Arab supporters, who usually belonged to cooperating, prominent families. During the first general elections of 1949, Mapai was the most active party politically among the Arabs, sponsoring two Arab lists. The Israeli Communist Party was next in influence among the Arabs, and Mapam third. During subsequent elections Mapam made a minor change by always having one Arab candidate rather than a list. A look at Arab representation in the Knesset, the 120-member Israeli parliament, reveals that during the nine general elections since Israel's creation, the Arabs have had six to eight Knesset members (MKs), with the exception of the 1949 election when they had only three seats.

The various parties vied for Arab votes through many techniques. To capture those votes and promote its Arab candidates, Mapai made use of the military government apparatus when it was in effect, of the office of the adviser to the prime minister on Arab affairs, and of the Arab department in the Histadrut (the General Federation of Workers), using its Arabic newspaper *al-Yom* to promote its positions and make them known to the Arab population.

Mapam, the United Workers' Party, for a long time the only Zionist party to accept Arabs as members, also tried to capture a share of the Arab vote by appealing to them on ideological bases. However, the party appeared insincere in character and took ambivalent positions, attempting to accommodate all sides at once.

Other Zionist parties also attempted to win over Arab support but very inconsistently.

The Israeli Communist Party (Rakah), a non-Zionist group and in fact the only party in which Arabs have had access to party power, has played an important role in the political life of the Israeli Arabs and has had a great appeal among them in protecting Arab interests and leading the Arab opposition to Israeli domestic policy, that is to say, the military government and the expropriation of Arab land. The party has consistently appealed to Arab nationalism. Indeed, as early as its twelfth party congress in 1958, the party advocated "the right of the Arabs in Israel to self-determination, even to the extent of seceding."[24]

Rakah has had substantial appeal for and support from among the Arab youth and has established branches in every Arab group it could reach. Its Arabic newspapers, magazines, and other literary and cultural publications helped it gain influence among the Arabs. The reason for its appeal is that the party is interested "not so much [in] Marxism as Arab nationalism and a chance to protest what many Israeli Arabs feel is second-class citizenship."[25]

Rakah members of the Knesset, particularly the Arab members, have consistently shown great interest in any Arab problem, addressing questions to the proper officials, introducing dozens of bills (few passed) to improve the lot of the Arabs, and actively participating in debates relating to Arab matters.

Recognizing the role of the Communist Party among the Arabs, the Israeli authorities tried to limit its activities by enforcing military government restrictions against its Arab members, being cautious to keep their interference within limits. Yet, Rakah has been viewed as a safety valve: it has not been outlawed and is considered by many Israelis as a weathervane of Arab concerns.

The party has not been effective in bringing about change or in securing legislative redress of Arab grievances. Since the 1965 Communist Party split, after which most Jewish Communists left what is now Rakah, the party has been almost completely isolated from the essence of Israeli politics. "Indeed, the separation of Rakah from the rest of the society is so complete and its illegitimacy so widely accepted that its existence serves basically to reinforce the institutional isolation of Arabs from the Jewish sector."[26] Thus, Israeli Arabs and Rakah, in increasing their mutual support, are reinforcing their own illegitimacy. Israeli government pressure to support the Zionist parties rather than Rakah is widespread. For example, Minister of Labor Moshe Baram warned, in a local election in Nazareth, that "only residents stand to lose if they identify with a list that reflects Communist imperialism and reactionary Arab nationalism."[27] Indeed, when Tawfiq Zayyad was elected mayor of Nazareth, the central government imposed a "financial blockade," cutting off government revenues to the municipality.

The speed with which Israel's Arabs are associating with Rakah is impressive. The Israeli Communist Party split in 1965. At that time, Rakah received 23.6 percent of the Arab vote. This support rose to 29.6 percent in 1969 and to 37 percent in 1973. In the recent (May 1977) elections, Rakah received approximately 50 percent of the Arab vote.

Communication

Prior to 1967, Israeli Arabs were linked to the rest of the Arab world only through the press, the mass media. However, since the 1967 war, communication and direct contact between Israeli Arabs and Palestinian Arabs in the occupied West Bank and Gaza Strip, and through them with the rest of the Arab world, have conduced to the greater assertiveness of Israeli Arabs. Before the occupation, the Arab world commonly perceived Israeli Arabs as collaborationists who had "sold out" to the Israeli enemy. Similarly, the stated aims of the Arab states with regard to Israel before 1967 were considered by Israeli Arabs as both threatening and unrealistic.

The occupation of the West Bank and Gaza, East Jerusalem, the

Sinai, and the Golan began shortly after the end of the military administration. Consequently, Israeli Arabs who had previously been unable to circulate found themselves able to move around their country and interact with other Arabs at the same time they were brought into contact with large numbers of Arabs in the occupied territories who then took jobs in Israel by the thousands.

Communication between Arabs within and outside Israel took place on four levels: in the media, and among students, intellectuals, and workers. Newspapers became the principal mass medium of communication, as the Arabic newspapers of Jerusalem were widely read in Galilee. Just as Rakah attracted Arab support as a licit protest organization that allowed Arabs to work together, *al-Ittihad* and *al-Jadid*, the party newspapers, became the principal printed media for the circulation of issues and ideas. Many Israeli Arab leaders wrote (and write) in *al-Ittihad* under pseudonyms.

The only type of Israeli Arab organization the government did not ruthlessly stamp out immediately was the student organization. Israeli Arab students formed an Arab Students Committee at the Hebrew University of Jerusalem as early as 1958. Although the authorities have traditionally refrained from recognizing (and thereby excluded use of facilities for) these organizations and have frequently harassed their leaders, the committees have not been eliminated. Interaction between Israeli Arabs and other Arabs has taken place, however, largely at campuses outside Israel in the past and, since 1967, in the West Bank. Its effect on attitudes is not clear, largely because the numbers involved are so limited.

Communication among Arab intellectuals has been indirect until recently. Israeli Arab novelists, men of letters, and poets have written of their attitudes and of their perceptions of discrimination and oppression in Israel. Although this literature was known to other Arab intellectuals, its circulation was somewhat limited. The events of Land Day—March 30, 1976—brought intellectuals from the occupied territory, who supported the Galilee protest, together with Israeli Arabs. Increasingly, these interactions have taken place in Rakah or other Communist-supported institutional contexts.

Finally, worker contacts are fairly extensive but elusive for assessment purposes. Given the large number of Arabs from the territories employed in Israel, one might expect these contacts to gain importance over time, but most of the participants are less politically conscious than the intellectuals, students, and media communities.

Palestinians of the occupied territories have had a definite reinforcement influence on the behavior of the Israeli Arabs, holding sympathy strikes to parallel those taking place within Israel proper: the March 30, 1976, Land Day strike and the September 1976 demonstrations backing the demands for the dismissal of Israel Koenig, the chief Israeli official in the Galilee and author of the controversial report recommending measures to curb the growth and influence of Israeli Arabs in the Galilee area. The September demonstrations were even more active in the West Bank town of Nablus than in Nazareth. The growing Palestinian nationalism is considered a crucial factor linking the West Bank and the Galilee disturbances of March 30, 1976, each group of Palestinians expressing solidarity with the other in the protests against the occupation in the West Bank and Gaza and against land expropriation and other forms of discrimination in Israel proper.[28]

ISRAELI ARABS AND THE LAND: POLICIES AND PERCEPTIONS

Any attempt to study the political attitudes of Israeli Arabs must take into consideration the land issue. Land has been the underpinning of the Arab minority's relations with state authorities for three decades, and official government policy regarding this land has shaped Arab attitudes toward the state. Arab land expropriation is a basic strategy, according to Tawfiq Zayyad, the mayor of Nazareth, who offers some statistics on land confiscation. Since the establishment of the State of Israel, the number of Arab villages has declined from 585 to just over 100 villages. Under military rule, the Arabs were deprived of many of their own lands, which were declared "closed areas." Israeli authorities thus seized more than 3.25 million *dunums* (812,500 acres) soon after the establishment of the state.* More recently, an additional 1.75 million *dunums* have been confiscated, and the government has announced plans to confiscate 1.5 million *dunums* from Arab-owned lands in the Negev. The sum of these figures is 6.5 million *dunums*, approximately one-third the area of Israel's pre-1967 borders.[29]

The Judaization of the Galilee ("settlement" and "development" are two of the more recent euphemisms used) is a government program designed to increase the amount of land available to Israeli Jews (depriving Israeli Arabs of more of their land through confiscation) and to alter the demographic composition of the Galilee, to move from an Arab into a Jewish majority. Referring to "develop-

---

*A dunum is approximately equal to a ¼ acre.

ment" or "Judaization," one observer has stated, "No matter how much the label changed, the goods remain the same: confiscation of land from the Arab population for the benefit of the Jewish population."[30] Reaction to the program led to the Land Day general strike of March 30, 1976, a demonstration of unprecedented magnitude.

Government expropriation of Arab lands, primarily in District 9 in Galilee, has forged a new national consciousness among Israel's half million Arabs. Simply put, Israeli Arabs perceive Israel's official policy of land expropriation as an unjustified, illegal, and systematic policy of discrimination against the Arabs. Israeli Arabs view this official policy of land confiscation as an effort by the Jewish state to make the lives of its non-Jewish citizens so uncomfortable as to lead to mass emigration. In support of this hypothesis, Israeli Arab elites offer several items of evidence:

They have been told many times that Israel is a state for the Jews in which Arabs can at best be a tolerated cultural minority;

Land expropriation has primarily meant taking Arab lands in order to build Jewish settlements on them. Arabs are legally banned from purchasing homes in these towns;

Israeli land policy has a twofold goal: to change the social structure of Israeli Arabs from farmers into unskilled workers, thereby creating a new class of "lumpen proletariat" and to alter the demography of such areas from an Arab majority into an Arab minority. If realized such a goal would perpetuate a situation in which the minority could be completely controlled and dominated by the government. The Arabs believe that this status was always assigned by the founders of the state to the Gentile citizens (goyim);

To many Israeli Arabs the confiscation of their lands indicates that the government has become uncomfortable with the increasing numbers of Israeli Arabs and their national awakening. Depriving them of their lands is seen as an attempt on the part of government to reassert the state's fundamental Jewishness;

Another indicator of the state's anti-Arab posture is seen in the official toleration and tacit approval of the virulently anti-Arab Koenig Memorandum written by a Jewish Ministry of Interior bureaucrat stationed in Galilee. The belief that Menachem Begin, head of the Likud Party which won in the May 1977 elections, contributed to the authorship of this memorandum has increased Arab apprehensions.

Over the years the government has justified its confiscation of Arab lands on the grounds of national security, regional development, and even environmental beautification, such as the establishment of national parks. Regardless of the reason given, most of the confiscated lands have been used to build Jewish settlements, towns, and cities such as Upper Nazareth and Karmiel.

ARAB RESPONSES

Israeli Arabs have continuously protested the expropriation of their lands. This protest has ranged from court action to open defiance in the form of rallies, strikes, and demonstrations. In the early 1950s, the inhabitants of Iqrit and Kafr Bir'im, two entire villages taken by the Israeli government and demolished by the Israeli army, took their case to the Israeli Supreme Court. The court ruled in their favor and ordered that they be allowed to return to their villages. The Israeli army refused to implement the court's decision for "security reasons." Since that time, several elderly men of Iqrit have held periodic sit-ins in the village church, but to no avail. The people of Iqrit and Kafr Bir'im have been living in the neighboring villages as "internal refugees," most of whom refused to sell their lands to the Israeli government in spite of pressure by the authorities. The one concession these people have received from the government is that some families have been allowed to bury their dead in the village cemetery. "Internal refugees" from other towns and villages have not been so fortunate. Neither cemeteries nor churches nor mosques have remained standing, and in place of the old Arab villages new Jewish settlements have risen.

Major Groups

In the late 1950s, Israeli Arabs attempted another method of response through the establishment of *al-Ard* (the Land) a coalition of intellectuals, workers, students, and farmers. (For *al-Ard's* concerns and more of its organizational history, see below.) However, the group was denied a permit to establish itself as a political party. The government has consistently refused to allow any independent Arab political party to operate in the state. Nonetheless, *al-Ard* held several rallies in the late 1950s, such as a May Day rally in 1958 in Nazareth and elsewhere. Economic and political pressures were applied against the leaders of the group; several were placed under house arrest or were denied travel permits, thereby forcing them to stay in their villages and towns. By the mid-1960s, *al-Ard* had practically disappeared.

Several other Arab political groups, committees, and organizations have appeared over the years protesting various facets of Israel's discriminatory policies against its Arab minority. Among the committees that became vocal and capable of capturing Arab public opinion, especially in the 1970s, there are three major ones: (1) *Lajnat al-Difă' 'an al-Arădi al-'Arabiyya* (Committee for the Defense of Arab lands); (2) *al-Lajna al-Qutriyya li Ru'asă' al-Majălis al-*

Mahalliyya (Regional Committee of the Heads of Local Councils); and (3) Lajnat al-Mubădara al-Durziyya (Druze Action Committee). The three committees came into being and became influential in the early to mid-1970s. Opposition to land expropriation has been a common theme of these committees, as has been the demand for equal rights and fair treatment for the Arab minority. An interesting characteristic common to these committees is the active involvement of relatively young intellectuals. These are second-generation Arabs, most of whom were born and all of whom were reared in the State of Israel. Their definite awareness of their Palestinianism attests to the failure of Israel's policies of integration of the Arab minority.

The Committee for the Defense of Arab Lands came into being in early 1975 as a result of the Galilee Judaization program announced by the government. In July 1975 a meeting was called in Haifa which was attended by intellectuals, heads of local councils, professionals, landowners, and journalists. Based on deliberations at the Haifa meeting, another meeting was held in August 1975 in Nazareth, at which time several resolutions were adopted. The most significant of these was to create a national committee for the defense of lands and to call for a mass rally to be held in Nazareth on October 18, 1975.

Thousands of representatives attended the mass rally, which was the largest Arab ever held in Israel. The rally produced several resolutions against land expropriation and in favor of equal rights for the Arab minority. These resolutions were carried by a delegation to the Knesset for action. Among the major resolutions passed by the October 18 rally were the following:

to deplore the government's policy of expropriating Arab lands;
to deplore the discriminatory, antihuman rights policy against Arab citizens;
to affirm the fact that Israeli Arabs, while demanding their equal rights in Israel, look toward a just and permanent peace between Israel and its Arab neighbors, believing that this peace must be based on U.N. resolutions calling for Israel's complete withdrawal from Arab territories occupied since June 1967 and on respect for the legal and national rights of the Palestinian Arab people and of the State of Israel;
to protest the government's systematic policy of transforming the Arabs from landowners into a people without a country in the name of development, industrialization, and settlement; and
to establish a standing committee to pursue the above resolutions and to coordinate all activities and efforts on behalf of Arab farmers, towns, and villages.

This, then, was the Committee for the Defense of Arab Lands in Israel. At its inception, the committee consisted of 121 members representing several strata of Arab elites. The committee represented 40 cities, towns, and villages and included 11 mayors (heads of local councils), 5 deputy mayors, 24 town councilmen, 18 lawyers, 1 member of the Knesset, and 13 doctors and other professionals.

By March 1976, when it became apparent to the organizers of the October rally that the government was not going to act on their earlier demands, another meeting was called for March 6, 1976. It was unanimously decided at that meeting that a general protest strike be organized for March 30, 1976.

The Regional Committee for the Heads of Local Councils came into being in June of 1970 as a collective response to the problems faced by Arab villages and towns. Those problems, according to a brochure issued by the committee in May 1974, were not ideological in nature. Rather they dealt with typical town issues, such as education, public services, government revenues, subsidies, and, of course, land expropriations. It must be noted that a vast majority of those mayors were status quo-oriented and invariably on good terms with state authorities.

The committee, which represented 16 towns, was first formed at a meeting held in Acre (Akko) on June 3, 1970. The demands raised at that meeting dealt with seven issues: the establishment of local councils in Arab towns and villages that had none; revenue sharing; the poor level of education, culture, and athletics in Arab towns; the lack of comprehensive land-use plans in Arab towns; the low tax base in Arab towns; and the limited industrialization of Arab areas.

The situation did not improve, and, according to the chairman of the committee, Mr. Hanna Mways, who was elected a member of the Knesset in May 1977, by 1976 many Arab villages and towns were on the verge of bankruptcy due to the favoritism the government had shown to Jewish towns at the expense of Arab towns. Consequently, the committee held a special meeting in Jerusalem in May 1976, following which a memorandum was sent to Yitzhak Rabin, then prime minister. The memorandum raised four major points.

First, it expressed deep concern regarding Rabin's statement that the Arabs in Israel constituted a cultural-religious minority rather than a political or national one. The memorandum called on the government to treat the Arabs, "who are the natives of this homeland," as citizens with equal rights.

Second, the memorandum called on the government to put an end to the "policy of depriving the Arabs of their lands." This policy "threatens the right of the Arab people to exist in this country and to own their land."

The memorandum went on to state that the government had totally ignored the authority of Arab local councils. Consequently, they have been reduced to "token authorities without power or significance."

Finally, the belief was expressed that the two peoples can coexist in one country; however, for this goal to be realized, Israeli Arabs would have to be accepted as a national minority with "the right to retain the land on which our fathers and our forefathers lived."

The Regional Committee of the Heads of Local Councils, like similar organizations, joined in the Land Day protest and has since become even more vocal in its demands on behalf of Arab towns.

The third major committee to join in the political struggle has been the the Druze Action Committee. This committee came into being under the leadership of a Druze imam, Shaykh Farhud Qasim Farhud, in March 1972. However, Shaykh Farhud's protest activities date back to 1956.

The Druze are a faction of Islam tracing their origins to tenth-century Fatimid rule in Egypt. Since that time, they have lived in isolated towns in the mountains of Palestine, Syria, and Lebanon.[31] Traditionally farmers, the Druze have practiced their religion in secret, and over the centuries they have often been ostracized and persecuted by orthodox Muslims. In 1948 Israeli leaders, in collaboration with the Druze religious hierarchy, forged an expedient special relationship with the Druze community which even permitted Druze youth to be drafted into the Israeli armed forces. Israeli policy has aimed at convincing the Druze that they were a special, non-Arab minority and that under Israel the Druze would no longer be subjected to discrimination. Certain privileges were bestowed upon Druze youth, particularly in the area of employment near the country's borders, where other Arabs could not go because they were denied travel permits.

In assessing this "special relationship," some Druze intellectuals and others concluded that the Druze community was being harmed rather than benefited by this arrangement. They pointed to several facts. First, the Druze are Arab in origin, tradition, culture, and language. The separate status granted them by Israel was in effect isolating them from their Arab kin, both in Israel and across the borders. Second, permitting Druze conscription resulted in Druze youth fighting Israel's wars against fellow Arabs; therefore, Druze youth were suffering loss of life and limb for a state created for the Jews. Third, the special relationship did not protect Druze villages from losing their lands to government expropriation. In fact, villages such as Kisra, Bayt Jann, al-Biqay's, Jath, Yanuh, Kafr Sumay', Yirka, and Daliat al-Karmil have lost thousands of acres in Galilee to

Jewish settlements. The more recent enclosure of District 9 also includes Druze lands.

It was with this background in mind that Shaykh Farhud began his protest with a letter written in 1956 to the president of Israel, then Yitshaq Bin Zvi. The letter carried 40 signatures, mostly of Druze farmers, and it protested the conscription of Druze youth into the Israel Defense Forces. The letter also strongly disputed the authority which the Druze religious hierarchy, under the leadership of Shaykh Amin Tarif, had used to commit the youth of that community to serve in the army.

However, these protest activities were restricted to a few individuals with little influence on Druze public opinion. Shaykh Farhud continued his activities with an open letter to the Druze community in November 1971, drawing attention to the two main issues, conscription and land expropriation. In the letter he called for unified action against the politics of discrimination.

Responding to Shaykh Farhud's call, several Druze intellectuals met in March 1972 to form the Druze Action Committee. The committee's founding declaration dealt with three issues which have remained at the heart of the Druze protest in Israel: conscription, land expropriation, and development and modernization of Druze villages. The committee called for an immediate halt to the drafting of Druze youth, for the return of expropriated lands to their Arab owners, for the expansion of developmental infrastructures (electricity, water, and roads) into Druze villages, and for depoliticization of the Druze religious hierarchy.

These demands were reiterated in another letter in 1974, which the Druze Action Committee distributed in Druze villages and towns. By the mid-1970s, however, the Druze Action Committee has become more vocal, more conscious of the Druze Arab heritage, and hence more nationalistic. In addition, more youthful elements came into positions of leadership within the committee, and more Druze youth became "draft dodgers" incarcerated in Israeli jails. Thus, by the 1970s, the members of the Druze Action Committee, like other Arabs in the country, became more aware of their Palestinianism and adjusted their demands accordingly. Recent Druze literature in articles, books, and poetry clearly reflects this new level of Palestinian awareness.

The Druze Action Committee strongly supported the Land Day strike and called on the Druze community to participate in all of the protests against the land policies. By March 1976 it was clear that the so-called special relationship Druze policy had failed and that the Druze were becoming more painfully aware of their minority status. There was, for example, increasing resistance to military conscription in the late 1970s. The new generation of Israeli Druze has, like the rest of Israel's Arabs, become "more numerous and more Palestinian."

Land Day and the Democratic Front

The Land Day events seemed to have fostered among the elite groups a new sense of the power of collective action. The most recent demonstration of this realization came in May 1977, when Knesset members were elected. Leaders of the three Arab committees joined forces with the Israeli Communist Party, Rakah, and the Black Panthers, a small leftist group of Oriental Jews, to form the Democratic Front for Peace and Equality [al-Jabha al-Dīmuqrātiyya li al-Salām wa al-Musāwā. Their platform, called the March 7 Program, included six points:

permanent and just peace between Israel and the Arab states based on the recognition of the rights of Israel and the Palestinian Arab people, on Israel's withdrawal from all territories occupied in 1967, on the recognition of the right of Palestinians to self-determination, and on the recognition of the PLO as the legitimate representative of the Palestinian Arab people;

defense of the rights and interests of workers in the production and services sectors;

eradication of the policies of national discrimination and persecution against Israeli Arabs;

elimination of religious discrimination in all fields;

defense of democratic freedoms; and

guarantee of equal rights for women in all fields.

In terms of program, organization, and execution, the Democratic Front was greatly influenced by Rakah, as was the makeup of the front's elected slate. Of the five candidates who won the election, the first two (a Jew and an Arab) are veteran Rakah members who have been Knesset members for several years. The third, Charlie Bitun, is a newcomer who represents the Black Panthers—a first for them in the Knesset. The fourth, Tawfiq Zayyad, is the mayor of Nazareth, an Arab Rakah member, and an active participant in both the Land Committee and the Local Councils Committee.

The interesting addition to this list is the fifth winner, Hanna Mways, who has been the mayor of Rama and the chairman of the Regional Committee of the Heads of Local Councils. For years Mways had been status quo-oriented and had cooperated with the authorities. He became nationally known among Israeli Arabs after the events of Land Day. Like many other traditionally bourgeois Arab elites in Israel, Mways sees his new militancy stemming from Israel's policies against the Arab minority.

The election results raised several serious considerations: First, the front captured a majority of the Arab vote in every large village, town, and city. Second, the front presented itself as the first Arab political slate independent of the government. Third, on May 3-4, a few days before the election, the front received the endorsement of the PLO at a meeting in Prague, Czechoslovakia, between representatives of Rakah and the PLO. Fourth, by electing Hanna Mways, Israeli Arab voters have in effect reaffirmed their opposition to Israel's policy concerning Arab lands and confirmed their demands for equal rights. Fifth, the front's sweeping victory on an essentially Palestinian platform might signal that Israeli Arabs have come of age politically—a prospect that does not hearten many Israeli Jews. This fact is brought home when one reviews the election returns. According to al-Ittihad (May 24, 1977), the front received 52 percent of the entire Arab vote in the country, for a total of 80,000 votes. The front received over 50 percent of the vote in 43 Arab villages, towns, and cities, of which 29 localities gave the front over 60 percent of the vote. In Nazareth, the largest Arab town in the country, the front received almost 66 percent of the vote.

These elections returns have conveyed a clear message to the authorities about the attitudes and perceptions of Israeli Arabs. Unfortunately, Israeli Arab elites do not expect any amelioration of their situation. It becomes interesting, therefore, to analyze certain indicators of the Jewish response to the rise of Palestinianism among Israel's Arabs.

ARAB GOALS

The crucial existential dilemma facing the Israeli Arab is that of identity—how to be loyal Israelis and remain true Arabs and, more recently, whether, as Arabs, to still try to be loyal citizens of the State of Israel. That members of one ethnic group can live in and contribute to a society dominated by another ethnic group is evident: both Arabs and Jews, for example, form active and constructive components of the United States. Israel, however, is not a secular state. Rather, it is self-avowedly Zionist. That Israel should be transformed into a secular state, that is, should move away from its Zionist philosophy, is the view of only a small minority of Israeli

Jews. Thus, the potential role of Muslim and Christian Arabs in the Jewish country is far less evident. We have pointed out above some of the problems of and discrimination against Arabs in a Zionist state.[32]

The conflict of loyalties for Israeli Arabs would be of little importance if it did not take place in the context of the Arab-Israeli conflict, of a Zionist state surrounded by Arab states in a hostile relationship in which each side views itself as the potential (and actual) victim of the other's aggressiveness and aggression. Therefore, the conflict of loyalties is less "religious" than it might be—and much more political.

How, then, do Israeli Arabs perceive themselves as a group? We have relatively little direct data from before 1965, but there is a growing body since that time. Although no comprehensive longitudinal study has been carried out, several discrete survey research initiatives have been undertaken. These are the only direct measures at our disposal, but they are adequate to isolate a clear-cut trend.

Research conducted from 1966 to 1968 on the "national identity of the Israeli Arab" employed intensive interviews of 500 male Israeli Arabs.[33] The sample was stratified by age, religious affiliation, place of residence, and geographic area.[34] The study attempted to demonstrate that the national Arab element and the Israeli element are integral parts of Israeli Arabs' identity. Social control factors—restraint from antagonizing the authorities and at the same time sanctions against any anti-Arab behavior—within the Arab minority helped to balance the contradictions in identity. The most extreme stands permitted in the past were being pro-Arab without being anti-Israeli and being pro-Israeli without being anti-Arab. This social control prevented "both the practical application of nationalism and the full-ideological legitimation of the existing situation."[35] One of the questions addressed to the interviewees dealt with self-description. In 1966, almost half the respondents preferred the term "Israeli" over "Arab" or "Palestinian." After the war, however, a similar sample chose "Arab" as the preferred descriptor, and placed "Israeli" last of five—following "Palestinian."[36]

Apart from the study cited above there are no firm data, but we do find a notable increase in protest literature after 1967.[37] Observers of the situation feel that Israeli Arabs, leaderless and isolated until then, began to experience an infusion of Arab nationalism or consciousness. Unquestionably, this developing group awareness is due to a variety of factors, not merely to the June War. It is important to note that the military government under which Arabs in Israel lived for 18 years after Israeli independence was also terminated in 1966. The abolition of the military government undoubtedly led to increased interaction among the Israeli Arabs.

The principal rallying causes of the Arabs in Israel are treated elsewhere in this chapter and in several other works.[38] What is important to note here is that new problems did not arise after 1967. On the contrary, the issues continued to be land, established forms of economic and social discrimination, and civil liberties. Yet the developing consciousness of the Arab minority did not abate or stagnate after the military government was disestablished.

The October 1973 war was another watershed in the evolution of Israeli Arab self-perception. By 1968, most Israeli Arabs viewed themselves as Arabs, Muslims, Christians, or Palestinians before Israelis. Yet, while the dominant descriptor was "Arab," "Palestinian" was far less common.[39] By contrast, a survey taken in 1974-75[40] found that only 14 percent of the sample of 342 respondents felt that the word "Israeli" described them very well, but fully 63 percent thought the term "Palestinian" did.[41] In this survey, "the term Palestinian was widely accepted and very rarely rejected as totally inappropriate. The term Israeli was rarely seen as completely suitable and almost a majority felt it described them only a little or not at all."[42]

Nominal self-identification is one aspect of identity. Clearly, another, and not less important, is the value-system that accompanies self-perception. Thus, we feel that an extremely significant component of self-perception is the Arab perception of Israelis. Indeed, so closely are the two subjects related that one must assume self-definitional change reflects growing alienation from Israelis. This hypothesis seems to be borne out by the data.

Once again the 1967 and 1973 wars seem to be turning points, perhaps because of the existential dilemma the Arab minority faces when Israel fights the "Arab" countries, when one's *state* directs the sum of its considerable military, psychological, and other resources against one's *nation*. The result seems to have been alienation and hostility, for three-quarters of the subjects interviewed before and after the June 1967 war underwent an increase in the level of their hostility toward Israel.[43] Ominously, in terms of the future of ethnic harmony, the greatest hostility was in the younger, the least in the older subjects. The more recent (1974-75) data show similarly dangerous attitudes. Unfortunately, we do not have post-1976 data reflecting the growing mobilization of Israel's Arab minority in the aftermath of the Yom al Ard demonstrations. The impressions of several of those who have visited Israel since Yom al Ard suggest that the Arab feelings of isolation and alienation from and hostility toward the Israeli state has continued unabated.

"Most of the Israeli Arabs see their future in Israel."[44] This has been the traditional wisdom. However, when 335 Israeli Arabs were asked whether they would move to a Palestinian state if one were established, only 33 percent indicated they definitely would not. By contrast 67 percent said they definitely would (29 percent) or might (38 percent) move there.[45] We have limited opportunity to monitor this trend, if indeed it is one, or to validate the recent findings. Certainly, however, if Israeli Arabs are inclined—or believe they are inclined—to leave Israel for a new Palestinian state, then many of the fundamental assumptions of analysts over the years are incorrect. Since there is no Palestinian entity, the correctness of the beliefs of the Arab minority cannot be tested, but if these data are correct it can be assumed that the commitment and loyalty of a sizable proportion of the minority is doubtful.

We have described the stages in the evolution of Arab Israeli attitudes above. They correspond to the phases in the development of their "collective identity systems" or self-perception.[46] After an 18- or 19-year period without leaders, organization, or communication (save for the short-lived al Ard movement) until 1967, the Arab minority developed a self-conscious Arabism after 1967. Partly as a result of the June War itself, partly as a consequence of the increased interaction with the Arabs of the occupied territories, and probably in part due to the increased intra-communication following the end of the military government in 1966, this sense of Arabism spread rapidly to encompass even Arabs in small villages (though less than those in the larger Arab locations). More importantly, a sense of "Palestinianism" also began to take root in the soil now already fertilized with Arab identity, and Palestinian symbols gained greater and greater currency among Israeli Arabs after 1970.

Thus, after the 1973 war, more Israeli Arabs perceived themselves first and foremost as "Palestinians." Taken in conjunction with the image of the "Palestinian" portrayed in the Israeli mind and spread in the Israeli media, cultural identification with Palestinian symbols is itself an act of extraordinary alienation from and hostility toward the Israeli system.

The Loyalty Issue

The result of increasing identity with a nationalism that is anathematized in the dominant Israeli political culture is to raise important conflicts in loyalties. To what extent are Israeli Arabs loyal Israeli citizens, and how may this be measured? There has been little incidence of seditious behavior, and it is in reference to this history that Israeli writers have attested to the loyalty of Israel's Arab citizens.[47] Yet, it may be argued that this approach is simplistic, taking little cognizance of psychological and institutional change in the context of the components of loyalty.

In the nation-state era, loyalty is certainly related in some degree to identification: the responsiveness of government to perceived needs and interests; the treatment by government of citizens and their grievances; the integration by government of individuals into state structures; and factors involved in generating feelings of loyalty. We have considered the nature of Israeli government behavior with regard to the Arab minority in other parts of this chapter. Here, we wish to evaluate the cumulative impact upon loyalty.

As Landau pointed out in his important study in 1969, Israeli Arab loyalty was unflinching both in the Suez War (1956) and the June War (1967).[48] The relative loyalty of Israeli Arabs seemed to disprove the contention of many Israeli Jews and the underlying assumption of government policy before 1967 that

> the Arabs of Israel are part of [the] Arab nation. They side with it; they would side with it even if they were not subjected to a daily barrage of broadcast propaganda against Israel; they would side with it even if they enjoyed twice as prosperous a life as they do now; they would side with it in the event of another war.[49]

However, the attitudinal and perceptual change that began after 1967—and possibly the increased communication with other Arabs—led to an upsurge in "subversive acts" between 1967 and 1972.[50] Tessler's 1974-75 study showed that one-quarter of the respondents felt that Israel had no right to exist, and 60 percent "had at least some reservations about the legitimacy of the Jewish State."[51]

Even with the growth of Palestinianism, the diminution in perceived legitimacy of Israel, and the increase in demonstrations and resistance to Israeli policies, the Arab minority in Israel has been and continues to be characterized by respect for and adherence to Israeli laws. While we have introduced what we believe to be clear signs of alienation from and hostility toward both the government and the very existence of Israel, these attitudes have not for the most part been translated into illegal acts. Thus, while Arabs seem to have a decreasing level of loyalty to Israel, this decline has not been matched by a rise in traitorous conduct.

Objectives

Nationalism among Israeli Arabs was evident soon after the creation of the state. In cooperation with the Communist Party, a group of intellectuals, including Sabri Jiryis, began in the early 1950s to form committees to defend the rights of the Arabs in Israel. The "Arab Front," established in 1957, announced the following aims:

equality between Arab and Jewish workers;
abolishing the military rule (terminated in 1966);
halting further confiscation of Arab lands and returning confiscated lands to owners;
improving education in Arab schools;
abolishing all manifestations of discrimination between Arabs and Jews; and
repatriation of Palestinian refugees.[52]

Shortly after, the front split with the Communists and evolved into an independent Arab nationalist movement under the name of al Ard (the Land). The word "ard" (land) encompasses all the values for whose sake the movement emerged and struggled—for the defense of and attachment to land as a national aim. The founders of al Ard announced that they were part of the Palestinian people who were in turn part of the Arab nation, that they were struggling for the sake of complete equality between the Arabs and the Jews, and that they demanded of Israel the following policy:

1. To recognize the nationalist movement as the established movement in this area;
2. To make an absolute separation between the state and Zionist ideology;
3. To follow a policy of positive neutrality and peaceful coexistence;
4. To recognize the Palestinian rights of self-determination and refugee repatriation.[53]

The al Ard movement was suppressed and finally banned in the mid-1960s; its founders were in constant conflict with the authorities who imprisoned them, placed them under house arrest, and finally deported them or convinced them to emigrate.

Following the 1967 war, there was a rise in national consciousness. The same demands and aims of al Ard were being echoed: equality between Arabs and Jews on all levels; total integration into the state's social, economic, political, and military structures; self-determination of the Palestinian people and repatriation of refugees; and cooperative coexistence.

The goal of equality was reiterated by many. An Israeli Arab and one of the co-directors of Mapam's Department for Arab Affairs said, "If the Arabs achieve full equality in the State, they can serve as a bridge for peace between Israel and the Arab States.[54] A similar comment was made by the deputy minister of health, Abdul Aziz Zuabi: "when there is peace and full economic and social equality in Israel . . . why should I leave Nazareth?"[55]

The Arabs in Israel wanted to integrate as a unit in the state. Bastuni mentions the necessity for complete integration within the educational system and with the military, for example.[56] Not unless Israel began to admit Arabs into its basic institutions, that is, in the government, in the Histadrut (the General Workers Federation), in its political parties, in the army, and in economic, cultural, and social organizations (as well as the "national institutions") could success- ful integration be achieved. As expressed by Shmuel Toledano, an Israeli MK and a former adviser on Arab affairs, "We must give Israeli Arabs a feeling of belonging and involvement in all that goes on in the State. They must not feel themselves separate from the State—they are part of it and participate in decisions."[57] The editor of New Outlook, Simha Flapan, similarly stated that if the Arabs are not integrated into the Israeli society and state, "the territorial continuity and integrity of the State of Israel will be in danger."[58] Mr. Flapan still believes that if Israel adopts a policy of integration then the attachment of the Arab minority to the state will prevail over their nationalist aspirations.

Israeli Arabs, too, continue to use integrationist language. Taw- fiq Zayyad, the Communist mayor of Nazareth, who spoke at the Arab American University Graduates conference in New York in October 1976, stated that the Arabs in Israel have an important role to play in the struggle for a just solution of the Palestinian national problem. Such a solution will create an atmosphere for continuing the democratic struggle in order to achieve full national equality, meaning that there has to be an end to land expropriation, a return of confiscated lands to owners, recognition of the right of the Arabs to exist and to develop on their land and in their homeland, respect for their culture and national dignity, full representation in official and public institutions, and participation in reshaping the general policy of the state and future relations with the Jews, relations which should be based on understanding, cooperation, and respect.[59]

Yet, integrationist language notwithstanding, the long-term objectives of Israeli Arabs are no longer integrationist. The majority of the Arabs in Israel favor either the PLO-supported "democratic, secular" state based on pluralist ethnic relations or the creation of a sovereign Palestinian state alongside Israel (and therefore presumably in the West Bank and, possibly, Gaza). This change away from integrationist philosophy was first evident after the June 1967 War, when a sizable minority of Israeli Arabs expressed its aims in terms of breaking away from Israel (possibly even seeing it destroyed) and establishing a Palestinian Arab state.[60]

For those who believe in the "democratic, secular" state, we can presume the motives to be both integrationist for some and Arab dominance-oriented for others. In reality, the language used to promote a democratic, secular state in Palestine embraces many of the values of the integrationists. However, a secular state must certainly be understood to become an Arab majority state in the short or long term. Thus, it becomes a majority Arab Palestinian state through democratic means.

> Their greatest expectations or hope is that all the political and military boundaries will be erased, and a single state will be created in which all those who are there now and all those who are entitled to return will live together as equals and in peace. This state would be secular and democratic, or, to use . . . the words of Nabeel A. Shaath, "a democratic, non-sectarian, secular, open, multiple, plural state" in lieu of "an expansionist, racist, ethnocentric, and closed state."[61]

An analysis of Arab-Jewish coexistence stipulates that certain conditions must prevail in a pluralistic society in order to achieve cooperative coexistence. Four conditions are delineated: First, a shared ideology of partnership which views coexistence as a desired goal preferable to the other patterns of assimilation, dissociation, and domination. The Arabs and Jews must accept the ideology that they are equals and integral parts of the same society. Second, cultural autonomy, wherein the minority is in command of its cultural institutions in order to protect and perpetuate its ethnic heritage and separate identity. Third, equality of resources, wherein the minority enjoys a proportional share of the socioeconomic and power resources. And fourth, interpersonal accommodation, wherein the minority and majority must have positive attitudes, mutual trust, and acceptance of each other in the public and private domains. The conclusion of the analysis is that although there are some apparent beginnings in this direction, the above conditions by and large do not prevail between Arabs and Jews in Israel.[62]

Most Israeli Arabs feel that a separate Palestinian state must arise. However, the views with respect to the nature and viability of this state, the boundaries, and future relations vary. An Iraqi Jew and one of the co-directors of Mapam's Department for Arab Affairs states that it must be understood that Israeli Arabs are part of the Palestinian people and that most of them, in his opinion, favor a Palestinian state alongside Israel, and not in lieu of it.[63] Recent survey data demonstrate that a majority or near-majority of Israeli Arabs prefer the separate state approach and that the vast majority support one or the other of these approaches rather than integration.[64]

NOTES

1. Israel, Central Bureau of Statistics, *Statistical Abstract of Israel 1975* (Jerusalem, 1976), p. II/1.

2. Edward E. Azar and R. D. McLaurin, "Demographic Change and Political Change: Population Pressures and Territorial Control in the Middle East," *International Interactions* 5, no. 2-3 (1978), table 11.

3. See Emile A. Nakhleh, "The Arabs in Israel and Their Role in a Future Arab-Israeli Conflict: A Perception Study," mimeographed, Abbott Associates SR17, June 1977. Parts of the present chapter are taken from this study.

4. In particular, the authors have paid close attention to *al-Ittihad* and *al-Jadid*, semi-weekly and monthly newspapers published by the Israeli Communist Party. These are important vehicles for the expression of contemporary political views among Israeli Arabs.

5. Figures representing only those fleeing to Jordan, Lebanon, Syria, and the Gaza Strip and classified as refugees (in other words, receiving some relief) amount to approximately 850,000. However, some refugees claimed no relief, others were not registered as refugees, and still others fled to places different from those named (especially Egypt and Iraq). These may add as many as 150,000 to the total. See Edward Hagopian and A. B. Zahlan, "Palestine's Arab Population: The Demography of the Palestinians," *Journal of Palestine Studies* 3, no. 4 (Summer 1974); 50-54; Palestine, *Statistical Abstract of Palestine, 1944-45* (Jerusalem, nid.) and *Vital Statistics Tables, 1922-45* (Jerusalem, n.d.).

6. Ian Lustick, "Arabs in the Jewish State: A Study in the Effective Control of a Minority Population" (Ph.D. diss., University of California at Berkeley, 1976), p. 72.

7. Khalil Nakhleh, "Cultural Determinants of Palestinian Collective Identity: The Case of the Arabs in Israel," *New Outlook* 19, no. 7 (October-November 1975); 36.

8. Article 125 of the military government regulations.

9. Article 124 of the military government regulations.

10. Lustick, "Arabs in the Jewish State," p. 128.

11. *Ibid.*

12. *Yehud HaGalil*, the "Judaization of the Galilee," has been stepped up since 1975 as a result of Jewish emigration from the Galilee. See Yehuda Arieli, "Judaising the Galilee—Plans and Reality," *Haaretz*, February 29, 1976; Yosef Goell, "Collision Course in Galilee," *Jerusalem Post Weekly*, March 6, 1976.

13. See Habib Qahwaji, "Al-Qissah al-Kamilah li-Harakat al-Ard," *Shu'un Filastiniyah*, no. 1 (March 1971); 112-25. Qahwaji was among the al-Ard leaders. See also Sabri Jiryis, *The Arabs in Israel* (New York: Monthly Review Press, 1976), pp. 185-96; Fouzi El-Asmar, *To Be an Arab in Israel* (London: Frances Pinter, 1975), pp. 65-75.

14. See, for example, K. Nakhleh, "Cultural Determinants," pp. 37-38, and see below.

15. Lustick, "Arabs in the Jewish State," is a brilliant analysis of the dynamics of the control mechanism.

16. Jiryis, The Arabs in Israel, pp. 65-68.

17. The issue of communication between these groups is discussed in greater detail below.

18. Lustick, "Arabs in the Jewish State," p. 91.

19. Ibid., passim.

20. Ellen Geffner and Joyce Kubersky, "Attitudes of Arab Editorialists in Israel, 1948-67: An Analysis of Al-Ittihad, Al-Mirsad, and al-Yawn" (Ph.D. diss., University of Michigan, 1973), passim.

21. See Jiryis, The Arabs in Israel, pp. 60-63.

22. Lustick, "Arabs in the Jewish State," pp. 156-57.

23. Frank H. Epp, The Palestinians: Portrait of a People in Conflict (Scottsdale, Penn.: Herald Press, 1976), p. 73.

24. Jiryis, The Arabs in Israel, pp. 181-82.

25. H. D. S. Greenway, "Israeli Arabs Express Alienation by Backing Communists," Washington Post, May 16, 1977.

26. Lustick, "Arabs in the Jewish State," pp. 162-63.

27. Eric Silver, "Israel Applies Pressure in Nazareth Election," Washington Post, December 9, 1975. Some appreciation of the view of many Israelis may be seen in part of the so-called Koenig Plan which suggests a "special team should be appointed to examine the personal habits of Rakah leaders and other negative people and this information should be made available to the electorate."

28. Washington Post, March 31, 1976, pp. A1, A10; Christian Science Monitor, April 2, 1976; New York Times, April 4, 1976, Section 4; New York Times, September 29, 1976, p. 4.

29. Tawfiq Zayyad, "The Fate of the Arabs in Israel," Journal of Palestine Studies 6, no. 1 (Autumn 1976); 94-95.

30. Peter Mansfield, "Galilee: Explosion on the Home Front," Middle East International, no. 59 (May 1976); 11, citing Victor Cygielman in New Outlook (February-March 1976).

31. See Peter A. Gubser, "Minorities in Isolation: The Druze of Lebanon and Syria," Chapter 5 of this volume.

32. See also the studies by Walter Schwartz, The Arabs in Israel (London: Faber and Faber, 1959); Don Peretz, Israel and the Palestine Arabs (Washington, D.C.: Middle East Institute, 1958); Jacob M. Landau, The Arabs in Israel: A Political Study (New York: Oxford University Press, 1969); Jiryis, The Arabs in Israel; and, especially, Lustick, "Arabs in the Jewish State."

33. Yochanan Peres and Nira Yuval-Davis, "Some Observations on the National Identity of the Israeli Arab," Human Relations 22, no. 3 (June 1969); 219-33. The work was sponsored by the U.S. Department of Health, Education and Welfare (Contract OE 621013).

34. Ibid., pp. 219-20.

35. Ibid., p. 226.

36. Ibid.

37. See Jiryis, The Arabs in Israel, chapters 1 and 2; and Lustick, "Arabs in the Jewish State," passim.

38. Cf. note 32 above.

39. Peres and Yuval-Davis, "Some Observations," p. 226.

40. Mark A. Tessler, "Israel's Arabs and the Palestinian Problem" (paper presented at the annual meeting of the Middle East Studies Association of North America, 1975).

41. Mark A. Tessler, "Israel's Arabs and the Palestinian Problem," *Middle East Journal* 31, no. 3 (Summer 1977); 317. This article is a partially revised version of the paper cited in the previous note. All further references to this author and title will refer to the article. The paper gives a fuller presentation of methodology employed, sample composition, and so forth.

42. *Ibid.*, p. 316. See also Sammy Smooha and John E. Hofman, "Some Problems of Arab-Jewish Coexistence in Israel," *Middle East Review* 9, no. 2 (1976-1977); 12-13.

43. Peres and Yuval-Davis, "Some Observations," pp. 228-32.

44. Israel's Arabs After October 1973," *New Outlook* 18, no. 7 (October-November 1975); p. 80.

45. Tessler, "Israel's Arabs," p. 325.

46. Khalil Nakhleh, "Cultural Determinants of Palestinian Collective Identity," pp. 31-40.

47. It must be emphasized that important differences exist *within* the Arab community as well. For example, a study conducted in 1967 indicated that at that time religious preference was the second most important descriptor Arabs applied to themselves in expressing their identity. A similar study in 1970 concluded that Muslim Arabs were hostile toward Israel, Christian Arabs moderate, and Druzes loyal (Edward Robins, "Attitudes, Stereotypes, and Prejudices Among Arabs and Jews in Israel," *New Outlook* 15, no. 9 [November-December 1972]; 36). Apparently, however, the growing Arab alienation in Israel crossed at least the Christian-Muslim lines, for data in 1974-75 suggest very similar self-definition by that time (Tessler, "Israel's Arabs," p. 321).

Self-Indentification in Percentages, 1974-75

(n = 335)

Religious Preference	Palestinian Only	Israeli Only	Palestinian and Israeli	Neither
Muslim	42	27	24	8
Christian	40	33	20	7

48. Landau, *The Arabs in Israel.*

49. Walter Schwartz, *The Arabs in Israel* p. 165. It is interesting to note that this prophecy was not borne out in the June 1967 War (nor even in the October War of 1973), if the author intended that the Israeli Arabs would undertake any actions to support these purported feelings.

50. Gideon Weigert, "Israel's Arab Minority," *World Jewry* 16, no. 3 (June 1973); 18-19.

51. Tessler, "Israel's Arabs," p. 318. See also Smooha and Hofman, "Some Problems," p. 12.

52. Qahwaji, "Al-Qissah al-Kamilah li-Harakat al-Ard," pp. 112-25.

53. *Ibid.*, p. 114.

54. "Israel's Arabs After October 1973" (Symposium), *New Outlook* 18, no. 7 (October-November 1975); 71.

55. Weigert, "Israel's Arab Minority," pp. 18-19.

56. Rustum Bastuni, "The Arab Israelis," in *Israel: Social Structure and Change,* M. Curtis and M.S. Chertoff (New Brunswick, N.J.: Transaction Books, 1973), pp. 410-14.

57. "Israel's Arabs After October 1973," p. 71.

58. *Ibid.,* pp. 75-76.

59. Zayyad, "The Fate of the Arabs in Israel," p. 103.

60. Peres and Yuval-Davis, "Some Observations," *passim.*

61. Epp, *The Palestinians,* p. 217.

62. Smooha and Hofman, "Some Problems," pp. 5-14.

63. Tessler, "Israel's Arabs," p. 73.

64. *Ibid.,* p. 325.

5

MINORITIES IN ISOLATION: THE DRUZE OF LEBANON AND SYRIA

Peter Gubser

Although the Druze constitute a relatively small religious minority, they have enjoyed a particularly rich history and have continually played a significant role in the Levant. The story of the Druze commences in the early eleventh century with the sect's founding in Cairo by the Sixth Fatamid Caliph, al-Hakim, and its propagation in Lebanon by Muhammad ibn Isma'il al-Darazi. By the mid-eleventh century, the religion was declared secret and no more converts were accepted. Druze history is subsequently dominated by the rise and fall of dynasties, their expansion into neighboring territories (notably under Fakhr al-Din ibn Ma'n II in the seventeenth century), their internal conflicts, and their relations with other Middle Eastern powers, such as the Mamluks and Ottomans. In the eighteenth and nineteenth centuries, the line of history shifts to an emphasis on relations between Druze and other Lebanese sectarian groups, the decline of Druze power, Druze relations with European (French, British) and Middle Eastern (Ottomans and the Egyptian Muhammad 'Ali dynasty) powers, and their settling of the Jabal al-Druze in Syria.[1] Finally, the history devolves into a saga of revolts and Druze relations with mandate powers and their often key role in the successor independent Arab states.[2]

Who are the Druze? What characteristics distinguish them from their neighbors? What is their role in the politics of Lebanon and Syria? How will they fit into the future of these two countries? Initially, this chapter will briefly describe the people and their regions and the unique Druze religion. Then, in greater detail, the

sociopolitical structure and leadership of their society will be investigated. Subsequently, a description and analysis of Druze political
trends will be presented.

THE PEOPLE AND THEIR REGION

The Druze are found in scattered but concentrated pockets in the
Levant. The largest and densest concentration is in the Syrian
province of Suwayda; the second largest group is found in Lebanon,
but in a more dispersed residential pattern in the districts of Shuf
and 'Aley in the province of Mount Lebanon, in the district of
Hasbaya in the province of South Lebanon, and in the district of
Rashaya in the province of the Biqa'. The third group is located in
two Israeli regions: western Galilee and Mount Carmel. In addition,
small numbers are found scattered all over the Levant, specifically,
in and around Damascus, in Jabal al-'Ala close to Aleppo, in the
Sytian province of Hauran, which includes the Golan Heights, in the
cities of Israel, especially the southern port city of Eilat, and in the
Lebanese capital, Beirut.[3] Druze population figures appear approximately as shown in Table 5.1. There are also about 1,000 Druze in
Jordan.

Until the end of World War I, all of these Druze areas were part
of the Ottoman Empire. Thus, there were no restrictive international
borders to impede social, economic, and political intercourse. Although current national borders do hinder intra-Druze relations,

TABLE 5.1: Population of the Druze Community, by Country
(approximate figures)

Country	Population	(Year)	Population 1970
Syria	c. 88,000	(1952)	c. 149,800
Lebanon	c. 88,131	(1953)	c. 145,650
Israel	14,500	(1950)	35,800
Total			331,250

Source: G. H. Blake, "Israel: Immigration and Dispersal of Population," *Populations of the Middle East and North Africa*, ed. J. I. Clarke and W. B. Fisher (New York:
Africana, 1972), p. 188; S. N. Eisenstadt, *Israeli Society* (New York: Basic Books,
1967), p. 392; Blanc, "Druze Particularism," p. 316; Charles Rizk, *Le Régime politique
libanais* (Paris: Pichon et Durand-Auzias, 1966), p. 22; Harvey Smith et al., *Area
Handbook for Israel* (Washington, D.C.: Foreign Area Studies Division, American
University; 1969), p. 55.

Druze do overcome even the most restrictive Israeli borders. Finally, like other Arabs, a significant number of Druze have emigrated to the Americas.

Each of the various regions in which the Druze live represents a different kind of terrain. The major Druze Syrian region, the province of Suwayda or Jabal al-Druze, is basically a basaltic dome, the result of long-past volcanic activity. Within this hilly region, there are pockets of rich soil where the Druze grow wheat, grapes, and other agricultural products. The Lebanese Druze, with the exception of those in Beirut, live primarily in the Lebanese and anti-Lebanese mountain ranges. Although many of the areas are not cultivable, others possess relatively rich valleys; also, the Druze have industriously terraced the sides of many mountains over the centuries, adding considerable arable land. The Israeli Druze live in two hilly to mountainous regions: Galilee and Mount Carmel.

The Druze are overwhelmingly a rural people. In the Syrian province of Suwayda, almost 75 percent are officially considered rural, and this includes numbers who live in the very small district capitals. In Lebanon, the same type of pattern holds, but no realistic figures are available. In Israel, 91 percent of the Druze live in villages, even though an increasingly large number work outside the villages.[4] Finally, virtually all of the Druze in each of these three countries live in mountains or at least rugged hills. Those in Syria have tended to continue to emphasize farming in their area of residence, while in both Lebanon and Israel much larger numbers have joined the nonagricultural sector of their economies, following the overall trend for both countries.

The rural pattern of the Druze is contrary to the predominant pattern found in the Islamic-Arab Middle East, where the culture has long emphasized the urban element. The lack of significant numbers of Druze in the major Middle Eastern cities indicates this group's weak conformity to the predominant culture. Historical reasons best explain this pattern of living. As a long-persecuted minority, the Druze sought a haven, and the mountains afforded a good defense. Even while they dominated the feudal system of Lebanon, it was their mountains which gave them a measure of autonomy under the Mamluks and the Ottomans. Those Druze who wished to live in the cities and took up residence there were usually made to feel unwelcome by the traditional urban population, which was mostly Sunni Muslim or Greek Orthodox. However, since the independence of Lebanon, Syria, and Israel, this is changing. Many Druze are now migrating to major urban centers in search of employment and education, but it is quite difficult to establish their numbers, for the

Druze tend to retain strong ties with villages and are often officially counted there.

Druze population movement—or the appearance of movement—over the past 100 years has been primarily the result of population pressures, individuals and groups seeking economic opportunity and avoiding repression, and numerous border changes over the entire Levant. First, following the 1860 crisis and during World War I, many Druze left the *Mutassarifiya* of Lebanon and moved to the Hauran and the Jabal al-Druze; second, in 1920, with the creation of Greater Lebanon, Hasbaya and Rashaya, both with substantial numbers of Druze, were taken away from the Ottoman governorate of Damascus and added to the *Mutassarifiya*. Also, the Druze in Palestine were cut off in the British Mandate of Palestine from their fellow sectarians in the French Mandates of Syria and Lebanon. Despite these new borders, many Druze continue to the present day to cross them (including the very restrictive Israeli border, but to a lesser degree) to visit their families and clans, to trade, and at times to find employment. Third, an unknown but not insignificant number of Druze have emigrated overseas, primarily to the Americas. The families of the emigrants have benefited from this movement through remittances sent to them by their relatives, usually sons and daughters, who have been able to gain some wealth in their new-found homes.[5] Fourth, as a result of the Israeli occupation of the Golan Heights in 1967, virtually all of the Arabs left, with the exception of the small Druze population residing there. Finally, the Druze, especially in the last two decades, have started to move around each of the countries (and occasionally across borders) to a much greater extent than before. Many have sought education, with sons, daughters, and at times whole families moving to the towns so that secondary and higher education would be available. Others, having joined the military, found new opportunities in new areas and remained there after the termination of their services. Many have gone to the major cities in pursuit of private and public employment.

RELIGION

Religion is the key factor setting the Druze off from the Muslim Arabs and other religious and ethnic groups in the Middle East. Because of its importance, it is appropriate to outline in some detail the Druze religious beliefs, the nature of their religious organization, and the meaning of the religion to Druze adherents. The Druze are supposed to keep their religious beliefs and dogmas secret to and among the Druze alone. However, well-known scholars have been able to trace many aspects of the sect's theology, and certain Druze have taken it upon themselves to reveal some of the creed either verbally or in written form. Thus, it is through a combination of these sources that the outside world has been able to gain a rudimentary knowledge of the Druze religion.[6]

Within the Druze religion, there exist four articles of faith which all the initiated believers must accept. The first and most important article of faith is the very strict unitarian concept of God. The Druze argue that God has no other attributes except being God, thus no thought of polytheism may arise. As a consequence of this strong one-God concept, the Druze prefer the name *al-Muwahhidin* (the Unitarians) for themselves.

The second article of faith is the belief in the deification of the Fatamide Caliph, al-Hakim. For the Druze, al-Hakim is the tenth, last, and most perfect incarnation of God. Related to this concept is the belief that al-Hakim is not dead but has only temporarily disappeared from view (occultation) and will reappear at some time in the future.

The third aricle of faith is the necessity to believe in the five divine ministers and the three inferior ministers. The ministers all represent specific theological concepts, although most are equated with important personages in Druze religious history. The five divine ministers are: (1) the Universal Mind who is Hamza, the most important theologian of the Druze religion; (2) the Opposer, who opposed Hamza; (3) the Universal Soul, a kind of alter ego of the Universal Mind; (4) the Precedent; and (5) the Follower, who is equated with another theologian, Baha al-Din. The three lesser ministers are more closely related to the spread of the Druze religion: the Propagator, the Licensed, and the Pioneer.

The fourth article of faith in the Druze religion is composed of seven precepts which closely resemble a moral code. This code of conduct is made up of the following principles which a Druze should always seek to uphold: (1) truthfulness, a concept which also makes it incumbent on an individual not to steal, not to kill, and not to commit adultery; (2) mutual aid for the members of the Druze faith; (3) rejection of other religions and gods; (4) maintenance of the secrecy of the religion and the detestation of the devil and all contact with evil; (5) belief in the oneness and unity of God; (6) submission to the acts of God; and (7) the resolution to and submission of one's self to God's will, whether for good fortune or bad, in secret or public.

Ancillary doctrines within the Druze faith include metempsychosis, dissimulation, and *bataniya*. Metempsychosis, or transmigration of souls, is a central, publicly espoused belief of the Druze. The Druze contend that there is a set number of souls; in Lebanon, they declare at funerals that if an individual has been good, his soul will reappear in China as a Chinese. Dissimulation, or *taqiya*, is a famous practice ascribed to the Druze. It is defined as the hiding of one's true faith and the profession of another for protection or convenience. As an often persecuted minority sect, the Druze have felt it prudent to fall back on this practice for their individual and collective welfare. *Bataniya* refers to the distinction between the exoteric and esoteric interpretation of written religious works. The exoteric is that which is apparent in the literal meaning of the word, phrase, or sentence, while the esoteric meaning or interpretation is only known to those who are initiated into the mysteries and secrets of the religion. The Druze also believe in predestination.

The question of whether or not the Druze are Muslim naturally arises, but it is always difficult to answer. Historically, the religion is an offshoot of the Isma'ili Shi'a Muslim sect, but just because a religion has its roots in another does not identify it with or make it the same as the other. Theologically, one would have to conclude that the Druze are not Muslims. They do not accept the five pillars of Islam. In place of these principles, the Druze have instituted the seven precepts noted above. Officially, the Druze have at different times been both accepted and rejected as Muslims by other Muslims. The Ottomans and other early Islamic rulers attempted to treat the Druze as part of Islam. However, by force of circumstances, they usually allowed the Druze considerable religious independence and freedom. Today, the Druze conduct their religious affairs under a code totally separate from the various Muslim sects. Socially as well, the other Muslims have treated the Druze ambivalently in terms of their Muslim identity. But what of the Druze themselves? Although no polls have ever been taken as to what they think, from the literature and other sources it may be concluded that the vast majority, while recognizing the Muslim origin of their religion, do not consider themselves Muslims.

In each of the Levant countires where Druze live, they have a similar religious organization. In each there is a formal head of the religion plus a number of officials who deal with religious and personal status law. The highest religious leaders are appointed by the head of state, but with the advice and concurrence of the Druze community. Each of the sect's communities also follows the same Law of Personal Status drawn up by Lebanese Druze and adopted in that country in 1948 and subsequently in Syria (1953) and in Israel (1961). This Druze law for personal status includes matters involving inheritance, marriage, divorce, protection of children, and so forth. The religious officials also control the institution of the *waqf* (a kind of religious endowment); they manage its shrines and supervise the expenditure of its income.[7]

Druze religious shaykhs are not a coherent group, however. They are distributed relatively evenly among the Druze villages in Lebanon, Syria, and Israel, where they lead the spiritual life of their fellow Druze. They enjoy the prestige of religious men in the Middle East, but as a rule, they do not have continual political power or influence. (Their political role, when they have one, is primarily that of an intermediary. In Lebanon, the highest Druze leader, Shaykh 'Aql Muhammad 'abu Shaqra, has often functioned in this capacity. He also attempts to protect the rights of Druze in the country, but the political leaders are much more important in this role.) Druze religious leaders, like their fellow Muslim shaykhs and Christian priests in the Middle East, have a residual political power in the sense that they quickly feel discontent among their flock or a challenge to their religion and react strongly to it. When they do so react, it has been known for them to build up and direct considerable discontent and even violence. This type of process is usually short-lived and only attains an adjustment in the previous situation, if that.

What is the meaning of the religion for ordinary Druze? On one level, there is little knowledge of the doctrine and theology among the majority of the Druze because they are not initiated into the secrets of the sect. In addition, against specific doctrines of the Druze religion, many hold beliefs in talismans, magic, and jinns. On another level, many Druze, especially the educated non-initiated (see below), state that they do not and cannot know anything about their religion and therefore it has little meaning for them. In actuality, this is a method of identifying with other members of the Druze religion, for Shi'a and Sunni Muslims and Christians can and often do know something about their religion. Looking at this problem from another viewpoint, Druze can emphasize or de-emphasize various publicly known doctrines or beliefs of their religion in order to identify with another religious group with which they wish to cooperate. Thus, they may stress their Muslim origins when they desire to work with Muslims or their common shrines with Jews when they desire to work with Israelis.[8] In sum, this is what some scholars call "situational selection," whereby an individual selects the group with which he wishes to identify in order to optimize his benefits in a specific situation. The Druze have followed this pattern quite closely.

SOCIOPOLITICAL STRUCTURE AND LEADERSHIP

Stratification Systems

The Druze community is subject to two forms of traditional social stratification with the addition of a new stratum in the last two to three decades. These systems are: first, the differentiation among the religious shaykhs, the religiously initiated, and the religiously uninitiated; second, the social, political, and economic distinction between the notable families and the balance of the society; and third, the rise and development of the new middle stratum.

At the top of the religious stratification system are the religious shaykhs. In a strict social sense, these men are not from any particular class or stratum; rather, in theory and practice, they may originate from any group. What separates them from the balance of society is their knowledge of the mysteries of the Druze religion and their ability to pass these on to future generations. In order to achieve this position, a man must study the secret doctrines of the sect and master the intricacies of the esoteric interpretation of the Druze books to a much greater degree than other members of the community. In addition, while becoming and after attaining this position, a religious shaykh must keep himself morally and socially pure as prescribed by the religion; also, he distinguishes himself by wearing a special form of clothing. In respect to politics, the shaykh does not play a very significant role. Even though almost all Druze villages are ridden by factionalism, most have only one shaykh— although of late some have acquired two, one for each faction. At times the shaykhs do perform certain functions in ensuring social control, but this usually reflects the values of the whole community. The next two levels of religious stratification concern initiation into the religious mysteries of the sect. Initiation is open to all Druze, both male and female. An individual who is initiated continues to function in the society as an ordinary person.* However, he or she possesses a certain aura of religiosity that is recognized and re-

---

*The initiated individual is termed 'aqil (pl. 'uqqal) or he who knows. The uninitiated individual is called jahil (pl. juhhal) or the ignorant. Thus, the religious shaykh is often termed shaykh al-'uqqal.

spected by the Druze society. It is not known what percentage of the Druze as a whole is initiated, but it is thought that a substantial number (though not a majority) are. Finally, the remainder of the society consists of those who are not initiated.[9]

In terms of socioeconomic stratification, the Druze are traditionally divided into two major strata, the peasants and the notables. The peasants are the majority of the population and should be considered to be those Druze who live in the mountain villages. Although they have a reputation for being a hard-working, disciplined, diligent people, their life cannot be considered exceptionally hard or harsh. In all three areas, Lebanon, Syria, and Israel (Palestine), there was considerable small holding, that is, many of the Druze peasants owned the land on which they worked. The only significant exception to this is in some limited areas of Lebanon and Syria, where peasants worked land owned by notables in sharecropping arrangements. In the past, the peasants showed considerable deference to the notable families, and this practice continues to some degree due to the high value put on tradition within Druze culture. Today, many Druze peasants are leaving agriculture for jobs in industry and commerce as a consequence of increased opportunities in these fields, changing values, and higher levels of education allowing them to go into these occupations.

The notable families form the upper stratum. In the nineteenth century and before, these families were the feudal elite; today, although in a formal sense they no longer have the feudal prerogatives, some of the families retain at least a hint of the old relationships. This is especially true of the current leading notable families, the Jumblatt and the 'Arslan in Lebanon and the al-'Atrash in Syria. Correspondingly, these families tend to maintain their traditional ways more than the next level of well-known families. The latter includes the following names: Talhuq, 'Alam al-Din, Nakady, 'Abd al-Malik, 'Imad, and 'Aid in Lebanon; Hanawy, Qala'any, Halaby, Hindiya, 'Abu 'Asaf, 'Azzam, and 'Issa in Syria. Families from both of these levels certainly tended to own more land, have more wealth, and exercise greater political power than the peasantry. It cannot be said, though, that they have held overly great "feudal" authority over the peasants in the last 50 years.[10]

The new middle stratum is a recent addition to the stratification structure of the Druze. Under many names, this feature has been recognized and investigated by students of the developing countries and the Middle East. Each has given it an important, often crucial or key position in the transitional societies.[11] What sets this group apart from the others is the at least intellectual commitment to achievement and a higher value put on modern skills and abilities attained through education. This is not to say that members of this group completely eschew ascriptive criteria and values, such as the family, the lineage, and religious group. However, they do emphasize them much less than other members of the society. This group has its origins in both the peasant and the lower notable strata, and its members' major assets for gaining new positions are education and technical abilities. On another plane, this group as a societal entity is competing strongly with the traditional ruling stratum for leadership positions. This competition has manifested itself in several ways. In Syria, members of the lower notable families led peasants in a number of insurrections against the al-'Atrash family in the 1930s and 1940s. By the 1950s, many Druze had joined the military and had started to participate in the numerous Syrian *coups d'état.* In addition, some members of this new stratum are beginning to win power on municipal and village councils and certainly increasingly are taking over bureaucratic positions where their skills are particularly valued. In Lebanon, new middle-stratum Druze have gained numerous bureaucratic positions and local council seats, as in Syria.[12]

Looking at the educated new middle stratum from another viewpoint, it cannot be said that it is a coherent group with corporate qualities, but subgroups within it do have these qualities. For example, individuals from this stratum are often members of the political parties, the officer corps, social and sports clubs, and informal associations. There are no figures to indicate the magnitude of this group, but it may be safely assumed that it is increasing, as suggested by statistics on education. The occupations of individuals in this group very considerably: lower and higher civil servants, teachers, military officers, government leaders, political operatives, and professionals. Accordingly, members of this group are concentrated where employment opportunities exist, that is, primarily in the urban centers. However, many of the teachers are scattered in the rural schools.

Because of the respect for education in the Middle East, these individuals enjoy varying degrees of prestige according to the level of education (and subsequent employment) they have received. But their political power is largely a function of their employment or membership in an organization. For example, if they are in the bureaucracy, they may be in a position to dispense favors. Or, if in the military, some may gain considerable power through their participation in *coups d'état,* as has been the case in Syria.

As with other Druze, most members of the educated new middle stratum consider their religion to be superior and give their ultimate loyalty to other Druze. Many members of this group in conversation with individuals of other sects deny their loyalty to their Druze brethren and the meaning of their membership in this sect, but, with few exceptions, when an issue involves fundamental loyalties they have joined with fellow Druze.

Kinship and Marriage

The Druze, like most Arabs, reckon kinship through the male line. Politically and socially this patrilineal pattern is significant, for it tends to create neat, segregated units and subunits within a larger group. Also, a man's identity is more strongly attached to these smaller units than any other group, for the behavior of an individual is considered to be the extension of that of his kin, and, conversely, the actions of a man's blood relatives heavily reflect upon him. In addition, it is usual in Druze society that all individuals with the same family name (often including members in several villages) consider themselves descendants of one man in the remote past. Actually, the lineage of four or five generations is the only true, coherent kin group.

The kin unit is further reinforced by the marriage preference for one's parallel cousin (father's brother's daughter). In traditional Arab law, even, an unmarried man has the legal right to marry his closest parallel (paternal) cousin; and not until he has given his permission may she marry another. If no first cousin on the paternal side is available, two other preferences become operative. Paternal cousins of a lesser degree are frequently chosen, and a cross-cousin (mother's brother's daughter or father's sister's daughter) is also sought. Qute often, because of the general marriage pattern, a cross-cousin is a paternal cousin as well, only of a more distant relationship. This marriage pattern, then, creates a web of both kin and conjugal ties within a relatively small unit, binding its members together and giving it some features of a bilateral kin system. The incidence of this kind of marriage may be partially indicated statistically. Of all marriages in one village, 11.5 percent were of the parallel cousin type. (Statistics of other Arab villages indicate the same level. Apparently, this percentage approaches the maximum number of marriages of this type possible given the demographic limit on the availability of parallel cousins.) Marriages within the larger lineage, usually a four or five-generation group and all descendants, are also sought. In two separate villages, they constituted 29 and 71 percent of all marriages.[13]

As a consequence of both the patrilineal and marriage patterns, all of the children in the male line of a man who lived four or five generations ago may be considered as a corporate group with a common identity and some political functions. Very often there will be one spokesman or leader for this kin group reinforced by marriage ties, and he will deal with the higher-level leaders in the Druze community.

For the most part, these lineages tend to be located in one residential area, a village (often just one part of a village, in a clan barrio fashion) or at most a few neighboring villages. This is due to the occupations—agriculture, local industry, and crafts—tying the individuals and families to a given area. However, a new pattern is beginning to emerge among members of the new middle stratum and those who move to other areas to seek employment. Their lineages have changed from a residential one to a functionally extended family, usually smaller than a lineage, but still maintaining extensive and intensive contact and cooperation.[14] Marriages in the functionally extended families tend to be contracted with individuals outside the kin group because the young men and their families are seeking brides who are educated like themselves and who will bring more to their families in a social and, ultimately, political sense.

For the more traditional Druze, marriage preferences (as was noted above) are endogamous according to kin group, village, region, and religion. There are two primary reasons for kin endogamy: to keep property within the family and to reinforce the large kin group as a political group. Allowing and contracting marriages outside of the family, but in the village or the near vicinity, also has strong social and political implications. On the one hand, it can create a link with another lineage which may help solidify an already tenuous tie, strengthening both groups through additional numbers. On the other, marriage ties are often used for communication between estranged groups: a woman has the right to visit her family, or a brother has the right to visit his sister. Looking at this subject from another standpoint, marriage and divorce are regulated by religious law. Unlike Muslims, Druze are not permitted multiple marriages. Divorce is allowed with the consent of a religious *qadi* (judge), but it is not practiced widely. Aside from ordinary social and family pressures not to divorce, there is a heavy financial burden involved. The man pays a substantial bride price in the first place, and upon divorce the standard contract is that he has to pay an even larger amount. Finally, there are very few marriages between Druze and other Middle Easterners, although they are starting to increase among the new middle stratum.

Almost all Druze villages are divided into two factions. In Lebanon, as was mentioned above, they identify with the Yazbaki and Jumblatti cross-country split. In Israel and Syria, there are similar village factions, some of which are associated with all the Druze in each of the countries and others of which are tied to non-Druze political groups in the given country. Each faction in the villages is usually composed of one major lineage tied to a number of allied clans and a few isolated families. These factions compete with each other on a number of levels. They vie with each other for prestige, accomplishments, and wealth. Politically, they put up opposing lists for village councils but usually end up sharing power with each other. Through their patrons in parliament and the bureaucracy, both factions try to obtain benefits in the form of general projects and personal services for their respective members. In a practical sense, the existence of two factions, each tied to opposing major politicians, ensures that the village will always receive some political patronage. Finally, from time to time the relations between the two factions degenerates into violence. This has occasionally necessitated the intervention of state police forces or even the military in order to control the situation. Peace is then usually realized through the mediation of a neutral outside force such as Druze religious leaders, provincial governors, or the like.[15]

Leadership

With this background on kinship, lineages, marriage, and factionalism, it is now appropriate to turn to the top Druze leadership as such. The typical term for these leaders, especially in Lebanon, is za'im (pl. zu'ama'). The base of one of the leaders' power is all those political assets which give him his position and which he brings to bear in his political activities. These political assets may be categorized as economic goods and services, status, information, force, and authority.[16]

A Druze za'im has various economic resources at his disposal in the political arena. From his family, he receives an inheritance, usually in the form of land, which throughout his lifetime he will attempt to maintain and increase and then pass on to his own son. This pattern is especially valid for Lebanon where large landholders still exist. Although small landholders are the norm in the Syrian Jabal al-Druze, the notable families, such as the al-'Atrash, do own significantly more land than the average Druze—their holdings are simply spread out under the names of many individuals. In Palestine and later Israel, there never were predominate lineages or notable families as in Lebanon and Syria, and thus there were no large estates. Equally important as an economic resource is the leader's access to the bureaucracy, whereby he obtains goods and services for the purpose of enhancing his own personal means and in order to maintain a political clientele. On the one hand, some members of his clientele, especially armed supporters, called *qabadays*, must be paid either directly or indirectly. On the other hand, individuals of his larger political following occasionally petition him for funds. These connections with the government, then, are especially important, for the *za'im* often exchanges administrative favors, government jobs, and economic benefits extended to his region for the political support of his clientele.

Status and prestige, when employed with wisdom, are certainly valuable social and political assets which may help a leader to gain and maintain authority and power. With the exception of Israel, which lacks notable Druze families, the very possession of a prestigious name automatically gives a leader a certain aura and stimulates social deference. In former days, the members of these well-known families were among the very few to receive primary or higher education, again a factor which gives a man status. But today, education in all three countries is much more widespread, and many individuals are more highly educated than the members of the leadership group. Through his family connections, a potential leader seeks out a proper "political" marriage, which is easily forthcoming due to the prestige of the family. This type of marriage, in turn, enhances the status of the leader and adds to his political assets. A leader's prestige and his place in the upper level of the social stratification system also give him access to the government bureaucracy and the highest government officials and, in respect to the general Druze population, almost automatically give him an opening to leadership positions if he uses his political assets properly. After the individual attains the position of *za'im*, his prestige and status are continually added to through his holding of elective offices and his serving the immediate and general interests of his constituents.

In any political system and especially in one with a developed bureaucracy, information is an indispensible resource for a leader. In Lebanon, Syria, and Israel, the *za'im* no longer has greater access to the broadcast or printed media, but, as a result of his occupation, he does devote more time to it and consequently has a greater mastery over it. He is, in addition, a member of the upper stratum where more and privileged information circulates. A leader also seeks out, through the medium of lesser leaders and employees, information about his followers' activities and opinions in order to keep himself abreast of events and possibly to take action accordingly. This enables a leader to have some potential control over his followers. However, a relatively more important informational resource is the leader's much greater contact with and knowledge about the government structure, which he can use on behalf of his clientele. Thus, knowing where and how to apply for jobs, to obtain services, and to aid individuals in trouble will work to the benefit of an individual's leadership position and in turn his authority and power among his constituents. On the other side, it is often upon these Druze leaders that higher leaders and members of the bureaucracy have relied for information about the respective Druze communities.

At various times throughout Druze history, leaders not infrequently have employed force as a political asset in conducting their roles as *zu'ama'*. Most leaders may be considered to have two circles of potential force at their command. First, they employ or support strongmen, *qabadays*. This group of men is used to maintain the leader's own security and potentially to harass his opponents. Second, in cases of national crisis, the *za'im* quickly recruits large numbers of young men who live in the various villages in his area of influence and who are usually under the command of lesser leaders from those villages. These men then are used to protect the leader's region and perhaps to aggress against his opponents. Examples of the use of force are numerous: the 1860 crisis in Lebanon; the 1910 revolt against the Ottomans in the Jabal al-Druze; the 1925 rebellion against the French in mandated Syria; the 1954 rising against President Shishakli in independent Syria; the 1958 crisis in Lebanon, in which Kamal Jumblatt led Druze forces against President Sham'-oun, his allies, and occasionally the Lebanese military; and the 1975-76 Lebanese civil war, during which Kamal Jumblatt's followers occasionally joined, it is reported, the left-wing Palestinian-Muslim alliance. In each of these events, the leader who was able to demonstrate that he could field considerable force was able to attract other followers and further augment his power and political assets.

Although authority is not a very tangible political asset, it is a significant one. Authority is the sum of all those political resources the leader may use in his activities. Additionally, however, the possession of this resource gives the leader the right in the view of his clientele to play certain important social and political roles in the Druze community. Thus, the leader is often the key person in dispute settling and in arranging marriages, both of which in turn may benefit the leader himself by healing wounds in his community and by consolidating or gaining potential support. The leader is also sought out for his advice on everything from personal to financial matters. Conversely, as a consequence of filling this role internally within his community of followers, the government looks upon him as an authoritative leader.

The Druze leaders use these resources in their competition with other leaders for followers and adherents. The sphere of competition is the Druze community in the specific country. Thus, on the highest level in Lebanon, it was between Kamal Jumblatt and Majid 'Arslan and their respective non-Druze allies. On the next but still very high level, the Talhuq, 'Alam al-Din, Nakady, 'Abd al-Malik, 'Imad, and 'Aid families compete among themselves and against lesser-known men. In the Jabal al-Druze, the al-'Atrash is the foremost family, but it faces strong competition from the 'Abu 'Asaf, Hanawy, Qala'any, Halaby, Hindiya, and 'Azzam, especially with the weakening of the traditional social, economic, and political systems there.

Viewing these traditionally oriented leaders from another standpoint. It may be noted that they have no common organization, internal cohesion, or political stand to unite them in either their individual country or among the various countries in which they live. The power of the Druze leaders does not rest in their numbers as a group but in their leadership of various clienteles. As was noted above, each leader has a following of ordinary Druze, and each also usually has attached to his service a small number of armed retainers.

Druze leaders possess a few common attitudes and values. Corresponding to one of the Druze religious precepts, Druze leaders give their ultimate loyalty to other Druze over members of any other sect. In addition, along with most Druze, the leaders believe in the superiority of their own religion. Another attitude of the leaders that is typical of most people in authoritative positions is their desire to preserve and enhance their roles within Druze society. The leaders do demonstrate some flexibility, however. The notable families have sent their children to school and university, making them eligible to become members of the educated new middle stratum and then to gain political positions in the new, changing political structures.

In this latter context, it should be stated that the political resources and, consequently, positions of traditional leaders are being seriously undermined and usurped by the members of the new middle stratum, especially in Syria and Israel. Working primarily through the government bureaucracy or governmentally sponsored organizations, these individuals, have taken over some of these leaders' political and social functions and assets. Thus, by controlling the distribution of goods, services, and economic benefits more as they see fit than as the more traditionally oriented leaders wish, they have partially gained control over the available economic resources. This phenomenon has been brought about by their increasingly staffing the bureaucracy and the new agricultural cooperatives (in Syria), and gaining positions on and at times controlling town and village councils. In respect to Syria, this newly developing pattern corresponds to the new policies of the government. The traditionally oriented Druze leaders in Syria have retained some political power despite the social revolution in that country, though there has been virtually no land expropriation in the Jabal al-Druze; so this political asset of the Druze chiefs still exists. Even among the individuals of the new educated middle stratum who are staffing the bureaucracy there is evidence that some retain ascriptive loyalties to traditional leaders, which, like the above, means this asset remains, although in diminished form. And, as noted above, sons of notable families have joined the ranks of the new stratum, again adding to these older leaders' political resources.

Communal and Regional Solidarity

Druze communal solidarity is a long-established phenomenon which continues in strength today for most Druze. On the one hand, this solidarity is required by the Druze religion: one of the sect's seven precepts (part of its moral code) orders all Druze to provide mutual aid to brothers in the faith. On the other, many observers have remarked that Druze of one country first look to Druze of another country. For example, many Druze of Lebanon identify with the Druze of Jabal al-Druze and see in the latter a model to emulate. Numerous houses contain pictures of the famous Jabal al-Druze leader, Sultan al-'Atrash Pasha, as well. This is equally true of the few Druze in Jordan. This sense of communal loyalty has often been manifested in substantive action. During the 1925 Jabal al-Druze revolt against the French, Lebanese Druze joined their Syrian brothers in the fighting. In the 1954 rebellion against Shishakli's government, Lebanese Druze again attempted to come to their Syrian brothers' aid, but were prevented from doing so by snow-blocked mountain passes. However, in the 1958 Lebanese crisis, Syrian Druze joined Kamal Jumblatt's men in the struggle. Consequently, it may be argued that almost all Druze will support another Druze over a member of another religion, irrespective of most other considerations.[17] This solidarity has certainly contributed to making this relatively small minority one of the forces to be reckoned with in any activity in Syria or Lebanon.

Along with this solidarity, a strong regionalism is prevalent in the Jabal al-Druze in Syria. Historically in the Middle East, the agro-city, or a central major city with its agricultural hinterland, has been a semi-independent economic unit and a political and administrative unit within which loyalty and identity developed.[18] This pattern of identity and loyalty became especially strong when a region was mostly made up of one religious group like the Jabal al-Druze. This regional loyalty has not been undermined by the introduction of modern education and radical political ideologies, which theoretically should be cross-regional. This is due to the fact that the Druze, especially the new, educated, middle stratum, are politicized while they are still in their provincial schools so that their "political and ideological loyalties reflect the local political situation in their particular" province.[19] Thus, this concept of regionalism has remained operative irrespective of the type of government: Ottoman, French or Arab, traditional or modern, capitalistic or socialistic, conservative or revolutionary.

POLITICAL TRENDS

The political relations between the Druze and other groups in Syria and Lebanon fall into two distinctive patterns, each reflecting the peculiarities and history of the given country. Thus, the patterns found in each of the countries are described separately below.

Druze in Syria

In postindependence Syria, the Druze have occupied a multifaceted position. Although significant segments have continued quite openly in their centrifugal ways for at least ten years, Druze have started to join the mainstream of politics, becoming involved in both traditional and revolutionary activity. They even have joined the military in large numbers and become a dominant force in Syria, second only to the Alawites.

The Syrian government led by President al-Quwatly attempted to suppress the centrifugal tendencies on the part of the minorities. It took steps initially to abolish the special status of the Druze and other minority groups (such as the Alawites). It reduced and then eliminated communal representation in parliament. It did, however, allow the Druze to retain separate juridical rights in matters of personal status, thus recognizing indirectly that the Druze religion is not truly part of Islam. The Syrian Druze community adopted the personal status laws drawn up by the Lebanese Druze.[20]

However, the Druze sect did not react favorably to the central government's attempt to deny it special privileges and to control it from Damascus. The Druze faction led by the paramount al-'Atrash family continually pushed for greater autonomy and at one time, in 1947, even invited King Abdullah of Jordan to annex the Jabal al-Druze. In reaction, President al-Quwatly tried to take advantage of the friction within the Jabal between the al-'Atrash faction and the 'Abu 'Asali family. He encouraged the latter to rise against the al-'Atrash, holding a battalion of the Syrian army in readiness to invade upon the success of the rebels. But the al-'Atrash were able to rally their forces and defeat the rebels. Later in 1947 parliamentary elections were held. The regime strongly backed the 'Abu 'Asali candidates, causing a virtual state of anarchy in the area. Only with the mediation of an outsider, the Lebanese Druze leader Kamal Jumblatt, did the elections take place. The result was a sweep for the 'Abu 'Asali, and the Al-'Atrash lost all of their offices in the government.[21]

The next major conflict between the Druze and the government was when 'Adib Shishakli was the dictator of Syria. During this period, many groups in Syria became very disillusioned with the Shishakli regime. Leaders of these groups met in Homs in the summer of 1953 and agreed upon a coordinated revolt to be initiated by a rising in the Jabal al-Druze. Unfortunately for the Druze, one group (the Ba'th Party) started passing out anti-Shishakli leaflets well before all the preparations were made. In reaction, Shishakli arrested leading Druze in Damascus and sent troops to the Jabal. As a consequence of misunderstandings, considerable fighting occurred in early 1954, resulting in a large loss of life and an army victory.[22]

With the crushing of this revolt, the relationship between the Druze and the Syrian government started to emphasize a new trend. The government proved its effectiveness to the public and established that state nationalism is superior to the autonomous aspirations of the Druze (and other minority groups) while the Druze became increasingly involved in the affairs of the Syrian nation.

As a part of the larger Syrian nation, the Druze took part in its politics which since the early 1950s have been dominated by the military and the Ba'th Party. Due to certain social, economic and political trends, by the 1960s the Druze had secured a significant role in the military, much larger than their proportion in the Syrian population would warrant. First, both before and after World War II, Sunni Muslim youth from the urban middle and upper middle classes did not want to join the army and often bought their way out. The Druze villager, in contrast, could not afford to bribe his way out of military service, but also this service was an opportunity for him to escape the poverty of the countryside and to see other parts of the country.[23] "The result was that while Arab Sunni Muslims formed the overwhelming majority of the Syrian population, most of the officers [by the mid-1960s] were Alawis [a heterodox Muslim sect] and Druzes of the mountains and rural areas."[24] Second, as Druze gained positions of authority within the military, they "attracted more of their relatives and others in their ethnic group into the military. The officer corps became an important center for the skilled and ambitous members of the minority groups."[25]

Another reason for the advancement of the Druze in the officer ranks was the high attrition rate of other officers for political reasons.

> After each revolution some of [the officers] rose rapidly in rank and then after the next turn of the tide were dismissed from the army, making way for others who in turn did not last long in their positions. Members of the minority groups were less active in the sphere of political strife in the 1950s, and thus suffered less from the wear and tear. Therefore in the 1960s they occupied important positions of command made vacant by the successive dismissals of the Sunnis by one side or the other. In 1963 and 1964 members of the minority groups reached the top ranks, and as good Syrians and typical Syrian officers, they too were infected with the spirit of politicization. They appeared generally—but not always—as rural rebels against urban supremacy and extremist supporters of nationalization and expropriations.[26]

Concomitant with these developments was the political parties' recruitment of Druze into their ranks. Due to the Druze's religious minority status, individuals of this sect were mostly interested in secular parties. These were the Syrian Social National Party (SSNP) and the Ba'th. The Muslim Brotherhood had no attraction for them because of its Sunni Muslim orientation. The Arab Nationalist movement, too, usually held little interest for them due to its Islàmic overtones and sponsorship by Egypt. The SSNP was purged from Syrian politics by the other political parties in the mid-1950s, leaving the Ba'th Party as the only political organization for young ambitious Druze civilians and officers.

By means of coups d'état, the Ba'th Party and the military came to power in Syria during the early 1960s. Within both the party and the military, loyalties based on sectarian identity and minority status were extensively used by the leaders of both the Druze and Alawites. However, in the initial period the Druze worked relatively closely with the Alawites.* Thus, in February 1966, Salah Jadid (an Alawite) and Salim Hatum (a Druze) led yet another *coup d'etat*, bringing the minorities into full control of the Syrian government. But the two men soon had a falling out and a struggle along Druze and Alawite sectarian lines ensued. In September 1966, Salim Hatum, in cooperation with many Druze officers, lead an abortive coup. As a consequence of the failure, he and a number of his fellow Druze were purged from the armed forces, leaving those Druze officers still in the military in a decidedly junior partner relationship with the Alawites. This pattern, despite other coups, persists.[27]

Druze in Lebanon

The story of the Druze in independent Lebanon may be looked at on two levels.[28] First, the major factional split between the Jumblattis and the Yazbakis continued; second, the Druze participated fully in the politics of Lebanon along with the other sectarian groups. The paramount leadership position of the Jumblatti faction fell to Kamal Jumblatt during and after World War II. That of the Yazbaki faction remained in the hands of Amir Majid 'Arslan.

In the elections, two Druze—Majid 'Arslan and the late Kamal Jumblatt—usually formed and headed electoral lists. Also, by virtue of their political power in Lebanon, they were able to influence the makeup of lists in districts in which they were not running for parliament. Even though both these men were descendants of true Lebanese "feudal" families, they practiced politics in contrasting ways. Majid 'Arslan was and still is the prototype of the traditional politician who negotiates with other politicians and services his clientele in time-honored ways. His political outlook is conservative and he eschews political parties. Kamal Jumblatt, while basing part of his power on his feudal patrimony and alliances with other leading political families, also worked through the only indigenous Lebanese socialist party, the Progressive Socialist Party, which he founded and headed. Despite these two politicians' different styles, both exercised considerable power in Lebanon. Majid 'Arslan held the position of minister of defense more times and longer than any other Lebanese politician; and Kamal Jumblatt had often held important portfolios—Interior, Planning, Public Works, and Education.

---

*The Druze were necessarily in a lesser position due to the Alawites' overwhelmingly greater numbers in both organizations. The Alawite population is over twice that of the Druze in Syria.

Of the two men, Kamal Jumblatt certainly had more impact on Lebanese society. As Bashara al-Khoury's regime became corrupt in the second term, Kamal rallied most of the Lebanese political forces against it, forcing President al-Khoury to resign. Again, after the next president, Camille Sham'oun, changed all of the Lebanese electoral districts (forcing many of the top leaders out of parliament) and started to take pro-Western positions, Kamal Jumblatt was at the forefront of the armed opposition in 1958. At first, his forces (mostly Druze) even clashed with those of Majid 'Arslan (also mostly Druze), but 'Arslan withdrew after the mediation of Druze religious personnel. Jumblatt's forces, joined by other Druze from Syria, attempted to attack the airport and to close the Beirut-Damascus highway, but they were stopped by the army and the militia of the Syrian Social National Party. However, Jumblatt and the other opposition leaders did attain their political aims by not allowing Sham'oun to succeed himself. Following the 1958 crisis, Lebanese politics returned to normal. Majid 'Arslan and his followers continued to adhere to the more conservative group, while Kamal Jumblatt and his political party, the Progressive Socialist Party, tended to support more liberal or leftist policies, such as social reform, Arab nationalism, and the cause of the Palestinian guerrillas.

Because of the late Kamal Jumblatt's crucial role in the history of Lebanon, an additional word should be said about him. To many, he was the personification of a contradiction. As the scion of the ancient and strong feudal house of Jumblatt, he owned considerable land upon which Druze peasants toiled. (In his youth, he did distribute some of his holdings.) As the leader of the only indigenous Lebanese socialist party, he spoke of fundamental reforms. As a prominent proponent of pan-Arabism, he competed effectively with established Sunni Muslims for the leadership in Lebanon. Essentially, he succeeded in his multifaceted role by practicing "situational selection." Among Druze followers, he acted politically as a za'im in the time-honored Lebanese manner. He was also initiated into the Druze religion, further adding to his aura. On the national level, he practiced much more than sectarian politics. He was able to persuade others by his words and deeds that he was sincere about socialist reform and the greater Arab unity.

As of this writing, the Lebanese civil war which started in spring 1975 has not ended.[29] As in all other major periods of Lebanese history since independence, Jumblatt was often central to the development of events. He was , for example, the spokesman for the National Movement which included, among others, the Ba'th Party, Communist Party, SSNP, Movement of the Deprived, the Nasserite party, and Jumblatt's own Progressive Socialist Party, and was allied with the Palestine Liberation Organization. Through this medium, until his assassination in March 1977, he demanded a series of fundamental political changes and reforms in the bureaucracy and social programs of the country. In addition, upon occasion during the civil war, his Druze followers joined in the fighting on the side of the National Movement.

Future Trends

Despite the above patterns of Druze interacting with the political systems of each of their countries of residence, most still consider themselves to be Druze before all other considerations. They continually communicate and intermarry with each other across borders. In practical political matters, they have come to the aid of fellow Druze during periods of crisis, such as in Syria in 1925 and 1954, and in Lebanon in 1958. Refugees from both the 1954 and 1958 troubles even travelled to Druze villages in Israel in search of safety. The strength of this religious and parochial identity, consciousness, and loyalty is quite common in the Middle East. For most, they are members of their family and religion first, with only secondary feelings of identity with political ideologies and the nation-state.

Consequently, one can anticipate that the Druze will continue in their dual role. On the one hand, Druzeness and the particular interests of the Druze will continue to dominate this group's loyalties and activities. On the other, the Druze will participate in national economies and politics. The degree to which they can succeed in the latter will depend largely on the fortunes and trends of the specific country. However, one no longer should anticipate major centrifugal rebellions due to the recent unsuccessful experience of the Druze in such efforts and due to their self-perceived weakness with regard to the larger nation. This is not to contend that the Druze will not protect their right to their own particularness. Such a defense, though, most likely will not require major violent action.

A more far-ranging scenario would be predicated on major changes in the Levant. In such an event, depending on the cause (establishment of an Alawite state, a deep invasion of Syria by Israel, the breakup of Lebanon), the group might perceive it to be in its interests to seek considerable autonomy or perhaps join a neighboring state.

A major reason for the considerable impact of the Druze on Lebanon in recent years was the stature of the late Kamal Jumblatt. Starting with his fundamental base among the Druze, by force of personality and of his thinking, he made himself into a true national leader and, in turn, gave the Druze a greater role in the country. A repeat of this pattern is problematic. Kamal's son, Walid, has acceded to Kamal's position as head of the ancestral house and the party. He has yet to prove his ability, personality, and thinking as did Kamal.

NOTES

1. References for this history are numerous. The most important are: Philip K. Hitti, *Lebanon in History* (London: Macmillan, 1962) and *The Origins of the Druze People* (New York: Columbia University Press, 1928); Kamal S. Salibi, *The Modern History of Lebanon* (London: Weidenfeld and Nicholson, 1965); Iliya Harik, *Politics and Change in Traditional Society: Lebanon, 1711-1845* (Princeton: Princeton University Press, 1968); Yusuf Mazhar, *Ta'rikh Lubnan al-'Amm*, 2 vols. (Beirut: n.p., 1953?); Muhammad Husayn, *Ta'ifa al-Duruz, Ta'arikhha wa 'Aqa'idha* (Cairo: Dar al-Ma'arif biMisr, 1968).

2. A few thousand Druze also live in Israel. Although they are touched upon in this chapter, they are dealt with at greater length as part of the Arab minority in Israel in Chapter 4.

3. Gabriel Baer, *Population and Society in the Arab East* (London: Routledge and Kegan Paul, 1964), pp. 83, 114; Haim Blanc, "Druze Particularism: Modern Aspects of an Old Problem," *Middle Eastern Affairs* 3, no. 11 (1952); 315-16; Hitti, *Origins*, p. 9.

4. J. C. Dewdney, "Syria: Patterns of Population Distribution," in Clarke and Fisher, eds., *Populations of the Middle East and North Africa*, p. 130; Jacob Landau, *The Arabs in Israel* (London: Oxford University Press, 1969), p. 12.

5. See Louise E. Sweet, "The Women of 'Ain ad-Dayr," *Anthropological Quarterly* 40, no. 3 (July 1967); *passim*. Ms. Sweet presents a census (p. 170) of a village, 'Ain ad-Dayr, which, first, demonstrates the fairly significant numbers of Druze overseas and, second, shows the resulting imbalance of the male-female ratio in the village.

Population of 'Ain ad-Dayr, Lebanon, 1965

	Males	Females
Resident	325	441
(Adults)	(145)	(241)
Overseas	135	29
In school or military	18	1
Total	478	471

6. The earliest and still one of the best works is A. I. Silvestre de Sacy, *Exposé de la religion des Druzes*, 2 vols. (Paris: L'Imprimerie royale, 1833). Another invaluable source is Hitti, *Origins*, as is another work of a similar period, N. Bouron, *Les Druzes: Histoire du Liban et de la Montagne hauranaise* (Paris: Editions Berber-Levrault, 1930). In the 1960s a number of works, written by both Druze and non-Druze, have appeared in Arabic. Although some of these are apologetic or argumentative, they are

still valuable sources. See, for example, Amin Muhammad Tali', 'Asal al-Muwahidin al-Duruz was 'Usulhum (Beirut: Dar al-'Andalis-Maktab al-Bustany, 1961); 'Abdallah al-Najjar, Mathab al-Duruz wa al-Tawhid (Cairo: Dar al-Ma'arif bi Misr, 1965); Sami Nasib Makarim, Adwa' 'ala Masalak al-Tawhid (Beirut: Dar Sadir, 1966); Muhammad Kamil Husayn, Ta'ifa al-Duruz, Ta'rikhha, wa 'Aqa'idha (Cairo: Dar al-Ma'arif bi Misr, 1968).

7. 'Arif al-Nady et al., al-Waqi' al-Durzi was Hatmiyyat al-Tatawwur: Majmu'at Muhadarat (Beirut: Lebanese Ministry of Social Affairs, 1962), passim.; Tali', 'Asal al-Muwahidin, pp. 111-35; Baer, Population and Society, pp. 53-54; Landau, The Arabs, pp. 13-14, 202; Salman Falah, "Druze Communal Organization in Israel," New Outlook 10, no. 3 (1967); 43; Victor Ayoub, "Political Structure of a Middle East Community: A Druze Village of Mount Lebanon" (Ph. D. diss., Harvard University, 1955), pp. 104-06.

8. See, for example, Blanc, "Druze Particularism," p. 317; I. Ben Zvi, "The Druze Community in Israel," The Israel Exploration Journal 4, no. 2 (1954); 69.

9. Bouron, Les Druzes, pp. 144-45; Sweet, "The Women," p. 171; Baer, Population and Society, p. 82; Hitti, Lebanon, pp. 260-62; Ayoub, "Political Structure," pp. 97-102; Leonard Kasdan, "Isfiya: Social Structure, Fission and Faction in a Druze Community" (Ph.D. diss., University of Chicago, 1961), p. 107.

10. Blanc, "Druze Particularism," p. 320; Rizk, Le Régime, p. 22; Husayn, Ta'ifa al-Duruz, pp. 5-6.

11. John H. Kautsky, "An Essay in Political Development," in Political Change in Underdeveloped Countries: Nationalism and Communism, ed. John H. Kautsky (New York: Wiley, 1962), pp. 22, 24; William R. Polk, The United States and the Arab World (Cambridge; Harvard University Press, 1965), pp 215, 225-28, 288; David E. Apter, The Politics of Modernization (Chicago: University of Chicago Press, 1965), pp. 138-78; Edward Shils, Political Development in the New States (The Hague: Mouton, 1968), pp. 15-24, 87-89; Leonard Binder, "National Integration and Political Development" American Political Science Review 58, no. 3 (September 1964); 627-31; James A. Bill and Carl Leidin, The Middle East: Politics and Power (Boston: Allyn and Bacon, 1974), pp. 84-88.

12. For material that supports this point, see Michael Hudson, The Precarious Republic: Political Modernization in Lebanon (New York: Random House, 1968), p. 32; Albert Hourani, Syria and Lebanon (London: Oxford University Press, 1946), p. 138; Moshe Zeltzer, "Minorities in Iraq and Syria," in Peoples and Cultures of the Middle East, ed. Ailon Shiloh (New York: Random House, 1969), p. 24; Patrick Seale, The Struggle for Syria (London: Oxford University Press, 1965), pp. 74, 133; Gordon Torrey, Syrian Politics and the Military (Columbus: Ohio State University Press, 1964), pp. 97-100.

13. Ayoub, "Political Structure," p. 88; Kasdan, "Isfiya," p. 69.

14. Kasdan, "Isfiya," p. 50; and Samih K. Farsun, "Family Structure and Society in Modern Lebanon," in Peoples and Cultures of the Middle East, ed. Louise Sweet, 2 vols. (Garden City: Natural History Press, 1970), pp. 257-307, passim.

15. See, for example, Sweet, "The Women"; Ayoub, "Political Structure"; Kasdan, "Isfiya"; Victor Ayoub, "Conflict Resolution and Social Reorganization in a Lebanese Village," Human Organization 14, no. 1 (Spring 1965); passim, and iden, "Resolution of Conflict in a Lebanese Village," in Politics in Lebanon, ed. Leonard Binder (New York: John Wiley & Sons, 1966), passim. Each of these anthropological studies focuses on this Druze village factional problem among others.

16. The source material for this sub-section on Druze leaders, the zu'ama', is literally scattered throughout a number of works due to the lack of any recent study or studies specifically concerning the Druze. Thus, for the sources, see Arnold Hottinger, "Zu'ama' in Historical Perspective," in Binder, ed., Politics in Lebanon, pp. 85-106, and

"Zu'ama' and Parties in the Lebanese Crisis of 1958," *Middle East Journal* 15, no. 2 (Spring 1961); 127-40; Farsun, "Family Structure," pp. 257-307; Hourani, *Syria and Lebanon, passim.*; Hudson, *The Precarious Republic,* pp. 125-47, 183-90; Iliya Harik, *Man Yahakam Lubnan* (Beirut: Dar al-Nahar lil-Nashr, 1972), *passim;* Seale, *The Struggle, passim;* Torrey, *Syrian Politics, passim;* Kasdan, "Isfiya," *passim;* Michael Van Dusen, "Political Integration and Regionalism in Syria," *Middle East Journal* 26, no. 2 (Spring 1972); 123-36; Peter Gubser, "The Zu'ama' of Zahlah: The Current Situation in a Lebanese Town," *ibid.*, 27, no. 2 (Spring 1973); 173-89; Fahim Qubain, *Crisis in Lebanon* (Washington, D.C.: Middle East Institute, 1961), pp. 75-79, *passim;* Gabriel Ben Dor, "The Politics of Innovation and Integration: A Political Study of the Druze Community in Israel (Ph.D. diss., Princeton University, 1972), *passim.*

17. Joy Tarabulsi, "Charoun under Microscope," *The Daily Star Sunday Supplement*, February 11, 1973, pp. 4-5; Seale, *The Struggle*, p. 135; Qubain, *Crisis*, pp. 142-43; Eliezer Be'eri, *Army Officers in Arab Politics and Society* (New York: Praeger, 1970), p. 336; Iliya Harik, "The Ethnic Revolution and Political Integration in the Middle East," *International Journal of Middle East Studies* 3, no. 3 (July 1972); *passim.*

18. A. H. Hourani and S. M. Stern, eds., *The Islamic City* (Philadelphia: University of Pennsylvania Press, 1970), *passim.* See especially Hourani's introduction, pp. 16ff.

19. Van Dusen, "Political Integration," p. 27, *passim.*

20. Moshe Ma'oz, "Attempts at Creating a Political Community in Modern Syria," *Middle East Journal* 26, no. 4 (Autumn 1972); 399; Iliya F. Harik, "The Ethnic Revolution," pp. 310-11.

21. Zeltzer, "Minorities," p. 24; Torrey, *Syrian Politics*, p. 97; Seale, *The Struggle*, pp. 14, 133; George Haddad, *Revolution and Military Rule in the Middle East: The Arab States*, 2 vols. (New York: Speller, 1971), II; 202-03.

22. Seale, *The Struggle*, pp. 133-36; Haddad, *Revolution*, II; 214-17. Shishakli lost power in February 1954 as a consequence of a *coup d'état*. He took refuge in Brazil but was killed by a Druze, Nawas al-Ghazali, in 1964 in retaliation for his crushing of the 1954 Druze revolt. Seale, *The Struggle*, p. 147, fn. 20.

23. *Al-Hayat*, December 19, 1964, cited in Gad Soffer, "The Role of the Officer Class in Syrian Politics and Society" (Ph.D. diss., American University, 1968); Haddad, *Revolution*, II; 45.

24. Haddad, *Revolution*, II; 45.

25. Soffer, "The Role," p. 25.

26. Be'eri, *Army Officers*, p. 337.

27. Be'eri, *Army Officers*, pp. 167, 250, 337-39; Haddad, *Revolution*, II; pp. 190-201, 357; Van Dusen, "Political Integration," *passim.*

28. For the source material on Lebanon, see Harik, *Man Yahakam Lubnan, passim.*, especially pp. 73-76; Hudson, *The Precarious Republic,* pp. 110-15, 198-200, 249, *passim.*; Michael C. Hudson, "Democracy and Social Mobilization in Lebanese Politics," *Comparative Politics* 1, no. 2 (January 1969); 247-49; Farsun, "Family Structure," *passim.*, esp. p. 278; Michael W. Suleiman, *Political Parties in Lebanon* (Ithaca: Cornell University Press, 1967), pp. 213-27, 519; Rizk, *Le Régime*, p. 102; Ayoub, "Resolution of Conflict," pp. 125-26, fn. 8; Hottinger, "Zu'ama' and Parties," *passim.*; and Qubain, *Crisis, passim.*

29. For more detail on the civil war, see P. Edward Haley and Lewis W. Snoder, eds., *Lebanon in Crisis: Participants and Issues* (Syracuse: Syracuse University Press, 1979).

6

MINORITIES IN ASSIMILATION: THE BERBERS OF NORTH AFRICA

William E. Hazen

To the American public, the Berber of North Africa has been portrayed as a romantic, hard riding, desert warrior who gallops across the dunes singing lustily of his prowess in battle and love. The fictional Rif of Sigmund Romberg and George Bernard Shaw, however, must not be confused with the Berber who lives today in North and Saharan Africa. Nevertheless, the Rombergs and Shaws have captured much of the inherent spirit of the factual Berber, one who is gradually losing his identity as a result of the encroachment of modern civilization into his mountain fastnesses and of his belief in the paraphrase of the adage, "Every man is an island."

Berbers throughout North Africa have been found to have similar traits and language. Yet, as has been constantly stressed by scholars who have done extensive research on the Berbers, they are not an homogeneous group. They have a rich heritage but one that is regionally fragmented. There is no sense of Berber ethnic national pride as is found among the Kurds. And because of the policies undertaken by the governments of North Africa, the Berber as such may in fact soon cease to exist.

Because of the similarities across the various Berber groups scattered throughout North Africa, Berbers everywhere must be considered to belong to one ethnic minority. This chapter will delve into their origins, history, relations with the Arab-controlled governments of their region, and, most important, relations with one another. Such a survey reveals that Berbers as an ethnic minority are becoming an endangered species. There is no concept of Berber nationalism. Instead, Berbers are being drawn into Arab society to which their roots are irrelevant and in which their heritage is but a dim memory of a forgotten past.

DESCRIPTION

The name "Berber" was first applied to the people living in North Africa by the Greeks who established colonies there several centuries before Christ. However, "Berber" must not be confused with the term "barbarian," which is also of Greek origin and was meant to include those people living outside the civilized world (that is, the Greek world). Instead, "Berber" was used to denote a tribe of people by that name living in the vicinity of their colonies. One of the leading tribal groups of the Middle Atlas range is the Beraber, a name derived from one of the original Berber tribes to migrate westward.[1] Berbers, themselves, never used the term "Berber" to denote themselves, however. Instead, they used to refer to themselves as the *Imazigher*.[2]

Berbers presently live in all the countries of North Africa, from the Siwa oasis of Egypt to the coastal cities of Tangier and Rabat in Morocco. Since the Tuaregs are also considered ethnically Berber, the group is also to be found in all Saharan countries, from the Sudan to Mauritania. However, the Tuaregs are concentrated in four plateau locations: Ajjar, Ahaggar, Adrar Ahnet, and Air, which are in Algeria, Mali, and Niger.[3] Berbers are even to be found in Senegal, where the Zenaga tribe lives.

Morocco contains the largest number of Berbers. Berbers are principally located in the mountains, while the Arab population is settled more heavily in the plains. Nevertheless, there are Berbers in all parts of Morocco. The major cities, for example, all have substantial Berber populations. And the Sus Valley in southern Morocco is composed of large number of Berber-speaking people.[4]

There are two major areas of Berber concentration in Algeria. These are the Aurès Mountains in the northeastern part of the country and the Kabyle, a mountainous region near the capital, Algiers. A third Berber population center is the Oued Mzab oasis in central Algeria. Five cities, of which Ghardaya is the most prominent, have preserved an almost medieval Berber existence.[5]

The principal Berber communities in Tunisia are found on the island of Jerba and in some southern oases. Since they comprise less than two percent of the population, Tunisian Berbers should be considered curiosities rather than an important ethnic group. In fact, their towns, such as Chenini and Douriat, are now tourist sites, since they have been preserved as troglodyte historical peculiarities which are only now emerging into the twentieth century.[6]

Libyan Berbers are also a negligible ethnic group and are to be found in the towns of Sukhna, Aujela, and Zuwara. The largest concentration is in the Jabal Nafusa region, abutting the Tunisian border.

Non-Tuareg Berbers are also to be found living among the Tuaregs. Approximately 12,000 live in a triangular area with points at Ghadames and Ghat on the Algerian-Libyan border and Timbuktu in Mali.[7]

The origins of the Berbers are shrouded in the mysteries of time. Different authors provide varying theories. It is known, though, that Berbers have lived in North Africa since the Stone Age. Berber towns of neolithic vintage have been unearthed in Morocco, and a primitive Berber civilization existed on the Canary Islands until the Spaniards conquered the islands in the fifteenth century.[8]

There is a consensus among authors that the Berbers are of Mediterranean stock, that is, they belong to a race indigenous to the Mediterranean basin. Where authors tend to disagree is on their original stock. One states that Berbers are of Hamitic origins.[9] Another states they are of Western origin.[10] It is clear that Berbers differ from the Semites and other races that have invaded their homeland. Yet, because of the subsequent mixing of the races, there has been a trend toward eliminating racial characteristics among the peoples of North and Saharan Africa; so it is difficult at times to distinguish a Berber from an Arab.

There are two main Berber stocks: the Botr and the Beranes.[11] Each tribe should be able to trace its origins to one of these two groups. Their descendants are easily identified by their language. The Botr speak the Zenata dialect, while the Beranes speak Masmuda and Sanhaja. With this rule as a guide, one may discern that Botr stock resides in Libya, Egypt, Tunisia, Algeria (except the Kabyles), parts of north central Morocco, and some isolated oases of the Sahara. Beranes descendants are to be found in Morocco in the Rif Mountains, the western High Atlas, the Anti-Atlas, the Middle Atlas, the Sus Valley, and the Saharan zone; in Algeria, the Kabyles; in the Sahara as Tuaregs.

POPULATION

As is common in the developing countries, accurate population figures are invariably nonexistent. Current figures are estimates based on previous studies carried out by colonial administrations. However, these may be 30 years old, and, in the case of Algeria, where the number of casualties incurred during the fight for independence is conjecture, the estimates are rough approximations. It must be remembered, too, that current demographic figures published by the countries themselves do not show an ethnic breakdown because of the central governments' desire to de-emphasize ethnicity in order to reinforce the concept of a homogeneous national population.

The Berbers of North Africa number between 9 and 12 million. The breakdown is as follows: Algeria, approximately 3.5 million (or about 20 percent of the total population); Morocco, 7.5 million (35-40 percent); Tunisia, approximately 100,000; Libya, substantially fewer than 100,000; and the Sahara (Tuaregs), 500,000. These figures are only very rough estimates since demographers are unable to come to a consensus as to what constitutes a Berber. Some say his ethnic background, others, his language. However, because of a decrease in the number of those who speak Berber while still claiming to be ethnic Berbers, the figures show great variance.[12]

In Algeria, Berber concentrations are to be found in three principal departments: Aurès, with about 45 percent of the total department population; Sètif, with approximately 41 percent; and Tizi-Ouzou, the heart of the Kabyles, with about 80 percent.[13] Density figures indicate that there are approximately 640 per square mile in the Kabyle, as compared with 13.4 for the whole country.

Other figures pertaining specifically to Algerian Berbers are not available. However, statistics of the country in general would give some indication of the population structure of the Berbers. Sixty percent of the population is under 20 years of age. Furthermore, there is a disproportionately heavy ratio of women to men because of the war for independence and the migration of men to Europe.

Berber dislocation during the war for independence was intense. The French set up temporary encampments and forcibly relocated the inhabitants of the Kabyles and Aurès Mountains, which were guerrilla strongholds. Further population movements occurred because of the vast destruction meted out by French forces in their attempts to destroy guerrilla sanctuaries. Many fled to urban centers where they reside today. Others have left their rural homes to seek employment in the expanding industries being developed by the central government. However, the greatest number of people leave to find work abroad.

The principal reasons for such extensive labor migration are, first, the Berber regions are poor and underdeveloped, and, second, they are overpopulated. The Algerian government has recognized these facts. At the same time, there is concern about the loss of Algerian manpower. Unable to pay wages comparable to those earned in Europe yet unwilling to lose the revenue brought in by these workers, the government can only hope that the more dedicated nationalists will eventually return home to work in their country's industries.

Statistics on Morocco are not as complete as those of Algeria. In fact, only scattered figures are available for the Berber population. Since the majority of the population (approximately 70 percent) is rural[14] and since much of the Arab-speaking population lives in the urban centers, it may be surmised that the majority of the Berbers lives in rural communities. This is not to say that there are no sizable Berber populations in the urban centers. Each city has a large Berber quarter. In fact, the city of Tangier has a 70 percent Berber population.[15] The population is young, with approximately 50 percent under twenty years of age. The overall population density is listed at 70 per square mile. However, in parts of the Berber mountain zones, density figures rise to half again as much.

These figures are expected to change in the near future since the urban population is expanding at three times the rate of rural growth.[16] The flight to the cities has been prompted by a desire on the part of the rural population to seek a life that affords them a better income. The underdeveloped situation existing in the mountains remains static. Unemployment and underemployment are increasing as the standard of living decreases in rural areas. Recurring periods of drought have exacerbated the situation. Only the central government could ameliorate conditions. However, as in most Third World countries, development projects are given priority, and rural improvement has had to take a back seat to tourism and industry.[17]

As in Algeria, Morocco, too, has migrant laborers. Their exact number cannot be accurately determined because of illegal entry into European countries, but it is estimated that up to 50,000 are working in Europe. Their migration is not due to overpopulation but in order to find work outside a country in which it is estimated 40 percent of the labor force between the ages of 20 and 30 is unemployed. Berbers, no doubt, make up a majority of the migrant laborers since they form the majority of unskilled workers seeking employment.

Because of the relatively small numbers of Berbers in other countries, population statistics for this minority cannot even be evaluated. It would be sufficient to state that they reside mainly in rural communities and depend upon agricultural employment for their livelihood. A few, such as those living on Jerba Island, are small merchants and migrate to the Tunisian cities in order to establish their businesses. Libyan Berbers are predominantly nomads, as are the Tuaregs of the Sahara region.

As we have indicated, the Tuaregs are undergoing severe hardships because of a prolonged drought. Heretofore, they had lived a nomadic existence as masters of caravans or as agriculturalists. With crops and livestock depleted, many have been forced to leave their traditional camp sites and seek succor in the larger cities of the region. This displacement may be permanent since their entire social structure may be undergoing drastic and permanent changes.

HISTORY

Ancient Berber history begins with the establishment of colonies by Phoenicians on North African shores and the subsequent interaction between the two groups. Primitive in comparison to the invaders from the east, the Berbers were unable to oppose the seagoing colonizers effectively. Nevertheless, the Phoenicians did not penetrate the Berber hinterland but established amicable relations with the indigenous population. By the time of the Punic Wars, Berbers fought alongside their Phoenician allies against Rome's rising power.[18]

With the destruction of the Carthaginian empire, the Berbers found themselves pitted against an ever expanding nation. At this time, there were three Berber kingdoms: Mauritania (Morocco), West Numidia (Algeria), and East Numidia (Libya/Tunisia). As at other times through the centuries, there was no cooperation among the three to repel the Roman forces. Piecemeal, the kingdoms fell, and their leaders were either replaced by Roman governors or permitted to remain as satraps of Rome. There are recorded accounts of Berber chieftains who defied Roman expansion. One was Masimissa who ruled over all of Numidia. Another was his grandson, Jugurtha, who held out against Rome for six years. The last independent Berber king was Juba, who ruled over Mauritania. His son, Ptolemy, was eventually put to death by Emperor Caligula, thus ending Berber independence.[19]

Between the death of Ptolemy and the Arab invasion in the seventh century A.D., a separate Berber history did not exist. The Berber homeland was an integral part of the Roman empire; important cities were erected; the hinterland was invaded; and Romans were settled in the cultivable areas. The Berbers were pushed back into mountain fastnesses or otherwise subjected to Roman authority.

With the invasion of North Africa by the Vandals in the fourth and fifth centuries A.D., Roman order came to an end. After the vast destruction, even the restoration of order by the Byzantines in the sixth century only affected the coastal cities. The interior remained virtually free from outside rule. This situation led to a Berber uprising against the Byzantines which was soon quelled, with the Berbers retreating to the harsh mountain areas and the Byzantines to their coastal cities. The stalemate was to persist until the Arab invasion of North Africa from Egypt in the seventh century.

Arab penetration was, at first, exploratory. It was not until the late 660s that the Arabs began their conquest in earnest. Although he reached the Atlantic, the Arab leader Okba was killed by a Berber chieftain and his forces chased back into Egypt. This new Berber luminary, Kossayla, was to become leader of the Berber forces and to establish his capital at Kairouan.[20] However, the Arabs sent another force into North Africa which succeeded and stayed as conquerors.

The Berber protagonist this time was a woman, Kahina. Jewish, she was to lead the resistance for five years.[21] Eventually, though, she, too, was killed. The Berbers submitted and allied themselves with their new conquerors. Some Berber tribes helped to pacify all of North Africa for their allies and were instrumental in establishing the Arab kingdom of Spain.

Until the Hilalian invasion in the eleventh century, the Berbers, though a subjugated people, gained control of North African affairs. They helped to establish Fatimid rule in Egypt and, for their loyalty, were permitted to establish semi-independent kingdoms.* Yet the Arab religion and language permitted the Arabs to retain their supremacy without force of arms. Loyalty to the religious head of Islam was important to the newly converted Berbers, and use of Arabic as the official language permitted some affinity between the two groups.

Islam was also a divisive factor in North Africa, however. The more fanatical Muslims felt compelled to wage war against their unconverted or less fanatical Berber brethren, with fragmentation and constant warfare as the result. It must be remembered that the opposing sides were both Berber. Yet because of the adherence of one side to Islam, warfare took on a Berber-Arab image.

During this unstable period in North African history, three

---

*The Fatimids opposed the orthodox caliphs of Baghdad. Shi'as, they favored succession to the caliphate by descendants of Muhammad, the prophet, through his daughter, Fatima, and son-in-law, Ali. Their rise to power began in Tunisia and, after conquering Cairo with Berber support, they transferred their capital to that city.

important Berber kingdoms were established. All originated in Morocco, and their influence was to be felt throughout all of North Africa and Spain. The Almoravids (al-Murabitun) established their capital at Marrakesh and extended their sway over all of Morocco, Spain, and a great part of Algeria. Once in control of these vast lands, their power declined. They were soon challenged by the Almohads (al-Muwahidun) who, in their conquest of Almoravid territory, stressed the decadence of the rulers and their turning away from true Islam. Their empire was to spread over all of North Africa, including Tunisia and parts of Libya, and, of course, Spain. By 1269 A.D., the empire was no more. A new dynasty had arisen in Morocco, the Merinids, who were to retain power until 1465.

In the meantime, Arab resurgence into North Africa had begun in 1051 A.D. with the Hilalian invasion. Spurned by their Berber vassal states in North Africa, the Fatimid caliphs of Cairo unleashed their bedouin tribes—the Hilal and the Sulaym—who quickly overran North Africa to the Rif Mountains and left behind a veritable wasteland. Cities were razed, crops destroyed, and countless thousands slaughtered. A few cities were able to withstand these hordes, but the majority of the Berber population fled to its mountain or desert retreats. From this time on, population distribution in North Africa was to take on a specific characteristic: the Arabs or pro-Arab Berbers were to inhabit the coastal plains and larger valleys, while the Berbers were to retain control of the mountains and less hospitable desert areas.

In the sixteenth century, North Africa began to experience the encroachment of European powers. The last of the Muslim states in Spain fell in 1492. The war against what Christianity now viewed as the "infidels" was carried to their own shores, and small European outposts were established in Morocco, Algeria, and Tunisia. An inevitable conflict was to bring in the North African states. Calling upon their coreligionists, the independent Barbary States asked succor from the Ottoman Empire, which was also expanding rapidly at this time. The Spaniards and Venetians were forced to retreat from most of their North African outposts. However, the Ottomans stayed on. Once again, all but Morocco suffered foreign rulers.

Under Ottoman rule, the Barbary States became maritime principalities, each with an independent ruler owing nominal allegiance to the Porte. Their principal income was derived from piracy directed against the merchant ships of the European states.

In Morocco, one Arabo-Berber dynasty succeeded another. Two zones were recognized: the makhzen and the siba.[22] The first was that area controlled by the ruling sultan; the second, the zone outside his authority. Constant warfare existed between the two. Areas diminished or increased according to the strength of the sultan. In the mid-1600s the Alawi (sometimes called the Filali) dynasty came to power. This dynasty rules today in the person of Hassan II.

With the rise of the European empires in the eighteenth century, it was only natural that North Africa should come under the designs of certain European states. France, Spain, and Italy were most concerned since their territories were closest proximity to the North African states, although Germany, too, later had ambitions in the area. Under the pretext of an insulting incident, Algeria was invaded by the forces of Charles X of France in 1830 to save the Bourbon dynasty. The conquest succeeded, by Carles X was forced to abdicate. Tunisia was next to come under French domination in 1881. Morocco lost its independence in 1912, the French assuming responsibility for the lion's share, while Spain took suzerainty over the nothern part and enclaves in the south. Italy finally gained control of Libya from the Turks in 1912.

The occupation of North Africa was not peaceful. Resistance was especially strong in western Algeria under the Berber leader, Abd al-Qadir. However, his defeat in 1847, followed by the capitulation of the Kabyle Berber confederacies in 1857, ended the initial resistance in Algeria to French occupation. Rebellions were to arise throughout French rule, but were always soon quelled.

In Morocco, resistance began in the Rif Mountains in 1921, and continued until 1926. Abd al-Krim was the Berber leader of this resistance, and he became a national hero. Elsewhere in the Middle Atlas, resistance continued until 1934, when the last Berber tribe capitulated to French forces.

In spite of the inferiority of their arms, the Berbers were able to hold out against European invaders for many years, principally because of the terrain. It was not until the French won the support of certain Berber chieftains and effectively employed their knowledge and manpower that final conquest was achieved. The French had sought in 1930 to appease the Berbers by issuing an edict, entitled *dahir*, meant to favor the Berbers over the Arab population. The *dahir* exonerated Berbers from Islamic law as exercised by the sultan. Furthermore, Berber customary law was substituted for Sharifian law, and all criminal cases were tried by French magistrates. In this way, the French hoped for Berber support, while instigating a divide-and-rule tactic, an approach which enjoyed some success in the Levant. Because most of the Berbers refused to lay down their arms and cooperate with French, it was a failure.

With the initial defeat of the French by Germany in World War II, the North African populations sought to expand their self-government perhaps as far as independence. Many Arabs and Berbers fought alongside Frenchmen during the war. Given the right to die for France, the North Africans felt they had the right to govern themselves. Rioting and bloodshed spread across the countries. The sultan of Morocco was deposed by the French (with the help of Berbers) and replaced by one more amenable to French policy; leaders of the independence movements were imprisoned. Yet strikes and rioting continued. By November 1, 1954, armed rebellion had broken out in Algeria.

The French first capitulated in Morocco on March 2, 1955, by declaring the protectorate at an end and reinstalling Mohammed ibn Youssef as sultan. On June 2, 1955, Tunisia was given internal autonomy. The Algerians had to fight for seven years before attaining independence, seven years of great suffering, bloodshed, and destruction. Throughout these turbulent times, Berbers played an important part. The Kabyles and the Aurès were guerrilla strongholds.[23] Many Berbers living in France gave monetary support to the independence movements. Berber leaders in Morocco paid open tribute to the deposed sultan, thereby persuading the French that most Moroccans were united behind their beloved sultan who was willing to sacrifice his throne for independence. A Berber army was mobilized in the Atlases but saw most of its action in the south, attacking the Spanish enclave of Ifni and Spanish territories of Saguia al-Hamra and Rio de Oro after independence had been proclaimed.

One thing must be clear. Throughout Berber history, there was little cooperation among the Berber populations in the four countries of North Africa.[24] During the struggles for independence, both the Tunisian and the Moroccan governments stood behind the Algerian independence fighters. However, these pledges of support must not be considered as Berber support for other Berbers but as governments supporting a cause. Even during the rebellions of Abd al-Qadir in Algeria and Abd al-Krim in Morocco, support was localized. In fact, some Berbers fought with French and Spanish troops against these two leaders, as they did against their brethren during the struggles for independence. The Berbers have not been united as a people. Instead, they remained fragmented, owing their allegiance to local leaders rather than national causes.

As we have indicated, Berber activities have been submerged into the mainstream of national events and policies of the states of North Africa. Only isolated incidents have highlighted Berber activity as such. For example, in Algeria in 1967, Abd al-Aziz Zirdani, minister of labor, enlisted the support of his fellow Berber Tahar

Zbiri, an army officer, in staging a coup against those in government opposed to his labor policies.[25] The attempt failed, but it should be noted that the Zirdani-Zbiri clique gained support from their fellow Aurès Berbers in the army.

Recent coup attempts in Morocco have brought to the fore prominent Berbers. Generals Oufkir and Medbouh were both Berbers, as were the other coup leaders of the attempt at Skhirat and the plane incident of the same era.[26] A revolt in the Rif Mountains in 1958 was crushed by Oufkir and King Hassan. In 1972, trouble again arose in the Rif and High Atlases. Army and air force officers deserted their posts and fled to the mountains, protesting against the regime of King Hassan.[27] They were encouraged and supported by the Libyan government and were successful in cutting communications, attacking gendarmerie posts, and setting off bombs. How much support these rebels received from the local population is unknown. But it may be surmised from past history that they did receive some support. Grievance committees, headed by some of the armed forces deserters, sued for assistance. Since the local community was well represented, it must be assumed that the population was listening to these men. There was no indication, though, that a Berber revolt as such was expected. The problem seemed to result from a general malaise about the central government, from the desire to eliminate corruption at the highest levels so that benefits might filter down to the people. As a result, the king personally investigated the allegations of corruption, dismissed several persons from office, and had several others imprisoned and tried. These efforts pacified the uneasiness of the military for some years. Later, with the take-over of the northern half of what had been Spanish Sahara and the resulting skirmishes with indigenous units of the Polisario Front, the army has had little time to lodge complaints against the government.

It should be noted that many members of the Polisario Front are of Berber origin. They are fighting, though, alongside their Arab counterparts in an attempt to gain independence for their land from Morocco and Mauritania. The rebellion is now in its fourth year with seemingly no end in sight, since the Algerian government continues to provide weapons and supplies to the front and Morocco has shown no indication that it will relinquish its claims to its section of the former colony. Mauritania, at first showing a willingness to appease the Polisario, hardened its position against the guerrillas after a coup ousted the Mokhtar Ould Daddah government.

In Algeria, too, Berbers have presented the government with some of its stiffest challenges in dissent. In 1963 and 1964, resistance to the regime of Ahmed Ben Bella was led by Berbers—though not *as* Berbers—from the predominantly Berber Kabyles. In particular, Ait Ahmed led a guerrilla campaign against the Ben Bella government for some time. Again, as in Morocco, however, *Berberism* was not the essence of the rebellion. Rather, the insurgency centered on dissent from Ben Bella policies.

POLITICS

Internal Politics of the Minority

Although the Berber population is located in ten countries (four of them with minimal Berber settlements), there is little transnational Berber political unity. For that matter, there is no single Berber policy or Berber leader in any country. The Berber communities prefer to limit their horizons to what they can see. Even then, different factions or tribes within the same area may be pitted against one another. In the past Berbers fought with the French against their fellow Berbers who were in rebellion against French rule. Or, in recent Moroccan events, Berber army leaders who rose against the central government were summarily executed by other Berbers loyal to the king. Only in immediate postindependence Algeria was there a hint of Berber support as such for an antigovernment leader.

There is contact among Berbers living in different countries. However, this occurs only during seasonal migrations of nomadic tribes and business transactions of Berber merchants, or when Berber migratory laborers find themselves living together in foreign cities. During Algeria's war for independence, Tunisian and Moroccan Berbers provided assistance for Algerian Berbers. However, the policies of the Moroccan and Tunisian governments were to give support to the rebellion. It was not an independent Berber policy.

Because of encroachments by the central governments, traditional Berber social structure is on the decline. Many headmen and representative councils have become firureheads whose authority has been replaced by officials appointed by the central government. With the elimination by decree of tribal feuds, vendettas, and tribal warfare, the need for arbiters decreased. In the realm of justice and conflict resolution, and in personal status matters as well, civil courts are supplanting Berber arbitration.

Those Berbers who seek political power have come to the realization that only political parties provide an opportunity for attaining power. Even the traditional noble families must use this means to regain their lost prestige. A few wealthy men have gained power by buying the favor of the central government. However, the norm is to run for election to local office.

The election process is complicated and filled with pitfalls because in Berber society there exists a system of patronage and support.[28] In this system, obligation is of paramount importance. If someone supports a candidate, it is expected of the candidate to eventually repay this debt. For it is a debt, since an obligation was incurred when the vote was cast.[29]

Complications occur when trying to win support. Usually families back their own members. But if a member of the family owes an obligation to a rival candidate, and the rival is pressing for his support, the result, more than likely, will be a split in family ranks.

By running more than one candidate from a single district, the traditional Berber checks-and-balances system comes into play.[30] Various groups support their candidates; however, if for advantageous reasons one group switches its support, another group may switch its backing to the rival candidate, thereby preserving the traditional system. Rivalry is constant, and fights are frequent.

Once in office, a successful candidate may begin to build up his support for more prestigious positions by dispensing favors or fulfilling election obligations. He himself is subject to pressures from those both in the party and the government to whom he is subordinate.

Party politics are handicapped in North Africa. The norm is a single party, with party-selected candidates competing for the same position. Only in Morocco is more than one party permitted. However, because of internal instability, no elections have been held recently. The parties are allowed to exist, but there are no offices for which to run. One Berber party came into existence following independence. The Mouvement Populaire flourished for a short time under the leadership of Mahjoub Ahardane. However, little has been heard from the party since the parliament was prorogued and constitutional power taken over by the king in the mid-1960s. Once party politics are normalized, the Mouvement Populaire could reorganize itself. However, only the Istiqlal and the Union Nationale des Forces Populaires (UNFP) have backing among the rural population. But even some branches of the UNFP were suspended by the government in August 1973.[31]

Relations with the Central Governments

Since the French occupation of North and Saharan Africa, Berber power has declined. Not only were the Berber lands conquered by military force; Berber administrative systems were put in tandem with the occupying French administration. Recognizing that authority in Berber communities was wielded by the headman as representative of the people, the French placed a counterpart to him in each community. The people soon recognized that their own representative was only a figurehead and that the real power lay in the French-appointed administrator. Allegiance, therefore, was transferred to the foreigner.

When independence was granted to these countries, the newly formed governments merely substituted their own administrators for the French.[32] This action formed part of the deliberate policy inaugurated by the central governments to loosen tribal ties, thereby weakening tribal structure. Another program with the same objectives was nationalization of tribal lands.[33] Tribal boundaries were eliminated and new regions established cutting across the old tribal limits, partitioning some and adding others to a single region. The land confiscated was then distributed to individuals or to a group.[34] Communal-type organizations were established to run these tracts, and the members then decided what should be done. The head of these communes, though, was a government appointee, from whom the benefits flowed and who, in reality, ran the groups. Entire tribes were sometimes brought in to farm tracts, plant orchards, or restore badly eroded lands. The tribal leaders had no say in what was to be done and therefore lost their traditional rights to the central government.

Development programs for Berber areas have also been initiated by the central governments. In Morocco, much has been promised but little provided. As a result, armed rebellions, five since independence in 1956, have arisen in the Atlas Mountains.[35] The last one finally dissolved in 1973. During this last outburst, grievances were presented to the king citing the unfulfilled promises made for new schools, roads, clinics, water supplies, and other needs vital to the Berber communities.[36] Sporadic roadblocks were set up, and strikes took place. Police stations were also attacked and bombs thrown.[37] Whether these activities were part of the tactics utilized by insurgents sent into Morocco from Libya and Algeria was never revealed. But the most serious clashes between government forces and insurgents took place in the High Atlases, which meant that some Berber support was given to the insurgents: to survive in these mountains, one needs assistance from the indigenous population. There is no question that some of the insurgents were followers of Muhammad Basri, a UNFP leader, and dissident Berber officers from the Moroccan Air Force.[38]

The Algerians have also promised aid to their Berber regions.

However, they have attempted to meet their pledges. Massive government funds were allocated for agricultural and industrial development in the Kabyles.[39] New housing and schools are also being constructed. In the region populated by the Tuaregs, the Algerian government has constructed houses and schools and installed electric power. As inducements to settle, the Tuaregs are offered credits toward the purchase of supplies and seed. They no longer need pay tribute to their ruling tribal chiefs nor bind themselves to the nobles with unequal sharecropping practices.[40]

The most important program utilized by the North African governments to weld their people together is that of Arabization. Arabization is two-pronged: to have one language, Arabic, and to stress those things that are Arab. To celebrate the twenty-ninth anniversary of the (Moroccan) Istiqlal Party's declaration for independence, the central committee of the Istaqlal declared that Arabization was necessary to complete Moroccan independence.[41] The school curriculum would be utilized to foster programs. Foremost would be the teaching of Arabic. Introduction of Arabic at all levels of the school curriculum has been desired for some time by the central government. Opposition arose to this policy, mainly from the Berber rural populations and from the French-educated urbanites. Now, however, with the full backing of the Istiqlal, a new emphasis has been given to Arabization for the forthcoming years.

Algeria also has declared an all-out war on those things not Arab and stressed the teaching of Arabic at all levels.[42] Although the program was primarily aimed at French-speaking groups, the Berbers received the brunt of the effort. Whether Arabization means an alignment of policy with the other Arab states is yet to be seen. Arab unity is looked upon with skepticism by North African leaders who nevertheless profess strong backing for it. Berbers are overtly critical of Arab unity and nationalism and believe it should not be stressed in North Africa.

These efforts by the central governments to bring the Berbers into the mainstream of society are scorned by the Berbers themselves.[43] They have lost their political independence to the central governments; they now fear permanent encroachment on their social and cultural lives which will lead eventually to the disintegration of all things Berber. Algeria has attempted to circumvent this scorn by bringing into the government a number of Berbers proportionate to that of their role in the total population.[44] The bureaucracy is composed of over 20 percent Berbers, while other government branches, such as the armed forces, have less. Overall, the average in government service is approximately 20 percent.

Berbers in Algeria have participated more actively in government than their counterparts in other countries. At the core of the Algerian rebellion were Berbers who rose to become prominent members in the movement.[45] As noted above, though, there was no single spokesman for the Berbers. Each acted independently from the others.

In Morocco, most Berber participation in government service is through the armed forces. The majority of officers are Berbers. Yet, here again, Berber fought Berber. Until a unified opposition emerges, the central government will slowly but irrevocably whittle away Berber traditional society to form a unified Arab society.

Relations with the General Society

The dominant attitude that has characterized relations between the Berbers and the Arabs, who comprise the majority of the population, is laissez faire. The desire to be left alone, to pursue their own affairs, is very strong among the Berbers. But since French intervention and the loss of their political freedom, Berbers have been drawn into the activities of the central governments, both as participants and as subjects of government policies. There has been no spectacular result of this increasing interaction—no wars or overt hostility on either side. Instead, there exists an atmosphere of resignation—"so be it"—tinged with disdain on both sides.

One result of interaction has been an increase in the rivalry between the two groups. The arenas in which this competition is most keenly evidenced have been politics and business.[46] In politics, Arabs have generally insisted upon giving orders, while the Berbers ended up doing the work. During the Moroccan elections in 1961, the Berbers saw and took the chance to turn the tables on the Arabs, winning important seats on several local councils that were considered to be the domain of the Arabs.

Business rivalry has existed for many generations, ever since the ambitious Berber began coming to the city and opening up his small shop. The most intense rivalry exists between the Fassis (Arabs from Fez) and Susis (Berbers from the Sus Valley).[47] The former became the wholesaler and the latter the retailer. However, Susis have been able to gain a toehold in the wholesale market with the purchase of Jewish businesses after 1948.

The Jews were always treated by the Berbers with deference. No hostility existed between the two groups. Whether this harkens back to the pre-Islamic era, when the Jews, fleeing from Jerusalem in the first century settled among the Berbers and converted many to Judaism, is open to speculation. Perhaps it was a feeling that they were two minorities who must band together against an aggressive external majority. Whatever the reason, the Jews preferred to turn to the Berbers for protection. Honor was thus invoked, and the Berbers scrupulously adhered to their code. When the Jews of North Africa began their mass exodus to Europe and Israel after 1948, they began to sell their businesses to Berbers instead of Arabs.[48]

Relations with International Powers

Berber relations with foreign countries have been limited primarily to France and Spain. As occupiers of Berber territory, their contact was continuous. The Spanish, having fought against the Berber Rifs in the 1920s, preferred to deal with the Arabs and left the Berbers to their own affairs.* The French, on the other hand, preferred to deal with the Berbers. A Berber policy was the key in governing Moroccan territory. Based on the principle of divide and rule, the French recruited Berbers for the Moroccan armed forces. A well-known decree in 1930 favored Berber customary law over the Shari'a. Moreover, the French elevated Berber chieftains to positions of grandeur so the latter would utilize their own forces in conquering dissident Berber tribes holding out in mountain sanctuaries.

French forces in Algeria treated Berbers very differently, though. Because the Berber homelands were centers for rebel concentrations during the Algerian war for independence, French troops destroyed many villages and interned the inhabitants in camps, where they lived for the duration of the war.

Since independence, Berber contact with the French has been on an individual basis. Migratory labor from North Africa has concentrated in France, although many have gone to work in other European countries. The choice of France was only natural since French had been taught in the North African schools, becoming a second language for many Berbers. Because of increasing opposition from French nationals to the presence of hundreds of thousands of North Africans, the French government in 1968 initiated a quota system whereby the number of migrant laborers permitted to enter France was 35,000 annually.[49] In 1973, the figure was dropped to 25,000.

The quota system only increased the number of illegal entries. Furthermore, there was no turnover of 35,000. Instead, many laborers stayed on year after year. Others applied for French citizenship

---

*The Spaniards were defeated by the forces of Abd al-Krim, and only through the intervention of the French were the Berbers pacified.

so that by 1970 some three-quarters of a million North Africans were resident in Europe, 80 percent of whom were in France alone.[50] In the summer of 1973, rioting against the North Africans broke out in several towns in southern France, and a number of migrants were killed. The rioting had been provoked by Arab/Berber laborers when they protested publicly about their wretched living quarters and their low salaries.[51] The Algerian government, in response to the attacks against their migrants, suspended the emigration of migrant workers to France until anti-Algerian perpetrations were curbed.

Currently, because of a lack of spokesmen for their minority, the Berbers have no special relationships with international powers; nor will they have any in the foreseeable future. The only contacts will be by individuals seeking business commitments or permission to enter host countries as laborers or immigrants.

FUTURE

The Berbers live in an Arab-oriented world. They have no press or periodicals. Their language, if written, is transliterated into Arabic script. Because of the high illiteracy rates, few could read Arabized Berber even if they wanted to do so. Furthermore, the central governments of the countries in which the Berbers live have de-emphasized the Berber language to such an extent that in most schools of the region the teaching of Berber is either frowned upon or forbidden.

This policy of de-emphasizing the Berber language is only one segment of the governments' programs to Arabize their populations. Tribal lands have been nationalized and redistributed, either to individuals or to collectives, over which government-appointed employees hold sway. Settlement programs also are attempting to eliminate migratory tribes to facilitate control. These are only a few of the efforts made by the central governments to eliminate Berber culture and identity.

Unemployment also has contributed to the breakdown of Berber culture, forcing rural people to migrate to foreign countries or to flock to the cities. In both instances, they are swallowed up by different cultures. The ever expanding slums of the cities, the bidonvilles, soon have an Arab patina in which Berber identity is alien.

As we have indicated, Berber identity is not a cohesive force. The Berber prefers to limit his horizon "to a small homeland; his plain, his valley, his mountain."[52] For this reason, "The idea of a national solidarity, encompassing all of Berbery, is foreign to his spirit." [53] And because of this "lack of solidarity," the Berber of North Africa will become, eventually, a rarity. His culture will be seen only in museums; his language will join the ranks of the "dead" languages only scholars study.

Unlike the Kurds who openly rebel against absorption into the general stream of alien nationalisms, the Berber seems to be content to be drawn gradually into and assimilated by his country's general ethos, to lose his identity in Arab society. Berber nationalism has become an outmoded doctrine, if it ever existed in the first place. The Berber of today may remember the tales of his father's father, of the glory of the Berber tribes; but he will not attempt to emulate his forebears. Instead, when asked his identity, he will say he is an Arab or an Algerian or Moroccan. *Imazigher* is a forgotten word.

NOTES

1. Carletoon Coon, *Caravan: The Story of the Middle East* (New York: Henry Holt and Company, 1951), p. 40.

2. Elaine Hagopian, "Morocco: A Case Study in the Structural Bases of Social Integration" (Ph.D. diss., Boston University, 1962), p. 7.

3. Coon, *Caravan*, p. 205.

4. John Waterbury, *North for the Trade: The Life and Times of a Berber Merchant* (Berkeley: University of California Press, 1972), p. 9.

5. Thomas Abercrombie, "Algeria: Learning to Live with Independence," *National Geographic Magazine* 144, no. 2 (August 1973); 209.

6. June Goodwin, "Home is a Whitewashed Cave," *Christian Science Monitor*, December 7, 1970, p. 15.

7. G. H. Bousquet, *Les Berbères* (Páris: Presses Universitaires de France, 1967), p. 17.

8. Coon, *Caravan*, p. 37.

9. *Ibid.*, p. 34.

10. Louis de St.-Quentin, *Algérie inconnue* (Algiers: Editions Baconnier, 1958), pp. 12-13.

11. Hagopian, "Morocco," p. 10.

12. G. Blake, in his article, "Morocco: Urbanization and Concentrations of Population," in *Populations of the Middle East and North Africa: A Geographical Approach*, ed. John Innes Clarke and W. B. Fisher (New York: Africana, 1972), p. 407, claims that 80 percent of the population speaks Arabic while only 10 percent speaks Berber and 10 percent is bilingual. On the other hand, Robert Mantagne, in *Révolution au Maroc* (Paris: Editions France Empire, 1953), states (p. 23) that 45 percent of the population speaks Berber while the rate is 30 percent in Algeria. Granted the 20 years between publication of the two works, those differences are perhaps slightly greater than one would expect.

13. K. Sutton, "Algeria: Changes in Population Distribution, 1954-66," in Clarke and Fisher, eds. *Populations of the Middle East*, p. 381.

14. Vincent Monteil, *Morocco*, trans. Veronica Hall (New York: Viking, 1964), p. 19. Hagopian, "Morocco," p. 5, places the figure at 75 to 80 percent.

15. David Hart, "Notes on the Rifian Community of Tangier," *Middle East Journal* 11, no. 2 (Spring 1957); 154.

16. Hagopian, "Morocco," p. 5.

17. Omar Annouari, "L'Exode rural restera toujours vérité," *L'Opinion* (Rabat), June 14, 1973, p. 7.

18. St.-Quentin, *Algérie*, p. 23.

19. *Ibid.*, p. 35.

20. *Ibid.*, p. 69.

21. *Ibid.*, p. 76.

22. Bernard Hoffman, *The Structure of Traditional Moroccan Rural Society* (The Hague: Mouton, 1967), p. 21.

23. William Quandt, "Berbers in the Algerian Political Elite" (Santa Monica: Rand, 1970), p. 4.

24. *Ibid.*, p. 3.

25. John Waterbury, "Land, Man, and Development in Algeria," *Reports of the American University Field Staff*, 17, part 3, no. 3, p. 2.

26. The attempted coup on the Skhirat palace in July 1971 was led by the Berber General Medboh, chief of the Royal Palace military staff. He and his fellow plotters were all eliminated by followers of the king and General Oufkir, himself a Berber. The attempted coup in August 1972, was this time led by General Oufkir and Major Kouera, another Rif Berber. Six of the pilots who strafed the king's plane were also Rifs. See John K. Cooley, "King Hassan's Task: Restoring Power Base," *Christian Science Monitor*, August 22, 1972, p. 3.

27. *Ibid.*

28. Ernest Gellner, "Patterns of Rural Rebellion in Morocco: Tribes as Minorities," *Archives européennes de sociologie*, 3, no. 2 (1962); 310.

29. Lawrence Rosen, "Rural Political Process and National Political Structure in Morocco," in *Rural Politics and Social Change in the Middle East*, ed. Richard Antoun and Iliya Harik (Bloomington: Indiana University Press, 1972), pp. 214-36, *passim*.

30. Ernest Gellner, "Independence in the Central High Atlas," *Middle East Journal*, 11, no. 3 (Summer 1957); 245.

31. *L'Opinion* (Rabat), August 18, 1973, p. 1. The Union Nationale des Forces Populaires (UNFP) of Morocco has not gained many adherents among the Berber. However, since it has been banned in the past and strongly restricted in 1973, its leader, Muhammad Basri, has called for outright confrontation with the central government. As a result, his adherents have formed the National Front for the Liberation of Morocco and have begun guerrilla-type operations. Based in the Berber stronghold of the central High Atlas, the front has caused some consternation within the government. The importance of this group, however, is not that it has party affiliation but that to exist in the High Atlas it must be receiving support from Berbers, whether or not they themselves are affiliated with the UNFP.

32. Gellner, "Independence in the Central High Atlas," p. 241.

33. Faith Willcox, *In Morocco* (New York: Harcourt, Brace, Jovanovich, 1971), p. 45.

34. Jean LeCoz, "Le Troisième age agraire du Maroc," *Annales de Géographie* 77, no. 422 (July-August 1968); 401.

35. Gellner, "Patterns of Rural Rebellion in Morocco," p. 297.

36. Cooley, "King Hassan's Task."

37. "Guerrilla au Maroc," *Jeune Afrique*, no. 650 (June 23, 1973); 31.

38. Cooley, "King Hassan's Task." Relations between Algeria and Morocco are constantly being strained and afford excuses for Algerian support of dissidents who act against the king's authority.

39. Quandt, "Berbers," p. 25.

40. Only recently are Tuaregs entering into the armed forces of Niger and Mali. Unwilling to do manual or agricultural work, the noble elites find army service rewarding since they are once again carrying a weapon and acting as guardians of the desert areas, a duty which the Tuaregs had assumed centuries ago. See P. Rognon, "La Confédération des nomades Kel Ahaggar," *Annales de Géographie* 71, no. 388 (November-December 1962); 617.

41. *L'Opinion*, January 11, 1973, p. 1.

42. Younes Berri, "Algérie: La révolution en arabe," *Jeune Afrique*, no. 639 (April 7, 1973); 14.

43. Hoffman, *Structure*, p. 99.

44 Quandt, "Berbers," p. 5.

45. *Ibid.*, pp. 9-15, *passim*.

46. Waterbury, *North*, pp. 125-36, *passim*.

47. *Ibid.*, p. 125.

48. Lawrence Rosen, "A Moroccan Jewish Community during the Middle Eastern Crisis," *Peoples and Cultures of the Middle East*, Louise Sweet, 2 vols. (Garden City: Natural History Press, 1970), II; 449.

49. Waterbury, "Land, Man, and Development in Algeria," part 2, no. 3, p. 14.

50. Migratory labor is important to the tribal areas because of the incomes sent by the migrants. Prior to the inauguration of the quota system, migrant Algerians in France sent approximately $300 million to their families. The amount of people supported was at least 1.5 million. The quota system curtailed the total of remittances. See John Waterbury, "Land, Man, and Development in Algeria," part 5, no. 3, p. 14.

51. "Europe's Own Bantu Labour Force," *The Economist* 246, no. 6762 (March 31, 1973); p. 54.

52. Lhaoussine Mtouggui, *Vue générale de l'histoire berbère* (Paris: Editions Larose 194-), p. 13.

53. *Ibid.*

7

MINORITIES IN PARTITION: THE CHRISTIANS OF LEBANON

Paul A. Jureidini and James M. Price

Lebanon, a land of diverse creeds and a meeting place for East and West, paradoxically has been at once a refuge for persecuted minority groups and a scene of virtually constant struggle among those same communities. It remains so today. With an area of only 4,000 square miles (no larger than the state of Connecticut) and a population of about 3 million, Lebanon today constitutes a mosaic of religious communities, has a large alien population numbering over 400,000, and has dozens of organized armed groups controlling various parts of its territory.* Lebanon is now involved in a struggle for its survival as a nation, as a haven for Christianity in the Arab world, and as a meeting place for Western and Arab interests.

Lebanon's unique status in the Arab world in the twentieth century, as well as its current predicament, are largely the result of the presence, activities, and thoughts of its Christian population. For a land so small, Lebanon has attracted disproportionate attention

---

*Most notably, the militias of the Phalange Party and the Parti national libéral; the Druze militias; the Muslim *Murabitoun* militia; a Muslim breakaway from the Lebanese Army called the Lebanese Arab Army and led by Ahmed al-Khatib; Christian breakaway forces from the Lebanese Army; 40,000 troops of the Arab Deterrent Forces (ADF), most of whom are from Syria; Palestine Liberation Army (PLA) forces; Palestine Liberation Organization (PLO) guerrilla fighters from several PLO constituent groups, and the United Nations forces (UNIFIL).

from historians and other scholars. Recently, renewed interest has blossomed as a result of the current Lebanese conflict. Most of these works have described Lebanon's modern history in terms of its more distant past. Some authors voice strong disapproval of the actions of Lebanon's Christian population; others praise them; few are neutral. However one chooses to view Lebanon's Christians—as classic examples of an elitist, bourgeois mentality, as the beneficent guiding lights of Western civilization, or in some less extreme perspective— the central role of the community in the development of the national character is clear.

Peoples of three religions, Islam, Christianity, and the Druze faith, constitute the vast majority of the Lebanese population. The Muslim population is divided between Sunni and Shi'a adherents, with the Sunnis slightly more numerous if Palestinians are included. (Without the Palestinians, the Shi'a slightly outnumber the Sunnis.) Muslims comprise at least 40 percent of the population, probably more.† The Christians are composed of numerous sects, which can be grouped into four classes: (1) the Roman Catholics ("Latin"); (2) the Uniates (those in communion with Rome), most notably the Maronites, Greek Catholics, Syrian Catholics, Armenian Catholics, and Chaldeans; (3) other eastern Christian denominations not in communion with Rome, such as the Greek Orthodox, the Armenian or Gregorian Church, the Nestorians (Assyrian Church of the East), and the Syrian Jacobites; and (4) various Protestant groups.[1] The Druze, who comprise about 6 percent of Lebanon's population, are not divided into various denominations, as are the Muslims and Christians. This does not mean that the Druze always act in a unified manner, for there are a variety of factors that periodically divide the Druze (especially, economics and family associations), but it is generally more accurate to speak in terms of "Druze" behavior than it is to speak of that of the "Christians" or "Muslims."[2]

The Lebanese adherents of those three religions have passed through many periods of conflict and cooperation. Although the issues among them have sometimes been purely religious, more often they have involved a combination of economic and political considerations which, when mixed with religion and family loyalties, have ignited Lebanon's internal conflicts. The focus here will be on the role the Lebanese Christians have played in making modern Le-

---

†The last complete census in Lebanon was taken in 1932. At that time Christians comprised 53 percent of the population, Muslims 40 percent, Druze 6 percent, and others 1 percent. No census has been taken since 1932; there is a fear of upsetting the delicate confessional balance of Lebanese society, despite the fact that many feel that the Muslim population has increased much more rapidly than that of the Christians.

banon, their role during the civil war, and their impact on Lebanon's future. Some background information about Lebanon and its Christian community is necessary to understand the nation's present situation and probable future.

Of the many Christian denominations found in Lebanon, the Maronites have made perhaps the most unusual and certainly one of the most important contributions to the area's social and political development.[3] Their role is due in part to their numbers—they are by far the largest Christian group in the country—but also to the entrepreneurial spirit exhibited by a number of well-educated Maronites, the Maronite Church's connections with the West, and the fact that the Maronite Church is indigenous to Lebanon, a fact which has had important psychological ramifications on Maronite actions.

The Greek Orthodox, Lebanon's second largest Christian community, have also played an important part in Lebanon's history. However, their role is not as extensive as that of the Maronites. The other Christian groups are much smaller than the Maronites and Greek Orthodox, and while each sect has produced individuals who have made a pronounced impact on Lebanese society, the limitations of their size have largely prevented them from playing a key role in Lebanon's overall development. When scholars discuss the unique role of Lebanon's Christians, they do so in terms of the Maronites and to a lesser extent of the Greek Orthodox.

HISTORICAL BACKGROUND

The Maronites

The Maronites trace their origin to an ascetic monk from the Syrian Church who lived in the late fourth and early fifth centuries. Most of his activities took place northeast of Antioch. After his death his disciples moved to what is today known as Qalat al-Mandiq on the Orontes. There the Maronites enjoyed tremendous growth and came into contact with a Monophysite[4] group, the Jacobites. Eventurally the Maronites adopted the Jacobite Christology, later moving into Jacobite territory in North Lebanon and giving the Jacobite community there the Maronite name. Labelled—and persecuted as—heretics by other Christians, the Maronites concentrated deep in the Mount Lebanon area where they were free to worship as they wished and from where they spread and "became until the present a dominant force in Lebanese affairs."[5] In the twelfth century, the Maronites entered a union with the Roman

Catholic Church, welcomed the French Crusaders, and even participated on the Christian side in the Crusades. The union ended shortly
thereafter but was reestablished in the sixteenth century and has
persisted to the present day.*

Despite their numerous triumphs and defeats during the twelfth
through fifteenth centuries, it was the Maronite experience under
Ottoman rule from 1516 to 1918 that shaped Maronite concepts of
themselves and Lebanon in the twentieth century.

The Greek Orthodox

The Greek Orthodox Church, more widely known as the Eastern
Orthodox Church, has approximately 370,000 Lebanese adherents,
making it Lebanon's second largest Christian community. Like the
Maronites, many Greek Orthodox have worked their way into
middle and upper-class professions. In fact, the professional classes
of Beirut are dominated not by Maronites but by the Greek Orthodox. Also like the Maronites, many Greek Orthodox have not
attained privileged positions in Lebanese society and instead eke out
meager existences in small villages in the mountains. Concentrations
of poor Greek Orthodox lie in the southern Shuf, on the slopes of Mt.
Herman, and in villages in southern Lebanon, as well as in other
areas where they live side by side with poor Druze and Muslim
families.

The Greek Orthodox can trace their Lebanese origins back to
when the split with the Western church became official. The Orthodox Church's history in Lebanon has many parallels with that of the
Maronites, especially since the coming of Muslim rule circa 640 A.D.
The three major Islamic empires, the Umayyads, the Abbasids, and
the Ottomans, which consecutively ruled over Lebanon until just
after World War I, incorporated within their political systems
methods of ruling religious minorities. As Christians, the Greek
Orthodox generally received the same treatment as the Maronites
under Islamic rule and shared with the Maronites a special hatred
for the treatment accorded to them under the *millet* system of the
Ottomans. (The *millet* system is discussed below.)

The historical common denominators between the Greek Ortho-

---

*The Maronites' union with Rome requires that the Maronites recognize the
suzerainty of the Pope and accept church dogma. In return the Maronites participate
in the Roman Catholic Church's administration (a Maronite may even be elected Pope)
and enjoy the other benefits of Roman Catholic membership. The Maronites are also
allowed to maintain their own liturgy.

dox and the Maronites are not sufficient to ensure complete cooperation between the two groups. A major factor inhibiting Maronite-
Greek Orthodox cooperation is the large Greek Orthodox population
residing in other Arab countries. The presence of their coreligionists
(as minorities) in other Arab lands limits the freedom of action of
Lebanon's Greek Orthodox in Lebanese affairs. Lebanon's Greek
Orthodox have been careful in expressing their views on issues that
could have repercussions on Greek Orthodox in nations like Syria,
Jordan, and Turkey. Their role in modern Lebanon is almost schizophrenic, although many Greek Orthodox have espoused ideas
similar to those of Camille Chamoun or of the latter-day Pierre
Gemayel, other Greek Orthodox have been in the forefront of pan-
Islamic parties and fought on the "Muslim" side in the Lebanese civil
war (see below).

Christians under Ottoman Rule

A brief review of Arab Christian experience under Ottoman rule
is necessary to understand later Christian actions. Their history
under Ottoman rule has been copiously documented, is intricately
interwoven with regional social and political developments and
therefore very complex, and for the purposes of this essay need not
be discussed in detail.[6] However, a survey of the general Lebanese
Christian experience under Ottoman governance will provide a
proper perspective for viewing Christian political thought in this
century.

When the Lebanese region (with boundaries similar to present-
day Lebanon's, though not clearly defined) initially fell under Ottoman dominion, the tiny area was under the control of several feudal
ruling families, the Sunni Shihabs, the Shi'a Harfushes, the Druze
Arslans and Jumblatts, and the Maronite Khazins, to name the most
noteworthy. The Christians' political strength, despite the community's large numbers, was limited to the Kisrawan area. The Druze
were then the dominant sect in Lebanon, and the leading Druze
family at that time, the Ma'n, was established as the ruling house.
Until the last Ma'ni heir died in 1697, the Ma'ns maintained authority in Lebanon, handling sectarian differences benevolently. The
Druze even encouraged Christian settlement in Druze districts,
particularly the Shuf, mixed with them, and served as a vehicle for
Christian vertical mobility in the political sphere.

When the last Ma'ni heir died in 1697, power gravitated to the
Shihab clan, a family related to the Ma'ns. Although publicly of
Sunni persuasion, the Shihabs made it known to their Druze subjects

that they were practicing Islam by dissimulation, that at heart they were really Druze.* In 1754, the current Shihabi ruler retired; his eldest son, installed in 1770 after reaching adulthood, had become a Christian. After a century and a half of generally beneficent Druze control, the Christians of Lebanon now had a Christian ruler. Christian security in Lebanon virtually reached its peak during the last third of the eighteenth century. Phillip Hitti records the impression Lebanon made upon the mind of Volney, a French nobleman and scholar.

> Here, unlike any other Turkish country, everyone enjoys full security for his property and his life. The peasant is not richer than in other countries, but he lives in tranquility. He fears not, as I have often heard him say, that the military officer, the district governor or the pasha should send their soldiers to pillage his house, carry out his family or give him the bastinado. Such oppressions are unknown in the mountain.[7]

Under the Ma'ns and Shihabs, Lebanon's ties with Europe—principally France and Italy—grew steadily. Not only did trade increase, but missionary activities became a major inroad for Western ideas into Lebanon. Numerous Jesuit schools were established, principally in Maronite areas. Relations between Lebanon's Christians and the French became close. Southern Lebanon, with its concentration of Shi'a and Druze communities, was not as affected by the commerical and cultural exchanges with France and Italy. However, during this time the various religious communities of Lebanon lived together in relative harmony. It is a period to which Lebanon's Christians often look back with favor.

It was during the reign of Bashir II (1788-1840), known as Bashir al Kabir (Bashir the Great), that relations with the West expanded most rapidly. In many ways a political genius, open-minded on matters of religion, often sensitive to his peoples' needs, other times cruel when political survival made oppression expedient, Bashir II both maintained a homeland for Christians in Lebanon and inadvertently sowed the seeds that led to the Druze massacre of the Christians in 1860.†

Taqiyyah or "dissimulation" is an acceptable practice among the Shi'a and Druze. It involves outwardly practicing the religion of the majority whenever it would be dangerous for one's self, one's family, or one's community to do otherwise.

†Bashir II's own religious life is somewhat of a mystery. He was born a Christian, married into a Muslim family, and was a practicing Druze. Hitti believes he was not a *believing* Druze, however.

Details of the reign of Bashir II, penultimate Shihab emir, have been treated adequately by a number of competent historians.[8] It will suffice here to point out that during Bashir's reign, Christians from other areas, most notably Syria, were attracted into Lebanon, settling principally in the Druze districts. With these new settlers came Christians from north Lebanon, who tended to settle in the Shuf area, the Druze heartland. These Christians were inclined to adopt relatively Western life styles and climbed ahead of their Druze counterparts socially and economically as a result of contacts with the West. This social change led to a number of problems between the Druze and the Christians, problems exacerbated by the Porte. Ironically, Bashir II's overthrow in 1840 came at the hands of a united Christian and Druze peasantry. The peasants revolted against excessive taxation, forced labor, and conscription, which came about as part of Bashir's alliance with Muhammed Ali of Egypt in the 1830s.

Despite the periodic upsurges in Lebanese Christian economic and social conditions, the general experience of all Christians under Ottoman rule was largely one of subservience to the Muslim majority; despite the benefits enjoyed by Lebanon's Christians as a result of the Ottoman policy towards religious minorities in general, and the situation of those living in Mount Lebanon in particular, the Christians of Lebanon resented being the vassals of any imperial power. They are particularly agitated by memories of the indignities heaped upon them under the Ottoman *millet* system. The *millet* system was designed to provide a relatively large level of autonomy for the minority religious communities, or *millets*, living under Muslim domination. In exchange for the payment of tribute, the minority religious communities were allowed freedom to worship and to govern themselves under their own laws and were represented by their leaders in Istanbul. Unfortunately, this system, which was never intended to provide the Christians or Jews with full rights as Ottoman citizens, also incorporated numerous unnecessary and humiliating restrictions towards the Christians and Jews which, when enforced, incurred lasting resentment from the *millets*. When these restrictions were enforced the Christians in Lebanon found, for example, that they were forbidden to ride horses, carry arms, or rebuild their churches and were required to pay extra taxes, all as reminders of their inferiority to their Ottoman rulers. The memory of these humiliations remains with their present-day descendants, having been passed and repeated in vivid terms from parent to child, and has played an important role in the psychology of Christian desires in and for Lebanon. The memories evoke fear and distrust of the Muslims and produce the determination never to permit others to rule the Christians again.

In 1842, the Porte officially ended Shihabi rule in Lebanon and established a new system which bisected Mount Lebanon into northern and southern districts using the Beirut-Damascus highway as the dividing line. The northern district was governed by a Christian *qam-maqam* (subgovernor), and the southern district was placed under a Druze subgovernor. Both subgovernors were directly responsible to the Wali of Sidon. Although Christians dominated the northern district, it still had a sizable Druze population. Similarly, the heavily Druze Shuf in the southern district held 8,000 Maronites. Disturbances between opposing religions became commonplace. In 1845 a major clash between Christians and Druze destroyed a number of villages belonging to both groups. In 1858-59 a Christian peasant uprising against their own feudal Christian leaders (the Khazins) in the north succeeded in relieving the feudal leaders of their land and influence. The success of their northern brethren whetted the southern Christian peasants' desire to free themselves of the Druze feudal overlordship. Druze leaders, however, were able to maintain the unity of the Druze peasants despite some unrest.* Furthermore, they had carefully marshalled support from Turkish authorities and Muslims in the area. By contrast, the Christians, lacking leadership and organization, were unprepared to face the Druze in armed conflict. Violence broke out initially in April 1860 in the Shuf and Metn areas. Occasional fighting soon escalated, much to the disadvantage of the Christians. By June, over 60 Christian villages had been destroyed. The larger towns were then attacked. On several occasions Christians surrendered their arms to Ottoman garrison commanders in order to accept their offers of asylum only to be massacred by the Druze under Ottoman eyes once thus disarmed.[9] By August, over 20,000 Christians had been killed in the mountains. In Damascus, repercussions of the Lebanese fighting resulted in the deaths of 11,000 more Christians.

The importance of the 1860 massacre in Lebanon's history—the massacre's effect upon the mentality of the Christians—cannot be overemphasized. The swift pace of the events, the extensive losses of life and property, and the collusion of the imperial authorities with

---

*Shortly before 1860 Druze peasants in some areas were revolting against their Druze landlords. However the Druze landlords were able to keep their coreligionist peasants united by appealing to a larger threat to the entire Druze community posed by the Christians. As a result, the peasant revolt of 1860 turned into a sectarian conflict, and all memories of peasant unity in the 1840 revolt were forgotten.

the petty local chieftains combined with other circumstances mentioned above to overpower the Christians completely. To this day many Lebanese Christians in general, and the Maronites in particular, feel that such an occurrence could be repeated if similar circumstances obtained. There is no question that the events of 1860 have made a permanent impression on the Christian mind.

It was the great powers that the Christians looked for protection. Finally, after over 30,000 had been killed, France, England, Austria, and Russia intervened, established a commission to punish those responsible (which it did only in a few cases), and set about devising a new system to govern Lebanon. The system they proposed was known as the Mutasarrifate. A Christian *Mutasarrife* (governor general) was to be appointed by the Ottoman sultan and approved by the four powers mentioned above and, after 1867, Italy. His jurisdiction extended over an area smaller than that governed earlier by the Ma'ns and Shihabs, for the intermountain plains and the land granting access to the sea were removed from his control. He was to have a council, composed of 12 representatives based upon the religious makeup of the area, to assist him in his duties. The territory was divided into seven districts, each with its own deputy-governor chosen by the dominant religious community in the district. Feudalism was formally brought to an end.

Although deprived of its most fertile land and its access to the sea, and having at best mediocre leadership during the entire Mutasarrife period, Lebanon enjoyed a good measure of success under the new formula.

> The surprising thing, as it turned out to be, is not only that the state survived till the first world war but that, thanks to the resourcefulness, industry, thrift and self-reliance of its citizens, it registered a record of prosperity, security, and progress that made it the envy of other provinces in the Ottoman Empire.[10]

The French Mandate

Ottoman sovereignty over Lebanon was brought to an end as a result of World War I, following which the area was transferred to French administration as a Class A territory under the League of Nations mandate system.[11] Lebanon and Syria were placed in the system with the alleged understanding that the area had "reached a stage of development where their existence as independent nations [could] be provisionally recognized subject to the rendering of administrative advice and assistance by a Mandatory until such time as they [were] able to stand alone."[12] However, the French (like other mandatory powers) proceeded to treat the area in essentially colonial terms.

An analysis of Lebanon under the mandate (1920-43) would focus on the very close ties that evolved between the French and the Lebanese, primarily the Christians. However, it would also reveal the limits to that relationship, for example, that the Christian Lebanese would not subvert their own interests as Lebanese citizens for the sake of the French. The mandate period also gave rise to the political framework for the modern Lebanese state, a framework so delicate yet so workable that the principles remained sacrosanct for over three decades as the foundation for balance in Lebanese society. The framework consisted of the Lebanese constitution and the unwritten national pact.

Several phenomena occurred under the mandate that led to the specific provisions incorporated in the constitution, which took effect in 1943, and the national covenant. The first important development was the expansion of Lebanon to include (along with the territory of the Mutasarrifate) Beirut and the Bekaa, Tripoli, Sidon, and Tyre regions. The inclusions of these areas, which (with the exception of Beirut) had predominantly Muslim populations, made Muslims a significant political factor and diminished the importance of the Druze. The second major development during the mandate period resulted from the nature of the territory's relations with France. French rule affected all areas of Lebanese life, often to the advantage of the Christians, particularly those Christians educated in the French and Roman Catholic schools. Businesses developed, and a Western-style middle class emerged. Third, a constitution— later superseded—was developed based on confessional representation. Although it did not set up ratios for confessional representation, the constitution did form the basis for the constitution of independent Lebanon.

The inclusion of the predominantly Muslim territory not only provided Lebanon with the human and territorial resources to function as an independent state; it also provided Lebanon with its major catalyst for political development. If Lebanon were to survive as a sovereign country, the Lebanese had to find a formula allowing the Christians, Muslims, and Druze to work together. The nature of this problem is best seen in light of the major political struggle between Lebanese during the mandate period, that between Emile Edde and Bishara al-Khuri.

Emile Edde, a Maronite from the predominantly Christian Jubayl district, French-educated, French in culture, "as much at home in

Paris as in Beirut,"[13] and far more proficient in French than in Arabic, typified the northern Maronite desire to maintain Lebanon as a Christian homeland. He held that Lebanon was part of the Mediterranean world of France rather than part of the Arab world. He had little appreciation for the significance of the Muslim population of Greater Lebanon. His views were of course quite welcome to the French, who desired to continue France's influence in the Middle East. Among the Lebanese, however, his only strong support was among the Christians and, in fact, among only some of them at that.[14]

Khuri, also a Maronite, was from the Jurd, a Druze region. Like Edde, he was French-educated. However, his cultural background remained Arab, and he excelled in the effective use of the rich Arabic tongue. He was also a great admirer of French culture, as was Edde, but insisted on the importance of finding a formula that would allow Muslim-Christian coexistence and cooperation. The Muslims in Lebanon feared that Lebanon's independence would cut them off from the Arab-Muslim world; they also rejected the idea of French political control.

> As a Maronite [Khuri] was devoted to the Lebanese entity; nevertheless, he could see that while an independent Lesser Lebanon stood little chance of survival, a Greater Lebanon could survive only through political and social partnership between Christians and Muslims. Like Edde, Khuri was no Arab nationalist, and he liked to think of Lebanon as part of a Mediterranean world. As a realist, however, he could not ignore the fact that his country was geographically inseparable from its Arabic-speaking surroundings. Consequently, he saw no wisdom in denouncing Arab nationalism but rather tried hard to come to terms with it.[15]

After years of bitter dispute, the tension between those advocating a Maronite-dominated Lebanon, personified by Emile Edde, and those, like Khuri, backing a Lebanon moderately associated with the Arab world of which it was geographically and linguistically a part, was resolved in favor of the latter group.

One reason for the victory of the second group was the disunity of the Muslims. The Shi'a, after initially appearing to back Arab nationalist claims calling for union of Lebanon with Syria, later backed the Constitutionalist Bloc led by Khuri, as they felt it was better to be a large minority in a small state than a smaller minority in a union with a predominantly Sunni nation. Nor were all the Sunnis in Lebanon completely behind the pan-Arabists. By the early 1940s some Sunni families who had become established in the forefront of Lebanese affairs advocated an independent Lebanon on the grounds of its unique national character. Some of these leaders perceived Lebanon's best interests as coming from a balance of its relations between the Arab states and the West. Many of these Sunni leaders were French-educated and did not feel as alienated from French culture as others of their sect. The leading family assuming this posture was the Sulh, led by the brothers Kazim, Taqi al-Din, and Riyad, who were largely responsible for formulating the details of the unwritten national pact.

A second reason Khuri's group realized its aims was that the Druze went the way of the Shi'a. The Druze, too, saw their best interests as a concentrated minority group in the relatively small state of Lebanon.

Another reason for the triumph of the Constitutionalist Bloc was the strong support of Christians of all denominations. It is true that the Syrian National Party (later the Syrian Social Nationalist Party, SSNP), the leading party advocating union with Syria, was dominated by Greek Orthodox and Protestants; however, those supporting the pan-Arabist stand hardly represented a majority of the members of their own sects, much less of Lebanon's Christian population. Moreover, unlike the Maronites, the Greek Orthodox and other denominations have significant numbers in other Arab countries who could be affected adversely by their respective Arab governments if these Lebanese sects were perceived to be taking an anti-Arab or at least an anti-pan-Arabist stand. Thus, some of the Christians' support for the pan-Arabist parties was half-hearted.*

As soon as the new government was formally installed, it began to negotiate with Jean Hellou, the French delegate-general, for an end to the mandate. When concessions from Hellou appeared to be very slow in coming, the Lebanese parliament met on November 8, 1943, and passed a number of constitutional amendments which deleted any reference to the mandate from the constitution, stressed Lebanon's sovereignty, and ended the status of French as the country's second language. Khuri immediately signed these amendments and had them published the next day.

Hellou, in a move that history can only regard as incredibly short-sighted and insensitive, had Khuri, Sulh, three cabinet members, and a Muslim deputy arrested and placed in prison. This action

---

*The same situation applies to some of the Christians fighting on the side of the predominantly Muslim groups in the Lebanese conflict. Some Lebanese families have found an interesting way to deal with problems of political-religious affiliations. The sons in a family will each join a different political party supported by one of the various religious groups. This way the family cannot be accused of partiality to any particular political-religious faction.

immediately united the Christians, Muslims, and Druze against the French. The result was a nationwide strike, the establishment of a new temporary government, adoption of a new flag, and the reaffirmation of parliamentary support for the new government (although parliament had been formally dissolved by the French). Hellou was recalled from his post and, on November 22, 1943, President Khuri and the others arrested with him were released from prison. The French mandate for all intents and purposes was at an end.[16]

THE CHRISTIANS' POLITICAL ROLE IN
INDEPENDENT LEBANON, 1943-75

After emerging triumphant over the French in 1943, Lebanon set a course of economic and foreign relations designed to ensure its stability in the Mediterranean area and in the world at large. The national pact, designed to provide adequate representation of Lebanon's major religious communities in the political system, and the Lebanese constitution were to guarantee that the country's affairs would not fall under the control of any one religious group.

The National Pact established a confessional political system.[17] By its terms, the Lebanese president was to be a Maronite, the prime minister a Sunni, and the speaker of the chamber of deputies (parliament) a Shi'a. Seats in the chamber of deputies were based on a six-to-five ratio of Christians to Muslims and Druze, as provided for in the Lebanese constitution. The national pact required that civil service appointments, as well, be made upon confessional lines. The basis for the ratios of confessional representation was Lebanon's last complete census, taken in 1932. No census has been completed since, largely to avoid disrupting the delicate balance of religious-political power.

Despite the divisions within Lebanon's Christian community, the apparent rapid growth of the country's non-Christian populations, and the appeal Egyptian President Nasser's pan-Arabism had among Lebanese Muslims, Christians, particularly the Maronites (but others, as well, notably members of the Greek Orthodox and Greek Catholic communities), gradually became the custodians of a disproportionate share of Lebanon's wealth and political power.

The Christians were able to outpace Lebanon's other religious communities in the race for political and economic strength for a variety of reasons. First, their close relations with the West generally, and France in particular, combined with the entrepreneurial traditions and commercial philosophies of Lebanese culture to produce a situation in which modernization in its most Western aspects was acceptable and indeed coveted, not suspect. In addition, the Christians took maximum advantage of Western educational institutions both in Lebanon and in Europe, recognized how to obtain maximum benefit from the position of national leadership in which they found themselves at the time of independence, organized effective political and paramilitary organizations bent on maintaining the status quo, optimally exploited governmental structures and processes favorable to Christian interests, played an instrumental role in establishing a service-based economy designed to take advantage of managerial and business skills belonging to the educated elite of Lebanon (largely, though not entirely, composed of Christians), and, almost paradoxically, did not attempt to dominate *completely* the country and its affairs. This last element is significant because the fact that the other communities did have a strong (although perhaps not strong enough) voice in planning Lebanon's course gave them, too, a real interest in the state.

Thus, Christian political domination of Lebanon has not been the result of a conspiracy. In fact, many Lebanese Christians, regardless of their denominational affiliation, are much less concerned with politics than they are with day-to-day survival. Many of them live in religiously mixed villages, are of the same economic status as the poorest elements of the non-Christian communities, and are much more tied to family loyalties than they are to the Lebanese state.[18] Rather, actions that have tended to increase Christian political power and economic security have been as much reactionary as planned and have often been undertaken with the poor in mind as well as or rather than the rich. Many also have been taken with the sake of the state of Lebanon in mind, if only to ensure Lebanon's survival as a Christian homeland in the Middle East. The political role of Lebanon's Christians up to the start of the civil war can best be described by an analysis of the Christian-led political parties, their leaders, support, and policies.

After 1958, with the formation of the Parti National Libéral (PNL) of Camille Chamoun, there were in Lebanon three active and influential Christian political parties, often vying with one another, whose leaders or families are still playing active roles today.

Before going on to discuss these individuals, families, and parties, mention must be made of the Lebanese Crisis of 1958, as it brings to light the nature of the confessional struggles in Lebanon which contributed in no small part to the civil war. The historical details of the crisis have been clearly set forth by K. S. Salibi, Phillip Hitti, and even by its most important participant, Camille Chamoun, in his book *Crise au Moyen-Orient.*[19] Here we will mention the most important events, political trends, and concepts that led to the invasion of Lebanon by U.S. Marines on July 15, 1958, and the significance of the crisis in Lebanon's political development.

By the start of 1958, Lebanese President Camille Chamoun's last year in office, Camille Chamoun had succeeded in aligning a wide range of Druze and Muslim leaders against him, very much as a result of his own desire to remain more powerful than they. Coalition formation against a president is hardly an unusual occurrence in parliamentary politics, and often it leads to a democratic change in government. However, other factors were at work which virtually polarized Lebanon along sectarian lines. These developments created an atmosphere in which violence became increasingly prominent in and common to political issues. The two most important elements in this volatile mixture were the popularity of Egyptian President Abd al-Nasser's pan-Arabism and Camille Chamoun's desire to amend the constitution to allow him to succeed himself as president.

After consolidating his power in Egypt in 1954, Nasser slowly emerged as the leading political figure in the Arab world, based upon his pan-Arabist policies. Soon, leading Lebanese Muslim politicians, such as Rashid Karami and Sa'ib Salam, had drifted into Nasser's camp. Nasserite propaganda spread throughout Lebanon posing as an only slightly veiled threat to the Chamoun regime. After the Suez War in November 1956, Chamoun was pressured to end diplomatic relations with Britain and France, the two European countries intervening in the Canal area. Not only did Chamoun categorically reject this idea, he filled the cabinet posts of those who then resigned from his government with pro-Western politicians. Most significantly he placed the staunchly pro-Western Charles Malik as minister of foreign affairs.

Meanwhile, Nasser was beginning to make overtures to communist powers. Chamoun countered Nasser's efforts immediately by courting the United States for its aid against real and imagined Egyptian insurgents. In 1957 Chamoun accepted the Eisenhower Doctrine, thus virtually isolating himself from his internal opposition and almost leading to a break in relations with Egypt.

Within Lebanon, Chamoun's actions as president were further scandalized in the eyes of the opposition when opposition leaders became convinced that Chamoun intended to succeed himself as president. Sunni, Shi'a, and Druze leaders organized an opposition National Front to run against Chamoun's supporters in the next parliamentary elections. However, Chamoun had the backing of the Kataib, the National Bloc, the SSNP, and his own large personal following, and he crushed the oppositions in the summer elections. That the vast majority of Lebanon's Christians united behind Chamoun for this election reflected the widespread Christian concern about and distaste for pan-Arabism, Nasser, and the increasing tendency of some Arab leaders to move toward the socialist countries. Oddly enough, the defeat of the National Front at the polls, which left a number of its leaders without seats in the chamber of deputies, contributed to the situation precipitating the call for U.S. intervention. Their efforts to bring about change in the governmental process frustrated, some National Front leaders adopted violence as a means of expression. In Druze districts, Jumblatt supporters began to blow up roads and bridges. Bombs exploded in Beirut on a regular basis, and other acts of violence sprang up intermittently throughout the country.

Before long the Lebanese government began to lose control over its functions, while arms were imported to the rebels from abroad. The army, under General Foad Shihab, would not crush the rebellion but would merely contain it, on the premise that its role was to maintain order and not to serve as a bulwark for any particular government. By mid-summer the threat from the Druze and Muslims appeared, at least on the surface, to have become serious. Then, on July 14, a revolution in Iraq replaced the pro-Western Hashemite monarchy with a regime which propounded pro-Egyptian themes in radical rhetoric. Chamoun then notified the United States that unless he received U.S. military assistance within 48 hours, his regime would be overthrown by outside forces if not by forces from within Lebanon. U.S. Marines landed the next day.

Apparently as early as the first week of June, Chamoun had decided not to try to succeed himself. In the aftermath of the U.S. landing, most political elements on both sides determined that Shihab would be the most logical choice as the next president. His stand during the crisis appealed to the Muslims, and although many Christians had reservations over his conservative stance they also understood the army's precarious situation. On July 31, 1958, he was elected president of the chamber of deputies and assumed office on September 23, according to the constitution.

The 1958 crisis foreshadowed events in Lebanon in the mid-1970s. Although virtually all the Muslims as well as many Christians feel that Chamoun substantially overplayed his hand by setting a precedent for external intervention in Lebanese affairs, Chamoun's actions came as no surprise to those familiar with the Christian ethos in Lebanon. Christian memories of the Ottoman Empire, of the Druze Massacre, and of having become pawns in international power struggles make them extremely wary of pan-Arab and pan-Islamic movements.

After leaving office, Chamoun formed his own political party (discussed below), and has kept himself (now joined by his sons Dory and Danny) in the forefront of Lebanese politics. The Christian mentality of 1958 was little different than that of 1975 or of the present and therefore provides an introduction to our discussion of Christian political roles in Lebanon before the civil war.

The Phalange

When Fuad Shihab assumed the presidency in 1958, Christian political power was in the hands of four groups: the Phalange Party (al-Hizb al-Kata'ib), the PNL, the National Bloc, and a coalition of influential Christians under Shihab himself.

The Phalange Party, organized as a paramilitary organization along Spanish, Italian, and German lines in 1936, by the Maronite, Pierre Gemayel, had become a political party in 1949, although it maintained its own militia. For most of its existence the Phalange has not been a cadre-type institution, unlike other Lebanese parties. Adopting a social democratic program, well organized with a tight party structure, the Phalange appealed to uprooted Maronites in major cities whose parochial affiliations had waned, to ambitious Christians who saw it as an avenue for political advancement, as well as to Christians from Gemayel's home town, Bikfiyya. Although certainly pro-Christian, the party advocated "Lebanon first," as opposed to other loyalties, be they tribal, religious, or pan-Arab. Phalangist attitudes were to change considerably in the 1970s, but during the 1950s and 1960s the party maintained a nationalist character.

The Phalangists became strong supporters of Fuad Shihab, whose presidency—although marred by corruption and its reliance on the deuxième bureau (army intelligence) to maintain order—was popular among Sunnis, Shi'as, and Druze due to its Arab nationalist rhetoric and its de-emphasis of Maronite exclusivity.

The policies of Shihab, which came to be known as the Nahj (method), were continued during the presidency of Charles Hilu (1964-70). The Phalange remained the only major organized Christian political party supporting the Nahj. From 1958 to 1968, the Phalangists were at odds with the Nationalist Bloc and the PNL. Events after 1968 were to change the role of the Phalange in Lebanese political life considerably. We shall turn to these after discussing the other major Christian groups.

Parti National Libéral

Soon after leaving the presidency in 1958, Camille Chamoun formed his own political party, the Parti National Libéral (PNL). The PNL, lacking the tight organization of the Phalange, represented a loose grouping of political leaders from many religious communities, including representatives of the Sunnis and Shi'as. The PNL has always been more of a cadre-type party, grouped around Chamoun (and now his sons as well), with little direct control over its many followers.

> Nevertheless, the PNL emerged after 1958 as the unrivalled representative of the Christian ethos in Lebanon. Its support came from all social levels, and from every part of the country. Christians, villagers from the mountian regions and the Bekaa, leading bankers and businessmen and small merchants, contractors and brokers, clergymen and monks of every Christian sect, and slum dwellers in the humblest quarters of Beirut and its suburbs, were all "Shamunist" by sentiment, unless they happened to be recruited by the Kataib party.[20]

The PNL stood in opposition to the *Nahj* and played an instrumental role in aligning members of parliament against *Nahj* presidents, culminating in the 1970 election of Suleiman Franjieh. Forming its own militia in the late 1960s, the PNL played a major role on the Christian side in the Lebanese civil war.

The National Bloc

The third major Christian party, which plays a smaller role today than in the 1960s, is the National Bloc, originally led by Emile Edde. Leadership of the bloc passed to Edde's eldest son, Raymond, who along with his younger brother, Pierre, brought the party back into the forefront of Lebanese affairs in the 1950s. Their appeal, largely among Maronites and the Greek Orthodox, was based less on the old bloc's anti-pan-Arabism than on an opposition to the militancy of the Shihabists. The National Bloc combined the Christian desire for a secure homeland with opposition to Shihab policies, without becoming completely unpalatable to the Muslim population in Lebanon. In fact, the National Bloc under Raymond Edde's leadership had much in common with the Kata'ib ideology of a Lebanese state that in theory tried to place religion outside of politics. Edde "was essentially a liberal of the Jeffersonian school, and a firm believer in open parliamentary politics."[21] His liberal attitudes made it impossible for him to accept the militancy of the *Nahj* and the Phalangists; nor could he accept the role Shihab gave to the *deuxième bureau*.

In 1968 the National Bloc, the PNL, and the Phalange united into a Christian coalition which they called *al-Hilf al-Thulathi* (the Triple Alliance), a union which typifies the working of Christian politics as the national level. The issue central to unification was the question of the freedom of action of Palestinian refugees in Lebanon, especially regarding Palestinian raids against Israel. The formation of the Palestine Liberation Organization (PLO) in 1964, its militant character, the support it received from Arab governments, and the influx of Palestinian refugees into Lebanon after the June 1967 conflict (which increased the size of the Lebanese Palestinian population to 400,000) aroused fears among Lebanese Christian leaders over Lebanon's security, stability, and sovereignty. The dilemma the Palestinians posed affected the very core of the Lebanese state—confessionalism—and presented Lebanon with a "state within a state," as the Christians often described the Palestinian presence. Lebanon, unlike other Arab states, was not in a position to offer the Palestinians entry into the country's political process, as such a change would upset the Christian-Muslim balance (the great majority of the Palestinians being Sunnis). Furthermore, Palestinian raids into Israel brought Israeli reprisals, not just on staging areas, but on the refugee camps and on Lebanese civilians, as well. Lebanon's small army, though well trained, could not control the entire Lebanon-Israel border region unless it had the authority and the equipment to engage Palestinian forces. Yet, such a confrontation would have ramified significantly both on Lebanon's relations with the Arab world and on the understanding that formed the basis of the country's confessional system. Practically, it might have split the army along Christian-Muslim lines, a split which did in fact occur later. Many Christians suspected that the Palestinian presence in Lebanon was being used by radicals (Communists, the Ba'th, and others) to sabotage the Lebanese system.[22] Many also believed that the Palestinian cause was supported by Muslim Lebanese in order to advance their own interests in Lebanon at the expense of the Christians.[23]

Thus, the *Hilf*, organized before the 1968 parliamentary elections, stood out in opposition to the *Nahj* and radicalism in the Arab world. The Phalange joined the *Hilf* rather than face losses at the polls. However, the Phalangists were becoming concerned about the future of Lebanon's Christians. The election of 1968 resulted in large gains for the *Hilf* coalition, and while the *Nahj* maintained a majority in parliament, a number of its key supporters were removed.

The Maronite Church

Before proceeding to Lebanese politics on the national level, mention must be made of the Maronite Church's role in Lebanese society. From birth to death the Maronite Church plays a significant part in a Maronite's life. It baptizes him, marries him (one does not marry outside one's own sect), and buries him. It also grabs at least some of his attention during Sunday sermons, provides him with his cultural identity, and can provide a helping hand in times of trouble. The church reinforces and deepens the political socialization the young receive at home, recalling the lessons of the past, commiserating over present problems, and providing guidance for the future based upon a clear-cut sense of cultural uniqueness first developed in the home but nurtured and further refined through the far-reaching activities and interests of the church. Moreover, the church has close ties to upper-class Maronites. Its bishops come from the leading Maronite families and hold a great deal of wealth. The church owns, for example, 30 to 40 percent of the most fertile Lebanese land.

The church's influence on Maronite life makes the Maronite patriarch an often-courted figure of Lebanese politicians. The church serves as a vehicle for political mobilization and recruitment for the Christian-dominated parties. In fact, during the civil war, the church played a role in unifying the Christians, recruiting for the militias, and disseminating propaganda; its monasteries and churches were even used to store weapons and ammunition and house militiamen.

National Politics

The Christian role in the pre-civil war Lebanese political process permeates all phases of Lebanese political activity. The election of presidents, formation of cabinets, makeup and strength of the chamber of deputies, structure of the army, and foreign and domestic policy formation all involve substantial input from, and often control by, Christian politicians. The presidential election of 1970 illustrates the powerful Christian role in Lebanese affairs on the national level.

In the spring of 1970, a few months before the chamber of deputies was to elect a new president, any one of five Maronite leaders had a reasonable chance to be elected: Fuad Shihab, Pierre

Gemayel, Camille Chamoun, Raymond Edde, and Suleiman Franjieh. The final election of Franjieh in August was the result of seemingly endless secret negotiations among the Christian, Muslim, and Druze political leaders.

Shihab had announced he would not run, leaving the door open for Gemayel who had harbored presidential ambitions for years. Gemayel had a history of not giving in to extreme Palestinian wishes but had also agreed to abide by the 1969 Cairo Accords, which allowed a large degree of Palestinian autonomy in Lebanon.[24] His combination of commitment to the Palestinian cause, on the one hand, and sense of moderation regarding Palestinian movement within Lebanon, on the other, enhanced Gemayel's appeal to many Christians and Muslims. However, the leaders of the *Hilf* coalition, who had political ambitions of their own, did not completely agree with Gemayel's position regarding the Palestinians. They would only give Gemayel their support if he could also enlist the backing of the *Nahj*. The *Nahj*, despite its good relations with the Phalange, sought to run a candidate from its own ranks. The *Hilf* then refused to back Gemayel and began to consider the alternatives.

Neither Chamoun nor Edde was acceptable to the Muslims. Chamoun's activities in 1958 were too well remembered. Nor did the Muslims and Druze forget the former stands of the National Bloc under Raymond Edde's father. The only suitable alternative was Suleiman Franjieh, a strong Maronite from north Lebanon who enjoyed good relations with the Muslims, both Sunnis and Shi'as. The reasons Franjieh was suitable to the *Hilf* demonstrate the ephemeral character of political alignments in Lebanese national politics.

In the 1950s, Franjieh had been at odds with then-President Chamoun. For a while he even fled to Syria as a result of the dispute. When he returned he adopted a Nasserite stand, allying himself with pro-Nasser Muslims in the 1958 crisis. However, during the Shihab regime the Franjieh clan was neglected while favor was shown to Franjieh's Muslim allies. The family soon became anti-Shihabist, reconciled itself with Chamoun, formed another anti-Shihabist coalition called the Central Bloc with conservative Muslim leaders in 1969, and thus became an ally of the *Hilf*. Franjieh was acceptable to the Muslims because of his pro-Nasser stands and acceptable to the Christians because of his determination to limit Palestinian freedom of movement in Lebanon. The *Hilf* and the Central Bloc chose Franjieh as the anti-Shihabist candidate with the most likely chance of winning.

That a man such as Suleiman Franjieh was chosen by the *Hilf* and Central Bloc as their candidate reflects some of the limits of Lebanon's confessional system. Franjieh was certainly tough, a loyal Maronite who had the wisdom to enlist Muslim support, at least temporarily, but he was not a highly skilled politician who could formulate, develop, and guide national policies over the long term. He was not viewed by many Lebanese (Muslim or Christian) as a national leader. Once the civil war began, cries for his resignation were heard daily on the radio and appeared constantly in the newspapers.

When Shihab announced just before the elections that he would not run, the *Nahj* had to scramble to find an acceptable candidate. They settled on Elias Sarkis, a man whose integrity and talents were undisputed. However, the facts that Sarkis was a bureaucrat, not a politician, and that he disliked petty political maneuvering separated him from many members of parliament.

In spite of the diminishing appeal of the *Nahj*, the absence of a prominent politician to carry its banner, and the unity of the strong opposition it faced in the election, Suleiman Franjieh was elected president by a margin of only one vote in the last fully independent election Lebanon was to have until the present.

Local Politics

The success of a Christian politician on the local level is based on his family name, his party affiliation (if any), his stands on issues of local and national interest, but most of all on his ability to enlist the support of prominent politicians who can exert their influence in getting the local populations to vote for the "right" candidate.

District representation in the chamber of deputies is based upon population and its confessional composition. Each sect within the district is represented by one or more of its members depending upon the number of the sect's adherents in that district. A successful politician must first get his name on the electoral list. In this connection, he needs the assistance of the most influential man or men of his district. He must trade political favors. To win the election he must also obtain the support of one or more of the leading politicians in the country. For example, a Maronite running for office in a district heavily populated by supporters of Camille Chamoun would have to contact Chamoun and make the proper political agreements. He could, for example, offer to join Chamoun's PNL and to vote along PNL lines in exchange for Chamoun's public and financial support. After getting his name on the list and acquiring the necessary backing, the candidate begins his campaign based largely on issues of local concern as he is elected by the entire population of his district regardless of their religous affiliations.

Confessionalism also transcends national and local politics, appearing in many aspects of Lebanese daily life. Commercial licenses, jobs, and tax and business privileges, for example, are often secured through contacts within the government who share the same confessional affiliation as the person seeking such benefits. A typical example is that of a Greek Orthodox restaurant owner in Beirut who wanted to obtain a liquor license but wanted to avoid the often endless bureaucratic red tape. He went to a local Greek Orthodox official to whom he explained his "good standing" in the church and articulated the importance of maintaining the license for this area in the hands of one of the church's brethren. The official made several phone calls with the practical result of securing the license for the Greek Orthodox applicant and denying it to a previous applicant outside the faith. Commerce, like politics, follows the church.

It is precisely this close feeling within the confessional ranks that gives Lebanon its unique combination of Eastern and Western life styles and philosophies—social, commercial, and political. It is, however, also due in large part to the confessional way of life that Lebanese society broke down over the Palestinian presence.

Mobilization and Recruitment

Since Lebanon is a very small state, local and national politics are closely related. However, Lebanon's Christian political parties, unlike the political parties of many other democratic nations relatively small in size, are not tightly organized political machines. News travels quickly, and through word of mouth and the media local politicians are easily kept informed of events and of actions they are to take. Mobilization and recruitment are usually informal matters often accomplished quietly and behind the scenes. National leaders contact their political supporters privately to discuss issues on which action is to be taken. The masses learn of decisions through national media, party organs, the churches, and word of mouth.

Before the civil war began in April 1975, political mobilization and recruitment usually involved only those Christians who were at least moderately well off and thus had a reason to support the status quo. However, not long after the civil war began, many Lebanese Christians saw the major issue as Christian survival. Suddenly enlistments in the militias skyrocketed as Christian elements in the media worked with the major parties and churches to recruit fighters for the Christian side. As more and more Christians saw the civil war becoming a threat to their existence in Lebanon, the poor elements of Lebanese Christian society began to take an active role in the conflict. "Survival" became the biggest mobilizing factor on the Christian side. Whereas before the conflict recruitment and mobilization were effected on the basis of helping to maintain the status quo and were done under the guises of abstruse political ideas, the issue had become focused on the future of all Christians in Lebanon. Of course, not all Lebanese Christians actively supported the Christian side in the conflict. Many fled the major cities to live with extended family members in the mountains. However, many of those who did seek refuge from the fighting were at least sympathetic to the Christian side.

The Christians and Lebanon's Civil War

The Christian role in the Lebanese civil war has been discussed in numberous newspaper articles, journals, books and newscasts.[25] The role is complicated, sometimes even incomprehensible, and has been discussed from points of view ranging from pro-Palestinian to positions little different from those of the staunchest Israelis. Christian actions in the Lebanese civil war can best be understood, however, from Christian perspectives. Comprehension and analysis of Christian behavior can only be achieved through an understanding of Lebanese Christian attitudes concerning their place in Lebanon and in the Arab world. Lebanon's Christian communities are by no means of one mind in their actions or perceptions, as we have seen. However, the convergence of their interests and attitudes often outweighs the divergences.

During the first half of this decade, tensions within Lebanese society were building around the Palestinian presence in the country while the Palestinians continued to carry out raids against Israel from Lebanese territory. Israel often retaliated swiftly and severely, punishing not only Palestinians but Lebanese citizens as well. The Christian call for the Lebanese Army to curb Palestinian operations, personified in Lebanon's president, Suleiman Franjieh, was effectively countered by Sunni Prime Minister Rashid Karami. Karami, as prime minister, was the constitutional head of the armed forces; it would have been political suicide for him to allow the Christian-dominated army to attack the Palestinians, who were very popular with his own constituency.

The Maronites have tended to be the most militant of Lebanon's Christians regarding the civil war in general and the Palestinians in particular. An overwhelming drive among Lebanon's Maronite leaders and their supporters has been to maintain Lebanon as a haven for the Maronite faith and, more generally, for Christianity. Their biggest fear is being swallowed in a wave of pan-Arabism and becoming once more a tiny minority in an Islamic environment. Although Maronite leaders have taken different paths to help maintain the status quo, from the highly exclusionist National Bloc under Emile Edde to the "Lebanese Nationalism" of Pierre Gemayel and his Phalange Party, the desire for a safe home for the Maronites in the Arab world has been shared by them all. Not surprisingly, it was the Maronites who refused to allow the Palestinians to keep the relatively free reign they had developed in Lebanon, a refusal which led to the civil war.

The first major Christian militia to become involved in the fighting that later developed into widespread civil war belonged to the Maronite dominated Kataib or Phalange Party. The Phalange Party, the largest and best organized of the predominantly Maronite parties, is also the Christian political party most widely discussed in the literature.[26] The Phalange theme is a Lebanon in which religious and family loyalties play second fiddle to loyalty to the state of Lebanon itself. Pan-Arabism, says Pierre Gemayel, is little more than a euphemism for pan-Islamism, which if implemented in the fertile crescent would threaten the life style and culture of Lebanon's Christians.[27] The Phalange appeal to Lebanese nationalism also attracted well-to-do members of other Christian communities as well as some elite among the Sunni Muslims who did not desire to see Lebanon swallowed up by another Arab country.

The second major Christian militia to become involved in the fighting were the "Tigers" of Camille Chamoun's largely Maronite PNL. While the ideology of the PNL is little different from that of the Phalange, in practice the PNL represents the Maronite desire to maintain itself as the dominant force in Lebanese politics. When it became apparent by the end of the summer of 1975 that the Sunnis, Shi'as, and Druze from the lower classes were supporting the Palestinians cause in an effort to change the prescriptions of the National Pact; that these groups were receiving Palestinian and other foreign support; and that they were sincerely committed to change, Chamoun's militia entered the battle in full force on the side of the Phalangists. By then, in many Christian eyes, most certainly in the eyes of the Maronites, the issue had become Christian survival. Enlistments in the militias skyrocketed, while at the same time the Christian leaders did everything in their power to have the

Christian-dominated army brought into the conflict, hoping it would come in on their side. However, the president and the prime minister were deadlocked on the issue of using the army to intervene, and the army disintegrated along sectarian lines in the early months of 1976. By June 1, 1976, Lebanon no longer had a national army.

The concept of Christian "survival" can hardly be overemphasized in discussing the civil war, but it does need to be explained. The Christians were not worried they would literally be massacred on a national scale if they lost the civil war (although there were fears of retaliatory massacres on a smaller scale); nor were they afraid they would be exiled from Lebanon. The Christians did feel that they were in danger of losing the independent life they led under the constitution and National Pact, that they would be overwhelmed by ideologies which would once again render them at best second-class citizens and would threaten their ties with the West, which had in the past provided them with countless opportunities for vertical social, economic, and political mobility.

From the Muslim and Druze point of view, the conflict had the potential of becoming a vehicle for political, social, and economic changes in the country, changes which would allow them to share more equally the benefits of Lebanese prosperity. Many rallied to the side of the Palestinians as the Palestinians were strong, well organized, and could tip the balance in the conflict in their favor. They also rallied to the side of the Palestinians for ideological reasons, many of the poorer elements of Lebanese society having long supported the Palestinian cause.

Lebanon's non-Maronite Christians were caught between the opposing forces. The larger groups, such as the Greek Orthodox and Greek Catholics, had long contributed members to political parties on all sides of the conflict. Many Greek Orthodox, for example, are to be found in the Peoples' Socialist Party (PSP) established by the late Druze leader, Kamal Jumblatt. Since many Greek Orthodox did not share in the Christian prosperity, and since there was a large Greek Orthodox population in neighboring Syria (of which Lebanon was once a part), a significant number of Greek Orthodox adopted pan-Arabist stands, citing racial, historical, and linguistic ties of all Arabs and stressing Lebanon's ties with Syria.[28] The case for the Greek Catholics is similar.

For the most part, the non-Maronite Christian denominations in Lebanon played a sort of schizophrenic role during the civil war. In fact, the Greek Orthodox and the Greek Catholics typify the experience of the non-Maronite Christian communities. Unlike the Maronites both groups have substantial coreligionists in other Arab states, people who could suffer the consequences of unwise actions on the part of their coreligionists in Lebanon. An uprising of united Greek Orthodox or Greek Catholics or both, for example, against the Palestinians or Muslim parties would certainly have repercussions for their communities in other Arab countries. Furthermore, although the Lebanese political system did offer advantages for non-Maronite Christians, these smaller Christian groups were not satisfied completely with the role allotted to them in the Maronite-dominated system. This was particularly the case among the poorer elements of these communities, who sometimes felt more attachment to lower-class Sunnis, Shi'as, and Druze than to the more privileged members of their own communities.

Of course, other members of these two relatively large Christian communities had strong stakes in the status quo, were extremely cynical about any type of pan-Arabist claims, and enjoyed the freedom of Christians in Lebanese society. These people supported and often fought alongside the Maronites. The other smaller Christian communities often were divided similarly in their associations with the various groups in the civil war.

As the war dragged on into the summer of 1976, the Maronites became increasingly determined to eliminate the single biggest threat to their security, the Palestinians. Realizing that they did not have the strength to run the Palestinians out of Lebanon and that the Palestinians had nowhere else to go, the Christians carved out an area surrounding the Christian heartland in the north from which they expelled as many of the Palestinians as possible. The most notable effort in that regard was the capture of the Palestian refugee camp of Tel Zaatar in August 1976. After the camp had been taken and its inhabitants evacuated, the shantytown was completely razed so that the Palestinians could never return.

With the Christian heartland securely carved out of Greater Lebanon, the Christians have hoped to remain strong enough to keep themselves from having to submit to Muslim and Palestinian demands. If circumstances warranted, they conceivably could call for a separate Christian state. With radicalized Shi'as, Sunnis, Druze, and Palestinians united against them, the Maronites felt trapped in a corner. If they conceded to opposition demands their influence in Lebanon would certainly be reduced, other potentially subversive elements such as the Ba'th and the Communist Party would be strengthened, and the Palestinians would have virtually free reign. When the Syrians shifted their support and began to aid the Maronites' opponents, the Christian feeling of isolation itensified.

The Christians and Lebanon's Future

The Lebanese conflict, at first an internal affair involving the Lebanese and Palestinians living in Lebanon, soon engulfed the entire country, led to outside intervention by Syria and Israel on an ever increasing scale, and has left real control in Lebanon in the hands of outsiders. The Lebanese civil war has become a war by proxy between Israel and its Arab opponents, most notably Syria and the Palestinians. The government is virtually paralyzed, and order in the country is maintained by the various militias or foreign troops which occupy different sections of the country.[29] Political decisions of importance are made only ostensibly by the Lebanese government. The real "domestic" decisions come during discussions between Lebanese, Palestinian, Syrian, and other Arab leaders and then are formalized through Lebanon's executive or legislative channels.

The Maronites in control of the Christian heartland currently seek a federal or even confederal framework for all of Lebanon. Some actually favor a partition of Lebanon into Christian and Muslim states. There is a consensus among Christian leaders of all sects on the Palestinian question if on no other. A solution to Lebanon's problems must be found that does not include the Palestinians as an integral part of Lebanon. As far as the Christians are concerned, the Palestinians must behave as any foreigners would in another country—or leave. When asked recently what should be done with the several hundred thousand Palestinians in Lebanon, an influential Maronite recently responded, in an observation characteristic of Maronite leaders, "I don't know, it's not our problem, it is a problem for the Arabs to solve." He went on to say that he saw no way the Lebanese could solve the problem. The Arab world, which had for so long supported the Palestinian cause, must find a place for the Palestinians outside Lebanon.

At this moment the Christians, heavily armed and as determined as ever, await further developments, especially in regard to the recent peace agreement between Egypt and Israel. Although the Christians are determined to end the Syrian presence in Lebanon and to neutralize the effect of the Palestinians upon Lebanese affairs, the Christians are willing to wait in their fortresses until the world takes notice of their situation and takes effective action to resolve their problems.

Without outside military support, the Christians cannot achieve military success over their opponents, whether their opponents be Syrians on the one hand, or Palestinians and Lebanese Muslims and Druzes. Much has been said about the arms and training the Christians have received and continue to receive (primarily from Israel), which at best only provide the Christians with the ability to keep their opponents at bay. A military victory for the Christians can come about only by direct Israeli involvement in the conflict, an involvement the Israelis are not eager to find themselves dragged into at this time.

Until a reasonable political solution can be found, or until the Christians receive sufficient outside military support, they will bide their time and build up their inventories of food and munitions.

The military stalemate suggests at least two political conclusions, however. The Christians *have* been able to forge a foundation for themselves in the Arab world. Their determined resistance—or the aggressiveness with which they pursued their convictions—first established a Christian dominance in Lebanon and now has infused that political reality with military force. Yet, the use of force by minorities, though perhaps tactically necessary, has grave implications. For, as even the Christians of Lebanon recognize, the militancy of their position in recent years has engendered a new distance between the Arab world and self-concept and their own. The idea of a pluralistic Lebanon is further from realization than ever before, and the enmities and distrust to which the conflict have given rise will not soon dissipate. Given the long-established differences in patterns of Christian and Muslim emigration and demography, it is not at all clear that today's military victories are other than Pyrrhic, especially in terms of the fundamental Christian objectives. Sadly, neither is it clear, given those objectives, that the Christians had any viable alternatives in the face of what they perceive to be clear and proximate threats to their survival.

NOTES

1. Harvey H. Smith, et al., *Area Handbook for Lebanon*, (Washington, D.C.: The American University Foreign Area Studies Division, 1969), p. 124

2. See Sami N. Makarim, *The Druze Faith*, (Delmar, N.Y.: Caravan Books, 1974); and Selim H. Hichi, *La Communauté druze* (Beirut: s.n., 1973), for discussions of the Druze faith.

3. For historical discussions of Lebanon, see Phillip K. Hitti, *Lebanon in History: From the Earliest Times to the Present* (New York: St. Martin's, 1967); and *A Short History of Lebanon* (New York: St. Martin's, 1965); Adil Ismail, *Lebanon: A History of a People* (Beirut: Dar al-Makchouf, 1972); and Kamal S. Salibi, *The Modern History of Lebanon* (New York: Praeger, 1966).

4. After the trinitarian controversy was settled at the Council of Constantinople in 381 A.D., attention was focused on the nature of Jesus Christ. The Monophysites in general disclaimed that Jesus had two distinct natures, one human, one divine,

arguing instead that the two natures had been blended into one. Extreme forms of Monophysitism held that Christ's human nature was totally absorbed by his divinity. The controversy was settled in 451 at the Council of Chalcedon in favor of those advocating a Christology that held Jesus as "truly God and truly man, the same of a rational soul and body, consubstantial with the Father in Godhead, and the same consubstantial with us in manhood." Although possessing two natures, Christ remains "without division, without separation."

The Maronites are often quick to point out that there is no historical proof that their Maronite ancestors of the fourth and fifth centuries ever adhered to the heretical Monophysite position. If ever adopted by the Maronites, Monophysitism has been abandoned by them since at least the sixth century.

For a discussion of the Christological controversies of early Christianity, see J.N.D. Kelly, *Early Christian Doctrines* (New York: Harper & Row, 1960), pp. 280-343.

5. Hitti, *A Short History*, p. 91.

6. See footnote 3. Also see Iliya F. Harik, *Politics and Change in Traditional Society: Lebanon 1711-1845* (Princeton: Princeton University Press, 1968).

7. Hitti, *A Short History*, p. 170.

8. Salibi's account in *The Modern History* is the most concise in English.

9. Hitti, *A Short History*, p. 194.

10. *Ibid.*, p. 197. Lebanon was not without economic difficulties during this period, as the entire Ottoman Empire was in financial straits. As a result, an exodus of Lebanese began during the *Mutasarrifate* and continues to the present day.

11. On the institutions of the mandate system, see H. Duncan Hall, *Mandates, Dependencies and Trusteeships* (Washington, D.C.: Carnegie Endowment for International Peace, 1948); R.N. Chowduri, *International Mandates and Trusteeship Systems* (The Hague: Martinus Nyhoff, 1955); and Quincy Wright, *Mandates Under the League of Nations* (Chicago: University of Chicago, 1930). Although the fifth of Woodrow Wilson's "Fourteen Points" had generated substantial anti-colonial support, especially in the United Kingdom and the United States, there was little real support for independence of former central powers' territory within the Paris peace conference. Secret agreements on allocations of the territories had already been made. Conference rivalries reflected less a competition over the disposition of specific territories than domestic, international, and British Empire disagreements over the framework within which the dispositions should be institutionalized. Credit for submitting the first formal proposal concerning the mandate approach is given to Jan Christian Smuts, prime minister of the Union of South Africa. See Ernst B. Haas, "The Reconciliation of Conflicting Colonial Policy Aims: Acceptance of the League of Nations Mandate System," *International Organization* 6, no. 4 (November 1952): 521-36; Seth P. Tillman, *Anglo-American Relations and the Paris Peace Conference of 1919* (Princeton: Princeton University Press, 1961); and Jan Christian Smuts, *The League of Nations: A Practical Suggestion* (New York and London: Hodder and Stoughton, 1918).

12. Article 22 (4) of the League of Nations Covenant.

13. Salibi, *The Modern History*, p. 172.

14. *Ibid.*, pp. 172-73.

15. *Ibid.*, p. 173.

16. Salibi, *The Modern History*, p. 190.

17. For discussions of pluralism in Lebanese society, see Michael C. Hudson, *The Precarious Republic* (New York: Random House, 1968); "A Case of Political Underdevelopment," *Journal of Politics* 29, no. 4 (November 1967); 821-37; and "The Lebanese Crisis: the Limits of Consociational Democracy," *Journal of Palestine Studies* 5, no. 3-4 (Spring-Summer 1976); 109-22. Also see Enver M. Koury, *The Operational Capability*

of the Lebanese Political System (Beirut: Catholic Press, 1972); and The Crisis in the Lebanese System (Washington, D.C.: American Enterprise Institute for Public Policy Research, 1976); Halim Barakat, "Social and Political Integration in Lebanon: A Case of Social Mosaic," Middle East Journal 27, no. 3 (Summer 1973); pp. 301-18; and Michael Johnson, "Confessionalism and Individualism in Lebanon: Critique of Leonard Binder (ed.) Politics in the Lebanon," Review of Middle East Studies, no. 1 (1975); 79-91.

18. Interview with Edward Azar, Professor of Political Science at the University of North Carolina at Chapel Hill, and Senior Scientist, Abbott Associates, March 27, 1979.

19. See Camille Chamoun, Crise au Moyen-Orient (Paris: Gallimard, 1963); and Kamal Salibi, Modern History, pp. 198-202.

20. Kamal S. Salibi, Crossroads to Civil War (Delmar, N.Y.: Caravan Books, 1976), p. 4.

21. Ibid., p. 7.

22. Ibid.

23. Ibid., pp. 35-36.

24. The Cairo Agreement, signed on November 3, 1969, allowed the Palestiniams to establish armed positions in refugee camps in Lebanon, to recruit Palestinians for the Palestinian armed struggle, and in effect allowed Palestinian armed operations against Israel from Lebanese territory. See Salibi, Crossroads, pp. 42-44.

25. For discussions of the Lebanese civil war in general, see Halim Barakat, Lebanon in Strife (Austin: University of Texas Press, 1977); John Bulloch, Death of a Country (London: Weidenfeld and Nicolson, 1977); Guido Garosa, Libano: Tragedia de un popolo (Torino: Societa Editrice Internazionale, 1976); Koury, The Crisis in the Lebanese System; Pierre Vallaud, Le Liban au bout du fusil (Paris: Hachette, 1976); and Harold Vocke, The Lebanese War: Its Origins and Political Dimensions (New York: St. Martin's, 1978). Some of these works are highly partisan; they also vary greatly in quality. The best study is P. Edward Haley and Lewis Snider, eds., Lebanon in Crisis: Participants and Issues (Syracuse, N.Y.: Syracuse University Press, 1979).

26. See John P. Entelis "Structural Change and Organizational Development in the Lebanese Katâ'ib Party," Middle East Journal 27, no. 1 (Winter 1973); pp. 21-35; "Belief System and Ideology Formation in the Lebanese Katâ'ib Party," International Journal of Middle East Studies 4, no. 2 (April 1973). 148-62; and "Party Transformation in Lebanon: Al-Katâ'ib as a Case Study," Middle East Studies 9, no. 3 (October 1973); 325-40: Also see F. Stoakes, "The Supervigilantes: The Lebanese Kataeb Party as a Builder, Surrogate, and Defender of the State," Middle East Studies 11, no. 3 (October 1975); 215-36; Tewfik Khalaf "The Phalange and the Maronite Community: From Lebanonism to Maronitism," in Essays on the Crisis in Lebanon, ed. Roger Owen (London: Ithaca Press, 1976), pp. 43-57. For a "progressive" interpretation of the Phalange, see Adil S. Elias, "God, Family, and Fatherland: The Lebanese Phalangists," in Lebanese War: Historical and Social Background, ed. Third World Magazine (Bonn: Progress Dritte Welt, 197?), pp. 12-20.

27. Entelis "Belief System," p. 160; Khalaf "The Phalange," p. 46. Khalaf also quotes Pierre Gemayel regarding the racial-religious composition of Lebanon: "Pays phénicien, hellénisé, romanisé, croisé, chrétien, tout ce qu'on veut, mais pas pays arabe ... rêvant parfois encore, s'ils n'osent plus en parler, au bastion sionisto-chrétien appuyé à la Méditeranée contre le déferlement de la poussée arabo-musulmane" (p. 46).

28. For discussions pertaining to Syria's relationship to Lebanon, see Phillip Hitti, History of Syria (London: Macmillan and Company, 1951), pp. 667-77; and

Stephen H. Longrigg, *Syria and Lebanon under French Mandate* (London: Oxford University Press, 1958).

29. The situation in southern Lebanon of Major Saad Haddad, formerly of the Lebanese Army, is typical. Major Haddad's forces control a 270-square-mile area in southern Lebanon on the Israeli border. On April 18, 1979, Major Haddad declared the area to be "independent" and took military action against U.N. peacekeeping troops to underscore his point. Major Haddad and his forces are backed, supplied, and paid by Israel. Key Christian leaders such as Camille Chamoun have supported his actions. See Marvin Howe "Beirut Sends Toops South, Warily, to Militia Area," *New York Times*, April 18, 1979; and "U.N. Lebanon Force Seen to Be in Peril," *ibid.*, April 29, 1979; Jonathan Kandell, "Militia in Lebanon Declares Border Area Independent," *ibid.*, April 19, 1979; "Christian Militiamen Attack U.N. Forces in Southern Lebanon," *Washington Star*, April 19, 1979; and Helena Cobban, "Lebanon Embarrassed at Support Rebels Garner," *Christian Science Monitor*, April 23, 1979.

8

MINORITIES IN RETREAT: THE JEWS OF THE MAGHREB

Mark A. Tessler,
Linda L. Hawkins, and
Jutta Parsons

This chapter describes the political life of Jews in Tunisia and Morocco, looking at the character of each community and its institutions and at the political orientations of individual Jews in each country. In addition, and without minimizing the importance of this descriptive information, the study also has a comparative and theoretical focus. Similarities in the political life of Jews in Tunisia and Morocco will suggest generalizations which may apply to other minorities. Differences between the two communities will permit the introduction of variables aimed at accounting for this variance, leading to more elaborate propositions which may also apply in other settings.

Two interrelated considerations must be addressed prior to examining the political life of Jews in present-day Tunisia and Morocco. The first is the history of North African Jewry, a subject which cannot receive serious treatment here but which must be

This research was made possible by grants from the Social Science Research Council, the American Philosophical Society and the University of Wisconsin-Milwaukee. While in Tunisia, the senior author received administrative support from the Centre d'Études et de Recherches Économiques et Sociales. The assistance of each of these institutions is gratefully acknowledged. A more detailed account of both the descriptive and theoretical aspects of this work, along with an analysis of the political life of Israel's Arab minority, tentatively entitled *Three Non-Assimilating Minorities: Jews in Tunisia and Morocco and Arabs in Israel*, is scheduled for publication (Praeger, forthcoming).

discussed at least briefly if the present period is to be understood. The second is a definition of the social and political context to which North African Jewish history has given rise. This context is the stimulus to which the communal structures and political attitudes of Jews in Tunisia and Morocco are a response. It also specifies in conceptual terms the probable locus of applicability of generalizations derived from the study of these communities, identifying, in other words, the kind of minority group phenomenon they represent and to which findings about them are most likely to apply.[1] History and conceptual context are dealt with briefly in the next section. Following this, the chapter takes up the contemporary political life of Jews in Tunisia and Morocco.

HISTORY AND CONCEPTUAL CONTEXT

Some believe Jews entered North Africa as early as the destruction of the the first Temple in Jerusalem in 586 B.C. Much larger Jewish migrations to the area took place after the Romans destroyed the second Temple, in 71 A.D. Thus, almost 600 years before the arrival of the Arabs, thriving Jewish communities existed in the Maghreb. In addition, it is generally held that many of the indigenous Berbers converted to Judaism, although most later embraced Christianity and, subsequently, Islam.[2]

In medieval times, the position of Jews in the Middle East and North Africa was defined by Islamic law. Like Christians, Jews were "People of the Book," with specific rights and obligations but never full membership in the Muslim community. Jews fared reasonably well in this situation, although harassment and violence were by no means unknown. They were economically integrated into Muslim society yet generally free to follow their own law and to maintain their own communal institutions. In the western Maghreb, Jews lived as did their Berber neighbors, the latter being almost completely Islamicized by the eighth century. In the eastern Maghreb and elsewhere in urban areas, Arabism as well as Islam took root after the eleventh century, and Jews adopted attributes of Arab culture. On the other hand, Jews in most towns and many villages were increasingly required to reside in special quarters, adding an element of physical separation to the legal, religious, and institutional distance between them and the Muslim majority.

With the Spanish Inquisition, many Jews fled to North Africa from the Iberian Penninsula and Balearic Islands. Muslims arrived, too, introducing an Andalusian component into North African civilization. Spanish Jews rarely settled in the countryside. In the cities, however, immigrant and indigenous Jews came into direct contact, the result being conflict in some instances but, overall, a reorganization and enrichment of communal life. Literacy and religious education increased, for example, and Western ideas were introduced into Jewish society. In addition, the expansion of commercial relations with Europe after the sixteenth century created a class of prosperous and internationally connected Jews for which there was no counterpart in Muslim society. Finally, many Italian Jews arrived in Tunisia in the seventeenth century, increasing still further the European component of North African Jewry. All of these trends increased the social and cultural distance between Jews and Muslims in urban areas, even though Jews remained politically subject and many continued to live in impoverished conditions.

French colonial rule was established in Algeria in 1830, in Tunisia in 1881, and in Morocco in 1912. The French conferred many privileges on North African Jewry, partly to justify their claim to being liberators and partly to divide the indigenous population. In 1870, almost all Algerian Jews were given French citizenship, for example. Elsewhere, Jews were given preferential access to coveted places in French schools. Also, the Paris-based Alliance Israélite Universelle (AIU) began its work in North Africa about this time, building modern schools in cities and towns throughout the Maghreb and, later, cooperating with the colonial establishment. As a result of these developments, large number of Jews were drawn into the French cultural and political orbit, learning the French language and frequently coming to regard themselves as Frenchmen. This assimilation was particularly widespread in Algeria, but it also assumed major proportions in Tunisia and the urban areas of Morocco. Among Muslims, on the other hand, the dominant response to colonialism was nationalism. This response progressed at different rates in Algeria, Tunisia, and Morocco, but in all three countries intellectuals were calling for independence after World War I. Further, to provide an ideological foundation for opposition to the French and to rally the masses to their cause, the nationalists usually stressed Islamic themes. This approach however, excluded Jews from the mainstream of North African nationalism and served to increase Jewish identification with France.

Jewish communities prospered greatly during the colonial period. Economic opportunities increased, lingering tensions between Jews of different origins diminished, and new communal organizations came into existence. Also, though rural communities in Morocco and southern Tunisia were less affected by the new currents, a measure of unity emerged among the Jewish population of each Maghreb country. There were national networks of Jewish schools, clinics, and religious courts, for example. In the cities there were newspapers and radio programs designed for Jews, and even many smaller towns had Jewish clubs and youth groups.

Following World War II, there were approximately 100,000 Jews in Tunisia, 175,000 in Algeria, and 275,000 in Morocco. In all three countries, Jews were a significant national minority and constituted a particularly important component of the educated and professionally skilled urban population. Within a few years, however, large-scale Jewish migrations from North Africa were underway. Motivated by traditional religious convictions, Jews from the Moroccan interior and the Tunisian south began to leave when Israel became independent in 1948. A more important stimulus to migration was the cultural and political distance between urban Jews and the Muslim majority and the significance this distance assumed with the end of colonialism. Few Jews identified with North African nationalism; and official policies promoting Arabism and Islam after independence reinforced this alienation. For example, since Jews were rarely literate in Arabic, they naturally felt threatened by proposed Arabization schemes. In addition, Jews were relegated to a permanently inferior political position by constitutional provisions making Islam the state religion. Finally, to many Muslims, Jews were tainted by their association with colonialism. They were seen as collaborators or, at best, persons whose right to the benefits of independence was questionable. Thus, all but a handful of Algerian Jews left after the revolution, and large and continuing migrations from Tunisia and Morocco have been occurring since independence.

Other factors have also contributed to Jewish emigration from independent Tunisia and Morocco. Educational advances in both countries have reduced dependence on Jews and foreigners and created pressures for economic discrimination in favor of Muslims. Also, especially in Tunisia, government policies have disadvantaged the middle class and disallowed independent political institutions, religious or otherwise. These policies have been applied equally to Muslims, but this does not lessen their impact on Jews. Acts of harassment have been another consideration. Though officially discouraged, such acts occur with some regularity on popular levels. Rapid urbanization has brought to North Africa's cities many illiterate individuals without prior contact with Jews. Bitter about social injustice, these persons are often receptive to ideologies attributing problems to Zionism or colonialism, and this process generates hostility toward Jews. Finally, since the existence of the critical mass necessary to maintain communal institutions and carry out normal social and religious activities is increasingly in doubt, the diminishing size of Jewish communities has itself fostered emigration.

Most departing Tunisian Jews have gone to France. Perhaps 10 percent are in Israel, the majority being from small communities in southern Tunisia. The majority of Moroccan Jewry has settled in Israel, although the wealthiest and best-educated Moroccan Jews are also in France. In addition, some Moroccan Jews have emigrated to French-speaking Canada, and many from the northern Spanish-speaking zone have relocated in Spain or South America. Despite pressure for emigration, however, sizable numbers of Jews remained in Tunisia and Morocco after independence. Both countries became independent in 1956; both were ruled by regimes which encouraged Jews to stay; and both declared that the Jews would be protected as national minorities. Thus, five years after independence, there were still approximately 30,000 Jews in Tunisia and 80,000 in Morocco. Moreover, the position of these Jews was one of relative prosperity. Jews held high positions in government, business, journalism, and other professions; Jewish organizations operated with comparative effectiveness; and the fortunes of most wealthy Jews were left intact. Nevertheless, Jewish migration continued unabated, the result being that increasingly little remains of the prosperity and vibrance that characterized North Africa's Jewish communities prior to independence. In the next section, we shall examine the political life of those Jews who continue to live in Tunisia and Morocco. Before proceeding, however, the circumstances of these Jews will be defined in conceptual terms.

The social and political context of contemporary North African Jewry is defined by three principal attributes: non-assimilating minority status, a level of social mobilization higher than that of the Muslim majority, and small relative and absolute size. These attributes define the circumstances to which North African Jewish political life is a response and identify structural conditions whose presence or absence will tend to determine whether other minorities exhibit similar patterns. Similarities between Tunisian and Moroccan Jews will, in particular, suggest generalizations about the impact of these conditions. Differences will leave variance unexplained and require that generalizations advanced incorporate additional contextual attributes differentiating between Tunisian and Moroccan Jewry.

Non-assimilating minority status refers to the situation of religious minorities in non-secular states.[3] In Tunisia and Morocco, as in many other Middle Eastern countries, constitutions make Islam the official religion, and governments build mosques and cemeteries, provide religious education, conform officially to Muslim holy days, and operate on the basis of a legal code owing much to the Koran and its interpretations. Tunisian and Moroccan Jews are thus religious minorities in states declaring an association with the religion of the majority to be central to their raison d'être; accordingly, even if granted full civil rights, they are incapable of sharing completely in the mission of the state. It should be noted that a rejection of secularism does not necessarily lead to theocracy. In Tunisia and Morocco, as in other self-consciously Muslim countries, there are intense debates about Islamic issues. Nevertheless, the connection between the identity of the state and the religion of the majority necessitates a separate and inevitably inferior political status for religious minorities.

Secularism does not refer only to religion and politics. It implies a dissassociation of the state's political identity and the defining attributes of any group: religious, racial, cultural, or other. Alternatively, secularism is absent if an avowed purpose of political association is the defense and service on a priority basis of a particular community of individuals rather than all citizens of the state; and this obtains whether or not the dominant group is the numerical majority. In Tunisia and Morocco, Arabism is also a part of the national identity. Arabic is the official language, and the majority believes that the government has an obligation to deepen Arab consciousness and to serve Arab interests. But, again, this creates an inferior status for individuals who are not Arab and have no prospect of becoming Arab, as is the case for all but a handful of Jews. Thus, in sum, Jews in Tunisia and Morocco are non-assimilating minorities, communities incapable of embracing or being embraced by a dominant national ethic that is the basis of statehood and political legitimacy. In this they reside in a context similar to that of many other minorities, including Arabs in Israel, Blacks in the Sudan, and Asians in several African countries.

Jews in Tunisia and Morocco are more socially mobilized than the Muslim majority, and this is another important attribute of the context in which they reside. With respect to education, professional skills, and cross-cultural exposure, Jews rate higher than Muslims in both countries. There is of course considerable variation among Jews. Also, the gap between Muslims and Jews is narrowing, due to social mobilization among the majority and the departure of many affluent Jews. Nevertheless, the Maghreb's Jews are "mobilized" minorities—groups without a political status advantage but enjoying material and cultural advantages[4]—and thus are distinguished from most other minorities described in this volume, including Arabs in Israel, North Africa's Berbers, and the Kurds of Iraq, Iran, and Syria. Finally, Tunisian and Moroccan Jews constitute a very small proportion of the population of their host societies. It is true that their level of social mobilization gives them an influence disproportionate to their numbers, but they still have little significance in the overall scheme of society. They are incapable of independent political action, being rather dependent and vulnerable "minorities in retreat." This aspect also differentiates them from other groups examined in this volume. On the other hand, there are minorities whose situation is similar to that of North African Jews on all of the contextual attributes described. Asians in Black Africa, overseas Chinese in Southeast Asia, and Christians in some Islamic countries come to mind.[5] It is probable that an understanding of how Jews in Tunisia and Morocco respond to their situation will shed light on the political life of such groups; and it is thus to suggest the possible locus of our findings, as well as to identify forces affecting the minorities under study, that we have sought to define systematically the position of Jews in the Maghreb.

While similarities between Jews in Tunisia and Morocco will suggest generalizations about a particular kind of minority group experience, differences will indicate that dissimilar contextual attributes must also be identified and incorporated into explanations of minority behavior. Actually, similarities between the two Jewish communities are quite pronounced, including more than the common sociopolitical situation already discussed. The cultural traditions and historical experiences of the communities themselves are highly comparable. Politics and society in the two host countries also have many common elements. Both are Arab and Islamic. Both were colonized by the French and attained independence at the same time and in comparable ways. Both are relatively small countries with roughly equivalent levels of development. Both are pro-Western in their foreign alignment. On the other hand, there are two potentially important areas of difference between Tunisia and Morocco which should be noted.[6] The first concerns demographic and cultural patterns. Tunisia has a more unified population and a stronger tradition of Islamic orthodoxy than does Morocco. There are few tribes and only a handful of Berberphones in Tunisia. The country also has a high level of urbanization and a readily accessible interior. Morocco, by contrast, is more socially fragmented, and its culture is shaped to a greater degree by rural, tribal, and non-Arab influences. The second concerns government policy. Tunisia pursued radical social and economic policies during the early postindependence period. There were extensive reforms relating to law and religion, economic policies favoring cooperative socialism rather than private enterprise, and social programs emphasizing education, youth, and mass mobilization. Morocco, on the other hand, has pursued a more consistently conservative strategy of change and development. Should differences be observed in the political life of Tunisian and Moroccan Jewry, these national variations may help to explain their dissimilar responses to a common minority group situation.

THE PRESENT: DEMOGRAPHIC PATTERNS AND COMMUNAL ORGANIZATION

This account of the present period is based principally on thirteen months of field work carried out in Tunisia and Morocco in 1972 and 1973. A short return to the Maghreb in 1976 and communications with North African Jews and others familiar with their situation suggests that our characterization of Jewish political life is still applicable, though some details have changed. We are thus describing the life of Jews more than 20 years after Tunisian and Moroccan independence. We shall begin with the situation in Tunisia.

The total Jewish population of Tunisia was about 3,000 in 1972, and the number of Jews emigrating annually has been about 500-700 in recent years. Today there are probably no more than 5,000 Jews in the entire country.* In addition, few Jews live outside Tunis and its suburbs, the only significant exception being two old and adjacent Jewish villages on the island of Djerba. These communities have about 800 and 300 inhabitants respectively and their populations have been relatively stable in recent years, although there are early signs of change. There are also three other towns with approximately 100 Jewish residents, but these are largely within the cultural and economic orbit of Tunis. Finally, there are a few towns with three or four Jewish families. Thus, in sum, Tunis, with perhaps

---

*All figures should be viewed as approximate. Community officials in both Tunisia and Morocco regularly develop their own population estimates, but they readily acknowledge that their figures are subject to considerable error. Estimates presented in this chapter are based on community data, available statistics—such as school enrollments and persons on welfare—and conversations with individuals in a position to make reasonably accurate educated guesses.

3,500-4,000 Jews, is the only major center of Jewish life, and Djerba is the only other location with a significant Jewish presence.

Much of the population is inactive. There is a disproportionately high number of old people, children, and, in Tunis, uneducated immigrants from the interior. It is unlikely that there are more than 500 families in Tunis in which the father, or mother, is steadily employed. The small active population spans a reasonably broad socioeconomic continuum, however. There are many merchants and shopkeepers, some wealthy businessmen and respected professionals, and a substantial number of white collar workers, some employed in institutions of the community itself and some in agencies of the French government.

The community is educationally and culturally heterogeneous. Much of the inactive population, especially immigrants from the interior, have had little modern education. Their language is Judeo-Arabic, and many know no French at all. This category includes young as well as elderly persons, though some young immigrants are educated and gainfully employed. A second category includes well-educated and professionally active individuals. Among older persons in this group, Judeo-Arabic is the mother tongue, but French is usually preferred today. Younger, well-educated persons are highly Frenchified and rarely speak Arabic well. These two categories constitute about 40 and 20 percent of the adult population, respectively. The remaining 40 percent are persons with intermediate educational levels—primary schooling and possibly some high school training in French. Most are in their forties or fifties, of urban origin or longtime urban residence, and gainfully employed, often in commerce. They are usually bilingual and bicultural, though their children identify strongly with French culture. As can be seen, there is an imperfect but generally significant correlation between high education, low age, longtime urban residence, successful professional activity, and familiarity with French culture. Though skewed toward the more traditional pole of the dimension defined by these characteristics, Tunisia's Jewish population is in general distributed fairly evenly over the entire spectrum.

Jewish community organizations are devoted primarily to the provision of social services. Some funds for these agencies are raised locally from taxes on kosher meat and wine. For the most part, however, they are supported by subsidies from international Jewish organizations, most notably the American Joint Distribution Committee. Though primarily institutions of social welfare, these organizations are also political in that they constitute the only existing form of organized communal activity. A Central Committee in Tunis serves as the administrative hub for communal service agencies. The committee operates several nursing homes, a nursery school and day-care center, a welfare program for needy and elderly, a *Talmud-Torah* primary school, and a cemetery. The committee also has administrative links to other institutions, such as clinics and some synagogues. Finally, it receives and dispenses modest income from a few pieces of property left by departing Jews. In theory the committee is a representative policy-making body chosen by Jews to direct community affairs and look after Jewish interests. Today, however, it is concerned primarily with administration.

A dozen or more synagogues continue to operate in Tunis. But most bear little resemblance to synagogues in the West. Few have activities other than worship, and only a handful are open during the week. Even on the Sabbath, many have difficulty obtaining the necessary ten men for a service. Most are little more than two or three rooms with an ark and a pulpit, and many have no rabbis. Worshippers conduct their own services as best they can. The large synagogue in Tunis operated by the committee is the principal exception to these generalizations, and one or two others also have more frequent and regularized activities. In Djerba there is a well-maintained synagogue frequented daily by the few rabbis who remain.

Schools are no longer a major part of the community's institutional network, as they once were. All AIU schools had closed by the mid-1960s. Declining enrollments due to emigration forced the AIU to turn its schools over to the government one by one. The Central Committee in Tunis runs one *Talmud-Torah* primary school, attended mainly by children of poor families. A private religious school maintained by representatives of an overseas hassidic organization offers modern and religious instruction at the primary and high school levels and is the most important Jewish school in Tunisia today. Children of the well-to-do usually attend the schools of the French University and Cultural Mission. Places in MUC schools are highly coveted, although a new requirement that Tunisian Jews (and Muslims) study Arabic has begun to change this. A vocational high school operated by O.R.T., an international Jewish organization, operated with minimal enrollment until 1973, when it finally closed its doors. There are very few Jews in Tunisian public schools—primarily because they do not wish to study Arabic—except in outlying communities. A few Jewish students do attend the French-speaking University of Tunis.

The only other major institution is a modern clinic in the former Jewish quarter of Tunis. Associated with O.S.E., an international Jewish welfare organization based in Geneva, it provides immediate aid to those who come in—including Muslims—and has beds for persons requiring special care. Part of the building is also a nursing home, and until recently there was another very small nursing home in one of the suburbs of Tunis. The O.S.E. clinic also attempts to help Jews in outlying areas, sometimes paying local doctors for treating them.

In the past there were other organizations, such as youth groups, sports associations, and scout troops. There were also Jewish newspapers and radio programs. But all of this has ended. In smaller towns, even most of what remains in Tunis has disappeared. The community school in Djerba, for example, provides only religious instruction after Tunisian public school. The one-room O.S.E. clinic, staffed by a male nurse from Tunis, closed in 1972 for lack of funds. It later reopened, but its future is uncertain. In Nabeul, to cite another example, about 100 Jews depend almost entirely on Tunis for communal organization. There is no Jewish school. A *Shoket* comes from Tunis about once a week to slaughter kosher meat. The head of the community lives in Tunis and returns to Nabeul when a problem arises.

The distinction between social and political functions is often blurred, but several institutions traditionally played more explicitly political roles. These are the Central Committee, which has already been mentioned, the Central Rabbinate, and the Rabbinical Courts. All have little political authority today. The Central Committee in Tunis was originally composed of 40 individuals chosen by popular election among Jews. Towns with smaller Jewish populations had smaller committees. In addition to coordinating the work of communal agencies, the committee set policy and spoke for the community when occasion dictated. After independence, however, the committee was held to be "a state within a state," and the Tunisian government forced it to reconstitute as the Temporary Committee for the Direction of the Jewish Religion. Elections are now prohibited. Many members who emigrate or die are not replaced, and when they are it is only upon appointment by the government. Today there are only four or five members of the Temporary Committee, and meetings are on an irregular basis. No central committees exist at all outside of Tunis, though some communities have one or two informally designated individuals who direct community affairs and maintain contact with the committee in Tunis.

The duty of the chief rabbi and his assistants is to represent the community in public and direct it in matters of worship and ritual; in theory at least, these functions are still carried out. The rabbinate is responsible for standards of *kashruth* in the preparation of wine and meat, for example, though instances of inspection appear to be few.

The chief rabbi, along with the president of the Temporary Committee, also continues to represent the community. Upon the death of the president of the committee in 1973, for instance, it was the chief rabbi who contacted the governor of Tunis about appointing a successor. Rabbinical courts, on the other hand, have been abolished. Shortly after independence, Tunisia integrated large bodies of civil and religious law and provided for unified judicial institutions to administer that law. *Shari'a* as well as rabbinical courts were affected; in fact, Muslim justices opposed the government at the time. In any event, all civil and criminal matters involving Jews are handled today in government courts.

Clearly the Jewish community of Tunisia has no meaningful political organization and only a minimum of institutional capacity and structural unity. It is wrong to see in this a policy of harassment aimed at Jews. Other independent political organizations (trade unions, the Communist Party, and the like) have also been disallowed, and traditional Muslim institutions have, if anything, been disbanded more thoroughly than Jewish ones. Moreover, much of the disarray in the Jewish community is due to emigration rather than official policy. Nonetheless, political activity by Jews is, at best, disorganized, intermittent, and informal.

In its broad outlines, the situation of Jews in Morocco is similar to that of Jews in Tunisia. Moroccan Jewry is experiencing emigration, an internal migration toward the cities, and steadily diminishing organizational complexity. Today the size of the community is only 6-7 percent of what it once was and dozens of towns that formerly had Jewish populations are now devoid of a Jewish presence. Jews who remain are concentrated in the largest cities, especially Casablanca, where about two-thirds of Morocco's Jews currently live. The institutional capacity of the community has diminished and become more concentrated, too. For example, every year witnesses the closing of additional Jewish schools. With students and teachers leaving, the number of Muslims in schools in small and middle-size communities rises each year until, finally, authorities turn some over to the government, which then pays for their operation and teaches according to its own curriculum. Remaining Jewish pupils and teachers are usually then shifted to other community schools, sometimes in different cities. Virtually every Jewish institution outside of Casablanca and Rabat experiences this kind of pressure. In Fez, for example, the local O.S.E. clinic closed in 1973, after an intense campaign by Fez Jews to keep it open. O.S.E. directors in Casablanca insisted that the clinic simply served too few people to justify expenses. Moreover, in at least a dozen towns of smaller size, communal institutions are totally defunct, and national Jewish organizations are trying to liquidate assets and transfer artifacts and religious objects to the capital. Finally, even in Casablanca, where the need to assist Jews coming from the interior permits the maintenance and even the expansion of some social services, many organizations have begun to shut down. In 1973, the O.R.T. vocational school system reluctantly closed two of its facilities, for example. One was a school for deaf mutes.

In the early 1970s, one could still witness among Jews in small and middle-size Moroccan towns processes of demographic dislocation and institutional atrophy that had already run their course among Tunisian Jews outside of Tunis and Djerba. The direction of these processes seems quite irreversible, and probably it will not be long before the overall situation of Moroccan Jewry comes to resemble that of Jews in Tunisia today. Nevertheless, for the present at least, these are important differences to be added to the similarities already noted between these two North African Jewish communities. Compared to Tunisia, the absolute number of Jews in Morocco is considerable; Jews are widely distributed throughout Morocco, and the magnitude of the active population is substantial. The community's own estimates of its population in 1973 varied from 25,000 to 30,000, occasionally even higher. Today, in 1978, there are probably 18-20,000 Jews in Morocco. Most Jews, of course, live in Casablanca, but over 2,000 Jews remain in Rabat, and four other cities—Fez, Marrakesh, Meknes, and Tangier—have something like 1,000 each, and at least six more towns have several hundred Jews. Morocco's Jewish population is also more heterogeneous than that of Tunisia. There are, of course, many indigent and elderly; but there are also many wealthy Jews, a large professional and white collar middle class, and numerous merchants and small businessmen. Thus the distribution of socioeconomic status within the active population is more even than in Tunisia, though somewhat skewed toward the middle class. Finally, there are far more Jews in their thirties and forties in Morocco.

Community institutions are likewise more active and better-structured. The Central Committee of Casablanca runs several modern nursing homes, has a staff of social workers caring for over 1,000 needy persons, and maintains a day-care center, a *Talmud-Torah* school, and community cemeteries. These activities do resemble those of the community in Tunis, but in Casablanca the staff and budget are much larger and the facilities far more modern. Moreover, comparable institutions exist in six or seven other Moroccan cities, several of which have structures more developed than those of Tunis.

The situation with respect to education is similar. In 1972-73 there were over 8,000 Jewish youngsters attending school; and while some were in French or other private schools, most attended schools run by Jewish organizations. The AIU's Ittihad Maroc remains the major educational system, with primary and secondary schools in a number of cities. Ittihad-Maroc receives a subsidy from the Ministry of Education. O.R.T. professional schools in Casablanca also have high enrollments, especially since they offer dormitory facilities for children whose parents live outside Casablanca. In addition, there are two independent religious school systems—one with schools in a number of cities—and community schools serving poorer children in several towns. Most Moroccan Jewish schools also offer many cultural and religious activities, such as pageants, sports events, and choral groups. All of this is virtually nonexistent in Tunisia.

Synagogues are better maintained and better attended than in Tunisia. In Casablanca, obtaining ten men for prayer is rarely a problem, and even in many smaller communities 75-100 persons attend the main synagogue on Saturday morning. The O.S.E. clinic in Casablanca dwarfs the facility in Tunis in terms of staff, budget, and equipment. Jewish scout troops and youth groups also operate in Morocco. Though diminished in size and in number, they are active all year and in summer camp alongside Muslim groups in government campsites. Finally there are several Jewish clubs in Casablanca and other cities.

Political activity and organizational complexity are greatly diminished but still significant by standards operative in Tunis. In Casablanca, the Central Committee meets regularly, has a full complement of officers and committees, submits a formal budget to Moroccan authorities, and maintains a staff of secretaries, accountants, and administrators. Central committees also operate on a smaller scale in Rabat and other cities, and there is a National Council in Rabat which coordinates their work and assists Jews in towns without these organizations. The secretary general of the council is the official head of Moroccan Jewry and, along with the president of the Central Committee of Casablanca, takes the lead in communicating Jewish concerns to the Moroccan government. The council is governed by representatives from the central committees of larger towns. An executive committee meets once or twice a month as the occasion requires, and a larger assembly of representatives convenes twice a year. The organization of both the council and the central committees is fixed by Moroccan law.

Unlike Tunisia, rabbinical courts continue to function in Morocco. The replacement of elderly personnel is a problem and the courts do not appear to be heavily used. Nevertheless, *dayyanim* in smaller communities, three-man courts of first instance in larger cities, and a supreme court located in Rabat continue to serve the populace. They are administered through the Ministry of Justice. The chief justice, who is also the chief rabbi of Casablanca, is an important dignitary and often represents the Jewish population to Moroccan society. Another Jew of political significance is a man who sits on the Casablanca Municipal Council. This individual is not chosen by Jews, but it is understood that he will speak for Jewish interests and take administrative action on behalf of Jews with special problems.

In both Tunisia and Morocco, the articulation of Jewish political demands is often carried out by individual Jews who use personal relationships with Muslim officials to secure desired political action. In Tunisia, however, such actions are relatively infrequent, limited almost entirely to Tunis, and often involve Jews who are not community officials. In Morocco, on the other hand, they occur on a wider scale and, most significantly, they often involve individuals who are fully familiar with the workings of the community and are regarded by Jews and non-Jews as its appropriate representatives. For example, it is accepted policy for the secretary-general of the National Council to request a formal interview with the prime minister or to prepare a formal memorandum setting forth Jewish concerns. Recent examples of such "interventions" are a request that the manditory retirement age for court justices be extended so that members of rabbinical courts who cannot be replaced may continue to serve and a proposal for disposing of Jewish property in towns where Jews no longer reside. Thus, in sum, there are both major similarities and major differences between the demographic and institutional character of the Tunisian and Moroccan Jewish communities. Increasing marginality and weakness is clearly the dominant trend in both instances. But it is far more advanced in the former, while the latter retains a greater degree of socioeconomic viability and institutional capacity.

Both similarities and differences between Jewish political life in Tunisia and Morocco are of interest. The sociopolitical context of each group involves non-assimilating minority status, that is to say, residence in a country where the political identity of the state is formally tied to the religious and ethnic identity of the majority. In addition, each minority is characterized by advantaged socioeconomic status relative to the majority and by small size. In North Africa such circumstances are clearly associated with communal instability, including a tendency toward emigration, an internal migration toward major urban centers, a disproportionately large inactive population, and the decay of community institutions. We would hypothesize that such tendencies exist among other minorities residing in similar circumstances, being a general response to their situation of privileged but vulnerable minority groups in societies where sceularism is absent.

Since these tendencies are more advanced in Tunisia than Morocco, factors that distinguish the two countries may be incorporated into hypotheses about the rate at which demographic and institutional dislocation occurs. One of these factors is the greater size and complexity of Morocco's Jewish community prior to independence. Given that this community was three times as large as that of Tunisia in 1956, it is not surprising that it remains more viable today. This suggests that, even among small minorities, larger and more institutionalized communities respond to comparable destablizing pressures in a less abrupt fashion. But the pressures upon Jews in Tunisia and Morocco are not fully comparable. Government policies and levels of social mobilization among the majority differ substantially. The Tunisian government has been more concerned with cultural reform, socialist economics, and mass mobilization than that of Morocco. As noted earlier, this concern has meant that independent religious organizations have been disallowed in Tunisia but not Morocco, that there has been more economic pressure on priviledged population categories in Tunisia than in Morocco, and that a higher proportion of citizens in the former country have been brought into the modern sectors of society and had their expectations raised. So far as Jews are concerned, fears about economic, political, and even personal vulnerability are greater in Tunisia than Morocco, and this variation undoubtedly does much to explain the more advanced state of demographic dislocation and institutional decay among Tunisian Jewry. Thus, we may add to the preceding hypothesis the proposition that communal disintegration among minorities like Jews in the Maghreb accelerates when the government of the majority pursues mobilization-oriented policies and slows when it follows a conservative and laissez faire political strategem.

THE PRESENT: INDIVIDUAL POLITICAL ATTITUDES

The response of North African Jewry to its sociopolitical situation is also reflected in the attitudes of individual Jews. To gather information about individual attitudes in Tunisia, 89 Jews were surveyed in Tunis and Djerba, this number being over 1 percent of the total Jewish population and over 5 percent of the active adult Jewish population. A matched sample of Muslims was also constructed for comparison purposes. In Morocco, 161 Jews were surveyed, about three-quarters being upper-division students in Jewish high schools. Adults were interviewed in Casablanca, Rabat, and Fez, and students, who represent about 5 percent of all advanced students in Jewish secondary schools, were surveyed in Casablanca and Meknes.

It was not possible to construct a random sample in either Tunisia or Morocco. Nevertheless, samples were balanced with respect to age, sex, educational level, and residence; and this balancing coupled with their size relative to the populations from which they are drawn, makes them generally representative of the active Jewish population in each country. In Tunisia, 350 Muslims were also surveyed, and from this pool an individual who closely resembled each Jewish respondent with respect to age, sex, education, and residence was selected. A Muslim match could not be found for three Jews from Djerba; all others were successfully paired, generating a "matched Muslim" sample of 86. In Morocco, high school students were surveyed primarily in Casablance, but some respondents were recent immigrants from the interior. Students were also drawn to a slightly disproportionate degree from professionally oriented schools serving the lower classes, although this was not sufficient to have detracted significantly from the representativeness of the sample.

The present paper examines responses to eight survey items identified by factor analysis as representative of two dimensions underlying respondent attitudes in each country. The items are listed below. The first four items pertain to esteem for traditional Arab-Islamic culture, a dimension which emerges with clarity in separate factor analyses of Tunisian and Moroccan data. The next four items concern attachment to the respondent's host society, a dimension which again emerges clearly and which includes similar political and social components in each country. Both dimensions represent shared variance among a substantial number of items, constituting themes reflected in responses to many questions. The items themselves load highly on the respective factors in each country and are therefore convenient indicators of these dimensions.

Some survey items were employed in both Tunisia and Morocco, and some were unique to the interview schedule used in each country. The two factors discussed above emerge clearly in both instances, however. In Tunisia, these dimensions are the first two factors to emerge in either a principal components or a varimax rotation solution, and in Morocco they are the second and third factors in each solution. The first factor identified from the Moroccan data measures personal isolation, reflecting estrangement from both Muslim and Jewish society and an intention to emigrate. The prominence of this factor in Morocco is attributable principally to the inclusion of a series of items too sensitive to ask in Tunisia. The third factor in Tunisia also pertained, though less directly, to satisfaction alienation at the individual level. Indicator items rather than factor scores are analyzed in the present paper for two reasons. The latter, though convenient for assessing variation on each dimension, give less descriptive information than do responses to actual items. They are also less suitable for comparisons between Tunisia and Morocco, since not all survey items used in each country were identical. Four indicator items have been selected for each dimension in order to reflect the substantive breadth and diverse tendencies associated with each. All were used in both countries and load highly on equivalent factors in each case.

The eight indicator items used, then, were:

High Esteem/Low Esteem for Arab-Islamic Culture

1. It is not acceptable for a married woman to go out socially without her husband.
2. It is important for Tunisian pupils to study classical Arab history.
3. It is not important for Tunisian pupils to study French history.
4. Europe has important lessons to learn from the Arabs.

Attachment to/Alienation From Respondent's Host Society

1. The government cares about people like respondent.
2. Respondent can identify a Tunisian cabinet minister.
3. Respondent can identify a prominent Jewish community leader.
4. Respondent characterizes relations with persons of different religions as good or excellent.

In analyzing data, respondents have been grouped on the basis of education, age, and, in Tunisia, residence. Education is used because it is strongly related to attitudinal variations in most settings and is an indicator of present and future socioeconomic status. Respondents are divided into those who are better educated and less educated. Age is employed to distinguish between respondents who grew up before and after independence and those whose career patterns are and are not, for the most part, established. Here respondents are divided according to whether or not they are over 35

TABLE 8.1: Responses to Selected Items of Respondents Classified by Residence, Age, Education and Religion

	Tunis								Djerba[a]				Morocco			
Age	Older				Younger				Older		Younger		Older		Younger	
Education[b]	High		Low		High		Low		Low		High		High	Low	High	Low
Religion[c]	J	M	J	M	J	M	J	M	J	M	J	M	J	J	J	J
Item (frequency)	10		11		26		9		10		23		15	11	63	72
Esteem for Arab-Islamic culture																
Percent believing a married woman should not go out socially without her husband	44	78	57	91	30	54	50	70	100	100	91	100	67	100	52	81
Percent considering it important for Moslem pupils to study classical Arab history	43	78	30	89	65	75	25	60	0	100	53	84	42	40	49	40
Percent considering it unimportant for Moslem pupils to study French history	0	44	10	67	38	38	13	50	0	71	5	61	58	13	45	25
Percent believing Europe has important lessons to learn from the Arabs	80	60	29	87	55	71	33	75	0	100	29	60	33	13	36	55

Attachment to Host Society

	J	M	J	M	J	M	J	M	J	M	J	M	J	M	J	M
Percent believing government cares about people like them	75	43	22	14	45	48	33	83	0	0	15	33	62	60	38	46
Percent able to identify Muslim cabinet minister	43	50	20	29	22	42	13	13	0	43	18	50	36	30	17	6
Percent able to identify Jewish community leader	71	22	40	20	31	13	25	0	0	0	5	10	79	40	33	33
Percent reporting good or excellent relations with persons of different religion	75	67	40	60	65	67	86	60	43	40	62	47	69	78	34	33

aIn Djerba, almost everyone with a primary school education or less is over 35, and only a handful of younger persons has completed high school. Thus, only two empirical categories based on age and education are discernable: older persons with primary schooling or, occasionally, a bit more. Not all Muslim respondents matched to Djerba Jews are from Djerba. Some are from comparable nonurban areas in other parts of the country.

bUnless otherwise indicated, younger persons are divided into those who have and have not finished high school and older persons are divided into those who have and have not finished junior high. The point of differentiation between those who are relatively well and relatively poorly educated varies because a high school education is much more common today than it was a generation ago. In Morocco, among younger respondents who are still attending high school, distinctions with respect to eduction are based on school and curriculum. Students in programs leading to the baccalaureate are rated as better educated and those in vocational or truncated academic programs are classified as less well educated.

cJ = Jewish and M = Muslim. Frequencies represent the number of Jews only. Three Jews from Djerba are not included in the analysis because they have not been matched to a Muslim respondent.

Source: Compiled by the authors.

years of age. Taken together, these dichotomizations provide useful categories for assessing intra-societal variation in politically relevant attitudes. Also, since the Tunisian and Moroccan samples are not identical, they delineate subsets of respondents on the basis of which valid inter-societal comparisons can be made. In Tunisia, respondents are also divided into those from Tunis and those from Djerba, the latter community being sufficiently homogeneous to yield only two subcategories based on education and age.

Table 8.1 presents the distribution of respondents in all categories, including matched Muslim respondents from Tunisia, and gives the proportion of persons in each who answer items in a fashion indicative of either high esteem for Arab-Islamic culture or attachment to Tunisia or Morocco. The table permits, first, an assessment of the nature and distribution of Jewish attitudes in Tunisia, including comparisons with matched Muslims to determine the degree to which attitudes are the result of minority status or other attributes unique to Jews, second, as assessment of the nature and distribution of Jewish attitudes in Morocco, and third, a comparison of Tunisian and Moroccan Jews in equivalent population categories.

The attitudes of Jews from Tunis will be considered first. Tendencies exhibited by each category of respondents will be noted, referring to both actual attitudes and orientations relative to matched Muslims and other Jews. Not every figure in table 8.1 will be discussed, though interested readers may consult it for additional detail. Our objective is to offer a general characterization of normative response of Jews from Tunis to the minority group context within which they reside.

First, well-educated, older Jews display considerable respect for traditional Arab-Islamic culture. Approval of traditional restrictions on women is higher among matched Muslims, as is the importance attached to studying classical Arab history. But support for these values is reasonably high in absolute terms, and these Jews are overwhelmingly of the opinion that Europe has important lessons to learn from the Arabs. Neither matched Muslims nor other Jews are as likely to hold this positive view of Arab culture. These Jews also distinguish themselves by their unanimous conviction that Tunisian pupils should study French hsitory, apparently believing that while Arab history and Islam are valuable components of Tunisia's legacy, other elements are important, too. Well-educated, older Jews also have comparatively positive feelings about Tunisian society. They are disproportionately likely to believe the government cares about them, their levels of political information are higher than other Jews and almost as high as comparable Muslims, and their personal relations with Muslims are usually good or excellent. Most also can identify a Jewish community leader—as a majority of Jews in no other category can do—and this ability suggests a strong Jewish communal identity. As with cultural orientations, these Jews apparently have positive feelings about the Muslims among whom they live, but their attitudes include the view that Tunisia is a society of diverse communities.

Second, poorly educated, older Jews hold Arab-Islamic culture in low esteem. Although more likely than other Jews to have traditional attitudes toward women, they rarely consider the study of classical Arab history to be important, are far less likely than others to believe Europe has something worthwhile to learn from the Arabs, and overwhelmingly believe that the study of French history is important. Also, in each of the latter instances, attitudinal differences between Jews and Muslims are greater than in any other respondent category. These Jews also have negative feelings about Tunisia. Most believe the government does not care about them, although similar ratings among Muslims suggest that government policies emphasizing education and youth may be as important as minority group status in fostering these attitudes. These Jews also have low levels of political information, even about the Jewish community, and are particularly unlikely to have satisfying personal relations with Muslims. In sum, older, poorly educated Jews are alienated from Tunisian society. Their attitudes may be attributable in part to policies affecting all Tunisians, but on the whole they compound an alienation which manifests itself on the cultural and personal, as well as the political, level.

Third, well-educated, younger Jews have more positive views of Arab-Islamic culture. They disagree with specific norms, such as those pertaining to women, but display respect in a broader sense. They are more likely than other Jews to consider the study of classical Arab history important, and a majority believes that Europe can learn valuable lessons from the Arabs. In addition, they are the only category of Jews that frequently regards the study of French history as unimportant. This opinion indicates not only a positive view of the majority culture but also a belief that other civilizations are peripheral in Tunisia. Attitudes toward Tunisia are less positive than those of well-educated, older Jews but more positive than those of poorly educated, older Jews. About half believe the government cares about them, and a majority has good relations with Muslims. On the other hand, information about both Tunisian and Jewish political life is low, suggesting little personal interest in Tunisian affairs. On balance, well-educated, young Jews from Tunis are not alienated and do not have negative attitudes about the majority and its culture. But they apparently see Tunisia as a society for Arabs and Muslims and accept the marginality of Jews.

Fourth, the cultural attitudes of poorly educated, younger Jews parallel those of poorly educated, older Jews and similarly set them apart from comparable Muslims. Specifically, most do not regard the study of classical Arab history as important; most do consider the study of French history to be important; and most believe that Europe has nothing valuable to learn from the Arabs. Attitudes toward Tunisia are similarly negative, with one interesting exception. These Jews almost all report good personal relations with Muslims. Nevertheless, most believe the government does not care about them, in striking contrast to comparable Muslims, who believe they will benefit from government programs, and few show any interest in either Jewish affairs or Tunisian politics. Thus, despite satisfactory relations with Muslims, these Jews hold Arab-Islamic culture in low esteem and display little attachment to Tunisian society.

Clearly not all Jews respond to minority group status in the same way. Esteem for traditional Arab-Islamic culture is associated with high education, the opposite of the pattern observed among Muslims, and a belief that French culture is important to Tunisia is generally associated with being older. Attachment to Tunisia also varies with education, although the relationship is stronger among older Jews. There is less variance among younger Jews and, especially among better educated individuals, Tunisian affairs are often seen as irrelevant. The positive attitudes of well-educated, older Jews and their emphasis on Tunisia's "Mediterranean" personality probably reflect the fact that these individuals were educated and socialized prior to independence, when the position of Jews was quite different. It also may reflect their decision to remain in Tunisia despite prospects for a good life elsewhere. The negative attitudes of poorly educated, older Jews are attributable in part to modernization policies affecting all Tunisians. But they also reflect a personal marginality compounded by their status as members of a vulnerable minority. Their future in Tunisia is not bright. Yet they probably consider themselves too old and unskilled to begin a new life elsewhere and hence are doubly frustrated. Most well-educated, younger Jews will eventually leave Tunisia, and this permits a degree of detachment which probably emplains both their positive attitudes and their lack of interest in Tunisian affairs. They assess Tunisian politics and society with minimal worry about what is good for Jews. This may also be the reason that Jewish and Muslim views are more similar here than in other respondent categories. The attitudes of poorly educated, younger Jews resemble those of comparably educated, older Jews but also reflect influences present among other, younger Jews. They disapprove of prevailing political and cultural currents, undoubtedly because of their marginality in Tunisia. At the sam time, while their prospects for success elsewhere are not bright, emigration remains a plausible option and limits their concern about developments among the majority.

The Jewish community of Djerba is more homogeneous and traditional than that of Tunis, as evidenced by a stronger correlation between age and education and by less educational variance within age categories. On the other hand, the circumstances of Djerban Jewry are changing, and greater diversity will be the result. French colonialism affected Djerban Jewry relatively little. Prior to independence Jews ran their own schools, emphasizing religion and Hebrew studies. Moreover, though they considered themselves Arabs, in contrast to most of their urban coreligionists, involvement in Muslim society was also limited. Few Jews were literate in Arabic, for example. In addition, Jews lived in their own villages. Contact with Muslims was particularly limited for women. Today the situation is changing, however. Young Jews attend Tunisian public schools and study both Arabic and French. Also, Muslims are beginning to settle in the Jewish villages, and aggregate social change has eroded the isolation of Djerba, fostering Jewish interaction with a broader spectrum of Tunisian society. With this introduction, the attitudes of Djerban Jews may be examined. As mentioned previously, the only respondent categories identified are older, poorly educated individuals and younger, better educated individuals.

First, poorly educated, older Jews support traditional prescriptions pertaining to women but otherwise hold negative attitudes about Arab-Islamic culture. They do not consider the study of classical Arab history important for Tunisian pupils; they do consider the study of French history important; and they believe Europe has nothing important to learn from the Arabs. These attitudes set them apart markedly from comparable Muslims. These Jews also display little attachment to Tunisian society. They do not believe the government cares about them, their levels of political information are low, and their relations with Muslims are usually limited or unsatisfactory. In addition, their inability to identify a Jewish leader from Tunis testifies to isolation from the mainstream of Jewish society. Since Muslim evaluations of the government are also low, Jewish attitudes may again reflect disapproval of policies affecting all Tunisians, policies perceived as particularly disadvantageous for nonurban areas. On the other hand, political information is much lower among Jews than Muslims, suggesting as much disinterest as active alienation.

Second, better educated, younger Djerban Jews have more positive views. With respect to cultural attitudes, they remain more traditional than comparable Jews in Tunis and differ substantially from Muslim respondents. But a majority considers the study of classical Arab history important, and almost a third believes that Europe can learn from the Arabs, a position not taken by any other Djerban Jews. With respect to attachment to Tunisia, a substantial majority has good or excellent relations with Muslims. Also, though the numbers remain low in absolute terms, these Jews are more likely to believe the government cares about them and to have information about Tunisian politics that older and poorly educated individuals. They are not more likely to have information about Jews in Tunis, however. In sum, while younger and better educated Djerban Jews do not have highly positive attitudes about Arab-Islamic culture and Tunisian society, their views are substantially less negative than those of others in their community.

Differences between respondent categories are generally similar in Djerba and Tunis. The principal dissimilarity concerns political information and the level of interest and salience it represents. Whereas the more positive attitudes of younger and better educated Jews in Tunis reflect detachment based on the likelihood of emigration, the more positive attitudes of comparable Djerban Jews are due to increased involvement in Muslim society. A new social order is emerging in Tunisia, and at least some younger and better educated Djerban Jews feel prepared to function effectively in it. Older and less well-educated Jews in both Tunis and Djerba fear the onset of a new social order. But the former are more likely to believe that their personal situation will deteriorate as a result. The latter, perhaps because their immediate social environment remains more traditional and stable, exhibit less intense alienation.

Turning to Morocco, the attitudes of urban Jews in the four categories of age and education can be examined. It will be recalled that, compared to Jews in Tunisia, Moroccan Jewry is characterized by a larger active population, a broader spectrum of residence patterns, and stronger community institutions. As previously mentioned, there are also differences between cultural traditions and government policies in Morocco and Tunisia.

First, well-educated, older Jews have mixed attitudes about Arab-Islamic culture. A majority accepts traditional prescriptions pertaining to women, and many, although not most, consider the study of classical Arab history important for Moroccan pupils. Also, a majority considers the study of French history unimportant, a characteristic not true of any other respondent category. On the other hand, only a third believes that Europe can learn from the Arabs. Thus these Jews appreciate the centrality of Arab-Islamic culture in Morocco, but hold that culture in only moderately high esteem. Older and well-educated Moroccan Jews display more positive attitudes toward their host society. They are more likely than other Jews to believe the government cares about them and to identify correctly a Muslim political official. Also, their personal relations with Muslims are usually good or excellent. Finally, as in Tunisia, they are more likely than others to be able to identify a Jewish leader, an ability suggesting a strong communal identity. Overall, then, while these Jews have mixed attitudes toward Arab-Islamic culture, they think well of Moroccan society more generally and have good personal relations with Muslims.

Second, poorly educated, older Jews have fairly negative views of Arab-Islamic culture. They hold traditional attitudes about women and are as likely as others to consider the study of classical Arab history important. But few believe Arab civilization has anything worthwhile to offer Europe, and most consider the study of French history important, suggesting a belief that Morocco should incorporate European elements into its cultural system as much as possible. Views about Moroccan society are much more positive. Most older and poorly educated Jews believe the government cares about them. They also have high levels of political information, in relative if not absolute terms, and the vast majority reports good or excellent personal relations with Muslims. Thus. these Jews maintain the disassociation between attitudes toward culture and society noted among better educated, older Jews. They do not hold the culture of the majority in high esteem, but they have positive feelings about other aspects of Moroccan society.

Third, well-educated, younger Jews are disproportionately likely to reject traditional prescriptions pertaining to women, about half think classical Arab history and French history are both important subjects for Moroccan pupils, and about a third believes Europe can learn from the Arabs. These attitudes resemble those of better educated, older Jews, suggesting that traditional culture is held in only moderate esteem but that European culture is accepted as peripheral in Morocco. Attitudes toward Moroccan society are even more negative. Most of these Jews believe the government does not care about them. Most have little political information about either

Moroccan politics or the Jewish community, and only a third has satisfying personal relations with Muslims. Thus they have low levels of attachment to Moroccan society, including weak identification with the Moroccan Jewish community.

Fourth, poorly educated, younger Jews have a more positive view of traditional Arab-Islamic culture. Most hold traditional attitudes about women; and though similar to other respondents with respect to views about studying classical Arab history, they are much more likely than others to believe that Europe can learn from the Arabs. Most also consider the study of French history important for Moroccan pupils, indicating a bicultural perspective. On the other hand, these Jews display little attachment to Moroccan society. Their views are almost identical to those of better educated, younger Jews, reflecting disinterest and detachment on both a political and personal level.

The distribution of Jewish attitudes is only partially similar among urban respondents in Tunisia and Morocco. As in Tunisia, esteem for traditional Arab-Islamic culture is related to high education among older Jews in Morocco. But, unlike Tunisia, the relationship is stronger and involves an association with low education among younger Moroccan Jews. Also, a belief that French culture is important in Morocco is associated with high education. In Tunisia it is associated with being older, or among younger Jews, with low education. Finally, positive attitudes toward the host society are related to being older in Morocco, there being little variation associated with education within age categories. In Tunisia, on the other hand, education is more important, especially among older individuals, where positive attitudes are associated with high education and negative attitudes are associated with low education.

Both similarities and differences between Jews in Tunisia and Morocco shed light on the origins of political attitudes. Both also suggest potentially generalizable insights about the minority group situation of Jews in the Maghreb. Well-educated, older Moroccan Jews are strongly attached to their host society, a phenomenon also observed in Tunisia and probably attributable to the same factors. These Jews were educated and socialized prior to independence, when the Maghreb's Jewish communities were strong and important. In addition, they are self-selected, having chosen to remain in North Africa. Finally, they have high status in communities with relatively few active and well-educated members and thus are afforded many opportunities to play useful and satisfying roles. In any event, it may be advanced as a general proposition that the context within which

North African Jewry resides produces positive attitudes toward the host society among older and better educated individuals.

Well-educated, older Moroccan Jews have mixed attitudes about Arab-Islamic culture, and most do not regard European culture as important for Morocco. This is in contrast to comparable Tunisian Jews who view Arabism and Islam in more positive terms and emphasize European as well as Arab culture. One reason for these differences may be the greater emphasis that Tunisia has placed on cultural reform and Francophonism since independence. A related possibility is that in Morocco traditional culture is bound up with a Berber as well as an Arab heritage, appearing as less of a sophisticated and urban civilization. For both of these reasons, Arab-Islamic culture may appear more conservative and inflexible in Morocco than Tunisia and also less compatible with European civilization; the circumstances of North African Jewry may produce among older and better educated individuals a view of the majority culture that is positive when this culture is perceived as sophisticated and dynamic and negative when it appears less suited to modern life.

Poorly educated, older Moroccan Jews have negative attitudes toward Arab-Islamic culture, as do comparable Jews in both Tunis and Djerba. This means that national variations in cultural tradition and government policy do not affect significantly cultural attitudes among this sector of Jewish society. The same is true of variations in the viability of the minority community and of urban rural differences within Tunisia. These Jews, whose status is low and whose prospects for emigration are limited, consistently hold Arab-Islamic culture in low esteem, probably feeling threatened by it and possibly believing their life chances have been limited by an association with it. It is thus possible to hypothesize as a general proposition that the situation of North Africa's minorities in retreat leads to low esteem for the culture of the dominant among older and less well-educated individuals.

Older and less well-educated Moroccan Jews have positive attitudes toward Muslim society, while comparable Jews from Tunis and Djerba tend to be alienated. This is probably because of the limited government emphasis in Morocco on policies stressing youth, education, and economic reform and also because of the greater security offered by Morocco's better organized Jewish community. In the former regard, Moroccan Jews feel less threatened by social change than do comparable Jews in Tunisia. In the latter, perceived challenges are mitigated to a greater degree by the personal and political support provided by Morocco's more viable

Jewish community. These findings lead to the general proposition that older and poorly educated minority group members are less alienated from their host society if their country is not ruled by a reform and mobilization-oriented government and if their community remains more intact.

Attachment to the host society is generally low among younger and better educated urban Jews in both Tunisia and Morocco. The only exception is a relatively high instance of good relations with Muslims among Jews in Tunis which may in part reflect the greater self-containment of Morocco's community but which is also at least partly attributable to the fact that most young Moroccan respondents are students in Jewish high schools. In any event, major similarities between Tunisia and Morocco suggest that the social and political context of these countries' Jews produces low attachment to the host society among younger and better educated minority group members in urban areas. This is in contrast to nonurban Jews in Djerba who, in relative if not absolute terms, are more involved in and attached to their host society.

Younger and better educated Jews in urban Morocco have more negative cultural attitudes than similar Jews in Tunis. In absolute terms their attitudes are about the same as those of comparable Jews in Djerba, but relative to others in their community they are also more negative. As with better educated, older individuals, these differences between Tunisia and Morocco are probably attributable to variations in government policy, which may be particularly significant among individuals who have grown up since independence, and to the dissimilar cultural traditions of the two countries. On the other hand, younger and better educated Jews in both Tunis and Morocco are disproportionally likely to regard French culture as unimportant for their host society, unlike comparable Djerban Jews whose perspective is more consistently bicultural. This difference is very possibly due to the likelihood of emigration among young urban Jews, a circumstance which reduces their personal stake in pluralist definitions of culture and social identity, and to the greater involvement in Muslim society of Jews and Djerba. A generalization that emerges from the latter observations is that the minority situation of North African Jewry creates a preference for cultural pluralism among younger and better educated individuals only if they are involved with the majority and fairly unlikely to emigrate.

The positive cultural attitudes of less well educated young Jews in Morocco contrasts with those of comparable Jews in Tunisia, the opposite of the pattern observed among better educated, younger Jews. This time, among individuals who grew up in independent

North Africa but are less well educated, being faced with a more conservative and less dynamic majority culture is associated with higher esteem. Attachment to the host society is low among poorly educated, younger Jews in both Tunisia and Morocco, as among better educated, young, urban Jews in each country. Thus, despite some differences in cultural attitudes, detachment and disinterest appear to be a common response among all young urban Jews to their minority group situation.

SUMMARY AND CONCLUSION

The future of North African Jewry is uncertain. The Jewish presence in the Maghreb is ancient, and as recently as 25 years ago there were strong and vigorous Jewish communities in Morocco, Algeria, and Tunisia. Today, however, only a few Jewish families remain in Algeria, and Jews in Morocco and Tunisia number barely 5 percent of their former total. Moreover, emigration, demographic dislocation, and institutional decay are continuing trends in Tunisia and Morocco, raising the possibility that a communal Jewish presence might disappear altogether from contemporary North Africa. This prospect is also reflected in generational differences noted among Tunisian and Moroccan Jews. Compared to older individuals, younger Jews have little interest in or attachment to their host societies. Indeed, there is evidence that many have come to think of themselves not as North African but as members of a foreign civilization who simply happen—temporarily—to reside in the Maghreb.[7] Thus, young Jews are unlikely to remain in North Africa, and their departure will leave the communities that remain that much less viable and self-sufficient.

There are a few reasons to posit a more hopeful future for North African Jewry. One is the difference between Jews in Djerba and the Maghreb's urban centers. Emigration and demographic dislocation, though significant, have been less intense in Djerba than in urban Jewish communities. In addition, young Djerban Jews are more involved in Muslim society than older individuals, a pattern opposite to that observed in the cities. Nevertheless, Djerba is at best a special case, notable precisely because it differs from other nonurban Jewish communities, almost all of which are now defunct. Moreover, the institutional capacity of the Djerban community is very low, lower in fact than in most urban centers. Indeed, the increased involvement of young Jews in Muslim society is probably attributable largely to this institutional weakness. Finally, as noted earlier, pressures on Djerban Jews have increased in recent years, raising questions about whether even the relative stability of this special community can endure much longer. Thus, even if Jews remain in Djerba and prosper, it is unlikely that they will constitute a viable and cohesive minority community as they have in the past.

Another more encouraging possibility derives from the observation that government programs and policies can either intensify or retard the rate of communal disintegration and produce either positive or negative political attitudes among minority group members. Thus, the fact that politics among the majority in Morocco appears to have slowed the disintegration of that country's Jewish community might mean that a government could reverse present trends were it to choose to do so. Moreover, following this logic, it is particularly noteworthy that Moroccan authorities have recently addressed themselves to precisely this objective, encouraging departed Jews to return and sponsoring visits by prominent Israeli Jews of North African origin. Yet again the prospects for a Jewish renaissance in the Maghreb, or even a stabilization of the present situation, are more illusory than real. For one thing, government policy has hardly been determinative in Morocco. Indeed, in the years immediately following independence, governments in both Tunisia and Morocco encouraged Jews to remain, to little avail. In addition, among younger individuals, whose predispositions will determine the character of their communities in years to come, differences associated with national variations in government policy are very limited, there being widespread disinterest and detachment among young Jews in Morocco as well as Tunisia.

A final possibility for the maintenance of Jewish communities in the Maghreb might be realized under conditions of an Arab-Israeli peace. Although the conflict has been a relatively unimportant factor in the decline of North African Jewry, peace could lead to increased trade and other contacts between Jews and Arabs; and Jews from the Maghreb, who are familiar with the Arab world, might be expected to play a special role in maintaining such contacts on the Jewish side. But, once again, this probably would not change things very much for Jews in North Africa. The principal focus of Arab-Jewish contacts would be the Arab East, not the Maghreb. Moreover, any increased Jewish presence in the Arab world would be on an expatriate basis, not through the expansion of national minorities in Arab countries. Thus, in sum, while it is always difficult to forecast the future and while there may be reason to hope for better Arab-Jewish relations generally, it is unreasonable to predict anything other than continued decline and disintegration for the Jewish communities of Tunisia and Morocco.

If the preceding is correct, the last 25 years have witnessed the unfolding of the final chapter in North African Jewish history. This chapter will not close for another generation or so, and individual Jews will remain in the Maghreb even after that. Nevertheless, the lesson of this inquiry is that conditions structuring the lives of Jews in independent North Africa, the absence of secularism, mobilized status, and small numbers, create irresistible pressures for communal disintegration. The present account of North African Jewish political life is thus a study of minority group response to these forces, of the character of communal life and political attitudes among a vulnerable minority under pressure and in retreat. In addition, however, and as made clear at the outset, this inquiry aspires not only to provide descriptive information about North African Jews during this period of this history, 20 years and more after the revolution of independence that established the conditions of their present-day life. It seeks also to define in conceptual terms the major determinants of political life among North African Jews and to develop propositions relating these determinants to minority group politics generally. A fundamental hypothesis is that small and privileged minorities in nonsecular states are confronted with irresistible pressures for communal disintegration. More focused propositions regarding the rate of this disintegration and the nature and distribution of attendant minority attitudes toward the culture and society of the dominant majority have also been advanced. Naturally these propositions are tentative, in need of independent empirical confirmation. Nevertheless, they give theoretical meaning to descriptive findings and suggest the general as well as the particular significance of conclusions about Jews in the Maghreb.

NOTES

1. The logic of presenting the sociopolitical context within which a minority resides in conceptual rather than descriptive terms, making its principal defining attributes independent variables in theories of minority group behavior, is discussed in John A. Armstrong, "Mobilized and Proletarian Diasporas," *American Political Science Review* 70, no. 2 (June 1976); pp. 393-408; Leo Kuper, "Plural Societies: Prespectives and Problems," in *Pluralism in Africa*, ed. L. Kuper and M. G. Smith (Berkeley: University of California Press, 1969), pp. 7-26; and "On Theories of Race Relations," in *Ethnicity and Peace Relations*, ed. Wendell Bell and Walter Fremman (Beverly Hills, Calif.: Sage, 1974); and Pierre Van den Berghe, "Pluralism and the Polity: A Theoretical Exploration," in Kuper and Smith, eds., *Pluralism in Africa*, pp.

67-81. For a fuller discussion applying this logic to the groups under study, see Mark A. Tessler, "Ethnic Change and Non-Assimilating Minority Status: The Case of Jews in Tunisia and Morocco and Arabs in Israel," in *Ethnic Change*, ed. Charles Keyes (forthcoming).

2. For general histories of North African Jewry, see H. Z. Hirschberg, *A History of the Jews in North Africa* (Leiden: Brill, 1974); and André Chouraqui, *Between East and West: The Jews of North Africa* (Philadelphia: Jewish Publication Society of North America, 1968). An extensive bibliography is available for the interested reader: Robert Attal, *Les Juifs d'Afrique du Nord: Bibliographie* (Leiden: s.n., 1973).

3. For a survey of politics in nonsecular states, see Donald Smith, *Religion, Politics and Social Change in the Third World* (New York: Free Press, 1971). Discussions relevant to the Middle East in general and the groups under study in particular may be found in Mark A. Tessler, "Secularism in the Middle East?" *Ethnicity* 2, no. 2 (June 1975); 178-203, and "The Identity of Religious Minorities in Non-Secular States," *Comparative Studies in Society and History* 20, no. 3 (July 1978); 359-73.

4. See Armstrong, "Mobilized and Proletarian Diasporas," for an elaboration of the distinction between mobilized and preletarian ethnic communities.

5. See, for example, G. William Skinner, *Chinese Society in Thailand* (Ithaca: Cornell University Press, 1957); Pierre Rondot, "Minorities in the Arab Orient Today," in *Man, State and Society in the Contemporary Middle East*, ed. Jacob Landau (New York: Praeger, 1972), pp. 267-81; Richard Coughlin, *Double Identity: The Chinese in Modern Thailand* (Hong Kong: Hong Kong University Press, 1960); Floyd Dotson and Lillian Dotson, *The Indian Minority of Zambia, Rhodesia and Malawi* (New Haven: Yale University Press, 1968); H. S. Morris, *The Indians in Uganda* (Chicago: Weidenfeld and Nicolson, 1968); and Pierre Van den Berghe, *Race and Ethnicity* (New York: Basic Books, 1974).

6. For the best general studies of politics and society in Tunisia and Morocco during this period, see the works of Clement Henry Moore, *Tunisia Since Independence* (Berkeley: University of California Press, 1965) and John Waterbury, *The Commander of the Faithful* (New York: Columbia University Press, 1970). Clement Henry Moore, *Politics in North Africa* (Boston: Little, Brown, 1971), and Elbaki Hermassi, *Leadership and National Development in North Africa* (Berkeley: University of California Press, 1972), advance comparisons between the two countries. For a summary of changes in Tunisian politics during the years following 1978, see Mark A. Tessler, "Single Party Rule in Tunisia," *Common Ground* 2 (Spring 1975); 55-64.

7. For a fuller discussion, see Tessler, "The Identity of Religious Minorities" and "Ethnic Change and Non-Assimilating Minority Status."

9

MAJORITIES AS MINORITIES: THE ARABS IN ISRAELI OCCUPIED TERRITORY

R. D. McLaurin

During the brief June War of 1967, Israel seized from Jordan East Jerusalem, which was soon annexed to Israel, and the West Bank of the Jordan River; from Syria, the Golan Heights; from Egypt, the Sinai peninsula; from Saudi Arabia, the islands of Sinafir and Tiran; and the Gaza Strip, which had been an international territory administered by Egypt. Of these territories, only East Jerusalem has been incorporated in Israel.* The rest are "occupied territories," or, as Israel calls them, "administered territories."† All had populations virtually exclusively Arab, although a considerable number of Druze inhabit the Golan. (Druze are viewed as Arabs by the Arab world but treated as non-Arabs by Israel.)[1] The establishment of *Kibbutzim* and *Nahals* (armed settlements) by Israel in the territories has

---

*The precise legal status of Jerusalem is a matter of dispute. Soon after capturing the city in June 1967, Israel passed a series of laws and implementing legislation "extending the law, jurisdiction and administration of the State" of Israel to East Jerusalem and some neighboring Arab communities (21 Laws of the State of Israel 75, 76, June 27, 1967). Since that time the government of Israel has never claimed—indeed, it has denied—that these measures amounted to "annexation" (see the letter from Abba Eban, Minister for Foreign Affairs, to the Secretary General of the United Nations, July 10, 1967. However, most observers have long viewed these Israeli laws and subsequent practice as constituting de facto annexation of East Jerusalem; moreover, numerous statements by Israeli officials suggest they, too, perceive East Jerusalem as having been annexed.

†Israeli occupation and control of Sinafir and Tiran islands have not been officially acknowledged by Saudi Arabia. In view of their limited size and significance, they will not be considered in this chapter.

had little effect on their overall demographic character, since two of the territories, the West Bank and the Gaza Strip, were (and remain) very populous.

This chapter analyzes the evolution of occupied territory Arabs' self-perception, goals, and attitudes toward Israel. It examines their views of their possible futures and the critical factors that have influenced these attitudes over time.

The analysis is based upon three main sources. Although each provided different perspectives, the conclusions have been integrated for the purposes of the report.

The first source consists of observations derived from a number of largely unstructured, open-ended interviews conducted by Emile Nakhleh among Gaza and West Bank Arabs in the summers of 1976 and 1977. The interviews involved local Arab leaders and many others, as well, and touched on a variety of subjects. A similar series of discussions was held by Edward E. Azar among West Bank and Gaza Strip Arabs and their leaders in the fall of 1976. These form the second basis of the chapter. The third source of data was the writings of West Bank and other Arabs, Israelis, and other observers.

ARAB ATTITUDES IN THE TERRITORIES

As in the case of Israeli Arabs—and for that matter other large groups—attitudes of Arabs in the occupied territories vary greatly. Nevertheless, it is possible to discern certain attitudinal eras and trends. Unfortunately, the occupied territories are more diverse and consequently less amenable to generalization. Most commonly, analysts use the West Bank as a model of the occupied territories. Yet, the West Bank situation is quite different from that of Gaza, or of the Sinai, and even further removed from those of Jerusalem and the Golan.

The decade of Israeli occupation may be divided into three periods: occupation and resistance, June 1967 to late 1970; regional and territorial transition, 1970 to 1973; and the current phase, one of organization and consciousness, which began in late 1973.

Stage 1: Occupation and Resistance, 1967-70

The June War was a military rout. Israel's seizure of the West Bank, the Sinai, the Gaza Strip, Jerusalem, and even the topographically formidable Golan Heights was effected quickly, efficiently, and decisively. Arab armies in Egypt, Jordan, and Syria were in total disarray; indeed, government authority was largely nominal in Jordan, Syria, and Lebanon. (That the Palestine Liberation Organization and its constituent groups grew to prominence during this period is hardly surprising. In many areas it was Fatah or other groups rather than the regime that held real power.) There was then little opportunity to organize an effective underground in the territories captured by Israel, an underground connected to the surrounding Arab states.

On Israel's side, the future of the territories was unclear. Many if not most Israelis believed the newly occupied areas would be used in postconflict negotiation to secure the historic Israeli aims: peace treaties, recognition, normal interstate intercourse, the right to send goods and flag ships through the Suez and the Straits of Tiran, and so forth. (Public and private Israeli statements from 1967 until the Jordanian civil war frequently addressed the possibility of using the territories as a "bargaining chip.") A small segment of the Israeli population sought the annexation of the West Bank to move toward borders they believed to be biblically ordained; the religious parties have consistently adhered strongly to this position, and most Israeli leaders referred frequently to the religious importance of Judea. Some Israelis felt the Golan Heights could never return to Syrian control untrammelled by conditions relating to Israeli security; indeed, one of the reasons Syrian leaders consistently pushed for a military approach to the conflict was their belief that Israeli statements about the nonnegotiability of the Golan were sincere.[2] In addition, virtually all Israeli Jews looked upon the annexation of East Jerusalem (which Israel annexed soon after the June War) as reasonable and desirable. Nevertheless, despite these attitudes the territories as a whole were not widely coveted.

Thus, as Syrian (Golan Heights), Jordanian (East Jerusalem, West Bank), and Egyptian (Sinai and the Gaza Strip, which had been administered by Egypt though not a territory subject to Egyptian sovereignty) administration was superseded by Israeli governance, there was no administrative goal or set of guidelines in the absence of a consensus as to the territories' future.[3]

Similarly, within the occupied lands, there was little cohesive concept of the role individuals might play in interaction with the occupier, less an agreed idea of workable interface with Arabs in the surrounding countries, and few communication or transportation links between the territories to develop or orchestrate either. Moreover, the Israeli military victory followed by occupation led to a large-scale Arab emigration from the territories, an exodus which further undermined social organization and both intra and inter-territorial communication. Thousands fled in each of the territories occupied, and the Arab emigration continued until mid-1969 in most of the areas.[4]

The first period of occupation was therefore one of social change bordering on chaos. Remarkably, even during the chaos, resistance was active in Gaza, Sinai, and the West Bank.[5] The resistance was initiated by organized committees, led principally by a spontaneous coalition of Baathists, Arab nationalists, and Communists, and concerned primarily with passive resistance: strikes, demonstrations, petitions, and protests.[6] Although this coalition gave rise to more active resistance in some quarters, it remained largely unorganized, and contacts with outside support continued to be limited.

East Jerusalem and the Golan Heights underwent an immediate social metamorphosis, the former as a result of its legal annexation to Israel, the latter because its remaining inhabitants were almost exclusively Druze, a minority group with whom Israelis have until very recently been able to develop cooperative ties.[7] Thus, the Golan Heights and East Jerusalem saw little resistance to Israeli control throughout the first period, while the other three territories were the site of continuing resistance in both legal and illegal forms.

The year 1970 was a critical year of change in the Middle East; that it greatly affected attitudes in the occupied territories should not be surprising.[8] New regimes in Syria and Egypt, the death of Nasser, the War of Attrition, massive influx of Soviet advisers in Egypt, futile pursuit of the so-called Rogers Plan, and the civil war in Jordan in September 1970—the aftereffects of many of these developments continue to ramify on regional interests to the present. All except the growth of the Soviet presence in Egypt directly affected the occupied territories. The new regimes were not as militant; indeed, Assad had made it abundantly clear before he took power that he intended to control completely Palestinian groups launching attacks from Syrian territory. The death of Nasser left a great vacuum in pan-Arab leadership, for Nasser was truly a transnational leader. His influence, although dimmed in the last years, was of great importance to Arab consciousness in and beyond the occupied territories. In some respects, then, Nasser's death allowed Arabism and Palestinian activism to pass beyond the "cult of personality" and take on more coherent and less national forms. The War of Attrition kept Israel on a quasi-war footing[9] and necessitated a variety of economic and administrative initiatives affecting all the occupied territories, especially the West Bank. Its effect on the Sinai was more direct but perhaps of less attitudinal significance. The abortive Rogers Plan provided a glimpse of an integrated settlement approach which has remained relatively close to likely parameters of any eventual solution. Yet, the initiative was important because it created standards against which other plans could be compared; because it served to mobilize individuals into groups (in support or opposition) which have remained largely identifiable and whose value systems have been reasonably consistent; and because in rejecting the annexation of the territories it reaffirmed to important members of the international community the inadmissability of geographical expansion through military act.[10]

Certainly, the most important of the many developments in 1970 was the Jordanian civil war, however. As a consequence of the large-scale fighting between Hussein's forces and those of the Palestinian resistance, Jordan and the PLO entered a cold war. Jordan was largely isolated from most of the Arab world, the Palestinian movement was in disarray, and Jordan was identified with Israel as the prime target of the Palestinian resistance.[11]

Stage 2: Regional and Territorial Transition, 1970-73

Dilution of enmity and organizational confusion after 1970 led to a definite erosion in the active resistance in the territories. If the Jordanian regime was to be as much the enemy as Israel, and if Israeli withdrawal were to lead to a return to Jordanian sovereignty over the West Bank, what was the point of hastening Israeli withdrawal? Thus, during most of the period from 1971 until the October War in 1973, Israeli authorities confronted little active resistance. Since this avenue was the sole route the PLO had concentrated on, with minimal attention on "the political struggle" in the territories, the 1970-73 phase can be viewed as the low period of the resistance.

In February 1973, the Palestinian National Council passed a resolution favoring the establishment of a unified front in the occupied territories. This organization, the Palestinian National Front (PNF), was founded on August 15, 1973, less than two months before the October War. This was the first organization to attempt to bring together the peoples in all the occupied territories. The war and the establishment of the PNF led to major changes in Arab attitudes in the territories.

Stage 3: Organization and Consciousness, 1973 to the Present

The October War breathed fresh air into the resistance in the occupied territories, a breeze which accelerated after the Rabat Conference in 1974 consecrating the new-found international strength of the Arab world. National pride was restored, and an intense Arab consciousness grew rapidly.

The close relationship between the PNF and the PLO and the more visible, or resuscitated, resistance after 1973 constitute warnings to Israel that the costs the latter must expect to bear in order to maintain the occupation will be higher than during the preceding period. Strikes, demonstrations, and other overt acts are merely one side of the coin; covert organization and planning are proceeding apace. In elections Israel forced onto the West Bank populace, for example, the winners were for the most part adherents to the PLO program.

The PNF is, however, moving to advance concrete ideas of peaceful settlement; in this respect, it is considerably in advance of the PLO, which, in order not to compromise its negotiating position, remains publicly firm on the necessity of dismantling Israel in its current form. Many senior PLO leaders have acknowledged privately at one time or another the desirability of a peaceful settlement and the acceptability of one providing for the coexistence of a Zionist Israel and a Palestinian entity. These leaders do not find it politically or diplomatically feasible to publicly advance such a proposal without Israeli concessions of similar magnitude, however.

The occupied Golan Heights, with its largely Druze population, has remained generally outside the mainstream of developments in the occupied territories. However, within Israel, Druze Israelis are in the process of developing an even greater consciousness of their Arabism,[12] and it is too early to predict what if any effect this may have in the Golan.

PERCEPTION OF ISRAEL AND ISRAELIS

The Arabs of the occupied territories would not be expected to hold the same view of Israel and Israelis as those living within Israel. The latter have lived in close proximity to Israeli Jews for 30 years, and to the extent Israel's continued existence is assured so is their status as a non-Jewish minority in a Jewish state. The inhabitants of the occupied territories, however, live in a transitional and unsettled status. Whatever the ultimate disposition of the territories captured by Israel in 1967, neither of the parties projects perpetual military occupation.

The uncertainty of the territories' status is reminiscent of the indecisive treatment of Israeli Arabs for many years after independence. Yet, there is no indecision on the part of the territories' Arab populations. Their long-term expectation is to return to Arab governance. That this should condition their views is hardly surprising.

We shall first consider some of the actions taken by Israel affecting the occupied territories and the views of their inhabitants. Then, we shall review their attitudes toward Israel, perceived Israeli goals with respect to the territories, and Israel's future.

Israeli Behavior in the Occupied Territories

From the time the Golan Heights, East Jerusalem and the West Bank, the Sinai, and the Gaza Strip were captured, the future of these territories has played an important role in domestic Israeli or in regional politics. We shall not review the debate—nor all the decisions, policies, and actions—of the Israeli government here, for that has been done elsewhere. Instead, it can be said briefly that the future of the territories has been influenced by considerations of security and religion. Although individual views have fluctuated over time, those Israelis principally concerned with security have sought to retain the Golan Heights and at least some Israeli presence in the West Bank; those whose views are principally influenced by religion have been more interested in the West Bank, including East Jerusalem. The Sinai's importance has been economic and military; it is a large area and serves as a buffer between Israel and her most powerful enemy. Yet, the security compromises that could be easily made in the Sinai, despite Egypt's military strength by contrast with Syria or Jordan, are far less practicable in the West Bank or the Golan.

Only East Jerusalem has been the subject of Israeli actions tantamount to annexation. (However, East Jerusalem's annexation has not been recognized or accepted by the international community. On the contrary, most countries, including the United States, have explicitly rejected it.)

A catalog of the types of Israeli actions that have gone into attitude formation may be useful. We must preface such a list with the notice that there is little Israel could have done to avoid Arab opposition in the occupied territories, for "the main source of unrest," as Moshe Dayan correctly observed, "is that they [West Bank residents] don't want to see us [Israelis] here, they don't like the occupation."[13] The most benevolent administration would have been unpopular, and Israeli occupation, while far from inhuman, was not wholly benevolent by any standards.

Among the actions that aroused concern of the occupied territory population were many of the same tactics employed so successfully over almost two decades from 1948 to control Israel's Arabs. The attempted use of segmentation, co-optation, and dependency— the triad correctly identified by Ian Lustick as the key elements in the control of Israeli Arabs—was clear in such actions as:

promotion of local government autonomy;
discouragement of territorial organization;
financial control over local governments;
intervention in educational curricula and materials;
use of financial grants to influence local cooperation;
undermining of industrial activity and deflecting Arab industrial
   workers to the agricultural sector;
control over Waqf land and finances;
seizures of Arab land;
establishment of Nahals and Kibbutzim;
destruction of homes, even whole villages, and eviction of their inhabitants;
deportation of individuals and groups;
refusal to allow return of large numbers of refugees;
prohibition of political strikes and demonstrations.

Although each of these activities has aroused a degree of opposition, none has been more potent than the establishment of Jewish settlements in the territories.[14] Israeli intervention in local religious and cultural affairs may be deeply resented; Israeli economic policy in the territories, which directly affects the well-being of their inhabitants, may be resolutely opposed; but these are functions of territorial *occupation*, which is a temporary phenomenon. Establishment of Jewish settlements is looked upon as a program of territorial annexation. Arabs in the occupied territories know enough of the fate of Israeli Arabs to recognize it as a fate they do not wish to share. (We cannot address the Golan Heights since the views of its Druze inhabitants are not known.)

The expropriation and purchase of Arab land and dwellings by Zionist organizations in Israel, then, when taken in conjunction with the establishment of Nahals and Kibbutzim and the destruction of Arab homes, raises the hackles of the Arab Palestinian residents of the occupied territories and has led to increasingly open opposition to Israeli military rule in the territories, especially since 1973.

Arab Attitudes

We have indicated that the Arab population of the occupied territories was largely quiescent between 1970 and 1973. Following the October War, however, the territories became much more active;

they were the scene of numerous strikes, demonstrations, and other forms of protest. Israeli occupation policy has likely crystallized the view of many territory residents that Israeli military superiority will inevitably be used for Israeli territorial expansion. Those aware of the demographic problem confronting the Zionist state recognize that Israeli expansion can lead ultimately only to mass deportation from the new areas. Moreover, while it may be true, as many Israelis point out, that Israel's occupation policy is "constructive and enlightened" by contrast with others in history,[15] it is also true both that its actions are still frequently cruel to the occupied and that a number of the more painful aspects of Israeli policy are subtle.

How, then, do the residents of the occupied territories view Israelis? And, more important, what is their attitude toward Israel itself? Are they reconciled to Israel's existence, or do they cling to and operate on the hope that the Zionist state eventually will be eradicated from the Middle East?

It must be said at the outset that these are difficult questions to answer. The real question might be, how has association with Israel affected the answers to these questions? There are no systematic surveys of Arabs in the territories to guide us. Moreover, we cannot rely overmuch on public comments of the leadership since the leaders are frequently responding to the demands of internal political dynamics in their public statements. We have therefore looked largely to conversations, first, with residents of the West Bank by Ian Lustick in early 1974 and Emile A. Nakhleh in 1976 and 1977, second, with residents of the Gaza Strip and the West Bank by Edward E. Azar in 1977, and last, to the Arabic literature, to assess the attitudes of occupied territory residents toward Israel.

Palestinians in the "administered areas," as Israel calls the territories, are, on the whole, strongly anti-Israeli. Despite Israeli economic exploitation,[16] the territories may well be in a better financial position today than if they had remained under Jordanian control. This is a point of contention, but it is certainly true that many or most individual Arab workers in the occupied territories, despite blatant Israeli economic discrimination against them,[17] have enjoyed a higher standard of living under Israeli occupation than they would otherwise have known. To recognize and acknowledge, then, as many Israelis do, the degree of hostility toward Israel in the occupied territories in spite rather than because of socioeconomic conditions is to come to grips with the depth of anti-Israeli feeling.

Yet, Israel's presence in the occupied territories is a realistic testament to Israeli military superiority. Arabs in the confrontation states may speculate as to the adequacy of Israeli offensive or defensive capabilities, but the daily lives of residents of the occupied territories are constant evidence of Israel's strength and determination. Thus, it might be expected that Arabs in the West Bank, Gaza, Sinai, and the Golan (to the extent the Golan, with its new sociological composition, can even be included with the other territories in psychological assessments) would hold far less to the idea of eradicating Israel as an essential condition of peace. These peoples have far more to gain and far less to lose by accepting Israel's "right to exist" in return for concrete territorial concessions: withdrawal.

Congruent with this expectation, most of the Arabic language literature on the occupied territories deals with short-term issues, political tactics, and personality and ideological questions. There is relatively little coverage given to Israel's future or to the acceptance or rejection of Israel as a state. Despite substantial attention to alleged Israeli abuses, illegal acts, and expansionist aims in the territories, condemnation of these practices and precepts does not lead to a demand to disestablish Israel. Indeed, we were unable to find any direct references to such an objective in the literature on the occupied territories. However, a few references to an undefined "final solution within the framework of the revolutionary movement of the Arab people in their struggle to liquidate imperialism"[18] and to similarly vague "liquidation solutions"[19] were encountered. These allusions are rare and generally limited to the more radical leaders and groups.

More commonly, one finds among the occupied West Bank residents scenario building that assumes the continued existence of Israel. The Azar, Lustick, and Nakhleh interviews all seemed to establish the necessity of creating a West Bank Palestinian entity or state that would not detract from Israeli sovereignty.[20] Some interviewees go even further to advocate "the creation of a Palestinian state with East Jerusalem as its capital; a state that would have normal diplomatic and economic relations with Israel."[21] This view is in fact quite compatible with the official Israeli aspirations as to the nature of their future relations with Arab states and more forthcoming (particularly with respect to economic relations) than most Arab regimes have seen fit to be in advance of negotiations.

It should be added that a small number of Arabs continue to hold to the goal of eradicating Israel. That this objective is not limited to the radical or Marxist elements, such as the Popular Front for the Liberation of Palestine (PFLP),[22] can be seen in the Azar talks, which note that some Muslim Brotherhood adherents, politically extremist on the opposite side of the spectrum from the Marxists, believe that Jews (and Christians, for that matter) should remain in the Middle

East only as subjects of pure Muslim states. Such views of the left and right are restricted to a minority, however.

POLITICAL SITUATION IN THE OCCUPIED TERRITORIES

The Status Issue

The key political question in the occupied territories—the question around which other issues, such as mobilization, leadership, organization, and role revolve—is that regarding future status. The status issue is highly complex, depending upon the political evolution of relations among several states in the region, domestic politics, local mobilization, superpower priorities and pressures, and a host of other factors. It is important to recognize, too, that while choice of political future options logically should influence leadership preferences on this highly salient issue, exogenous factors may create constraints too great to permit this expectation to be realized.

It seems clear from all sources used in this report that the desired future political status of West Bank and Gaza residents is to be citizens of a Palestinian state. The state is not envisioned as "the democratic, secular state" of which the Palestine Liberation Organization has spoken in all of Palestine, that is, a state replacing Israel. Rather, it is conceived of as an Arab state comprising the West Bank or the West Bank and the Gaza Strip, but precise borders are unclear in these discussions.[23]

The principal issue is whether or to what extent this Palestinian state would be independent of, federated with, or linked in some other way to Jordan. Since the 1973 war, attitudes toward Jordan seem to have softened somewhat, but the dominant view nevertheless seems clearly to favor the formation of an independent state—not a return to Jordanian rule.[24] While the idea of some sort of integral relationship between the East and West Banks of the Jordan is still supported by some West Bank leaders and notables,[25] others strongly oppose any ties to the Hashemite monarchy.[26] The Palestine National Front, which seems to have captured an important role in articulating and supporting the views of West Bank and Gaza Palestinians, recognizes and accepts, however, that links to Jordan will be close—based upon participation, cooperation, and common destiny.[27] The dominant view across all sectors is that, ideally, the Palestinian state will be sovereign, whatever the nature of the ties it chooses to establish with Jordan.

Leadership and Organization

Given the widespread support in the West Bank and the Gaza Strip for some form of Palestinian entity, it is hardly surprising that the residents of these areas support the Palestine Liberation Organization.

Although Israeli leaders have'frequently questioned the representativeness of the PLO, all recent studies agree that the PLO is widely seen as the most representative negotiator for the West Bank (including East Jerusalem) and Gaza Arabs.[28] Indeed, it is interesting that support for the PLO is undiminished by the fact that very few Arabs adhere to its professed goal of a "democratic, secular state" throughout Palestine. As we have seen, in fact, most reject this concept in favor of an Arab state in the West Bank and Gaza, yet apparently see little contradiction between their support for such a state and their support for the PLO as their representative.

The Palestine National Front, established in mid-August 1973, has rapidly gained adherents in the West Bank and Gaza.[29] The PNF is an outgrowth of the Palestinian National Council and, for all intents and purposes, a part of the PLO. It does not compete with the PLO for leadership of the West Bank and Gaza. However, the PNF has frequently maintained positions that conflict with those of the PLO. A careful review of these positions reveals that they may be more accurately reflective of future PLO viewpoints. For example, the Palestinian National Front is prepared to accept Israel's existence (see below) and even praised the Sinai I disengagement.[30] Before the PLO deigned to show any interest in the reconvened Geneva Conference, the PNF urged the PLO to take a positive position on the conference and, later, to participate.[31] Almost since its inception, the PNF has pronounced itself in favor of a *peaceful* settlement of the Palestinian problem.[32] Since 1974, both the PNF and the Jordanian Communist Party, to which the PNF also has close ties, have consistently supported the establishment of a Palestinian national authority in whatever territories might be returned by Israel, rather than insisting on the return of all Palestinian territory prior to undertaking preparations for administrative control.[33]

These leadership alternatives were not the only possibilities. Had Israel moved earlier to establish autonomous local leadership, such a move might have precluded the attitudinal shift toward the PLO. However, as local leaders gathered popular support they were—representing their constituencies' views—opposed to the occupation and consequently viewed as a threat by the occupier. Thus, the most effective leaders were deported, imprisoned, or undermined. By the mid-1970s, when Israeli authorities appeared to have realized the process that had taken place as a result, it was too late: popular attitudes were firmly behind the PLO as representative of West Bank and Gaza residents. A post-October War policy of establishing "civil administration" in the West Bank and Gaza was widely viewed as an attempt to set up collaborationist leadership groups in these areas.[34] Recent efforts by King Hussein to reassert Jordanian sovereignty over the West Bank are regarded with similar distrust.

The communist movement in the occupied territories has followed earlier communist precedents by aligning itself largely with the nationalist forces and providing them an organizational framework and infrastructure. Thus, local communist leaders have strongly supported and helped to accelerate the popular movement toward the PLO; moreover, they are prominent in PNF leadership. It is not yet clear whether the nationalist movement will swallow its communist supporters or vice versa, although the former is more likely in view of the relative size of each group. The critical point is that there is little "progressive" schism in leadership; only the "rejectionist" elements, which are very small, diverge from the unity of the front ranks.

Communication

Communication between Israeli Arabs and the Arabs of the occupied territories has changed significantly. The even more important changes in the nature of contacts with the rest of the Arab world since the occupation began have all been in the direction of limitation. In fact, however, very little effective constraint has been placed on communications channels.

Land

As we have indicated above, the principal rallying point for the Arabs in the occupied territories (as well as those in Israel itself) is the land issue. Similar to the Arab lands problem within Israel, the subject arises as a result of Israeli and Jewish acquisitions of land in Arab territory through legal, quasi-legal, and illegal means. It involves all of the territories—East Jerusalem, the West Bank, the Golan, Gaza, and the Sinai—although most of the controversy surrounds the first two areas.

Israeli land acquisitions are of four types: traditional sales agreements, expropriations and other seizures, operational use of state-owned land, and appropriation of abandoned land.

Occasionally, land has been sold by individual Arab owners to

Israeli state or Zionist land authorities. (Some transfers have in fact been made from Arab individuals to Israeli Jews, but more commonly the Jewish National Fund or the Israel Lands Authority has been the buyer.) Individual transactions have played a greater role in East Jerusalem than elsewhere. Jordanian law makes it a capital offense for Arabs to sell land to Israel or Israelis, and Arab pressure generally leads to Arab sellers' seeking secrecy.

Very substantial amounts of land have been expropriated. The extensive expropriated areas of the West Bank and the Gaza Strip have not resulted in as much international attention as the expropriation of virtually all Arab property in the Jewish quarter of Jerusalem, where Arabs are being removed—often physically evicted—solely in order to create a wholly Jewish area. Expropriation laws are general and have been used in even broader ways than the legislators originally intended.

State-owned land has been interpreted to include all land not officially owned. This stands in contrast to custom in the Arab countries, which has encouraged and protected villagers' use of nearby "public" lands for farming. Thus, lands traditionally used by Arab farmers are now viewed as state land, which Arab farmers have no right to use. As an occupying power, the Israeli state does not have the legal right to carry out such social changes under the Geneva conventions to which Israel is a signatory.

Finally, "abandoned" lands have been taken over by the state for "public use." Abandoned lands are those lands the owners of which are not in the territory. Thus, lands belonging to Palestinians who fled during or after the 1948 or 1967 wars, or who have been deported, are seized by the state—by Israel.

The issue that has aroused greatest concern in connection with the disposition of the lands in occupied territories other than Jerusalem has been and continues to be the creation of Israeli agricultural and paramilitary settlements and new urban centers. The reason for the concern is the widely shared view that the growing Israeli presence in occupied territories may impede significantly the process of Arab-Israeli peacemaking. The settlements have proliferated to the point that over 70 now exist, housing more than 9,000 Israeli Jews. Viewing this spreading presence as evidence that Israel intends to remain in the territories, Arabs in the occupied lands have consistently protested the settlements, but to no avail. The current government is composed of individuals likely to continue the settlements.

It has been suggested that the settlements approved to date form what may be the future boundaries of Israel in the leadership's perspective. If this hypothesis should prove to be well-founded, it should be noted that sizable Arab populations are currently within these lines. Recognizing the demographic constraints on implementation of the Zionist concept, many analysts suggest large numbers of Arabs will have to be "resettled," possibly within the next 10 to 15 years, in order to meet Israeli "security needs." Such a suggestion is, to say the least, an ominous prospect.

ARAB GOALS

Self-Perception

The issues of Arab goals and self-perceptions are far less complex in the occupied territories than in Israel because except in the Golan Heights there is no Israeli loyalty to provoke existential conflict. The Arabs of the territories other than the Golan view themselves as Arab Palestinians (in the case of the West Bank and Gaza Strip) or Egyptians (Sinai), not Israelis. Israelis among them in the military government and in the settlements established since 1967 are seen as unwanted foreign elements depriving the Arab residents of their rights, some of their liberties, and their national identity.

The Golan Heights, with the vast majority of its pre-1967 population in refugee status, is certainly a separate case. Virtually all those who remained after the Israeli capture of the area were Druze and were aware that the Druze in Israel had always been distinguished from and favored in treatment over other Arabs. Thus, those who remained expected—and to a large extent received—much more liberal treatment than the Arabs in the other occupied territories. At least up to the 1973 war, and for a time thereafter, the residents of the Golan Heights benefited from and at least tacitly supported Israeli occupation, With the growth of Arabism and Palestinianism among the Israeli Druze population, the Golan Druze's attitudes may change, although we have no evidence to support or refute the likelihood of such a change at this time.

For the Arabs of the Sinai there has been no conflict of identities. Traditionally seen by themselves and others as Egyptians, no one has attempted at any time to dissuade them from this allegiance or persuade them they should hold some other loyalty. The legitimacy of Egypt as a nation-state has never been in question.

In East Jerusalem and the West Bank, however, and in the Gaza Strip, wholly different circumstances prevail. Gaza Arabs have always been considered Palestinians, whether as refugees or habitual residents of the region. At no time before 1967 did Egypt, nor after 1967 did Israel, claim sovereignty over Gaza. Indeed, many of the Palestinian leaders (including Yasser Arafat) have worked in Gaza to build their Palestinian constituency.

By contrast, East Jerusalem and the West Bank, although incorporated into the Hashemite Kingdom of Jordan after 1948, had been part of the Palestine mandated territory. Thus, when Israel conquered the West Bank in June 1967, it captured a population nominally both Jordanian and Palestinian. Because in the years immediately following the 1967 military rout some Arab governments—including Jordan—in practice retained little capacity for control over their territory, the Palestinian resistance and guerrilla groups exercised de facto sovereignty in certain areas or for certain functions. The resurgence of Palestinianism was directly related to the renaissance of a Palestinian movement with real power. Indeed, Jordan became a Palestinian state in some ways, and the ties of West Bank Arabs were torn between the newer—and less "nationally" representative—Jordanian official states, on the one hand, and the more appealing, but still unlegitimized, Palestinian consciousness. This conflict only grew after the 1970 civil war in Jordan.

Black September, black because it was viewed as Hashemite oppression of Palestinians, however, combined with the absence of Arab government control over the West Bank territory conducing to the strength of a resistance movement, moved the West Bankers closer to a full-fledged self-perception as Palestinian. That there was residual support for a return of Jordanian administration cannot be denied, but the dominant tone of Arab identity in the West Bank after 1971 was clearly Palestinian.

Objectives

As we have indicated above, residents of the occupied territories aspire, for the most part, to Palestinian statehood. That is, they seek an independent Palestinian state located in the West Bank and Gaza Strip. Druze in the occupied Golan have not been surveyed or even widely interviewed; consequently, their desires are not known. It is believed that those still living in the Golan do not object strongly to Israeli governance, but given the growth in Arab consciousness among Druze in Israel a substantial degree of attitude change must be allowed for.

There is no contradiction in pressing directly for the realization of the political objectives of the territories' inhabitants, again unlike the case of Israel's Arabs. The former recognize that the alternatives are either incorporation into Israel (whether de facto or de jure), a return to previous status, or Palestinian sovereignty in the West Bank (with Gaza being absorbed by Israel, Egypt, or the new Palestinian state) combined with Israeli withdrawal from the Golan. East Jerusalem is probably amenable to no more than face-saving solutions that put the cloak of internationalism over the body of Israeli control. The alternative futures above are listed in order of Israeli preference and inverse order of Arab resident preference. The more aggressive are the Arabs in pursuing their objectives the more costly the Israeli preference schedule and the more benefits inhering in the Arab preference schedule. Thus, resistance has a reasonable incentive structure.

Specifically, the West Bank Arabs, most of whom prefer an independent future for their territory as a Palestinian state, are inclined to look to the PLO for institutionalized leadership. (That this fact has major advantages for Israel, as well as the more frequently discussed disadvantages, should be clear and is addressed in our final report.) The conclusion that most West Bankers anticipate is that once Israeli withdrawal has been secured, government of the West Bank—whatever its sovereign status—will be in the hands of leadership aligned with what is now called the PLO. No indigenous leadership is expected to contest PLO leadership effectively in the West Bank before a settlement (or for the next few years in the event Israel does not withdraw) because public support behind the PLO is strong.

The future of the Gaza Strip is more open to question. Although Israel has no strong religious incentive to move toward its annexation, and although the very large Arab population also argues forcefully against annexation, the return of the Gaza Strip to potential enemy control is a threatening concept to many Israeli leaders. Its location and the geographic and logistic constraints it places on Israeli strategy make the Gaza Strip a unique problem in the settlement process. Thus, the objectives of the Gaza population— which are clearly accession to independence as part of a Palestinian state—are not likely to figure prominently in Israeli decisions on the territory's future. Thus, the Gaza Strip will continue to support strongly the Palestine National Front and through it the PLO. In Gaza, there is no real alternative to PLO influence.

NOTES

1. See Peter Gubser, "Minorities in Isolation: The Druze of Lebanon and Syria," and Suhaila Haddad, R. D. McLaurin, and Emile Nakhleh, "Minorities in Containment: The Arabs of Israel," Chapters 5 and 4, respectively, in this volume.

2. See R. D. McLaurin and Mohammed Mughisuddin, Cooperation and Conflict: Egyptian, Iraqi, and Syrian Objectives and U.S. Policy (Washington, D.C.: American Institutes for Research, 1975), chap. 4.

3. Cf. Ann Mosely Lesch, Israel's Occupation of the West Bank: The First Two Years (Santa Monica, Calif.: Rand Corporation, 1970), passim.

4. Edward E. Azar and R. D. McLaurin, "Demographic Change and Political Change" International Interactions 5, no. 2-3 (1979); pp. 279-80. Cf. Edward Hagopian and A. B. Zahlan, "Palestine's Arab Population: The Demography of the Palestinians," Journal of Palestine Studies 3, no. 4 (Summer 1974); 32-73.

5. Cf. I. ash-Shu'aybi, "Ad-Daffah al-Gharbiyyah: Ihtilal Muqawamah, wa Nazra ila al-Mustaqbal (Nadwah)," Shu'un Filastiniyyah, no. 32 (April 1974); 30-55; Mamduh Bakr, "Sina' Taht al-Ihtilal al-Isra'ili," at-Tali'ah, no. 7 (July 1973); 45-48.

6. Dunia Nahas, "La Résistance palestinienne dans les territoires occupés," Travaux et jours, no. 55 (April-June 1975); 35-54.

7. See Chapters 4 and 5 of this volume.

8. Abraham S. Becker, "The Superpowers in the Arab-Israeli Conflict, 1970-1973," Rand Paper P-5167, December 1973, pp. 4-18.

9. See Lawrence L. Whetten, The Canal War: Four-Power Conflict in the Middle East (Cambridge, Mass.: MIT Press, 1974), passim.

10. Thus, the Rogers Plan had a greater symbolic than diplomatic significance. As we have pointed out elsewhere, the plan was later—and not because of its substance—considered the epitome of chimeric thinking by many in the Department of State. See R. D. McLaurin, Mohammed Mughisuddin, and Abraham R. Wagner, Foreign Policy Making in the Middle East (New York: Praeger, 1977), chap. 2.

11. See Paul A. Jureidini and William E. Hazen, Six Clashes: An Analysis of the Relationship Between the Palestinian Guerrilla Movement and the Governments of Jordan and Lebanon (Kensington, Md.: American Institutes for Research, 1971).

12. See Chapters 4 and 5 in this volume.

13. Quoted in the Jerusalem Post, October 27, 1968.

14. See the comments of 'Abd al-Muhsin Abu Mayzar, in Shu'aybi, "Ad Daffah," pp. 33-40.

15. Avi Shlaim, "Israel and the Occupied Territories," The World Today 29, no. 10 (October 1973); p. 422. It should be noted that Mr. Shlaim also describes Israeli military rule in the territories as "harsh."

16. See Abdul Ilah Abu-Ayyash, "Israeli Regional Planning Policy in the Occupied Territories," Journal of Palestine Studies 5, no. 3-4 (Spring-Summer 1976); 83-108; Sheila Ryan, "Israeli Economic Policy in the Occupied Areas: Foundations of a New Imperialism," MERIP Reports, no. 24 (January 1974); 7-8; and especially Brian van Arkadie, Benefits and Burdens: A Report on the West Bank and Gaza Strip Economies Since 1967 (New York: Carnegie Endowment for International Peace, 1977).

17. Van Arkadie, Benefits and Burdens. A more polemic, but also interesting and useful treatment is Jamil Hilal, "Class Transformation in the West Bank and Gaza," MERIP Reports, no. 53 (November 1976); 9-15.

18. A. 'Awwad, et al., "Hiwar ma' al-Jabbah al-Wataniyah fi al-Ard al-Muhtallah," at-Taliah, no. 3 (March 1974); 44-45.

19. Comments of 'Arabi 'Awwad in Shu'aybi, "Ad-Daffah," pp. 54-55.

20. Emile A. Nakleh, "The Arabs in Israel and Their Role in a Future Arab-Israeli Conflict," Abbott Associates Special Report, no. 17, June 1977; Ian Lustick, "What Do the Palestinians Want? Conversations in the Occupied Territories," New Outlook 17, no. 2 (February 1974); 25-28. The Azar and Nakhleh discussions were conducted principally with political leaders and other opinion elites; Lustick interviewed

journalists, students, and professionals, but also blue and white collar workers and farmers.

21. Lustick, "What Do the Palestinians Want?" pp. 26-27.

22. "Attitude of Palestinians in Occupied Areas," *The Arab World*, March 6, 1974, p. 12.

23. Ian Lustick, "What Do the Palestinians Want?" pp. 25-28.

24. See "A Decision for Palestinians: Self-Rule," *The Arab World*, February 14, 1974, pp. 11-12.

25. *Ash-Sha'b*, November 20 and 29, 1973. See also Richard Yaffe, "Among Jerusalem and West Bank Arabs: Disappointment and Gloom," *The National Jewish Monthly* 86, no. 7 (March 1973); 42. Cf. Hamdi Kanaan article in *al-Quds*, December 7, 1970; interview with Kanaan, *al-Ahram*, March 3, 1974. Rashad ash-Shawwa, mayor of Gaza, spoke frequently, too, of the Gaza Strip's joining in a confederation. (See various issues of *The Arab World* for example, August 17, 1972.) Unfortunately, the Lustick interviews excluded notables with ties to the Hashemites.

26. Compare, for example, the interview with Abu Iyad in *As-Safir*, May 31, 1974; *Maariv*, November 23, 1973; Yaffe, "Among," p. 39; I. ash-Shu'aybi, "Ittijihat as-Suhuf fi ad-Daffah al-Gharbiyah 'at-Taharrukat as-Siyasiyah Ba'd Harb Tishrin al-Awwal-'Sukkan ad-Daffah La Yuridun al-'Aysh fi Zill Nizam al-Malik Husayn;" *Shu'un Filastiniyah*, no. 30 (February 1974); 166-73.

27. See the PNF's bulletin of January 1974, and paragraph 11 of the PNF program, which affirms the unity of the Palestinian and Jordanian people while supporting the development of a popular struggle to transform the nature of the regime. Although the PNF's opposition to the Hashemite regime softened after the October War, 'Arabi Awwad, a PNF leader, was quoted in *an-Nahar* as late as the spring of 1974 as supporting "the establishment of a liberated, nationalist regime in East Jordan."

28. Shu'aybi, "Ad-Daffah," *passim*; A. Awwad et al., "Hiwar ma' al-Jabhah al-Wataniyah fi al-Ard al-Muhtallah," *at-Tali'ah*, no. 3 (March 1974); 12-45; Shu'aybi, "Ittijihat," pp. 167-69; Edward Mortimer, "Why the Arabs Rallied to the Cause of Palestine," *The Times* (London), January 29, 1974; Lustick, "What Do the Palestinians Want?" p. 26.

29. "Attitude of Palestinians in Occupied Areas," p. 11.

30. *Al-Anwar*, March 5, 1974.

31. *An-Nahar*, December 17, 1973.

32. Nahas, "La Résistance palestinienne dans les territoires occupés," pp. 48-52.

33. *An-Nahar*, March 3, 1974.

34. Musa Budeiri, "West Bank's Firm Answer," *Middle East International*, no. 56 (February 1976); 10-12; "West Bank Voices," *New Outlook* 18, no. 8 (December 1975); 19-24.

10

MINORITIES AND POLITICAL POWER IN THE MIDDLE EAST

Lewis W. Snider

The war in Lebanon, the Kurdish uprisings in Iraq, and the growing assertiveness of the Kurdish and Arab minorities in post-Shah Iran demonstrate how communal solidarities can trigger political conflict. They underscore the intensity and resilience of minority identifications and loyalties in the face of modernization and central government attempts to weaken, coexist, or complete with these intensely held corporate identifications.

The durability of minority loyalties is supported by the sobering observation of one student of ethnic nationalism that no examples of significant assimilation can be cited that have occurred since the advent of the age of nationalism and the propagation of the principle of self-determination.[1] Prior to the nineteenth century, those people who were attracted to another culture—those who were assimilated—were not aware of belonging to a separate culture group with its own proud traditions and myths. Thus there was no intense competition for group allegiance to a broader corporate entity.

By contrast, peoples today are more likely to be aware of their membership in a group having its own mythical genesis, its own values, customs, and beliefs, and possibly its own language which distinguish that group from all others. Competition for group allegiance is likely to be keenly felt, particularly where ethnic loyalty and ethnic identity do not correspond to the broader identity of the state in which the group is located.

In short, the available evidence suggests that minority identities may continue to be an irreducible problem for several Middle Eastern states, a problem which under certain circumstances could become a threatening, destructive force. Entrenched minority identification is likely to limit the extent to which the central government can extend its authority over the entire population. The state's vulnerability to foreign penetration through minority collaboration with an external adversary is one likely consequence for which there is ample precedent in the Middle East. The prospects for international conflict will be increased as political minorities seek external support for their causes and as these outside powers perceive it advantageous to undermine an adversary regime by supporting minority dissidence within that regime's borders.

The purpose of this chapter, then, is to identify conditions and circumstances that are associated with the magnetism and apparent staying power of minority political identities. The specification of these characteristics will then permit some assessments of the prospects and scope for cooperative coexistence between political minorities and the majority societies, and how the processes of modernization and social mobilization may affect these prospects.

LIMITS TO ASSIMILATION: THE ATTRIBUTES OF THE STATE

The political minorities described in this volume are ethnic groups in that they are self-differentiating peoples who view themselves as discrete primary social groups, culturally distinct from the majority populace. They share a common ideology, common institutions, and a strong sense of homogeneity upon which their political identity is based. Those minorities who aspire to political autonomy for a community within a definable geographic area can be considered a nationalist movement.

A basic obstacle to assimilation—and in some cases even to peaceful coexistence—is the way political legitimacy is defined in the Middle East. The legitimate political order, writes Michael Hudson,

> ... requires a distinct sense of corporate selfhood: the people within a territory must feel a sense of political community which does not conflict with other subnational or supranational communal identifications. If distinct communal solidarity may be understood as the necessary horizontal axis for the legitimate political order, there must as well be a strong, authoritative vertical linkage between the governors and the governed. Without authoritative

political structures endowed with "rightness" and efficacity, political life is certain to be violent and unpredictable.[2]

The principal sources of political legitimacy and political identification are ethnic and religious. In the Arab world the hallmark of political identity on the ethnic dimension is the Arabic language and culture, and on the religious dimension is Sunni Islam. In Israel political legitimacy is based on Judaic religion, Jewish history and culture, and the Hebrew language. In short a common barrier to assimilation of political minorities in the Middle East is the fact that there are no secular states in the region.

The political identities of the majority populations in the Arab states and Israel are based on ethnic religious nationalism. There is an intimate connection between the identity of the state and religion and culture of the majority which inevitably assigns an inferior political status for religious or ethnic minorities.

It was pointed out in Chapter 8 of this volume that secularism involves a disassociation of the state's political identity and the defending attributes of any group, be they religious, racial, cultural, or other. Secularism is absent if the avowed purpose of political life is the defense and service, on a priority basis, of a particular community of individuals instead of all citizens of the state on an equal basis.

The absence of secularism in this strict sense severely restricts the possibilities for the assimilation of political minorities, for even if they enjoy full civil rights they cannot share completely in the mission of the state. The constraint applies even in situations where the minority enjoys a privileged position and controls the reins of power. The position of the Maronite community in Lebanon is an example.

Another example is the Alawite-dominated regime in Syria. Evidence that the regime is aware of the problem is suggested by Peter Gubser elsewhere in this volume. He cites efforts by the regime to diminish the role of Islam and the position of the Sunni Muslim religious leaders in the state and society, and by President Hafez al-Assad to strengthen the Alawites' Arab-Muslim identity in the eyes of the majority population. These efforts include obtaining affirmation from Syrian Sunni 'ulama and a declaration from Lebanese Shi'a 'ulama that Alawites are Shi'a Muslims.[3]

The political and social consequences of being unable to share in the mission of the state, however, are most clearly illustrated in the situation of the Arab minorities in Israel where the mission of the Zionist state is totally incompatible with the Arabs' political existence. A similar problem exists for the Jews of Morocco and Tunisia and elsewhere in the Arab world. The most apparent difference between the two communities' situation is that the Jews do not feel the Arabs seized their patrimony.

Political Implications

The incapacity of minorities to share in the mission of the state may explain why secular ideological parties in the Middle East usually show a higher proportion of minority members than their percentage in the population. The Ba'ath Party traditionally has had a high proportion of minority membership (mainly Alawites, Druze, and Greek Orthodox Christians) relative to its percentage of the population. The Syrian Social National Party (SSNP), with its emphasis on secular criteria for political identity reportedly had wider appeal to the Christian minorities than to the Muslims. Indeed the party's founder, Antun Sa'adith, and many of its leaders were Christian. The doctrine of Syrian nationalism was articulated mainly by Christians and other minority groups in Syria and Lebanon who opposed Arab nationalism out of fear of Muslim hegemony.[4] Conversely, the SSNP failed to attract large numbers of Arab Sunni Muslims precisely because they were opposed to any movement that did not accept Arab nationalism.

Similarly the Communist Party of Syria and Lebanon with its strong nonsectarian orientation struck a particularly responsive chord among the Kurds and Armenians.[5] The Progressive Socialist Party (PSP), founded by the late Druze leader Kamal Jumblatt ostensibly to propagate the principles of socialism in Lebanon, emphasizes a nonsectarian view of Arab nationalism. The majority of its members are Druze. The PSP also attracted a number of political activists from other minorities however, because of its nonsectarian orientation and because Jumblatt was one of the indispensable traditional leaders in Lebanon by virtue of his leadership of the important Druze community. Thus, the PSP had the kind of access to Lebanese institutions that no other "radical" (radical by prevailing Lebanese standards, at any rate) organization enjoyed. At one time the party's leadership comprised 13 Christians, 2 Druze, and 1 Sunni Muslim.[6]

The most pronounced example of minority attraction to secular parties is Arab support for Rakah, the Israeli Communist party. This is a non-Zionist organization and the only party in which Arabs in Israel have had access to party power. However, as pointed out in Chapter 4 of this volume, the departure of most of the Jewish communists from Rakah after the split in 1965 has left the party almost isolated from the essence of Israeli politics. The effect of this isolation has been to underscore the illegitimacy of the party thereby reinforcing the isolation of Arabs from Jewish political life.

True, there are exceptions to the tendency of political minorities to broaden their participation in political life via membership in secular political parties. The Kurdish Democratic Party is an example, but then the Kurds are basically in opposition to the societies in which they are a sizable minority. The Alawite, Druze, and other minorities are not. If the practice is not more widespread it is because official tolerance for the existence of political parties in many countries (for example, Iran, Egypt, Algeria, Morocco, Yemen) has been very low. Nevertheless, the available evidence suggests that for the politically conscious minorities the most promising hope for achieving more complete and active participation in the mission of the state lies in working toward a redefinition of its mission so that the political identity of the state becomes disassociated from the defining attributes of any social group. With the exception of the Alawites in Syria and the Druze in Lebanon, however, these efforts have so far met with indifferent success.

Yet, the very fact that Middle Eastern minorities—even alienated minorities like the Arabs in Israel—have attempted to obtain legitimacy from the larger society may be an optimistic sign. For this type of political activity, carried on within channels sanctioned by the majority, implies minority acceptance of the legitimacy of the state. The fact that this positive participation occurs further implies that on balance the sacrifices and constraints imposed on ethnic minorities by their integration into a larger state are overshadowed by the perceived advantages of the situation. Such behavior at least leaves open the possibility that peaceful and cooperative political coexistence can be achieved between the minority and majority communities. The mere presence of a nonassimilating minority by itself need not mean the existence of a continued threat to the integrity of the state.

The consequences of minority political power become more threatening, however, if the minority believes it is unique in a most vital sense. In the absence of such a popularly held awareness there is only an ethnic group.[7] Its presence means the development of a separate national identity and the growth of minority nationalism. At that point the perceived benefits of belonging to a larger state may diminish substantially. Once people become committed to the belief that their community should govern itself, they come to view politics from an entirely different perspective with an entirely different purpose; and it is not likely that their minds will be changed by piecemeal concessions.[8] The long history of Kurdish wars for independence, and the existence of Kurdish political parties devoted to securing autonomy and independence, support this conclusion. Renewed Kurdish unrest has begun in the wake of the Islamic revolution in Iran. Promises of greater autonomy for the Kurdish community by officials of the amorphous Islamic Republic of Iran in the wake of clashes between Iranian troops and armed Kurds in the northwest provincial capital of Sanandaj are unlikely to reverse this new drive for secession.

A more recent example concerns the continuing conflict in Lebanon where the Maronite Christians, unable to eliminate their Palestinian opponents and restore their dominant political and economic position in Lebanese politics, appear to have given up their cherished concept of a pluralistic Lebanon. Instead, they appear to be establishing a *de facto* secessionist polity in the parts of Lebanon under their control.

The distinction between an ethnic group and an ethnic nationalist movement and the possible transformation of the former to the latter alert one to the possibility that the above examples may not be isolated incidents, but harbingers of what may occur elsewhere in the Middle East. The Arab minority in Iran located in the southwestern province of Khuzistan (the Arabs refer to it as Arabistan) began to voice its growing dischantment with the revolutionary government's treatment of minorities soon after the post-shah regime was established. At least three Arab organizations seeking autonomy for Khuzistan reportedly held discussions in May 1979 on self-determination within a "federal Islamic republic" in the Persian Gulf port of Khorramshahr, according to news releases from one of the groups, the Front for the Liberation of Ahwaz (FLA).

The Iranian Arabs, representing about 20 percent of the work force in Iran's oil industry, threatened strikes and sabotage of key oil installations unless the government halted its attacks and agreed to safeguard minority rights. In addition to grievances concerning alleged suppresion of their rights, the Arabs insisted on priority allocation of the top jobs in their region. The discontent went beyond complaints of Iranian discrimination against Arabs, and escalated to Arab demands for autonomy. The leader of the FLA, Sayyed Abbas al-Mahar, warned the Khomeini government that unless self-rule were granted the Arabs of Khuzistan would resort to "armed struggle and the oil weapon."[9] In June fierce fighting broke out in Khorramshahr and the refinery port of Abadan between Iranian government troops and Arab guerrilla forces. A state of emergency was declared in Khorramshahr—the first anywhere in Iran after the overthrow of the shah.

Precisely what these events portend—greater autonomy, return to the status quo, or the birth of an active and permanent Arab separatist movement—is impossible to predict. What is important for the purposes of this discussion is that the outcome could be decided by changes in the Arabs' political identity. Iran's Arab population (estimated to number about two million)—or at least that part of it which is native to Iran—is Shi'a rather than Sunni Muslim. The neighboring Arab governments of Iraq and Saudi Arabia are Sunni or Sunni-dominated. The Shi'a attachment may inhibit Arab separatist inclinations to turn to Iraq for support against perceived oppression. Iraq may be equally disinclined to offer support. In Iraq the Shi'a Arabs outnumber the Sunnis who nevertheless have traditionally governed the country, both under the Hashemite monarchy and under the republic. Sunni-Shi's rivalry within Iraq must be taken into account in Iraq's response to whatever happens in Khuzistan.

On the other hand, continued friction between the Arab minority and the Iranian majority could lead to increased emphasis on the Arab dimension of the minority identity. That would likely accelerate the centrifugal separatist tendencies already set in motion as it would stress the ethnic difference between the Arab and Persian communities. An appeal to Iraq for support on Arab nationalist grounds may have the effect of blurring the Sunni-Shi'a dimension and place more pressure on the Baghdad government to respond positively. Under the shah, Iraqi inclinations to intervene on behalf of the Arab community in Khuzistan would have been discouraged by Iranian military superiority. By the spring of 1979 when fighting broke out in Khuzistan, however, the fighting ability of the Iranian armed forces was highly questionable. Not only had the army's ranks been severely depleted by desertions and AWOLs—discipline and morale were so low as to leave serious doubts in the minds of observers on the scene whether the army could function effectively as a fighting force.[10] Much of its equipment is no longer in working condition and the air force had been grounded for lack of spare parts. Thus, there is no serious military deterrent to Iraqi intervention. Yet, there is no serious military deterrent to Iraqi intervention. Yet, any government in Tehran would be expected to fight to prevent the loss of its vital oil province. Faced with the prospect of military defeat even if no power intervened on the side of the Arab nationalist forces, it could be expected to call on foreign assistance to reverse the disaster. The result could be an interstate war.

The potential for a secession of a different sort concerns the

Alawites of Syria should they be displaced from political power by a Sunni Muslim majority regime. In that case the idea of autonomy or secession may be attractive to the Alawites if they believed they would suffer unequal treatment at the hands of a nonsympathetic Syrian government. The establishment of an autonomous (and possibly independent) Maronite regime in Mt. Lebanon sets a precedent for the Alawites to follow in the Latakia province of Syria. Thus, Peter Gubser points out that the current regime's heavy investment in Latakia may not only be for the benefit of the Alawites under a Syrian government but in preparation for the time when the Alawites fall from power.[11]

The foregoing observations apply to minorities who are in power as well as those whose status is that of second—or third-class citizens. If the inferences drawn from these observations are valid, they challenge one of the dominant assumptions of many political scientists and sociologists who are students of nation building and political integration: that nation building is an evolutionary process in which local loyalties are eroded and replaced by a wider loyalty to the state as a result of social mobilization, industrialization, improved communications, and the like.[12] The nonsecular criteria for political identification with the state would seem to forestall, if not preclude altogether, such an evolutionary process toward assimilation.

Furthermore, speculation on possible reactions to a loss of political power in Syria suggests that the weakening or strengthening of minority political identification does not necessarily have to be a unidirectional process. Trends toward assimilation can be reversed.[13] If the political position of the Alawites in Syria and the Assad regime's continuing efforts to gain legitimizing approval from the Sunni and Shi'a 'ulama imply that the processes of political integration and assimilation are at work, the possibility that this trend—if, indeed, it is a trend—can be reversed is illustrated by the real possibility of Alawite separation should they lose power to an unsympathetic Sunni majority.

The Israeli Arabs offer a more developed instance of reversal in assimilation of minorities. Survey research on the national identity of Israeli Arabs, reported elsewhere in this volume, revealed that in 1966 over half the sample of Arab respondents preferred the term Israeli over Arab or Palestinian. After the 1967 war, however, a similar sample chose Arab as the preferred description and placed Israeli after Palestinian. The change in the Israeli Arabs' political consciousness is documented by a third survey taken in 1974-1975. The one revealed that only 14 percent of the respondents felt the word Israeli described them well, but fully 63 percent thought the term Palestinian did. Almost a majority believed the term Israeli described them very little or not at all (see Chapter 4). The Israeli government believed that with a government-approved education system the new generation of Arabs would be properly integrated into Israeli society and forget its Arab political identity. Israel's wars with the Arab states apparently have contributed to just the opposite result.

Conversely, what appears to be Arab separatist agitation in Iran could be reversed *if* this nationalist sentiment has arisen as a consequence of specific grievances. In that case separatist inclinations could possibly be halted or reversed by remedying the specific grievances. This sort of reversal assumes, however, that the perceived benefits of belonging to a larger state have not diminished in the meantime. But even if these perceived benefits remain, what was said earlier concerning the attraction of political minorities to secular-oriented political movements suggests that they may not be sufficient to end Arab agitation. The Arabs of Khuzistan could join forces with more secular-oriented political groups in Iran who are becoming increasingly alienated by the severely conservative and authoritarian rule of Ayatollah Khomeini and his Islamic fundamentalist followers. The oil fields in Khuzistan and the refinery at Abadan have long been the site of Iran's best organized trade unions which are subject to leftist, secular influence. The oil workers have already clashed with Muslim fundamentalists in Abadan. The 200,000 oil workers there whose general strike in the winter of 1978-1979 was decisive in overthrowing the shah, are predominantly of Arab origin. Oil worker strikes could be used to bring down the Khomeini regime or to gain a measure of autonomy for the Arab community.

Whether Arab nationalist sentiment in Khuzistan can be contained and separatist inclinations reversed may depend in large measure on how the central government responds to Arab grievances. Yet the upsurge in minority consciousness in the 1970s in the Middle East and elsewhere suggests that it may be easier to reverse progress made toward assimilation than contain growth of minority national consciousness. The reasons for this asymmetry lie in the sources of minority corporate cohesiveness and the factors that have the effect of reinforcing this cohesion.

LIMITS TO ASSIMILATION: MINORITY COHESION AND MODERNIZATION

If the nonsescular nature of Middle Eastern states has the effect of sustaining or reinforcing minority identities, so apparently do certain attributes and conditions associated with the minorities themselves.

Cultural distance *per se*, even if it could be precisely measured, does not have very much explanatory power either in accounting for minority cohesion or communal conflict. The Berbers in North Africa and Kurds in Iraq, for example, are both non-Arab Sunni communities living in Arab Sunni states. Both have their own languages. Yet the Kurds are in opposition to the societies in which they reside— Arab, Iranian, Syrian, and Turkish alike—while the Berbers seem to be far more advanced toward assimilation than any other major minority group in the Middle East. The Maronities of Lebanon may appear culturally closer to the Sunni Arab majority than the Armenians and no more distant from the majority than the Greek Orthodox community. Yet the Maronites have maintained a virtually uncompromising stand in their ongoing conflict with the largely Muslim-leftist and Palestinian forces, preferring to risk the dismantling of Lebanon as an independent state altogether to the conceding of political privileges they held in prewar Lebanon.

Geographical and demographic circumstances are more salient. First the most cohesive minorities are concentrated in a distinct territorial location: The Arabs of Iran, Alawites, Druze, Maronites, Berbers, Kurds, and Zaydis of Yemen all have distinctive territorial "heartlands." Many of these have the added topographical advantage of a mountainous base from which defense or domination can be supported.

A prominent social trait common to many of these groups is a predominantly rural lifestyle in societies that are primarily urban. The predominantly rural lifestyle applied to the Arabs in Israel until the early 1970s, the Arabs in Khuzistan, the Alawites in Syria, the Druze in Lebanon and Syria, the Maronites in Lebanon, the Kurds in Iraq, Syria, Iran, and Turkey, the Zaydis in Yemen, and, to a lesser extent, the Berbers in Algeria and Morocco. The contrast in lifestyle has undoubtedly reinforced the insulation of many of these communities from the majority population. In other words, the clash between the "alien rule" of the states and the minority groups' determination to preserve their unique cultural patterns and lifeways is minimized. The effect has been to perpetuate minority cohesion while diluting any countervailing influence of the majority identity.

Relative size of the minority may be an important attribute when considering the potential for communal conflict. Hudson points out that in the conflict involving the Kurds, the Maronites, and the Zaydis the contending parties are not very unequal in size. Consequently each side poses a potential threat to the other.[14] Hudson's observation would also apply to the Arabs in Israel, particularly when the difference between Arab and Jewish Israeli rates of natural increase is considered.[15] it does not apply, however, to the Arabs in Iran who constitute a tiny fraction (less than one percent) of the total population of Iran, though a majority in southwestern Iran.

The Role of Communications and Modernization

Geographical concentration, topographical advantage, or predominantly rural lifestyle do not provide a very complete explanation for minority cohesion or communally-based conflict. The Berbers, for example, possess many of these traits. (The exception is territorial concentration.) Yet they are the closest to an assimilated minority of all those surveyed in this volume.

The Berbers exhibit another trait, however, which alerts one to the importance of social mobilization in general and the role of communications in particular: the Berbers are decentralized, scattered along several isolated mountain locales, have no strong horizontal communications links between their communities within the same state, and no history of cooperation among their settlements in Tunisia, Algeria, and Morocco. More important, the Berber language is mainly oral not written. Hence one vehicle of cultural transmission remains almost dormant. Compare this situation to another non-Arab, Sunni minority, the Kurds. This group has maintained close contact among its communities across national boundaries— the Kurds have an active press in their own language.

The state of communication links among members of a minority community provide only a partial glimpse of the impact of communications and ease of transportation on minority cohesion. Equally, if not more important, is ease of the communications and transportation between central government and the majority, on the one hand, and the minority community, on the other.

Presumably the central governments of the Middle East states have long sought to make their rule effective throughout their entire territories. Advances in communications and transportation links however, were necessary before central government presence could be introduced in the remote territories of minorities. As communications and transportation links improve, central government presence is further extended into remote minority communities. The increasing contact between majority and minority communities may confront the minority with the problem of cultural preservation. An unintegrated state poses no serious threat to the cultural patterns or lifestyle of various minorities. But, as Connor has noted, improvements in the quality and quantity of communications and transportation progressively erode the cultural isolation in which an ethnic minority could formerly shield its cultural purity from the subverting influences of other cultures within the same state. The result of such erosion is likely to contribute more to xenophobic hostility than assimilation or integration.[16]

Television may be particularly effective in accelerating minority self-consciousness and hostility. Television, as Birch has indicated, differs from other media because it brings the majority culture right into the viewer's living room. It captures the imagination of children more effectively than does radio or the printed word.[17] Television also differs from the printed word because minorities seldom have access to this medium in the way they do to publishing firms. Apart from the fact that television production costs are enormous relative to print media, television in the Middle East is almost always government controlled.

If improvement in communications and transportation increase the cultural awareness of minorities by making their members more aware of the distinctions between themselves and others, then not only do individual minority members become more aware of alien ethnic groups; they also become more aware of those who share their own identity. Thus prior to 1966 the Israeli Arabs were unable to interact with one another because of the constraints imposed by the presence of the Israeli military government upon Arab freedom of movement. It was during this period when the Arab or Palestinian identity was weaker than the sense of being Israeli. The Israeli identity was able to take root among Israeli Arabs in spite of the siren calls of propadanda broadcast from neighboring Arab countries, particularly the Voice of the Arabs from Cairo. Between 1967 and 1973 when, according to survey results reported earlier, the Israeli identifier apparently became displaced by the Arab label, Israeli Arabs were able to interact more freely with one another, travel around Israel and come in contact with Arabs from the occupied territories. The continued shift in specificity of identity from Arab to Palestinian reported after the 1973 war is attributed by Haddad, McLaurin, and Nakhleh to proliferation of contacts among Israeli Arabs within and outside Israel through institutionalized channels of communication (see Chapter 4).

Communications are a prerequisite for social mobilization, "the process in which major clusters of old social, economic and psychological commitments are eroded or broken and people become available for new patterns of socialization."[18] Mobilization not only involves making people available for new patterns of behavior; it also means "putting them in situations where they have new needs and new learning experiences."[19] Thus mobilization denotes three properties: availability, needs, and learning situations. Karl Deutsch has listed a number of specific processes of changes denoted by social mobilization including change of residence, of social setting, of occupation, of face-to-face associates, of institutions, of experiences, and of expectations.[20] Since social mobilization is a multidimensional process of change that happens to large segments of a population in countries that are moving from traditional to modern life, one indication of this concept is the percentage of the population exposed to the mass media; another is the percentage of the population that is literate.

By most criteria of social mobilization (that is, percentage of the population who have changed residence, total population living in towns, the percentage of the population engaged in nonagricultural occupations), social mobilization has been taking place in the Middle East—especially in Lebanon, Iran, and Israel—for several decades, as communications have continued to improve. What is important for the purposes of this discussion is that as social mobilization has proceeded apace, so, apparently, has minority political consciousness. Yet much of the literature on nation-building assumes that social mobilization will contribute to assimilation. It further assumes that modernization will also strengthen the momentum toward assimilation. In fact these assumptions have been given almost official approval in Israel where it was believed that as Arabs became more modernized, better educated (more secular?), and more advanced economically they would beocme more accepting of Israel.[21]

It is often assumed that modernization is the handmaiden of assimilation and political integration.[22] But modernization involves the ability to absorb and generate change, to *adapt*, a process where advanced nontraditional practices, technology, and economic life are introduced and accepted by an increasingly larger proportion of the population. The process does not necessarily mean the repudiation of values, loyalties, and corporate identities.

Similarly, social mobilization and assimilation are causally separate processes. Their relationship to each other, according to Deutsch, is mainly chronological:

> If assimilation stays ahead of mobilization or keeps abreast of it, the government is likely to remain stable, and eventually everybody will be integrated into one people.... On the other hand,

where mobilization is fast and assimilation slow the opposite happens. More and more highly mobilized and disgruntled people are held at arms length from the politics and culture of their states, and they easily become alienated from the government, the state, and even the country to which they thus far had belonged.[23]

That social mobilization and modernization are compatible with traditional loyalties and identities, and need not inevitably lead to their erosion is suggested in the following passage by Deutsch:

> We have seen that the more gradually the process of social mobilization moves, the more time there is for social and national assimilation to work. Conversely, the more social mobilization is postponed, the more quickly its various aspects—language, monetization, mass audience, literacy, voting, urbanization, industrialization—must eventually be achieved. But when all of these developments have to be crowded into the lifetime of one or two generations, the chances for assimilation to work are much smaller. The likelihood is much greater that people will be precipitated into politics with their old languages, their old outlook on the world and their old tribal loyalties still largely unchanged; and it becomes far more difficult to have them think of themselves as members of one new nation.[24]

The outcomes Deutsch described summarize conditions in Lebanon between 1955 and 1975 and what may be taking place among the Arab communities in Israel. Lebanon is a small country where mass communications have become well developed, in which short distances mean relative ease of travel, and where many of Lebanon's Christian minorities live in religiously mixed villages. It is also a country in which one of the most specialized institutional channels of communication and political socialization—the schools—is heavily sectarian.[25] During the mid-1960s the pace of social mobilization and modernization accelerated, characterized by rapid urbanization and growing poverty belts in which the gaps between the wealthy privileged minority and the burgeoning urban poorer strata became increasingly conspicuous. As the increase in peasant migration to the cities continued unabated, the job market in the cities became incapable of absorbing more new migrants. The number of unemployed and dispossessed was disproportionately high among the Muslim (mainly Shi'a) communities. Hence, their frustrations accentuated the cleavages in the confessional society. The Muslims, and particularly the Shi'ites, suffered most acutely from poverty and low social and political status. Conversely the most prominent positions in the socioeconomic and political structures in Lebanon were occupied by, and often reserved for, the Christians, particularly the Maronites. The result was that the Lebanese sectarian communities, and not just individual Lebanese, became "arranged into hierarchical, stratified structures of privileged and deprived communities."[26]

The same accelerated process has taken place among the Israeli Arabs since 1966 when the military government control over Arab freedom of movement was lifted. Israel's policy of Arab land confiscation has largely destroyed the Arab village agricultural economy in many areas, and contributed to a burgeoning Arab landless proletariat. The accelerated rate of transformation is illustrated by the fact that in 1963 75 percent of the Arabs in Israel were located in rural areas. By 1973 56 percent were residing in urban areas, and it is estimated that 90 percent of Arab village workers commute daily to Jewish cities in order to work.[27] Arab incomes and consumption have declined in relation to the rest of the economy while many disparities between Arab and Jewish economic sectors have increased. These circumstances may help to explain why the Israeli policy of de-Arabization and Judaization through the school system, designed to reduce Arab national consciousness (described in Chapter 4 of this volume), has so far met with indifferent success.

The causal linkages between social mobilization, ethnolinguistic fragmentation, and assimilation specified by Deutsch are supported by empirical evidence by Douglas Hibbs, Jr., in a cross-national study of mass political violence (n=108 countries). Using multiple regression techniques, Hibbs looked at the impact of ethnolinguistic fractionalization, social mobilization, and the interaction effect of the two on frequency of political separatism. The results strongly support the position that a mobilized *and* differentiated population is a particularly volatile combination. Ethnolinguistic fractionalization alone had no significant impact on separatism when controlling for mobilization. Social mobilization alone appeared to have a moderately dampening influence on separatism when controlling for ethnolinguistic fractionalization. However the *conjunction* of social mobilization *and* ethnolinguistic fractionalization totally eclipsed the inverse bivariate relationships between mobilization and separatism and fractionalization and separatism.[28] Separatism, in turn, was shown to be a strong predictor of internal war (a composite measure indexed by frequency of deaths from political violence, armed attacks, and assassinations). Thus Hibbs concludes that the conjunction of high levels of social mobilization and a highly differentiated population contributes indirectly to internal war through its

strong direct effect on political separatism. Ethnolinguistic fractionalization was also shown to have a strong impact on group discrimination. In other words, the more differentiated the population, the
higher the level of group discrimination. Group discrimination in
turn was found to have a strong causal impact on collective protest
(a composite measure indexed by riots, antigovernment demonstrations, and political strikes). Thus ethnolinguistic fractionalization
was mediated through group discrimination to indirectly affect the
incidence of collective protest.[29] The direct and indirect linkages are
diagrammed in Figure 10.1.

The linkages in Figure 10.1 underscore a point made earlier that
cultural distance *per se* does not have any direct effect in communal

FIGURE 10.1

**Summary of Causal Linkages between Ethnolinguistic
Fractionalization, Social Mobilization, and Political Violence**

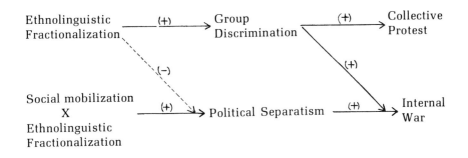

──────→ denotes strong causal relationship

------→ denotes weak causal relationship

Source: Compiled by the author.

conflict but is mediated through other variables. Note that two critical mediating influences—level of social mobilization and group discrimination—are to some extent subject to influence by state policy.

Implications for Assimilation and Cooperative Coexistence

That social mobilization need not lead to a transfer to primary loyalties from the minority group to the state, paritcularly in the Middle East, seems abundantly clear. If anything, Deutsch's theoretical scheme accounts for the apparent ascendancy of ethnic nationalism as political force. But what of the future? Recall that large segments of several prominent political minorities discussed in this volume are concentrated in relatively isolated rural areas. Thus, they have not yet been significantly mobilized in the sense of being made available for new behavior patterns, and being put in new situations where they acquire new needs and new learning experiences. The rapidity with which they are mobilized may unleash more centrifugal forces in the political system, perhaps raising the level of collective protest in some cases and weakening political stability in others.

The juxtaposition of empirical evidence with the theoretical orientation just reviewed suggests that primordial loyalties and identities are likely to be reinforced as communications and transportation media progressively curtail the cultural isolation of additional segments of minority populations and as these people become more aware of the distinction between themselves and others. The one possible exception is the Berbers for whom the process of assimilation may have proceeded far enough to where social mobilization will only accelerate the prevailing trend. If the Berger populations were mobilized at a fairly rapid rate, however, the assimilation trend that Hazen describes could be reversed.

The rate at which minority populations are mobilized, the kind of new needs that confront them, and the institutional channels of communication that are open to them for expressing their needs, are highly likely to color their view of politics. They can also be expected to affect the perceived trade-offs between the advantages of belonging to a larger, multiethnic state and self-government. The new learning experiences encountered by these populations are likely to be shaped by their increasing contact with members of the political majority and with one another. What seems certain, however, is that the corporate cohesiveness of political minorities in the Middle East is not likely to decrease.

Dimensions of Assimilation and Political Conflict

Communal tensions between minority and majority populations in the Middle East obviously exist. Yet, none of what has been said so far warrants the conclusion that the region is seething with communal unrest or that it is highly susceptible to Balkanization. Communal tensions do not in themselves generate conflict. But the Middle East has witnessed several fierce and prolonged conflicts between opposing forces arrayed along communal lines and which appear to be primordial in nature:

The civil war in Yemen in the mid-1960s pitted the royalist Zaydis on the side of the deposed imam against the orthodox Shaf'is who comprised the bulk of the republican forces.

The Kurdish war of secession against the Iraqi Republic was intensified by the fact that the predominantly Kurdish territories in northern Iraq include Iraq's major oil fields.

The Lebanese civil war of 1975-76 and beyond found Maronite forces engaged in what amounted to almost a class struggle with a coalition of mostly Muslim forces seeking a different distribution of social, economic, and political benefits and a shift in Lebanon's foreign policy orientation in the Arab world.

Both Arab and Kurdish minorities in Iran have clashed with Iranian troops loyal to the new Islamic republican government. The Arabs in particular accuse Tehran of trampling on minority rights and are demanding autonomy.

In March 1979 Zaydi-Shaf'i tensions in Yemen were on the verge of erupting into armed hostilities once again when South Yemen invaded the north, in an apparent attempt to bring down the government of President 'Ali 'Abdullah Saleh. The Shaf'is who are the majority population in the southern part of Yemen were extremely discontented with President Saleh, which raised the spectre of Shaf'i collaboration with South Yemen in the overthrow of the government in Sana.

Note that the origins of these conflicts are political and economic, not directly communal. Similarly, continuing tensions between Israel's Jewish majority and the Israeli Arabs stem mainly from continued Israeli seizure of Arab land for Jewish settlement and from other economic disparities between the majority and minority communities most of which appear to be the direct result of official Israeli policy.

One feature common to all these conflicts is the presence of external support for the minorities, and sometimes for both rival communities. If one or both sides have access to neighboring sanctuaries and supply lines and if there are external powers committed to the support of the rival communities, then the conflict is likely to intensify and become protracted and communal hatreds further inflamed. Nowhere is this outcome more apparent than in Lebanon. The Maronites were supported by Israel, Syria (eventually), the United States, and some European states, while the Muslim-progressive coalition was backed by Syria (at first), Iraq, Libya, and other Arab countries. In Yemen, Egyptian forces supported the Shaf'i republicans while Saudi Arabia backed the Zaydi royalist forces. The Kurds were supported by Iran, Israel, and the United States in their struggle with Iraq until Baghdad was able to resolve its differences with Iran in 1975. At the time this essay was written (June 1979) the Arab separatist forces in Khuzistan were allegedly receiving support and training from Iraq. The Arabs in Israel have the support of the PLO, however limited the effectiveness of this support may be. In Yemen, the Shaf'i threat to the government of President Saleh was only credible in conjunction with the invasion by South Yemen whose military effectiveness had been improved by the presence of Soviet, East German, and Cuban advisers.

A minimal level of political compatibility among ethnic communities is necessary in order to prevent protracted conflict and political disintegration of the state. In countries where that minimal level of compatibility cannot be sustained without a high degree of assimilation, political conflict triggered by communal tensions is likely to increase.

Assimilation, however, is not a unidirectional phenomenon. For this reason only a limited degree of assimilation may be necessary in order to achieve sufficient cooperative coexistence to forestall social conflict and separatist tendencies. Deutsch divides assimilation into four autonomous dimensions: assimilation of needs; assimilation of aspirations; assimilation of capabilities; and assimilation of attainments.[30] To these I would add a fifth dimension—assimilation of political identity. It is in regard to this last dimension that most students of nation-building and political integration seem to be confining their discourse.

The notion of assimilation connotes a process whereby unlike, highly differentiated objects become undifferentiated according to some given set of defining attributes. In the context of this discussion the process of becoming undifferentiated in treatment by the state in meeting basic human needs is an important defining attribute. This connotation is not the same as equality. It simply means that where discrimination exists it exists on the basis of criteria (that is, wealth, social status, personal connections, and the like) other than communal or ethnic affiliation.

Assimilation of needs refers to wants which, if not satisfied, are followed by a relatively high probability of observable damage to the individual or the community. Needs include such services as clean water, public health services, and security of one's property and person. Needs should not be confused with *desires*, for the latter may be unmet without observable damage. Minority demands to have their own language used in the schools in their locales may be highly desirable. If this want is unmet however, it may lead to frustration and resentment without noticeable damage. Assimilation of needs is the *sine qua non* for cooperative coexistence between communities. Where the state cannot or will not provide for the basic needs of the community there are no real benefits of belonging to this broader corporate entity, and sentiment in favor of secession and self-government seem almost inevitable.

Assimilation of *aspirations* simply means people—regardless of political identification of communal affiliation—want the same things. The presence of this attribute however, does not automatically imply peaceful coexistence. In Lebanon under the mandate, for example, the Muslim communities were not interested in close collaboration with the French mandatory authority as were the Maronite Christians. Neither were they interested in commercial and economic success to the same extent (possibly because of Islamic strictures against usury and interest rates) as the Christians. This condition meant that the Maronites, with aspirations grounded on industry and commerce, secured a disproportionate share of rewards available in Lebanese society. It may very well be that confessional tensions in Lebanon *increased* as the Muslims began to aspire to the same things since the political and social order could not adequately accommodate these aspirations. Thus, one qualifying consideration should be kept in mind: assimilation of aspirations may have to proceed in rough symmetry across communities of intercommunal conflict is to be minimized. A useful working hypothesis can be stated as follows: If assimilation of aspirations means that their fulfillment for one group is associated with their nonfulfillment for another group *as a group*, then assimilation of aspirations will be associated with increases in communal tensions. If, however, the fulfillment or denial of aspirations occurs on an individual rather than on a communal basis, assimilation of aspirations is likely to strengthen political compatibility and cooperative coexistence.

Assimilation of *capabilities* emphasizes a rough equality in education and skills. In this regard, assimilation of language appears to be a crucial factor in facilitating the assimilation of capabilities, particularly via a homogeneous education system. Assimilation of capabilities implies an undifferentiated ability across ethnic communities to compete for the social, economic, and political rewards of society. The absence of this dimension suggests that when differentials in capabilities are distributed disproportionately across ethnic communities rather than across individuals, gaps between affluent and disadvantaged will become conspicuous according to communal affiliation. Such conditions are likely to promote communal stereotyping and generate communal resentments and suspicions. This is exactly what happened in Lebanon prior to the war in 1975-1976. The result was that with the passage of time, fewer and fewer groups had any strong commitment to uphold the prevailing social and political order.

Assimilation of *attainments* occurs where a group has already become assimilated in needs, aspirations, and capabilities, and appears to be almost a derivative of the previous three dimensions. According to Deutsch a major cause of political disintegration occurs in situations where a minority has become assimilated in needs, aspirations and capabilities only to be denied a significant share of the attainment.[31] Attainments include not only social and economic rewards, but access to political power and a share in determining the destiny of the state.

None of these four dimensions of assimilation *a priori* a submersion of minority corporate identity with that of the majority. For analytical purposes that condition should be treated as a fifth and separate aspect of assimilation.

A critical breakpoint for achieving political compatibility seems to occur between assimilation of aspirations and assimilation of capabilities. If the basic aspirations of the minority diverge significantly from the majority, then it is difficult to conceive of the two communities having a shared view of politics or of what the destiny of the state ought to be. Figure 10.2 summarizes an intuitive rating of the principal political minorities in the Middle East in these five dimensions. Note that almost all the minorities listed appear to have achieved at least an assimilation of aspirations. The one exception is the Kurds, who are opposed to the societies in which they reside. Given the persistence of Kurdish secessionist activities, this one exception lends support to the proposition that assimilation in the first two dimensions is probably a prerequisite to a minimum of political compatibility in states comprising sizable and potentially disruptive political minorities.

A related consideration is the possibility that assimilation of aspirations can be either conflict-reducing or conflict-promoting. Assimilation in any of these dimensions cannot be accomplished by the minority without the cooperation or at least the acquiescence of

FIGURE 10.2

Degrees of Assimilations of the Principal Minorities in the Middle East

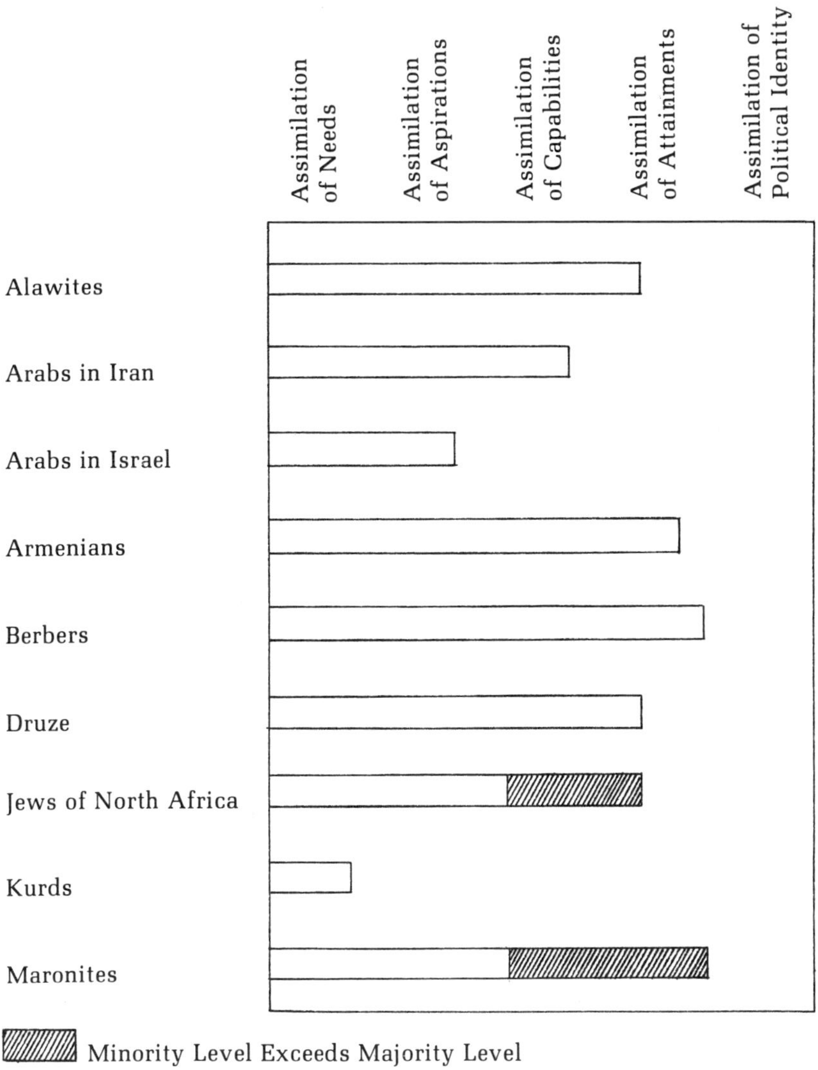

Minority Level Exceeds Majority Level

Source: Compiled by the author.

the majority and the state apparatus. Thus, assimilation on the last three dimensions may be conditioned in large measure by minority assessments of how further assimilation will expand opportunities for influencing the destiny of the state. But where the very *raison d'être* of the state is in opposition to further advancement of a community, the prospects for and advantages of further assimilation are meager. In such instances protracted conflict appears to be highly probably sooner or later. This appears to be the case of the Israeli Arabs. The nonsecular nature of the defining attributes of Middle Eastern states imposes varying degrees of opportunities for or barriers to assimilation of capabilities or attainments of their respective minorities.

Figure 10.2 further suggests that the number of dimensions on which assimilation has been achieved is not necessarily associated with a corresponding decrease in the likelihood of severe conflict or secessionist tendencies. Prospects for secession are subjectively rated higher for the Maronites, Alawites,[32] or the Arabs in Khuzistan than for the Arabs in Israel. In this regard the bar graphs underscore an observation made earlier, namely, that apparent progress toward assimilation can be reversed.

CONCLUSIONS

Those who count on modernization and social mobilization to lead to the eventual extinction of minority political identities and the eventual absorption of these ethnic-religious communities by the majority populace will have found little in this essay to support their convictions. The nonsecular nature of Middle Eastern states is almost an impossible barrier to such an outcome. The degree to which the nonsecular national identity of the majority facilitates officially sanctioned group discrimination eventually may make a crucial difference between cooperative coexistence between communities and minority unrest, protracted armed conflict, and possible political disintegration. This condition may be particularly critical for minority groups that have become assimilated in needs, aspirations, and capabilities only to be denied a share of the attainments including a share in the participation in the political mission of the state. For these minorities may be the most capable of mounting sustained collective protest and separatist drives. The fact that many minorities are concentrated in distinct geographical locations which are often relatively easy to defend against military assault means that secession is often a viable realistic option for minorities who no longer see any compelling advantage to belonging to the state.

Modernization and social mobilization appear to have had a reinforcing influence on minority corporate identities and cohesion in the Middle East. Quite possibly these processes have meant that the origins of conflicts involving primordial loyalties have been political and economic and not directly communal per se. But social mobilization cannot be said to have *caused* these conflicts. They have only contributed to the solidarity of political minorities in most instances and are likely to do so to an even greater extent in the future.

Yet, this chapter has also striven to show that conflict and separation are not an inevitable outcome of the presence of political minorities in the Middle East. The multidimensional view of assimilation suggests that there is sufficient scope for minimum political compatibility if state policy does not have the effect or the intention of threatening the welfare and political, social, and economic advancement of minorities. What is important is that Middle Eastern policy makers recognize that political minorities are unlikely to be assimilated. Therefore, it is in their interest to continue striving to develop policies that will at least emphasize basic compatibility of interests between minority and majority communities and underscore the benefits to the minority of belonging to the state and participating in its destiny; demonstrate that the national destiny of the state is not inimical to the welfare and prosperity of minorities; and encourage the minorities to develop a common view of politics with the majority. Such a policy orientation is not just ethically commendable, it may help to avoid the outbreak of future communal conflict, exposure of the state to penetration by external powers, the possible overthrow of the regime, and the political disintegration of the state itself.

NOTES

1. Walker Connor, "Nation-Building or Nation-Destroying," *World Politics* 24, no. 3 (April 1972): 350.

2. Michael C. Hudson, *Arab Politics: The Search for Legitimacy* (New Haven: Yale University Press, 1977), p. 4.

3. See Peter Gubser's Chapter 2, "Minorities in Power: The Alawites of Syria."

4. Labib Zuwiya Yamak, *The Syrian Social Nationalist Party: An Ideological Analysis* (Cambridge, Mass.: Harvard University Press, 1966).

5. Michael W. Suleiman, *Political Parties in Lebanon: The Challenge of a Fragmented Political Culture* (Ithaca, N. Y.: Cornell University Press, 1967), p. 78.

6. Labib Zuwiya Yamak, "Party Politics in the Lebanese Political System," in *Politics in Lebanon*, ed. Leonard Binder (New York: John Wiley & Sons, 1969), p. 161.

7. This distinction is made by Connor, "Nation-Building," p. 337.

8. Anthony H. Birch, "Minority Nationalist Movements and Theories of Political

Integration," World Politics 30, no. 3 (April 1978): 338-41, for further discussion of the point.

9. John K. Cooley, "Iran Oil Flow May Halt Again," Christian Science Monitor (May 16, 1979): 1, 9.

10. See Kenneth Freed, "Iran's Once-Proud Army Reduced to Motley Crew," Los Angeles Times (June 2, 1979): 1, 6.

11. See Gubser's Chapter 2, "Minorities in Power."

12. A partial list of this literature would include Karl W. Deutsch, "Social Mobilization and Political Development," American Political Science Review 55, no. 3 (September 1961): 493-514; Karl W. Deutsch, Nationalism and Social Communication: An Inquiry into the Foundations of Nationality, 2nd ed. (Cambridge, Mass.: MIT Press, 1966); Karl W. Deutsch and William Foltz, eds., Nation-Building (New York: Atherton Press, 1966); Clifford Geertz, "The Integrative Revolution: Primordial Sentiments and Civil Politics in New States," in Old Societies and New States, ed. Clifford Geertz (Glencoe, Ill.: The Free Press, 1965), pp. 104-157; Jason Finkle and Richard Gable, eds., Political Development and Social Change, 2nd ed. (New York: John Wiley, 1971); Kalman H. Silvert, Expectant Peoples, Nationalism and Development (New York: Vintage Books, 1963); Myron Weiner, "Political Integration and Political Development," Annals of the American Academy of Political and Social Science 358 (March 1965): 52-64.

13. Connor points out that Scottish and Welsh people have undergone generations of acculturation, including almost total linguistic assimilation. Yet the upsurge of Scottish and Welsh nationalism during the 1960s shows how "assimilation may indeed be reversed so long as some glimmer of a separate ethnic identity persists." Connor, "Nation-Building," p. 348.

14. Hudson, Arab Politics, p. 79.

15. This is covered in Edward E. Azar and R. D. McLaurin, "Demographic Change and Political Change: Population Pressures and Territorial Control in the Middle East," International Interactions 5, nos. 2-3 (1978): 267-87.

16. Connor, "Nation-Building," p. 329.

17. Birch, "Minority Nationalist Movements," p. 336.

18. Deutsch, "Social Mobilization and Political Development," p. 494.

19. Karl W. Deutsch, Tides Among Nations (New York: The Free Press, 1979), p. 285.

20. Ibid., p. 91.

21. A thorough review of the thinking and literature in Israel reflecting these notions is found in Benjamin Beit-Hallahmi, "Some Psychosocial and Cultural Factors in the Arab-Israeli Conflict: A Review of the Literature," Journal of Conflict Resolution 16, no. 2 (June 1972): 270-80.

22. This view is reflected in Karl Deutsch, "Nation-Building and National Development: Some Issues for Political Research," in Nation-Building, ed. Deutsch and Foltz, pp. 5-6, 8-9.

23. Karl W. Deutsch, Nationalism and Its Alternatives (New York: Alfred A. Knopf, 1969), p. 27.

24. Ibid., p. 73.

25. Halim Barakat, a sociologist who has conducted considerable empirical research in Lebanon, reports that the proportion of students in private (sectarian) schools increased from 66 percent to 86 percent between 1955 and 1968; in Mount Lebanon (a Maronite stronghold), the proportions of students in private schools jumped from 58 to 78 percent. See Halim Barakat, "The Social Context," in Lebanon in Crisis: Participants and Issues, ed. P. Edward Haley and Lewis W. Snider (Syracuse: Syracuse University Press, 1979), p. 11.

26. *Ibid.*

27. Suhaila Haddad and R. D. McLaurin, "Evolution of the Attitudes of Israel's Arab Minority," Abbot Associates Special Report 23 (October 1977), pp. 24-25.

28. Douglas A. Hibbs, Jr., *Mass Political Violence: A Cross-National Analysis* (New York: John Wiley & Sons, 1973), pp. 77-78.

29. *Ibid.*, pp. 77-80.

30. Deutsch, *Tides*, pp. 286-87. The elaboration of the definitional characteristics of these dimensions borrows heavily from Deutsch's discussion.

31. *Ibid.*, p. 287.

32. The Alawites are depicted as being slightly less assimilated than the Armenians, Berbers, or Jews since the Alawites, even though they dominate the regime in Damascus, have not yet attained the same socioeconomic position as the Sunni majority.

APPENDIX A
INTRODUCTION

These appendixes bring together some population estimates of major religious, ethnic, and linguistic groups in the Middle East. The data are presented for the 20 independent states we have included in the "Middle East" for our purposes. Excluded are the territories occupied by Israel since 1967: Jordan west of the Jordan River, the Golan Heights, the Gaza Strip, and part of the Sinai. Population estimates are uniformly for 1978.

Most of the countries included in these tables have never experienced a thorough census. In only one or two cases are figures very dependable. For the rest, data—these or other data—are speculative, sometimes almost wildly speculative. They are "order of magnitude" figures—and sometimes may not even be that close.

The data in Appendixes B and C derive from numerous sources, including interviews. We do not pretend the data are accurate. We do believe they constitute one of the first serious attempts to bring together population figures of this type for the Middle East.

APPENDIX B
COUNTRY DATA

TABLE B.1: Algeria: Population Data

(population 18,000,000)

Group	Population (thousands)	Percent of Population
Religious		
Islamic: Sunni*	18,000	99.4
Christian: Roman Catholic (Latin), Protestant	75	0.4
Ethnic		
Arab*	14,200	78.5
Berber	3,520	19.4
European	75	0.4
Linguistic		
Arabic*	14,215	78.5
Berber	3,500	19.3
European	80	0.4

*Majority group, representing over half the country's total population.

TABLE B.2: Bahrain: Population Data

(Population 282,000)

Group	Population (thousands)	Percent of Population
Religious		
Islamic: Shi'a	135	47.9
Islamic: Sunni	125	44.3
Christian: Protestant	10	3.5
Christian: Roman Catholic (Latin)	3	1.1
Hindu	9	3.2
Ethnic		
Arab*	250	88.7
European/American	10	3.5
Persian	8	2.8
Pakistani/Baluchi	8	2.8
Indian	5	1.8
Linguistic		
Arabic*	250	88.7
South Asian	13	4.6
English	10	3.5
Persian	8	2.8
Nationality		
Bahraini*	220	78.0
Alien	60	21.3
Arab	30	10.6
Other	30	10.6

*Majority group, representing over half the country's total population.

TABLE B.3: Egypt: Population Data

(population 39,890,000)

Group	Population	Percent of Population
Religious		
Islamic: Sunni*	36,590,000	91.7
Christian: Copt	3,000,000	7.5
Christian: Other (Roman Catholic/Latin, Greek Orthodox, Eastern Orthodox, Protestant)	300,000	0.8
Judaic	500	—
Ethnic		
Arab/Eastern Hamite*	39,300,000	98.5
Bedouin	50,000	0.1
Nubian	50,000	0.1
Greeks, Italians, Syro-Lebanese	300,000	0.8
Linguistic		
Arabic*	39,300,000	98.5
English, French	500,000	1.3
Beja	10,000	—
Berber	5,000	—
Nubian	3,000	—

*Majority group, representing over half the country's total population.

TABLE B.4: Iran: Population Data

(population 35,286,000)

Group	Population (Thousands)	Percent of Population
Religious		
Islamic: Shi'a[a][b]	31,120	88.2
Islamic: Sunni	3,460	9.8
Christian		
Gregorian	250	0.7
Assyrian ("Nestorian")	30	—
Chaldean	30	—
Roman Catholic (Latin), Protestant	30	—
Baha'i [c]	200	0.6
Judaic	80	0.2
Zoroastrian	40	0.1
Ethnic		
Persian	25,000	70.8
Turkic	6,000	17.0
Azerbaijanis	3,000	8.5
Arab	2,000	5.7
Kurd	1,100	3.1
Bakhtiari	500	1.4
Lur	460	1.3
Armenian	270	0.8
Jewish	80	0.2
Assyrian	30	—
Linguistic		
Farsi and other Persian[a]	25,000	70.8
Farsi	18,150	51.4
Turkic	6,000	17.0
Arabic	2,000	5.7
Kurdish	1,000	2.8
Baluchi	600	17.0
Armenian	250	0.7

[a] Majority group, representing over half the country's total population.

[b] Included among the Shi'a are many Isma'ilis ("Seveners"). Unfortunately, no breakdown as to the proportion of "seveners" and "twelvers" is available at this time.

[c] The estimated figures of Baha'i followers varies between 30,000 or fewer, on the one hand, and 400,000, on the other.

TABLE B.5: Iraq: Population Data

(population 12,470,000)

Group	Population	Percent of Population
Religious		
Islamic: Shi'a*	6,550,000	52.5
Islamic: Sunni	5,050,000	40.5
Christian:		
Chaldean	475,000	3.8
Syrian Catholic	35,000	0.3
Gregorian	25,000	0.2
Assyrian ("Nestorian")	20,000	0.2
Syrian Orthodox	12,000	0.1
Armenian Catholic	5,000	0.1
Roman Catholic (Latin)	3,500	—
Greek Orthodox	2,000	—
Protestant	2,000	—
Greek Catholic	1,000	—
Yazidi	30,000	0.2
Gnostic: Mandaean	6,000	—
Judaic	2,500	—
Ethnic		
Arab*	9,350,000	75.0
Kurd	2,820,000	22.6
Turkic	330,000	2.6
Persian	220,000	1.8
Lur	100,000	0.8
Armenian	30,000	0.2
Circassian	8,000	0.1
Jewish	2,500	—
Linguistic		
Arabic*	9,350,000	75.0
Kurdish	2,000,000	16.0
Persian	300,000	2.4
Turkic	250,000	2.0
Nationality (Aliens)		
Iranians	50,000	0.4
Palestinians	25,000	0.2

*Majority group, representing over half the total population.

TABLE B.6: Israel: Population Data

(population 3,660,000)

Group	Population	Percent of Population
Religious		
Judaic*	3,100,000	84.7
Islamic: Sunni	430,000	11.7
Christian		
Greek Catholic	40,000	1.1
Greek Orthodox	22,000	0.6
Roman Catholic (Latin)	12,000	0.3
Maronite	6,000	0.2
Protestant	3,000	0.1
Druze	45,000	1.2
Baha'i	300	—
Ethnic		
Jewish*	3,100,000	84.7
Arab	430,000	14.5
Circassian	5,000	0.1
Other: Armenian, Kurd, European, American	115,000	3.1
Linguistic		
Hebrew*	3,000,000	82.0
Arabic	530,000	14.5
European	120,000	3.3

*Majority group, representing over half the country's total population.

TABLE B.7: Jordan: Population Data
(population 2,183,000)

Group	Population[a]	Percent of Population
Religious		
Islamic: Sunni[b]	2,000,000	91.6
Islamic: Shi'a	2,000	0.1
Christian		
Greek Orthodox	90,000	4.1
Greek Catholic	50,000	2.3
Roman Catholic (Latin)	5,000	0.2
Armenian Catholic, Syrian		
Catholic	500	—
Ethnic		
Arab[b]	2,150,000	98.5
Circassian	25,000	1.1
Chechen	2,000	0.1
Linguistic		
Arabic[b]	2,180,000	99.9
Other Origin[cd]		
Palestinian[b]	1,150,000	52.7
Jordanian	1,030,000	47.2

[a]Figures exclude the West Bank and include the 20,000 Lebanese Christians who migrated to Jordan during the Lebanese conflict.

[b]Majority group, representing over half the country's total population.

[c]Palestinians resident in Jordan who wish Jordanian nationality are legally entitled to it. Figures under "other origin" represent *all* Palestinians, irrespective of their actual nationality.

[d]Another origin breakdown is relevant: Bedouin origin/South—230,000 (Bedouin, 60,000); Urban origin/North—1,960,000.

TABLE B.8:   Kuwait: Population Data

(population 1,205,000)

Group	Population (thousands)	Percent of Population
Religious		
Islamic: Sunni*	1,020	84.6
Islamic: Shi'a	125	10.4
Christian	25	2.1
Hindu	10	0.8
Ethnic		
Arab*	1,050	87.1
Persian	60	5.0
South Asian	25	2.1
Europeans and other	25	2.1
Linguistic		
Arabic*	1,050	87.1
Farsi and other Persian	60	5.0
English	25	2.1
South Asian	25	2.1
Nationality		
Alien*	630	52.3
Palestinian	250	20.7
Iraqi	65	5.1
Iranian	60	5.0
Egyptian	40	3.3
Syrian	35	2.9
Kuwaiti	575	47.7

*Majority group, representing over half the country's total population.

TABLE B.9: Lebanon: Population Data

(population 3,300,000)

Group	Population (thousands)	Percent of Population
Religious		
Christian		
Maronite	850	25.8
Greek Orthodox	370	11.2
Greek Catholic	200	6.1
Gregorian	120	3.6
Protestant	25	0.8
Syrian Catholic	22	0.7
Roman Catholic (Latin)	22	0.7
Armenian Catholic	20	0.6
Assyrian ("Nestorian")	15	0.5
Chaldean	8	0.2
Islamic: Sunni	890	27.0
Palestinians	300	9.1
Islamic: Shi'a	600	18.2
Druze	150	4.5
Judaic	10	0.3
Ethnic		
Arab[a]	2,910	88.2
Palestinian non-Lebanese	330	10.0
Armenian	200	6.1
Kurd	100	3.0
Assyrian	15	0.5
Linguistic		
Arabic[a]	3,015	91.4
Armenian	150	4.5
Kurdish	80	2.4
Nationality		
Lebanese[ab]	2,920	88.5
Alien	380	11.5
Palestinian[b]	330	10.0

[a]Majority group representing over half the country's total population.

[b]About 70-100,000 Palestinians have become Lebanese citizens and are included in that category only.

TABLE B.10: Libya: Population Data

(population 2,760,000)

Group	Population	Percent of Population
Religious		
Islamic: Sunni*	2,730,000	98.9
Christian	30,000	1.1
Ethnic		
Arab*	2,000,000	72.5
Berber	110,000	4.0
Tuareg	10,000	0.4
African	70,000	2.5
European and others	30,000	1.1
Tebu	1,500	0.1
Linguistic		
Arabic*	2,600,000	94.2
Berber	110,000	4.0
Tebu	1,500	0.1
European	20,000	0.7
Nationality		
Libyan*	2,410,000	87.3
Alien	350,000	12.7
Egyptian	230,000	8.3
Tunisian	65,000	2.4
Other	55,000	2.0

*Majority group, representing over half the country's total population.

TABLE B.11: Morocco: Population Data

(population 18,915,000)

Group	Population (thousands)	Percent of Population
Religious		
Islamic: Sunni*	18,540	98.0
Christian: Roman Catholic (Latin)	300	1.6
Christian: Protestant	50	0.3
Judaic	20	0.1
Ethnic		
Arab*	11,280	59.6
Berber	7,480	39.5
European and others	140	0.7
Jewish	20	0.1
Linguistic		
Arabic*	11,450	60.5
Berber	7,300	38.6
European	140	0.7

*Majority group, representing over half the country's total population.

TABLE B.12: Oman: Population Data

(population 800,000)

Group	Population (thousands)	Percent of Population
Religious		
Islamic		
Ibadi*	400	50.0
Sunni	200	25.0
Shi'a		
Christian	150	18.8
Hindu		
Ethnic		
Arab*	700	87.5
Baluchi		
Indian		
African/Negro		
Pakistani	75	9.4
Persian		
Qara		
Shihuh		
Linguistic		
Arabic*	700	87.5
Qara		
Shihuh	50	6.3
Other	50	6.3
Nationality		
Omani*	725	90.6
Alien	75	9.4
Tribal		
Hinawi (Yemeni)	?	
Ghafiri (Adnani)	?	

*Majority group, representing over half the country's total population.

TABLE B.13: Qatar: Population Data

(population 185,000)

Group	Population (thousands)	Percent of Population
Religious		
Islamic: Sunni*	130	70.3
Islamic: Shi'a	45	24.3
Ethnic		
Arab*	100	54.1
Persian	40	21.6
Pakistani	20	10.8
Linguistic		
Arabic*	100	54.1
Farsi and other Persian	40	21.6
Urdu, Bengali, other Pakistani	15	8.1
Nationality		
Alien*	150	81.1
Arab	65	35.1
Non-Arab	80	43.2
Qatari	35	18.9

*Majority group, representing over half the total population.

TABLE B.14: Saudi Arabia: Population Data
(population 7,000,000)

Group	Population (thousands)	Percent of Population
Religious		
Islamic: Sunni*	6,450	92.1
Islamic: Shi'a	350	5.0
Ethnic		
Arab*	6,400	91.4
Afro-Arab	350	5.0
Linguistic		
Arabic*	6,750	
Nationality		
Saudi*	5,500	78.6
Alien	1,500	21.4
Yemeni	800	11.4
Palestinian	50	0.7
U.S.	35	0.5

*Majority group, representing over half the country's total population.

TABLE B.15: Syria: Population Data

(population 8,375,000)

Group	Population[a] (thousands)	Percent of Population
Religious		
Islamic		
Sunni[b]	6,025	71.9
Palestinians	225	2.7
Shi'a: 'Alawi	1,050	12.5
Shi'a: Isma'ili	70	0.8
Shi'a: "Twelvers"	70	0.8
Christian		
Greek Orthodox	330	3.9
Gregorian and Armenian Catholic	180	2.1
Syrian Orthodox	100	1.2
Greek Catholic	85	1.0
Syrian Catholic	40	0.5
Maronite	35	0.4
Assyrian ("Nestorian")	30	0.4
Protestant	15	0.2
Roman Catholic (Latin)	5	0.1
Chaldean	5	0.1
Druze	240	2.9
Yazidi	15	0.2
Judaic	4	—
Ethnic		
Arab[b]	7,590	90.6
Kurd	500	6.0
Armenian	240	2.9
Turkic	120	1.4
Circassian	110	1.3
Assyrian	30	0.4
Jewish	4	—
Linguistic		
Arabic[b]	7,150	85.4
Kurdish	620	7.4
Turkic	200	2.4
Armenian	180	2.1
Syriac	160	1.9
Nationality		
Palestinians	250	3.0

[a]Reflects influx of Lebanese refugees, 1975-78, and Palestinian refugees, 1948-78.
[b]Majority group, representing over half the country's total population.

TABLE B.16: Tunisia: Population Data

(population 6,250,000)

Group	Population (thousands)	Percent of Population
Religious		
Islamic: Sunni*	5,980	95.7
Christian: Roman Catholic (Latin)	40	0.6
Christian: Protestant, Greek Orthodox,		
and others 10	10	0.2
Judaic	5	0.1
Ethnic		
Arab-Berber*	6,000	96.0
European	50	0.8
Jewish	5	0.1
Linguistic		
Arabic*	6,200	99.2

*Majority group, representing over half the country's total population.

TABLE B.17: Turkey: Population Data

(population 43,059,000)

Group	Population (thousands)	Percent of Population
Religious		
Islamic: Sunni*	38,730	89.9
Islamic: Shi'a†	4,000	9.3
Christian		
Greek Orthodox	100	0.2
Gregorian	85	0.2
Roman Catholic (Latin)	40	0.1
Protestant	30	0.1
Judaic	45	0.1
Ethnic and Linguistic		
Turkic/Turkish*	38,840	90.2
Kurd/Kurdish	2,990	6.9
Arab/Arabic	510	1.2
Zaza/Zaza	200	0.5
Circassian/Circassian	75	0.2
Greek/Greek	65	0.2
Georgian/Georgian	45	0.1
Armenian/Armenian	40	0.1
Laz/Laz	38	0.1
Ladino/Ladino	10	—

*Majority group, representing over half the country's total population.
†Includes almost 200,000 'Alawis.

TABLE B.18: United Arab Emirates: Population Data

(population 800,000)

Group	Population (thousands)	Percent of Population
Religious		
Islamic: Sunni*	500	62.5
Islamic: Shi'a	120	15.0
Ethnic		
Arab*	400	50.0
South Asian	350	43.8
Linguistic		
Arabic*	400	50.0
South Asian	350	43.8
Nationality		
Alien*	600	75.0
Arab	200	25.0
South Asian	350	43.8
U.A.E.	200	25.0

*Majority group, representing over half the country's total population.

TABLE B.19: Yemen Arab Republic: Population Data

(population 6,670,000)

Group	Population (thousands)	Percent of Population
Religious		
Islamic		
Sunni	3,300	49.5
Shi'a	3,200	48.0
Shi'a: Isma'ili	50	0.7
Ethnic		
Arab*	6,150	92.2
Afro-Arab	500	7.5
Linguistic		
Arabic*	6,650	99.7

*Majority group, representing over half the country's total population.

TABLE B.20: People's Democratic Republic of Yemen: Population Data

(population 1,735,000)

Group	Population (thousands)	Percent of Population
Religious		
Islamic: Sunni*	1,730	99.7
Hindu	4	0.2
Ethnic		
Arab*	1,680	96.8
Somali	25	1.4
Socotran	8	0.5
Pakistani	8	0.5
Indian	4	0.2
Linguistic		
Arabic*	1,710	98.6
Himyarite	10	0.6
South Asian	10	0.6

*Majority group, representing over half the country's total population.

APPENDIX C
TABLES

TABLE C.1: Religious Groups in the Middle East

Group	Number of States in which Group Is					Number of States in which Group Numbers More than				
	Majority	Plurality	More than (percent)			1 million	500,000	100,000	50,000	25,000
			25	10	1					
Islam	18	18	19	20	20	15	17	20	20	20
Sunni	12	14	18	19	20	14	16	20	20	20
Shi'a	2	3	3	10	13	5	6	10	10	12
'Alawi	0	0	0	1	1	1	1	2	2	2
Isma'ili	0	0	0	1	1	1	1	1	2	2
Ibadi	0	1	1	1	1	0	0	1	1	1
Christianity	1	1	1	2	10	2	4	8	12	14
Roman Catholic (Latin)	0	0	0	0	2	0	0	1	3	5
Greek Catholic	0	0	0	0	4	0	0	1	3	3
Greek Orthodox	0	0	0	1	5	0	0	3	5	5
Maronite	0	1	1	1	1	0	1	1	1	2
Coptic	0	0	0	0	1	1	1	1	1	1
Assyrian	0	0	0	0	0	0	0	0	0	2
Gregorian	0	0	0	0	2	0	0	3	4	5
Chaldean	0	0	0	0	1	0	0	1	1	2
Protestant	0	0	0	0	1	0	0	0	0	3
Armenian Catholic	0	0	0	0	0	0	0	0	0	1
Mandaean	0	0	0	0	0	0	0	0	0	0
Syrian Orthodox	0	0	0	0	1	0	0	1	1	1
Syrian Catholic	0	0	0	0	0	0	0	0	0	2

TABLE C.1: Religious Groups in the Middle East

| | Number of States in which Group Is | | More than (percent) | | | Number of States in which Group Numbers More than | | | | | |
	Majority	Plurality	25	10	1	1 million	500,000	100,000	50,000	25,000
Group										
Judaism	1	1	1	1	1	1	1	1	2	3
Hinduism	0	0	0	0	2	0	0	0	0	1
Zoroastrianism	0	0	0	0	0	0	0	0	0	1
Baha'i	0	0	0	0	0	0	0	1	1	1
Yazidi	0	0	0	0	0	0	0	0	0	1
Druze	0	0	0	0	3	0	0	2	2	3

Note: Figures for Isma'ilis do not include those in Iran. 'Alawis are included with Isma'ilis for the purposes of this table, but Isma'ilis and 'Alawis are not combined with Shi'a (except in Iran).

TABLE C.2: Ethnic Groups in the Middle East

Group	Majority	Plurality	Number of States in which Group Is — More than (percent) 25	10	1	Number of States in which Group Numbers More than 1 million	500,000	100,000	50,000	25,000
Arab	17	17	17	18	20	14	15	20	20	20
Berber	0	0	1	2	3	2	2	3	3	3
South Asian	0	0	1	2	5	0	0	1	1	2
Persian	1	1	1	2	5	1	1	2	3	4
Kurd	0	0	0	1	5	3	3	4	4	4
Turk/Turkic	1	1	1	2	4	2	3	5	5	5
Assyrian	0	0	0	0	0	0	0	0	0	2
Jewish	1	1	1	1	1	1	1	1	2	2
Armenian	0	0	0	0	2	0	0	3	3	5
Bakhtiari	0	0	0	0	1	0	1	1	1	1
Lur	0	0	0	0	1	0	0	2	2	2
Circassian	0	0	0	0	2	0	0	1	2	3
Afro-Arab	0	0	0	0	1	0	1	1	1	1
Zaza	0	0	0	0	0	0	0	1	1	1
Georgian	0	0	0	0	0	0	0	0	0	1
Somali	0	0	0	0	1	0	0	0	0	1

TABLE C.3: Linguistic Groups in the Middle East

Group	Number of States in which Group Is					Number of States in which Group Numbers More than				
	Majority	Plurality	More than (percent)			1 million	500,000	100,000	50,000	25,000
			25	10	1					
Arabic	17	17	17	18	20	14	16	20	20	20
Berber	0	0	1	2	3	2	2	3	3	3
Persian/Farsi	1	1	1	2	5	1	1	2	3	4
English	0	0	0	0	4	0	0	1	1	3
Kurdish	0	0	0	1	5	3	4	4	5	5
Turkish/Turkic	1	1	1	2	4	2	2	4	4	4
Baluchi	0	0	0	0	1	0	1	1	1	1
Aramaic/Syriac	0	0	0	0	1	0	0	1	1	2
Armenian	0	0	0	0	2	0	0	3	3	4
Hebrew	1	1	1	1	1	1	1	1	1	1
French	0	0	0	0	0	0	0	0	0	2
Zaza	0	0	0	0	0	0	0	1	1	1
Circassian	0	0	0	0	0	0	0	1	1	1
Greek	0	0	0	0	0	0	0	1	1	1
Georgian	0	0	0	0	0	0	0	0	0	1
Laz	0	0	0	0	0	0	0	0	0	1

TABLE C.4: Religious Minorities in the Middle East

Minority	Number of States in which Minority Is		More than (percent)			Number of States in which Minority Numbers More than				
	In Power	Plurality	25	10	1	1 million	500,000	100,000	50,000	25,000
Islam	0	0	1	2	2	1	2	2	2	2
Sunni	3	2	6	7	8	4	5	8	8	8
Shi'a*	1	1	2	7	9	2	3	8	9	10
'Alawi	1	0	0	1	1	1	1	2	2	2
Isma'ili	0	0	0	0	0	0	0	0	2	2
Ibadi	0	0	0	0	0	0	0	0	0	0
Christianity	0	0	0	1	9	1	3	7	11	13
Roman Catholic	0	0	0	0	2	0	0	1	3	5
Greek Catholic	0	0	0	0	4	0	0	1	3	3
Greek Orthodox	0	0	0	1	5	0	0	3	5	5
Maronite	1	1	1	1	1	0	1	1	1	2
Coptic	0	0	0	0	1	1	1	1	1	1
Assyrian	0	0	0	0	0	0	0	0	0	2
Gregorian	0	0	0	0	2	0	0	3	4	5
Chaldean	0	0	0	0	1	0	0	1	1	3
Protestant	0	0	0	0	1	0	0	0	0	3
Armenian Catholic	0	0	0	0	0	0	0	0	0	1
Mandeaen	0	0	0	0	0	0	0	0	0	0
Syrian Orthodox	0	0	0	0	1	0	0	1	1	1
Syrian Catholic	0	0	0	0	0	0	0	0	0	2

TABLE C.4: Religious Minorities in the Middle East

| Minority | Number of States in which Minority Is | | | | | Number of States in which Minority Numbers More than | | | | |
| | | | More than (percent) | | | | | | | |
	In Power	Plurality	25	10	1	1 million	500,000	100,000	50,000	25,000
Judaism	0	0	0	0	0	0	0	0	1	2
Hinduism	0	0	0	0	2	0	0	0	0	1
Zoroastrianism	0	0	0	0	0	0	0	0	0	1
Baha'i	0	0	0	0	0	0	0	1	1	1
Yazidi	0	0	0	0	0	0	0	0	0	1
Druze	0	0	0	0	3	0	0	2	2	3

*'Alawi and Isma'ili faiths are treated as independent of Shi'aism and of each other.

TABLE C.5: Ethnic Minorities in the Middle East

Minority	Number of States in which Minority Is					Number of States in which Minority Numbers More than				
	In Power	Plurality	More than (percent)			1 million	500,000	100,000	50,000	25,000
			25	10	1					
Arab	0	0	0	1	3	1	2	3	3	3
Berber	0	0	1	2	3	2	2	3	3	3
South Asian	0	0	1	2	5	0	0	1	1	2
Persian	0	0	0	1	4	0	0	1	2	3
Kurd	0	0	0	1	5	3	3	4	4	4
Turk/Turkic	0	0	0	1	3	1	2	4	4	4
Assyrian	0	0	0	0	0	0	0	0	0	2
Jewish	0	0	0	0	0	0	0	0	1	1
Armenian	0	0	0	0	2	0	0	3	3	5
Bakhtiari	0	0	0	0	1	0	0	1	2	3
Lur	0	0	0	0	1	0	0	2	2	2
Circassian	0	0	0	0	2	0	0	1	2	3
Afro-Arab	0	0	0	0	1	0	1	1	1	1
Zaza	0	0	0	0	0	0	0	1	1	1
Laz	0	0	0	0	0	0	0	0	0	1
Georgian	0	0	0	0	0	0	0	0	0	1
Somali	0	0	0	0	1	0	0	0	0	1

TABLE C.6: Linguistic Minorities in the Middle East

Minority	In Power	Plurality	Number of States in which Minority Is More than (percent)			Number of States in which Minority Numbers More than				
			25	10	1	1 million	500,000	100,000	50,000	25,000
Arabic	0	0	0	1	3	1	2	3	3	3
Berber	0	0	1	2	3	2	2	3	3	3
Persian/Farsi	0	0	0	1	4	0	0	1	2	3
English	0	0	0	0	4	0	0	1	1	3
Kurdish	0	0	0	1	5	3	4	4	5	5
Turkish/Turkic	0	0	0	1	3	1	1	3	3	3
Baluchi	0	0	0	0	1	0	1	1	1	1
Aramaic/Syriac	0	0	0	0	1	0	0	1	1	2
Armenian	0	0	0	0	2	0	0	3	3	4
Hebrew	0	0	0	0	0	0	0	0	0	0
French	0	0	0	0	0	0	0	0	0	2
Zaza	0	0	0	0	0	0	0	1	1	1
Circassian	0	0	0	0	0	0	0	0	1	1
Greek	0	0	0	0	0	0	0	0	1	1
Georgian	0	0	0	0	0	0	0	0	0	1
Laz	0	0	0	0	0	0	0	0	0	1

BIBLIOGRAPHY

Abu-Ayyash, Abdul Ilah. "Israeli Regional Planning Policy in the Occupied Territories." *Journal of Palestine Studies* 5, no. 3-4 (Spring-Summer 1976): 83-108.

Antoun, Richard, and Harik, Iliya, eds. *Rural Politics and Social Change in the Middle East.* Bloomington: Indiana University Press, 1972.

Apter, David E. *The Politics of Modernization.* Chicago: University of Chicago Press, 1965.

Arfa, Hassan. *The Kurds: An Historical and Political Study.* London: Oxford University Press, 1966.

Armstrong, John A. "Mobilized and Proletarian Diasporas." *American Political Science Review* 70, no. 2 (June 1976): 393-408.

El-Asmar, Fouzi. *To Be an Arab in Israel.* London: Frances Pinter, 1975.

Attal, Robert. *Les Juifs d'Afrique du Nord: Bibliographie.* Leiden: s.n., 1973.

Ayoub, Victor. "Attitude of Palestinians in Occupied Areas." *The Arab World,* March 6, 1974, p. 12.

——. "Conflict Resolution and Social Reorganization in a Lebanese Village." *Human Organization* 14, no. 1 (Spring 1965): 11-17.

——. "Political Structure of a Middle East Community: A Druze Village of Mount Lebanon." Ph.D. dissertation, Harvard University, 1955.

Awwad, A., et al. "Hiwar ma' al-Jabbah al-Wataniyah fi al-Ard al-Muhtallah." *At-Tali'ah,* no. 3 (March 1974): 12-45.

Azar, Edward E., and McLaurin, R. D. "Demographic Change and Political Change: Population Pressure and Territorial Control in the Middle East." *International Interactions* 5, no. 2-3 (1978): 267-87.

Baer, Gabriel. *Population and Society in the Arab East.* London: Routledge and Kegan Paul, 1964.

Bakr, Mamduh. "Sina' Taht al-Ihtilal al-Isra'ili." *At-Tali'ah,* 7 (July 1973): 45-53.

Barakat, Halim. *Lebanon in Strife.* Austin: University of Texas Press, 1977.

——. "Social and Political Integration in Lebanon: A Case of Social Mosaic." *Middle East Journal* 27, no. 3 (Summer 1973): 301-18.

Becker, Abraham S. "The Superpowers in the Arab-Israeli Conflict, 1970-1973." Rand Paper, P-5167, December 1973.

Be'eri, Eliezar. *Army Officers in Arab Politics and Society.* New York: Praeger, 1970.

Bell, Wendel, and Freeman, Walter. *Ethnicity and Race Relations.* Beverly Hills, Calif.: Sage, 1974.

Ben Dor, Gabriel. "The Politics of Innovation and Integration: A Political Study of the Druze Community in Israel." Ph.D. dissertation, Princeton University, 1972.

Benjamin, Charles. "The Kurdish Nonstate Nation." In *Nonstate Nations in International Politics: Comparative System Analysis*, edited by Judy S. Bertelsen, pp. 69-97. New York: Praeger, 1977.

Ben-Tzur, Avraham. "The Neo-Ba'th Party in Syria." *New Outlook* 12, no. 1 (January 1969): 21-37.

Ben Zvi, I. "The Druze Community in Israel." *The Israel Exploration Journal* 4, no. 2 (1954): 65-76.

Bertelsen, Judy S., ed. *Nonstate Nations in International Politics: Comparative System Analysis*. New York: Praeger, 1977.

Bill, James A., and Leiden, Carl. *The Middle East: Politics and Power*. Boston: Allyn and Bacon, 1974.

Binder, Leonard, ed. *Politics in Lebanon*. New York: Wiley, 1966.

Birch, Anthony H. "Minority Nationalist Movements and Theories of Political Integration." *World Politics* 30, no. 3 (April 1978): 325-44.

Blanc, Haim. "Druze Particularism: Modern Aspects of an Old Problem." *Middle Eastern Affairs* 3, no. 11 (1952): 314-21.

Bouron, N. *Les Druzes: Histoire du Liban et de la Montagne hauranaise*. Paris: Editions Berber-Levrault, 1930.

Bousquet, G. H. *Les Berbères*. Paris: Presses Universitaires de France, 1967.

Budeiri, Musa. "West Bank's Firm Answer." *Middle East International* 56 (February 1976): 10-12.

Bulloch, John. *Death of a Country*. London: Weidenfeld and Nicolson, 1977.

Chamoun, Camille. *Crise au Moyen-Orient*. Paris: Gallimard, 1963.

Chouraqui, André. *Between East and West: The Jews of North Africa*. Philadelphia: The Jewish Publication Society of North America, 1968.

Chowdhuri, R.N. *International Mandates and Trusteeship Systems*. The Hague: Martinus Nyhoff, 1955.

Clarke, John Innes, and Fisher, W. B., eds. *Populations of the Middle East and North Africa: A Geographical Approach*. New York: Africana, 1972.

Claude, Inis L., Jr. *National Minorities: An International Problem*. Cambridge; Harvard University Press, 1955.

Condit, D.M. *Modern Revolutionary Warfare: An Analytical Overview*. Kensington, Md.: American Institutes for Research, 1973.

———. and Cooper, Bert H., Jr. *Strategy and Success in International Conflict*. Kensington, Md.: American Institutes for Research, 1971.

Connor, Walker. "Nation-Building or Nation-Destroying?" *World Politics* 24, no. 3 (April 1972); 319-55.

Coon, Carleton. *Caravan: The Story of the Middle East*. New York: Henry Holt and Company, 1951.

Coughlin, Richard. *Double Identity: The Chinese in Modern Thailand*. Hong Kong: Hong Kong University Press, 1960.

Curtis, Michael, and Chertoff, M. S. *Israel: Social Structure and Change*. New Brunswick, N.J.: Transaction Books, 1973.

Dann, Uriel. "The Kurdish National Movement in Iraq." *The Jerusalem Quarterly*, no. 9 (Fall 1978); 131-44.

"A Decision for Palestinians: Self-Rule." *The Arab World*, February 14, 1974, pp. 11-12.

Deutsch, Karl W. *Nationalism and Social Communication: An Inquiry into the Foundations of Nationality.* 2nd rev. ed. Cambridge, Mass.: MIT Press, 1966.

Dotson, Floyd and Dotson, Lillian. *The Indian Minority of Zambia, Rhodesia and Malawi.* New Haven: Yale University Press, 1968.

Dussaud, René. *Histoire et religion des Nosairis.* Paris: Bovillion, 1900.

Eagleton, William. *The Kurdish Republic of 1946.* London: Oxford University Press, 1963.

Eisenstadt, S. N. *Israeli Society.* New York: Basic Books, 1967.

Elias, Adil S. "God, Family, and Fatherland: The Lebanese Phalangists." In *Lebanese War: Historical and Social Background,* edited by Third World Magazine, pp. 12-20. Bonn: Press Dritte Welt, 197?.

Emerson, Rupert. *Self-Determination Revisited in the Era of Decolonization.* Occasional Papers in International Affairs, no. 9. Cambridge; Harvard University Center for International Affairs, 1964.

Enloe, Cynthia H. *Ethnic Conflict and Political Development.* Boston: Little, Brown, 1973.

——. "Police and Military in the Resolution of Conflict." *Annals of the American Academy of Political and Social Science* 433 (September 1977); 137-49.

Entelis, John P. "Belief-System and Ideology Formation in the Lebanese Katâ'ib Party." *International Journal of Middle East Studies* 4, no. 2 (April 1973); 148-62.

——. "Party Transformation in Lebanon: Al Kataib as a Case Study." *Middle East Studies* 9, no. 3 (October 1973); 325-40.

——. "Structural Change and Organizational Development in the Lebanese Kataib Party." *Middle East Journal* 27, no. 1 (Winter 1973); 21-35.

Epp, Frank H. *The Palestinians: Portrait of a People in Conflict.* Scottsdale, Penn.: Herald Press, 1976.

Falah, Salman. "Druze Communal Organization in Israel." *New Outlook* 10, no. 3 (1967); 40-44.

Garone, Guido. *Libano: Tragedia de un Popopla.* Torino: Societa Editrice Internazionale, 1976.

Gavan, S. S. *Kurdistan: Divided Nation of the Middle East.* London: Lawrence and Wishart, 1958.

Gellner, Ernest. "Independence in the Central High Atlas." *Middle East Journal* 11, no. 3 (Summer 1957); 236-52.

——. "Patterns of Rural Rebellion in Morocco: Tribes as Minorities." *Archives européennes de sociologie* 3, no. 2 (1962); 297-311.

Glazer, Nathan, and Moynihan, Daniel P., eds. *Ethnicity: Theory and Experience.* Cambridge; Harvard, University Press, 1975.

Gubser, Peter. A. "The Zu'ama' of Zahlah: The Current Situation in a Lebanese Town." *Middle East Journal* 27, no. 2 (Spring 1973); 173-89.

Gurr, Ted. *Why Men Rebel.* Princeton: Princeton University Press, 1970.

——, with Charles Ruttenberg. *Cross-National Studies of Civil Violence.* Washington, D.C.: Center for Research in Social Systems, The American University, 1969.

Haddad, George. *Revolution and Military Rule in the Middle East: The Arab States.* 2 vols. New York: Speller, 1971.

Hagopian, Edward, and Zahlan, A. B. "Palestine's Arab Population: The Demography of the Palestinians." *Journal of Palestine Studies* 3, no. 4 (Summer 1974); 32-73.

Hagopian, Elaine. "Morocco: A Case Study in the Structural Bases of Social Integration." Ph.D. dissertation, Boston University, 1962.

Hah, Chong-do and Martin, Jeffrey. "Toward a Synthesis of Conflict and Integration Theories of Nationalism." *World Politics* 17, no. 3 (April 1975); 361-86.

Haley, P. Edward, and Snider, Lewis W., eds. *Lebanon in Crisis: Participants and Issues.* Syracuse: Syracuse University Press, 1979.

Hall, H. Duncan. *Mandates, Dependencies and Trusteeships.* Washington, D.C.: Carnegie Endowment for International Peace, 1948.

Harik, Iliya. "The Ethnic Revolution and Political Integration in the Middle East." *International Journal of Middle East Studies* 3, no. 3 (July 1972); 303-23.

——. *Man Yahakam Lubnan.* Beirut: Dar al-Nahar lil-Nashr, 1972.

——. *Politics and Change in Traditional Society: Lebanon, 1711-1845.* Princeton: Princeton University Press, 1968.

Harris, George S. "Ethnic Conflict and the Kurds." *Annals of the American Academy of Political and Social Science* 433 (September 1977); 112-24.

Hart, David. "Notes on the Rifian Community of Tangier." *Middle East Journal* 11, no. 2 (Spring 1957); 153-62.

Hass, Ernst B. "The Reconciliation of Conflicting Colonial Policy Aims: Acceptance of the League of Nations Mandate System." *International Organization* 6, no. 4 (November 1952); 521-36.

Hermassi, Elbaki. *Leadership and National Development in North Africa.* Berkeley: University of California Press, 1972.

Hewitt, Christopher. "Majorities and Minorities: A Comparative Survey of Ethnic Violence." *Annals of the American Academy of Political and Social Science* 433. (September 1977); 150-60.

Hichi, Selim H. *La Communauté druze.* Beirut: s.n., 1973.

Hilal, Jamil. "Class Transformation in the West Bank and Gaza." *MERIP Reports*, no. 53 (November 1976); 9-15.

Hinnebusch, Raymond A. "Local Politics in Syria: Organization and Mobilization in Four Village Cases." *Middle East Journal* 30, no. 1 (Winter 1976); 1-24.

Hirschberg, H. Z. *A History of the Jews in North Africa.* Leiden: Brill, 1974.

Hitti, Phillip K. *History of Syria.* London: Macmillan, 1951.

——. *Lebanon in History: From the Earliest Times to the Present.* London: Macmillan, 1962.

——. *The Origins of the Druze People.* New York: Columbia University Press, 1928.

——. *A Short History of Lebanon.* New York: St. Martin's 1965.

Hoffman, Bernard. *The Structure of Traditional Moroccan Rural Society.* The Hague: Mouton, 1967.

Hottinger, Arnold. "Zu'ama' and Parties in the Lebanese Crisis of 1958," *Middle East Journal* 15, no. 2 (Spring 1961); 127-40.

Hourani, Albert H. *Minorities in the Arab World.* London: Oxford, 1947.

———. *Syria and Lebanon.* London: Oxford, 1946.

———, and Stern, S. M., eds. *The Islamic City.* Philadelphia: University of Pennsylvania, Press, 1970.

Hudson, Michael C. *Arab Politics: The Search for Legitimacy.* New Haven: Yale University Press, 1977.

———. "A Case of Political Underdevelopment." *Journal of Politics* 29, no. 4 (November 1967); 821-37.

———. "Democracy and Social Mobilization in Lebanese Politics." *Comparative Politics* 1, no. 2 (January 1969); 245-63.

———. "The Lebanese Crisis: The Limits of Consociational Democracy." *Journal of Palestine Studies* 5, no. 3-4 (Spring-Summer 1976); 109-22.

———. *The Precarious Republic: Political Modernization in Lebanon.* New York: Random House, 1968.

Hurewitz, J. C. "The Minorities in the Political Process." In *Social Forces in the Middle East,* edited by Sydney Nettleton Fisher. Ithaca; N.Y.: Cornell University Press, 1955.

Husayn, Muhammad. *Ta'ifa al-Duruz, Ta'arikhha wa 'Aqa'idha.* Cairo: Dar al-Ma'arif biMisr, 1968.

Hutchinson, Hugh. "Kurds in Turkey." M.A. thesis, Columbia University, 1967.

Isaacs, Harold. *Idols of the Tribe: Group Identity and Political Change.* New York: Harper & Row, 1975.

Ismail, Adil. *Lebanon: A History of a People.* Beirut: Dar al-Makchouf, 1972.

"Israel's Arabs After October 1973." *New Outlook* 18, no. 7 (October-November 1975); 31-40.

Jiryis, Sabri. *The Arabs in Israel.* New York: Monthly Review Press, 1976.

Johnson, Michael. "Confessionalism and Individualism in Lebanon: Critique of Leonard Binder (ed.), *Politics in the Lebanon.*" *Review of Middle East Studies,* no. 1 (1975); 79-91.

Jureidini, Paul A., and Hazen, William E. *Six Clashes: An Analysis of the Relationship Between the Palestinian Guerrilla Movement and the Governments of Jordan and Lebanon.* Kensington, Md.: American Institutes for Research, 1971.

Jurji, E. J. "The Alids of Northern Syria." *The Moslem World* 29, no. 4 (October 1939); 333-38.

Jwaideh, Wadie. "The Kurdish National Movement: Its Origins and Development." Ph.D. dissertation, Syracuse University, 1960.

Kasdan, Leonard. "Isfiya: Social Structure, Fission and Faction in a Druze Community." Ph.D. dissertation, University of Chicago, 1961.

Kautsky, John H., ed. *Political Change in Underdeveloped Countries: Nationalism and Communism.* New York: Wiley, 1962.

Kelly, J.N.D. *Early Christian Doctrines.* New York: Harper & Row, 1960.

Khalaf, Tewfik. "The Phalange and the Maronite Community: From Lebanonism to Maronitism." In Essays on the Crisis In Lebanon, edited by Roger Owen, pp. 43-57. London: Ithaca Press, 1976.

Kinnane, Derk. The Kurds and Kurdistan. London: Oxford University Press, 1964.

Koury, Ever M. The Crisis in the Lebanese System. Washington, D.C.: American Enterprise Institute, 1976.

———. The Operational Capability of the Lebanese Political System. Beirut: Catholic Press, 1972.

Kuper, Leo. "Plural Societies: Perspectives and Problems." In Pluralism in Africa, edited by Leo Kuper and M. G. Smith, pp. 7-26. Berkeley: University of California Press, 1969.

Landau, Jacob M. The Arabs in Israel: A Political Study. New York: Oxford University Press, 1969.

LeCoz, Jean. "Le Troisième Age agraire du Maroc." Annales de Géographie 77, no. 422 (July-August 1968); 385-413.

Lesch, Ann Mosely. Israel's Occupation of the West Bank: The First Two Years. Santa Monica: Rand Corporation, 1970.

Lustick, Ian. "Arabs in the Jewish State: A Study in the Effective Control of a Minority Population." Ph.D. dissertation, University of California at Berkeley, 1976.

———. "What Do the Palestinians Want? Conversations in the Occupied Territories." New Outlook 17, no. 2 (February 1974); 25-28.

Lyde, Samuel. The Asian Mystery. London: Longman, Green, Longman, and Roberts, 1860.

Makarim, Sami Nasib Adwa' 'ala Masalak al-Tawhid. Beirut: Dar Sadir, 1966.

———. The Druze Faith. Delmar, N.Y.; Caravan, 1974.

Mansfield, Peter. "Galilee: Explosion on the Home Front." Middle East International, no. 59 (May 1976); 10-12.

Ma'oz, Moshe. "Attempts at Creating a Political Community in Modern Syria." Middle East Journal 26, no. 4 (Autumn 1972); 389-404.

———. "Syria Under Hafiz al-Asad: New Domestic and Foreign Policies." Jerusalem Papers on Peace Problems, no. 15 (1975).

May, Pierre. L'Alaouite. Paris: Brokghausen, n.d. (late 1920s?).

Mazhar, Yusuf. Ta'rikh Lubnan al-'Amm. 2 vols. Beirut: n.p., 1953(?).

McLaurin, R. D., et al., eds. The Art and Science of Psychological Operations. 2 vols., Washington, D.C.: Government Printing Office, 1976.

McLaurin, R. D., and Mughisuddin, Mohammed. Cooperation and Conflict: Egyptian, Iraqi, and Syrian Objectives and U.S. Policy. Washington, D.C.: American Institutes for Research, 1975.

———. and Wagner, Abraham R. Foreign Policy Making in the Middle East. New York: Praeger, 1977.

Monteil, Vincent. Morocco. Translated by Veronica Hall. New York: Viking, 1964.

Moore, Clement Henry. Politics in North Africa. Boston: Little, Brown, 1971.

———. Tunisia Since Independence. Berkeley: University of California Press, 1965.

Morris, H. S. *The Indians in Uganda*. Chicago: Weidenfeld and Nicolson, 1968.

Moutafakis, George. "The Role of Minorities in the Modern Middle East Societies." *Middle East Review* 9, no. 2 (Winter 1976-77); 63-72.

al-Nady, 'Arif, et al. *Al-Waqi' al-Durzi wa Hatmiyyat al-Tatawwur Majmu'at Muhadarat*. Beirut: Lebanese Ministry of Social Affairs, 1962.

Nahas, Dunia. "La Résistance palestinienne dans les territorires occupés." *Travoux et Jours*, no. 55 (April-June 1975); 35-54.

al-Najjar, 'Abdallah. *Mathab al-Duruz wa al-Tawhid*. Cairo: Dar al-Ma'arif biMisr, 1965.

Nakhleh, Emile A. "The Arabs in Israel and Their Role in a Future Arab-Israeli Conflict: A Perception Study." Mimeographed, Abbott Associates Special Report, no. 17, 1977.

Nakhleh, Khalil. "Cultural Determinants of Palestinian Collective Identity: The Case of the Arabs in Israel." *New Outlook* 19, no. 7 (October-November 1975); 31-40.

"New Modus Vivendi." *The Middle East*, no. 43 (May 1978); 46.

Nyrop, Richard F., et al. *Area Handbook for Syria*. Washington, D.C.: Foreign Area Studies Division, American University, 1969.

O'Ballance, Edgar. *The Kurdish Revolt 1961-1970*. Hamden, Conn.; Archon, 1973.

Peres, Yochanan, and Yuval-Davis, Nira. "Some Observations on the National Identity of the Israeli Arab." *Human Relations*. 22, no. 3 (June 1969); 219-33.

Peretz, Don. *Israel and the Palestine Arabs*. Washington, D.C.; Middle East Institute, 1958.

Polk, William R. *The United States and the Arab World*. Cambridge; Harvard University Press, 1965.

Qahwaji, Habib. "Al-Qissah al-Kamilah li-Harakat al-Ard," *Shu'un Filastiniyah*, no. 1 (March 1971); 112-25.

Qubain, Fahim. *Crisis in Lebanon*. Washington, D.C.: Middle East Institute, 1961.

Ar-Razzaz, Munif. *Al-Tajriba al-Murra*. Beirut: Dar Ghandur lil Taba'a wa al-Nashr wa al-Tawzi', 1967.

Rizk, Charles. *Le Régime politique libanais*. Paris: Pichon et Durand-Auzias, 1966.

Robins, Edward. "Attitudes, Stereotypes, and Prejudices Among Arabs and Jews in Israel." *New Outlook* 15, no. 9 (November-December 1972); 36-48.

Rognon, P. "La Confédération des Nomades Kel Ahaggar." *Annales de Géographie* 71, no. 388 (November-December 1962); 604-19.

Rondot, Pierre. "Minorities in the Arab Orient Today." In *Man, State and Society in the Contemporary Middle East*, edited by Jacob Landau, p. 267-81. New York: Praeger, 1972.

Rustow, Dankwart. *A World of Nations: Problems of Political Modernization*. Washington, D.C.: Brookings Institution, 1967.

Ryan, Sheila. "Israeli Economic Policy in the Occupied Areas: Foundations of a New Imperialism." *MERIP Reports*, no. 24 (January 1974).

Said, Abdul Aziz, ed. *Ethnicity and U.S. Foreign Policy*. New York: Praeger, 1978.

———. and Simmons, Luis R., eds. *Ethnicity in an International Context*. New Brunswick, N.J.: Transaction Books, 1976.

Saint-Quentin, Louis de. *Algérie inconnue*. Algiers: Editions Baconnier, 1958.

Salibi, Kamal S. *Crossroads to Civil War*. Delmar. N.Y.: Caravan Books, 1976.

———. *The Modern History of Lebanon*. London: Weidenfeld and Nicolson, 1965.

al-Salih, Mahmud. *al-Naba' al-Yaqin 'an al-'Alawiyin*. N.p., 1961.

Schiffrin, H. Z., ed. *The Military and State in Modern Asia*. Jerusalem: Academic Press, 1976.

Schwartz, Walter. *The Arabs in Israel*. London: Faber and Faber, 1959.

Seale, Patrick. *The Struggle for Syria*. London: Oxford University Press, 1965.

"Setting the Record Straight." *The Middle East*, no. 43 (May 1978); 47.

Seymour, Martin. "The Dynamics of Syria Since the Break with Egypt." *Middle Eastern Studies* 6, no. 1 (January 1970); 35-47.

al-Sharif, Munir. *Al-Muslimun al-'Alawiyun: Man Hum Wa 'Ayna Hum*. 2nd ed. Damascus: al-Matba'a al-'Umumiya, 1960.

Shiloh, Ailon, ed. *Peoples and Cultures of the Middle East*. New York: Random House, 1969.

Shils, Edward. *Political Development in the New States*. The Hague: Mouton, 1968.

Shlaim, Avi. "Israel and the Occupied Territories." *The World Today* 29, no. 10 (October 1973); 421-29.

ash-Shu'aybi, I. "Ad-Daffah al-Gharbiyyah: Ihtilal Muqawamah wa Nazra ila al-Mustaqbal (Nadwah)." *Shu'un Filastiniyyah*, no. 32 (April 1974); 30-55.

———. "Ittijihat as-Suhuf fi ad-Daffah al-Gharbiyyah 'at-Taharrukat as-Siyasiyah Ba'd Harb Tishrin al-Awwal—'Sukkan ad-Daffah La Yuridun al-'Aysh fi Zill Nizam al-Malik Husayn.'" *Shu'un Filastiniyyah*, no. 30 (February 1974); 166-73.

Silvert, Kalman H. *Expectant Peoples, Nationalism and Development*. New York: Vintage, 1963.

Silvestre de Sacy, A. I. *Exposé de la religion des Druzes*. 2 vols. Paris: L'Imprimerie Royale, 1833.

Skinner, G. William. *Chinese Society in Thailand*. Ithaca: Cornell University Press, 1957.

Smith, Donald. *Religion, Politics and Social Change in the Third World*. New York: Free Press, 1971.

Smith, Harvey H., et al. *Area Handbook for Israel*. Washington, D.C.: Foreign Area Studies Division, American University, 1969.

———. *Area Handbook for Lebanon*. Washington, D.C.: Foreign Area Studies Division, American University, 1969.

Smooha, Sammy, and Hofman, John E. "Some Problems of Arab-Jewish Coexistence in Israel." *Middle East Review* 9, no. 2 (Winter 1976-77); 5-15.

Smuts, Jan Christian. *The League of Nations: A Practical Suggestion.* New York: Hodder and Stoughton, 1918.

Soffer, Gad. "The Role of the Officer Class in Syrian Politics and Society." Ph.D. dissertation, American University, 1968.

Stoakes, F. "The Supervigilantes: The Lebanese Kataeb Party as a Builder, Surrogate, and Defender of the State," *Middle East Studies* 11, no. 3 (October 1975); 215-36.

Sweet, Louise E., ed. *Peoples and Cultures of the Middle East.* 2 vols. Garden City: Natural History Press, 1970.

——. "The Women of 'Ain ad-Dayr." *Anthropological Quarterly* 40, no. 3 (July 1967); 167-83.

Suleiman, Michael W. *Political Parties in Lebanon.* Ithaca: Cornell University Press, 1967.

Tachau, Frank, ed. *Political Elites and Political Development in the Middle East.* Cambridge, Mass.: Schenkman, 1975.

Tali', Amin Muhamad. *'Asal al-Muwahidin al-Duruz was 'Usulhum.* Beirut: Dar al-Andalis-Maktab al-Bustany, 1961.

Tankut, Hasa. *al-Nusayriyun wa al-Nusayriya.* Ankara: Devlet Matbassi, 1938.

al-Tawil, Muhammad. *Ta'rikh al-'Alawiyin.* Beirut: Dar al-'Andalis, 1966.

Tessler, Mark A. "The Identity of Religious Minorities in Non-Secular States." *Comparative Studies in Society and Hsitory* 20, no. 3 (July 1978); 359-73.

——. "Israel's Arabs and the Palestinian Problem." *Middle East Journal* 31, no. 3 (Summer 1977); 313-29.

——. "Secularism in the Middle East?" *Ethnicity* 2, no. 2 (June 1975); 178-203.

Tillman, Seth P. *Anglo-American Relations at the Paris Peace Conference of 1919.* Princeton: Princeton University Press, 1961.

Torrey, Gordon. *Syrian Politics and the Military.* Columbus: Ohio State University Press, 1964.

U.S. Department of State. Office of the U.S. Coordinator for Refugee Affairs. *1979 World Refugee Assessments.* Washington, D.C., 1979.

Vallaud, Pierre. *Le Liban au bout du fusil.* Paris: Hachette, 1976.

van Arkadie, Brian. *Benefits and Burdens: A Report on the West Bank and Gaza Strip Economies Since 1967.* New York: Carnegie Endowment for International Peace, 1977.

van den Berghe, Pierre. "Pluralism and the Polity." In *Pluralism in Africa,* edited by Leo Kuper and M. G. Smith, p. 67-81. Berkeley: University of California Press, 1969.

——. *Race and Ethnicity.* New York: Basic Books, 1974.

Van Dusen, Michael. "Political Integration and Regionalism in Syria." *Middle East Journal* 26, no. 2 (Spring 1972); 123-36.

van Langenhove, Fernand. "Le Problème de la protection des populations aborigénes aux Nations Unies," *Recueil des Cours* (Hague Academy of International Law) 89, no. 1 (1956); 319-433.

Vaumas, Etienne de. "Le Djebel ansarieh. étude de géographie humaine," *Revue de Géographie alpine* 48, no. 2 (1960); 267-312.

Vocke, Harold. *The Lebanese War: Its Origins and Political Dimensions.* New York: St. Martin's, 1978.

Waterbury, John. *The Commander of the Faithful.* New York: Columbia University Press, 1970.

———. "Land, Man, and Development in Algeria." *American Universities Field Staff Reports* 17, no. 3 (1971).

———. *North for the Trade: The Life and Times of a Berber Merchant.* Berkeley: University of California Press, 1972.

Weigert, Gideon. "Israel's Arab Minority." *World Jewry* 16, no. 3 (June 1973); 18-19.

Weiner, Myron. "Political Integration and Political Development." *Annals of the American Academy of Political and Social Science* 358 (March 1965); 52-64.

"West Bank Voices." *New Outlook* 18, no. 8 (December 1975); 19-24.

Weulersse, Jacques. *Le Pays de Alaouites.* Tours: Arrault, 1940.

———. *Paysans de Syrie et du Proche-Orient.* Paris: Gallimard, 1946.

Whetten, Lawrence L. *The Canal War: Four-Power Conflict in the Middle East.* Cambridge, Mass.: MIT Press, 1974.

Yaffe, Richard. "Among Jerusalem and West Bank Arabs: Disappointment and Gloom." *The National Jewish Monthly* 86, no. 7 (March 1973); 37-42.

Willcox, Faith. *In Morocco.* New York: Harcourt, Brace, Javanovich, 1971.

Wright, Quincy. *Mandates Under the League of Nations.* Chicago: University of Chicago Press, 1930.

Zayyad, Tawfiq. "The Fate of the Arabs in Israel." *Journal of Palestine Studies* 6, no. 1 (Autumn 1976); 92-103.

INDEX

ABOUT THE EDITOR
AND CONTRIBUTORS

R. D. MC LAURIN, editor of this volume, is a Senior Staff Member of Abbott Associates, Incorporated. He is the author of *The Middle East in Soviet Policy* and coauthor of *Foreign Policy Making in the Middle East.* In addition, Dr. McLaurin has authored, coauthored, edited, or coedited over two dozen other books, chapters, professional journal articles, and research reports.

PETER A. GUBSER, currently President of American Near East Refugee Aid (ANERA), was formerly with the American Institutes for Research and the Ford Foundation. Dr. Gubser is the author of *Politics and Change in al-Karak, Jordan* and articles in the *International Journal of Middle East Studies* and *Middle Eastern Affairs.*

SUHAILA HADDAD is a consultant to Abbott Associates, Inc. Formerly on the staff of the U.S. Library of Congress, she has contributed to several studies dealing with Middle East language and society.

LINDA L. HAWKINS is a doctoral candidate in political science at the University of Wisconsin-Milwaukee. She is coauthor of several scholarly papers dealing with the Middle East and North Africa and has published a number of articles on U.S. politics and urban politics.

WILLIAM E. HAZEN is the coauthor of *The Palestinian Movement in Politics* and coauthor and coeditor of *Middle Eastern Subcultures: A Regional Approach.* Affiliated with Abbott Associates, Inc., Dr. Hazen has previously worked for the American Institutes for Research and the U.S. Library of Congress.

PAUL A. JUREIDINI, Vice-President of Abbott Associates, Inc., is considered one of the leading experts on the Levant, particularly Lebanon, Jordan, and Syria. Dr. Jureidini, a native of Lebanon, is coauthor of *The Palestinian Movement in Politics.* He lectures widely across the United States and serves as a consultant to numerous private and public institutions. His most recent publications are articles in *International Interactions,* the *Journal of Palestine Studies and Military Review* and contributions to *Crisis in Lebanon: Participants and Issues* and *Constructing Policy.*

EMILE A. NAKHLEH, Professor of Political Science at Mt. St. Mary's College, is generally recognized as one of the foremost experts on Israeli Arabs and on the Persian Gulf. Dr. Nakhleh is the author of *Arab-American Relations in the Persian Gulf*, *The Political Development of Bahrain*, and *The United States and Saudi Arabia*, and *The West Bank and Gaza: Toward the Making of a Palestinian State*.

JUTTA PARSONS is a doctoral student at the University of Wisconsin-Milwaukee. She is coauthor of several scholarly papers in the field of international relations.

JAMES M. PRICE, Research Assistant at Abbott Associates, Inc., has conducted studies on the Soviet role in the Middle East and, in particular, on religious and military aspects of the Lebanese civil war. His most recent publication is an article on OPEC current account surpluses in *Oriente Moderno*.

LEWIS W. SNIDER, Research Associate at Abbott Associates, Inc., is also Assistant Professor on the faculty of the Claremont Graduate School. Dr. Snider is the author of *Arabesque: Untangling the Patterns of Supply of Conventional Arms to Israel and the Arab States* and coeditor and coauthor of *Crisis in Lebanon: Participants and Issues*. He has also contributed articles to professional journals, books, research studies, and newspapers.

MARK R. TESSLER is Chairperson of the political science department at the University of Wisconsin-Milwaukee. He is coauthor of *Tradition and Identity in Changing Africa* and coeditor of *Arab Oil: Impact on the Arab Countries and Global Implications* and *Survey Research in Africa*. Dr. Tessler has also published numerous articles and chapters dealing with the Middle East and North Africa and is currently preparing a book on Jews in Tunisia and Morocco and Arabs in Israel.